T0334655

LEADERSHIP

The second edition of *Leadership* offers a unique, highly-applied academic treatise on leadership, uniquely blending a chronological analysis of the last 100 years of leadership theory with exclusive CEO interviews. The case studies, expert insights and other teaching aids are timely and hard hitting, making this textbook relevant, insightful and informative, while a research chapter empowers the reader to competently question the leaders that shape our world.

The world has turned on its political and corporate axis since the first edition of *Leadership* was published, and it became necessary to produce a second edition that fully encapsulated, respected and observed these changes. Numerous new case studies, discussion starters and examples subsequently reflect today's volatile technological, political, financial and social shifts, while exclusive interviews with successful CEOs powerfully blend theory with practice. Readers will learn the importance of navigating leadership in the most testing of times. A new chapter, "Researching leadership", offers the reader the opportunity to develop significantly as a leadership researcher and to ably question reality in a post-truth world. A self-leadership chapter equips the reader to develop their own leadership capabilities, while retaining the ability to avoid destructive leadership. Ultimately, readers will become empowered to appreciate the complex, intersectional nature of leadership and to learn what it takes to lead in today's politically, technologically and socially tumultuous world.

This book will be particularly engaging for students and educators at secondary school, college, undergraduate and postgraduate level, and for leadership/management consultants. While the book's primary role remains as a core text for leadership, management and business modules, it will also be of interest to students on many other courses (e.g. psychology, politics, sociology). Packed with teaching resources which educators will find particularly useful, *Leadership* is the only textbook of its kind to offer such an applied view of this subject via the inclusion of 12 (mostly CEO) expert insights. The first edition was an "Amazon Hot New Release", so this second edition might also hold interest for a general readership.

Elesa Zehndorfer PhD is the Research Officer for British Mensa. Author of four additional Routledge titles, Dr. Zehndorfer is an experienced writer and academic with international board level experience. A Quora Top Writer 2017 and 2018, Dr. Zehndorfer writes about physiology, politics, finance and leadership.

LEADERSHIP

Performance Beyond Expectations

2nd Edition

Elesa Zehndorfer

Routledge
Taylor & Francis Group

LONDON AND NEW YORK

Second edition published 2021
by Routledge
2 Park Square, Milton Park, Abingdon, Oxon OX14 4RN

and by Routledge
52 Vanderbilt Avenue, New York, NY 10017

Routledge is an imprint of the Taylor & Francis Group, an informa business

© 2021 Elesa Zehndorfer

First edition published by Routledge 2013

British Library Cataloguing-in-Publication Data
A catalogue record for this book is available from the British Library

Library of Congress Cataloging-in-Publication Data
Names: Zehndorfer, Elesa, 1975– author.
Title: Leadership : performance beyond expectations / Elesa Zhendorfer.
Description: Second Edition. | New York : Routledge, 2020. | Includes
bibliographical references and index.
Identifiers: LCCN 2020018464 (print) | LCCN 2020018465 (ebook) |
ISBN 9780367406165 (hardback) | ISBN 9780367374822 (paperback) |
ISBN 9781003011507 (ebook)
Subjects: LCSH: Leadership.
Classification: LCC HD57.7 .Z4644 2020 (print) | LCC HD57.7 (ebook)
| DDC 658.4/092-dc23
LC record available at https://lccn.loc.gov/2020018464
LC ebook record available at https://lccn.loc.gov/2020018465

ISBN: 978-0-367-40616-5 (hbk)
ISBN: 978-0-367-37482-2 (pbk)
ISBN: 978-1-003-01150-7 (ebk)

Visit the eResources: www.routledge.com/9780367374822

Typeset in Bembo
by Wearset Ltd, Boldon, Tyne and Wear

For Henry and Clemens

CONTENTS

ILLUSTRATIONS

Figures

Tables

ACKNOWLEDGEMENTS

I remain indebted to the leaders who have contributed their time and expertise to this book, and to the editing team at Routledge, who have supported me so effectively throughout the writing process.

With thanks to the following publishers for granting permission to reproduce the figures below:

Figure 3.1 Influence of leader characteristics on leader performance.
Mumford, M.D., Zaccaro, S.J., Harding, F.D., Jacobs, T.O. and Fleishman, E.A. (2000). Leadership Skills for a Changing World: Solving Complex Social Problems. *Leadership Quarterly*, 11(1), p. 16.

Figure 4.5 The self-determination continuum.
Ryan, R.M. and Deci, E.L. (2000). Self-Determination Theory and the Facilitation of Intrinsic Motivation, Social Development, and Well-Being. *American Psychologist*, 55(1), p. 72.

Figure 5.2 LMX Theory.
Groen, G.D. and Uhl-Bien, M. (1995). Development of LMX Theory over 25 Years. *Leadership Quarterly*, 6(2), p. 237.

Figure 9.1 The effect of authentic transformational leadership on follower and group ethics.
Zhu, W., Avolio, D., Riggio, R. and Sosik, J. (2011). The Effect of Authentic Transformational Leadership on Follower and Group Ethics. *Leadership Quarterly*, 22(5), p. 802.

Figure 9.2 The process by which authentic leadership impacts follower attitudes and behaviours.
Avolio, B.J., Gardner, W.L., Walumbwa, F.O., Luthans, F. and May, R. (2004). Unlocking the Mask: A look at the Process by Which Authentic Leaders Impact Follower Attitudes and Behaviours. *Leadership Quarterly*, 15, p. 803.

Figure 9.3 A conceptual framework for authentic leader and follower development.
Gardner, W.L., Avolio, B.J., Luthans, F., May, D.R. and Walumbwa, F.O. (2005). Can You See the Real Me? A Self-Based Model of Authentic Leader and Follower Development. *Leadership Quarterly*, 16(3), p. 346.

Figure 9.4 Authentic leader influence on eudaemonic well-being.
Ilies, R., Morgeson, F.P. and Nahrgang, J.D. (2005). Authentic Leadership and Eudaemonic Well-Being: Understanding Leader–Follower Outcomes. *Leadership Quarterly*, 16, p. 377.

Figure 10.1 A model of destructive and constructive leadership behaviour.
Einarsen, S., Aasland, M.S. and Skogstad, A. (2007). Destructive Leadership Behaviour: A Definition and Conceptual Model. *Leadership Quarterly*, 18(3), p. 211.

Figure 10.2 The toxic triangle: elements in the three domains related to destructive leadership.
Padilla, A., Hogan, R. and Kaiser, R.B. (2007). The Toxic Triangle: Destructive Leaders, Susceptible Followers, and Conducive Environments. *Leadership Quarterly*, 18, p. 180.

Figure 10.3 The susceptible circle: a taxonomy of followers associated with destructive leadership.
Thoroughgood, C.N., Padilla, A., Hunter, S.T. and Tate, B.W. (2012). The Susceptible Circle: A Taxonomy of Followers Associated with Destructive Leadership. *Leadership Quarterly*, 23, p. 902.

1

AN INTRODUCTION TO LEADERSHIP

"You can only succeed in life if you try, and leadership requires you to fail as well as succeed."

– Michael de Giorgio, OBE[1]

The world has always needed great leaders. From the heroes and legends of Ancient Rome and Greece, through to the study of leadership in modern politics, economics and warfare, one is able to traverse the landscape of heroes, myths, legends – in other words, those great leaders – that have ruled earth, sea and the human spirit – in a thousand different ways. From the time-honoured storytelling of great tales such as *Beowulf* and Homer's *Iliad*, to the study of religious texts, and the philosophical leadership of Epictetus, Plato and Aristotle, one is able to observe the motivation of society for leadership at every turn. Leaders come in every form: from the inspirational (Nelson Mandela) to the charismatic (Barack Obama), from the impeached (Donald Trump) to the unethical (Harvey Weinstein), from the groundbreaking (Greta Thunberg) to the utterly destructive (Adolf Hitler). The purpose of *Leadership: Performance Beyond Expectations* is to instil a passion for leadership in the reader by combining abstract theory with the views of real-world leaders, to develop the self-leadership of the reader and to encourage the critical deconstruction of key theories that together provide a comprehensive introduction to what is at once a seductive, complex, transformative and alluring topic.

Since the 1st Edition of this book was written, the world of leadership has shifted on its axis; students, scholars and educators are facing a different world, and the 2nd Edition seeks to reflect exactly those leadership challenges.

But before such a pedagogic journey can be undertaken, one must first ask the wholly important question: "Why study leadership?".

Why study leadership?

The reader is encouraged to heed the seminal words of Marcus Aurelius, who advises us that one must "look back over the past, with its changing empires that rose and fell, and you can foresee the future too".[2] The study of leadership allows us to learn from history, so that we are not consigned to repeating the mistakes of our forefathers, nor are we fated to ignore the lessons of their success. Developing self-leadership greatly enhances our lives by maximizing our human capital. Acting as role models and transforming others develops social capital, and carries the power to transform communities and nations. Most importantly, it allows us to be inspired to realize our own abilities as a leader.

The study of leadership equips us with the ability to understand the complex interplay of situational variables that contribute to leadership. Consider, for example, our role as electoral voters in a democratic society; we carry the right and responsibility to vote for a leader, yet our leaders often emerge as ineffective and corrupt. One reason for this might be explained by academic studies into leadership preferences; our instinct remains overwhelmingly to vote for candidates that we find physically appealing, as opposed to those who have the fairest policies or who possess the highest level of intelligence. In fact, studies of US presidents (discussed in Chapter 2, "Trait theories") report that presidents who have elicited high levels of intelligence during their tenure are less likely to win by a landslide in subsequent elections.

The rampant use of propaganda in the 2016 US and UK election and referendum cycles have amplified our understanding of the incredibly powerful role of tech and media in transforming – and manipulating – the world that we see around us, and in shaping our political realities; another factor reflected in updates to the 2nd Edition of this book.

Studying leadership also challenges us to confront the notion of how we measure leadership. It is interesting that the use of instruments such as the MBTI (Myers Briggs Type Indicator) remains popular among business consultants and corporate recruiters, despite the fact that they possess little predictive power. For this reason, each chapter includes a list of instruments that are considered reliable and generalizable and that possess a high level of validity and reliability, thus facilitating the effective measurement of leadership. A new chapter has been added to this 2nd Edition as a means of further extending the concept of how to measure, research and analyse leadership (Chapter 12, "Researching leadership").

The final purpose of studying leadership is to challenge the very notion of leadership success. Should it be measured by the power, authority and/or materialistic wealth that a business or political leader has accrued throughout their career (Mark Zuckerberg, Donald Trump)? Alternatively, should it be measured by the transformative effect that an individual has exerted over society (the hugely philanthropic investments of George Soros, founder of the pro-democracy Open Society Foundations), or in challenging discrimination and great injustice in society itself

(Steve Biko, Greta Thunberg, Elijah Cummings, Nobel prize winner Donald Woods)? The intellectual and technological contribution that an individual has contributed (Steven Hawking) might also provide an incontrovertible measure of leadership success, due to the manner in which their work has exerted a transformative and enriching effect on our understanding of the world in which we live. Finally, might leadership success simply be measured by the way in which we have demonstrated the effective use of self-leadership in the achievement of eudaemonia (happiness)?

Such questions will form the focus of debate throughout this book. The first step in this process is to define leadership.

Defining leadership

The *Collins English Dictionary* defines leadership as:

> 1. The position or function of a leader; 2. the period during which a person occupies the position of leader: during her leadership very little was achieved; 3. the ability to lead; 4. (as modifier): leadership qualities, and 5. the leadership of a group of a party, union, etc.; the union leadership is now very reactionary.[3]

While the dictionary definition above is useful, modern scholars of management and leadership have found it fundamentally problematic to reach a clear consensus on what they feel leadership actually is. Stogdill (1974), a theorist who believed in the 'Great Man' theory (that leaders are born with innate abilities – see Chapter 2, "Trait theories"), perhaps put it best when he commented succinctly that "there are almost as many definitions of leadership as there are persons who have attempted to define the concept" (p. 259).

Nevertheless, one might positively view such disagreements as a worthwhile representation of the rich intellectual activity that surrounds this field of study (which has now grown to include the unique contributions of neurology, business and management studies, behavioural finance, psychology and physiology). We will not seek to enter the debate of how to conceptualize leadership in this chapter; it remains instead the responsibility of the reader to consider intellectually the merits of the many theories of leadership (and their corresponding definitions) that follow in the remaining eleven chapters of this book, to understand their merits, to define their weaknesses and to adopt a personal stance relating to the definition(s) that they feel best encapsulate what leadership means to them.

Leadership timeline

> Look back over the past, with it changing empires that rose and fell, and you can foresee the future too.[4]

Marcus Aurelius (AD 121–AD 180)

Figure 1.1 provides an overview of the modern theories of leadership that feature throughout the book. These theories have been chosen due to their dominance within the field of leadership and management studies throughout the twentieth and early twenty-first centuries. Each theory has been assigned its own separate chapter.

Each chapter contains a range of interactive materials that facilitate and augment the reader's understanding of key theories. These materials constitute:

- *Discussion starters.* Brief statements or examples designed to stimulate brief discussion and debate.
- *Ideas in brief.* These provide a short, sharp observation of a particular topic, and serve as thought-provoking examples of leadership for the reader.
- *Quizzes.* End-of-chapter quizzes allow the reader to consolidate their learning of key theories.
- *Case studies.* These allow the reader to apply theory to practice via the use of real-world examples.
- *Expert insights.* Written by successful leaders, these provide a real-world, pragmatic complement to the academic theory included in each chapter.

Each chapter is now outlined in greater detail. Readers are encouraged to jump to those chapters that they find most interesting, or to take a leisurely sojourn through the chapters in order to gain a historic perspective of the way in which studies of leadership have progressed. Academics and students will benefit from interacting with the pedagogic materials that accompany each chapter.

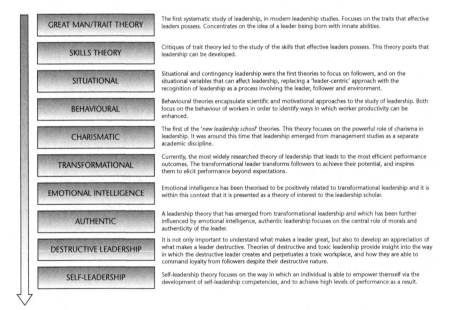

FIGURE 1.1 Leadership timeline.

Chapter 1: An introduction to leadership

This chapter provides an introduction to the textbook, and to the concept of leadership. A case study of leadership in Ancient Rome immerses the reader in the application of theory to practice and introduces key theories that will be studied later. The expert insight ("Changing lives") for this chapter is provided by Michael de Giorgio OBE, co-founder and former CEO of Greenhouse Sports.

Chapter 2: Trait theories

> Never give in – never, never, never, in nothing great or small, large or petty, never give in except to convictions of honour and good sense. Never yield to force; never yield to the apparently overwhelming might of the enemy.
>
> *Winston Churchill (1874–1965)*[5]

In Chapter 2, the reader is introduced to the 'Great Man' theory of leadership, also referred to as the *trait theory*. The trait theory asks whether great leaders are born or made, and whether effective leaders possess specific traits (such as intelligence, charisma or physical strength) that ineffective leaders do not. The reader is invited to define leadership, to identify leaders that have inspired them, and to consider what makes a leader great. The expert insight ("The role of personality traits in leadership success") that accompanies this chapter is provided by Bassma El Amir-Riley, former Head of Trading (Government Bonds & Repo) at a leading global universal bank. This precedes a case study of Winston Churchill ("Winston Churchill: born leader?").

Chapter 3: Skills theories

> Time is neutral and does not change things. With courage and initiative, leaders change things.
>
> *Jesse Jackson*[6]

Chapter 3 considers the skills theory of leadership, which asks whether great leaders become great due to the acquisition of extremely well-developed skills, talents and abilities. The fascinating question here is whether leadership can be taught and developed, or whether leadership is really an incontrovertible feature of nature, endowed upon a special few at birth. The expert insight for this chapter profiles Mavens & Moguls CEO Paige Arnof-Fenn, whose innovative, disruptive entrepreneurial approach inspired a *Harvard Business Review* case study and allows her to connect with clients across the globe. A case study entitled "Harbinger of fortune" profiles the changing fortunes of Philip Falcone, CEO of Harbinger Capital.

Chapter 4: Behavioural theories

> You and I, as citizens, have the obligation to shape the debates of our time – not only with the votes we cast, but with the voices we lift in defense of our most ancient values and enduring ideals.
>
> *Barack Obama*[7]

Behavioural theories include both the work of scientific management scholars, and motivational theorists. Scientific and classical approaches assumed that employees were essentially tools of work, from whom maximal productivity could be expediently extracted. Conversely, the motivational approach recognizes the role of motivational needs and goals in the maximization of employee productivity and performance. The expert insight for this chapter is provided by University of Oxford Wellness Research Group board member and CEO and co-founder of The 4 Day Week project, Andrew Barnes ("Challenging orthodoxy: the 4 day week"). This precedes a case study entitled "Tragedy at Longhua" that considers the damage that can be caused to human life when productivity and profit are placed before human well-being.

Chapter 5: Situational theories

> I claim not to have controlled events, but confess plainly that events have controlled me.
>
> *Abraham Lincoln (1809–1865)*[8]

Situational and contingency theories heralded a move away from exclusively 'leader-centric' approaches to the study of leadership as a process. Situational and contingency leadership theories (Fielder's Contingency Theory, House's Path–Goal Theory and Vroom and Yetton's Normative Theory) subsequently provide insight into the way in which a leader's style is contingent on the needs and preferences of their followers, and on the control that they exert over their environment. The quality of the leader–follower relationship and the emergence of 'in-groups' within organizational teams throws further light on the mechanics of the leader–follower relationship, and the reader is encouraged to consider the role that diversity might play in this process. The expert insight for this chapter ("From the Iron Curtain to Coca-Cola HQ") provides a first-person account of living with consumerism in pre- and post-Communist Bulgaria. The case study for this chapter offers an enthralling insight into how Wall Street has invested heavily in Las Vegas ("Casino bankers"), with both winners and losers walking out of the Strip.

Chapter 6: Charismatic leadership

> The ruler lacking intelligence multiplies oppression; but he who abhors greed will endure.
>
> *Proverbs 28:16*

Charismatic leaders are powerful revolutionary visionaries, able to inspire us beyond measure. They develop a strong emotional bond with followers, who subsume the identity, values and beliefs of the charismatic leader so powerfully that any critique of that leader is perceived as a personal slight on them, too. This removes all objectivity, raising the danger of cult-like worship, extreme political partisanship and a failure to hold that leader to account when they are clearly guilty of moral transgressions. It also provides a willing army of defenders for that leader who will fight their corner whenever it is needed. When people ask if leaders are 'born or made', it is often charisma that they are really alluding to.

Charisma is amoral, meaning that it can be extremely moral and principled, used only to mobilize action for social good via a motivation for socialized power (e.g. Martin Luther King, Steve Biko, Mahatma Gandhi). Conversely, it can be morally bereft, narcissistic and dangerous (the 'dark side' of charisma), where the power of the leader's charisma is used to pursue self-serving and immoral goals (e.g. Adolf Hitler, Harvey Weinstein), propelled forward by a deep motivation of personalized power. The reader will discover that charisma comes in many forms (e.g. rhetorical, or related to a specific position of authority). Charismatic leadership formed part of the *new leadership school* that encompasses visionary theories of leadership and set apart, for the first time, studies of leadership and management as separate fields of study (one will also find charisma as a constituent part of *full range leadership* which forms the basis of Chapter 7). The expert insight is written by the Managing Director of a leading investment bank and tells us what happens "When leadership fails". A case study of George Soros paints a timely and dark picture of the role of scapegoating in politicized charismatic rhetoric.

Chapter 7: Transformational leadership

> Meek young men grow up in libraries, believing it their duty to accept the views, which Cicero, which Locke, which Bacon, have given, forgetful that Cicero, Locke, and Bacon were only young men in libraries, when they wrote these books.
>
> *Ralph Emerson (1803–1882)*[9]

Transformational leadership (TL) facilitates performance beyond expectations through the communication of a vision, and via the intellectual stimulation, individualized consideration, idealized influence and inspirational motivation of followers. It is augmented by specific transactional behaviours (discussed in Chapter 7 under the auspices of *full range leadership*). A dominant theory in modern leadership studies, TL theory has been tested extensively across cultures, continents and professions (e.g. military, educational, corporate fields) and has been linked consistently to the elicitation of high levels of performance. A powerful and timely expert insight provided by Life After Hate CEO and co-founder Sammy Rangel precedes a case study of Nobel-prize winning South African journalist Donald Woods ("Sikhahlela Indoda Yamadoda" – We salute the hero of a nation).

Chapter 8: Emotional intelligence

> Success in investing doesn't correlate with IQ once you're above the level
> of 25. Once you have ordinary intelligence, what you need is the tempera-
> ment to control the urges that get other people into trouble in investing.
>
> *Warren Buffett*[10]

Emotional intelligence (EI) can be defined as the "ability to monitor one's own and
other's feelings and emotions, to discriminate among them and to use this information to guide one's thinking and actions" (Salovey and Mayer, 1990, p. 189). It is
also a concept that is believed, by many, to impact significantly on leadership
success. The field is somewhat divided, with supporters claiming that EI is critical
to workplace performance, and detractors claiming that the concept itself is nothing
but hyperbole. Such claims make study of the field of EI quite fascinating. The
chapter presents trait and ability approaches of EI and considers possible relationships between EI, transformational and authentic leadership. The expert insight for
this chapter is a lively exposition of CEO Lauren Grech's stellar rise in the luxury
wedding industry at the helm of LLG, accompanied by an entertaining look at the
mixed fortunes of two men – Masayoshi Son, founder of Softbank, and Adam
Neumann, former CEO of WeWork ("A tale of two visionaries").

Chapter 9: Authentic leadership

> What you leave behind is not what is engraved in stone monuments, but
> what is woven into the lives of others.
>
> *Pericles (495 BC–429 BC)*[11]

Authentic leadership focuses on the role of authenticity and morality in leadership,
and on the need for a leader to demonstrate consistency between their principles
and their actions. Authentic leadership is considered to be a *root construct*; that is, it
is considered foundational to all other forms of leadership. The chapter presents
self-based and developmental definitions of authentic leadership and highlights the
need for leaders to act as moral agents. The expert insight ("On the ATAQ") for
this chapter chronicles the passion and drive of ATAQ Fuel CEO Tammo Walter
– a man whose entrepreneurial drive was borne out of a need to follow his authentic vision for a transformative health product. An inspiring and timely case study of
the decorated Vietnam veteran and former FBI Chief Robert Swan Mueller III
("Tour of duty") concludes the chapter.

Chapter 10: Destructive leadership

> When bad men combine, the good must associate; else they will fall, one by
> one, an unpitied sacrifice in a contemptible struggle.
>
> *Edmund Burke (1729–1797)*[12]

It is a sad fact that many leaders throughout time, across cultures, sectors and national boundaries, have failed their followers by promoting the use of toxic leadership in their quest to fulfil a self-serving agenda. Referred to as a 'personality disordered' individual within the literature, destructive leaders are those who "by dint of their destructive behaviours and dysfunctional personal qualities generate serious and enduring poisonous effects on the individuals, families, organizations, communities, and even entire societies they lead" (Lipman-Blumen, 2005, p. 29).

Chapter 10 addresses the need to investigate not only what makes a leader great, but also what makes a leader destructive. The chapter opens with a discussion of Enron and then moves on to a presentation of three key theoretical models applied to case studies of the use of social media based propaganda in the 2016 US election cycle: *constructive and destructive leadership behaviour*, the *toxic triangle* and the *susceptible circle*. The expert insight for this chapter constitutes a deeply concerning look at the reality of day-to-day racism from the perspective of a senior professional. "Just show me the data" offers a fascinating case study of the stellar rise and momentous fall of the medical technology company Theranos Inc., and of the related choppy fortunes of its charismatic founder, Elizabeth Holmes.

Chapter 11: Self-leadership

> Courage is not always done on the battlefield. Courage is done when someone has the courage to right a wrong, even if it is not popular.
>
> *Gunnery Sergeant David A. Oswell*

How can we effectively lead others if we cannot first lead ourselves? This theory-driven chapter begins with theoretical observations in the field of self-leadership, then combines key trends that emerge from the previous 10 chapters to assist the reader in developing their own excellent self-leadership skills. A truly fascinating expert insight is provided by Gunnery Sergeant David A. Oswell ("Military lessons in self-leadership") while a case study, "Frank talk", based on the life of Steve Biko, a young South African man and a martyr to Apartheid, swiftly follows. Remembered as the father of Black Consciousness, Biko serves as a reminder that one man can make a difference even in the face and might of the most oppressive of evils.

Chapter 12: Researching leadership

This chapter offers a fascinating, detailed insight into the way in which leadership scholars can seek to create a detailed, theoretically-grounded, rigorous research strategy. You are unlikely to find another book chapter that offers a relatively simple explanation of the beauty, simplicity and critical uses of research philosophy in the context of leadership research. The expert insight for this chapter profiles Dr. Laslo-Baker, a PhD toxicology researcher-turned-entrepreneur who recently raised $6 million in seed funding for her innovative DeeBee's Organics company. Dr. Laslo-Baker shares with us why developing great research skills is so vital to achieving your dreams. The case study "Financial markets meltdown: the case of Value at Risk" offers an enthralling real-life scenario to which readers can apply their newly acquired research philosophy skills.

Summary

This chapter has introduced the reader to the modern academic study of leadership and provided an overview of both the structure and key foci of the book. Engagement with the case studies and other pedagogic materials associated with each chapter is recommended, as it will facilitate a richer appreciation of the applied value of the theories presented. It is hoped that the reader will enjoy traversing the chapters that follow, and that their journey will prove not only elucidating and informative, but also entertaining and pragmatic.

The next chapter introduces the reader to the first modern, systematic study of leadership, the Great Man theory, otherwise referred to as the trait theory of leadership.

The reader is now invited to engage with the first expert insight of the book – provided by co-founder and former CEO of the hugely successful Greenhouse Sports charity, Michael de Giorgio, OBE[13] – before tackling the case study "Ancient Rome" and the end-of-chapter questions that follow.

 **Expert insight**

Changing lives

**Greenhouse
Sports**

Michael de Giorgio founded the hugely successful Greenhouse Sports in 2002, stepping down as CEO in 2017 after 15 years at the helm. As CEO, de Giorgio built a financially strong, sustainable and profitable organization which continues to positively impact many lives. de Giorgio carried the Olympic Torch in 2012, chaired the Centre for Social Justice's report on how best to harness the power of sport to transform young lives and was recently awarded an OBE for his charitable work. Greenhouse delivers intensive sports coaching and mentoring, positively targeting the development of Social, Thinking, Emotional and Physical (STEP) abilities of young people from disadvantaged communities. Michael de Giorgio serves as an inspiring example of a man who has employed his significant professional expertise as a finance professional to build a profitable, sustainable charity. In 2020, Greenhouse Sports appointed highly respected city veterans Beatrice Butsana-Sita as CEO and Luke Ellis as Chair, with de Giorgio moving to the role of Trustee. Here, he shares with us his compelling thoughts on leadership.

On his leadership style

❝In terms of my leadership style, I think that I am relatively light touch, as far as I don't try to get involved too much in a lot of the details. I'm very keen to employ people who can help me, and, ultimately, help me perform better because they're good at what they do. So I'm very keen to have those people and I think that I delegate relatively well as a result. In terms of particular traits, I don't think that I was born with any, necessarily, but as I've gone from working with and advising rich people to working with relatively poor people, I've learned a hell of a lot from that. I have a lot of strengths and weaknesses, but I think that ultimately my biggest strengths are my vision of what I want to achieve, my tremendous optimism and the fact that I am clear in what I want to achieve, and where my expertise lies.

It is my opinion that 'better never stops'. I have very, very high standards for what I expect Greenhouse to do – at no stage have I compromised on things. If we have a coach, I want the best coach. If we have equipment, I want the best equipment. If we have kit, we want the best kit. We want it done very, very well, and as a result I don't accept second best. I don't accept second best for these kids. I think they are used to having second best but I think they should have the best, and I think that's how we can transform their lives. We can transform them by offering something that they don't normally get.

Ultimately, I have no one to impress but myself. I don't need to go in and run the programme and appear to be seen to be leader of an organization. The whole thing is to just go in and do the best thing possible for the kids. That's what I am working for – that's my goal. If I am not proud of something, I stop it. An expression that I use is 'Am I proud of it?' because I don't have the financial incentive to do something just to make money, so I need to feel proud of whatever I am doing in order for it to happen.

On leading a successful team

I think we do run this as a business and we try to run it in a very efficient way and people appreciate that, and they know that I'm not buying myself a Ferrari, if you know what I mean. And as a result, I don't have a great big salary, or any salary, and as a result they know that I'm putting my own money and time where my mouth is.

Probably the most important thing for me is to find the right coaches, the right leaders, the right mentors, the right people that would inspire the kids … because if I actually go in front of a programme myself, the kids wouldn't turn up a second time! So it's been a great challenge, not upgrading coaches as much as making sure that we have the right people. Over time, coaches have been replaced with better coaches and it's been a huge learning curve.

We now no longer have just an interview – we also have a rigorous practical session where we put the shortlisted candidates in front of the children, and they tell us what they thought of the coach. Obviously, people are inspirational and people have different coaching styles – and we've learned that people can be inspirational in different ways.

For me, to be a coach I think that you have to be technically good ... but actually for me, that's not enough. For me, a good coach is technically good, but also knows how to engage with the kids. It's different relating to a kid who is at Eton and a kid who is on one of our football programmes in Peckham. Children are different, they have different backgrounds, and you have to understand where they're coming from. To understand their backgrounds and what they are going through every day, to empathize with them, then be able to mentor them, and work with them, is crucial. I think that is as important as teaching them to kick the ball better.

Inspiring a vision

Essentially, I started this charity to give young people an opportunity to receive a very high-quality sports provision – which is something which I had been given as a child, and which was something that I felt that I had learned a lot from and that I wanted to pass on to other people. As a young teenager, probably like other teenagers, I had a lot of issues, [and sport] had given me a way of dealing with some of those issues. Having been inspired by various good coaches, and teachers, who, as a young person had inspired me and helped me, motivated me to develop something that would create that same valuable experience for others.

I am not silly enough to think we are taking on the world, and conquering the world, and changing the world, but we are changing some people, and helping some people, and as long as we are helping some people then I'm thrilled. The more hours that we spend with these kids, the better. I think the problem is that most people don't get the opportunity to do things. I think what I would say is that my dream is to give people the opportunity that they don't normally get. Ultimately, if you don't give people the opportunity, then they can't succeed.

In terms of getting other people to buy into my vision, I am lucky in that I have had a lot of people who I knew from my business life before, who have seen my 'moments of madness', as they would probably describe it, and they had seen what I am doing, as a volunteer. They know how much passion ... I have, and that obviously inspires them to want to be generous in terms of donating financially to the charity.

Ultimately the advice that I would give to others is this: don't be scared of trying. Don't be afraid of failure. There are so many people that don't succeed simply because they've never tried. If you want to be a leader, you've got to do things you wouldn't normally do, take every opportunity that arises. The worst thing that can happen is you fail, but you learn something from failure. You can only succeed in life if you try, and leadership requires you to fail as well as succeed. "

Find out more

- Greenhouse Sports official website: www.greenhousecharity.org.

Questions

1 Discuss, with a partner, what you think makes a leader successful.
2 Identify the leadership skills, traits and career experiences that de Giorgio exhibits, and those which have contributed to his success as a leader.
3 de Giorgio has achieved success as a leader in two very different scenarios (finance and as a charity CEO). What does this tell us about the transferability of leadership skills?
4 In de Giorgio's early professional career, he appeared to be motivated primarily by personalized power, whereas his charity work was motivated primarily by socialized power. In the case of founding Greenhouse Sports, de Giorgio is essentially leveraging his capital for good. Name some other CEOs that have sought to do the same.
5 What do you feel your greatest strengths and weaknesses as a leader currently are?

Case study: leadership in Ancient Rome

The world has always needed great leaders. However, history shows us that the world has needed very different kinds of leaders at different periods in its development. For example, in ancient times, leaders were required to defend their loved ones from wild animals, to lead their communities into battle, and to display physical strength and fortitude in order to protect and fortify their surroundings. The demands of leadership in the corporate arena differ sharply in their requirements, placing a far lesser requirement on physical strength, and a far greater notional requirement on intellectual and technical skills. Nevertheless, there are still notable parallels within antiquity and modernity. A brief sojourn into the history of leadership in the Ancient Roman Empire, for example, allows us to draw direct parallels between the leadership issues that exist both in antiquity and in modernity.

The fascinating thing about leadership is that history is awash with examples of how it can be practiced badly, or of how environmental factors can unseat an otherwise greatly effective ruler. Yet despite being in full possession of such historic data, we frequently seem to repeat the same mistakes. Let us refer, for example, to the case of the greatest empire the world has ever known; the Roman Empire. Founded in 753 BC, and until its ultimate destruction in AD 476, the Roman Empire became the greatest and most powerful empire the ancient world had ever seen.

Roman history is characterized by three eras of leadership: a monarchy, the Republic and the Empire. The Roman monarchy, which ended in 509 BC, was founded on the concept of *imperium*, a legal concept that allowed the king to put to death any individual that disobeyed him, and valued self-discipline, order and simplicity over individual freedom. On a micro-level, the common-law concept of *paterfamilias* allowed each Roman male to effectively rule over their household, allowing him to kill, or sell into slavery, anyone in his household (including his wife and children!) that disobeyed him.

The monarchical rule eventually ended with the driving out of King Tarquinius Superbus, a man regarded as proud, arrogant and tyrannical by his followers. Modern-day parallels perpetuate within the corporate sector – for example, within the corrupt and arrogant culture of Enron (Chapter 10, "Destructive leadership"), or among the words of a Managing Director of a leading investment bank quoted earlier in this chapter (expert insight, "When leadership fails", see p. 119):

> it is not uncommon to come across very autocratic leadership styles, where the leader at the top of an organization is very charismatic, has a very strong grip on his (sometimes quite inexperienced and easily impressed) employees, and typically himself has an opportunistic and flexible approach to getting things done and is not limited by a strong moral compass.

Two magistrates, elected by a senate, and guided by a constitution, took the king's place, transforming Rome into a republic for the next 500 years. The Republic, consisting of patricians (the wealthy, born into aristocratic lineage) and plebeians (the poorer, working classes), was governed by magistrates, the senate and assemblies. Interestingly, any patrician wishing to enter the political sphere had to begin at its lowest rung and work their way up by a mixture of merit, significant lobbying to win votes and what one might, in the modern day, refer to as the ability to demonstrate charisma and power (via the staging of gladiatorial fights, banquets and so forth; or, in a modern guise, political rallies) in order to appeal to voters (Chapter 6, "Charismatic leadership"). The political use of charismatic rhetoric, rallies, glittering fundraising events and black-tie dinners remain a stalwart of many modern political campaigns, with many of those rallies often becoming violent (e.g. President Donald Trump's visit to India which was characterized by major riots in Delhi).

The Republic underwent a period of social reform when plebeians demanded a greater legal and political voice; these rights were granted by the powerful patricians in a bid to retain order and avoid civil war. In times of trouble, Romans appointed a dictator. This is a fascinating concept, with Max Weber's conceptualization of charisma *in statu nascendi* (Chapter 6, "Charismatic leadership") detailing a pattern that has occurred throughout history, and which involves individuals and societies looking to a strong, charismatic leader at times of uncertainty. When charisma becomes routinized, the appeal of the charismatic leader falls, and they often need to resort to force and a dictatorial approach to retain their hold on power (recent examples include Daniel Ortega, Recep Tayyip Erdoğan and Fidel Castro).

The Republic expanded first by diplomatic means – extending citizenship and protection to its neighbours – and, later, via military conquest (including Greek city-states and, then, Carthage – from whom they learned great lessons regarding leadership of, and preparation for, battle, in lands as far afield as Egypt and Britain). One might compare the historic practice of invading a country to the modern corporate practice of the hostile takeover, where battles are fought not on the field but in a boardroom.

As the Republic matured, and its prosperity grew, the model of governance changed. The *Lex provinciae* (a code of regulations) was utilized by a network of governors. Unfortunately, these positions were allocated largely on the basis of nepotism, influence, bribery and friendship (Chapter 10, "Destructive leadership"), problems compounded by the significant financial cost of military campaigns. Bribery, a negative use of one's influence and corruption are all problems that continue to blight society, and remain prevalent in the worlds of business and politics. One might refer to the recent impeachment proceedings launched by the US House of Congress against President Donald Trump for a useful contemporary example, or to the FBI's investigation into Russian interference in the 2016 US Presidential elections.

By this point, many individuals throughout the Republic had lost land and money in the campaigns, and migrated to Rome to seek greater prosperity. At the same time, wealthy plebeians who had prospered greatly from Rome's expansion began to demand greater political and administrative powers. This culminated in a period of political and civil disobedience that surpassed anything previously experienced within the Republic, with growing polarization evident between social reformers and the ruling elite who favoured keeping the status quo. While revolutionary activity has clearly perpetuated throughout political history, forming the fabric of societal change, its inclusion in corporate life remains more recent. Perhaps the financial crisis of 2008 escalated protests against capitalism, and distinct blame towards corporate 'masters of the universe' that many blamed for the economic problems led to widespread riots and protests that included the Occupy Wall Street and Occupy London movements. Interestingly, the ability to challenge the status quo forms a hallmark of successful leadership (Chapter 7, "Transformational leadership"), a phenomenon considered at length later in this book.

Expanding aggressively into new territories bought tremendous prosperity to Rome, but at the same time created the costly and complex problem of how to defend an increasingly vast range of new territories (Chapter 5, "Situational theories"). Certainly, this is a problem that has blighted many leaders, posing problems for Churchill and the maintenance of the Empire in post-World War II Britain, for example, and for President Obama in the defence of American overseas territories and campaigns. In corporate terms, Toyota provides an interesting case of a company that (by its own admission) grew too fast and subsequently faced reputational, logistical and financial difficulties.

The emergence of Marius, a war hero who ran the Roman military campaign in Africa, heralded a new era for Rome. Marius was later to quash the 'Social War' of Roman allies who had become disillusioned with what they felt was exploitation by the Empire, with the help of his assistant, Sulla. Sulla was to eventually betray Marius, and take Rome into its third period of leadership after being declared dictator of Rome for life. Sulla removed (via confiscation of wealth, exile and execution) all liberal elements of society. After installing his followers in the Senate and eventually retiring, his protégé Pompey took on his dictatorial position. Pompey was a conservative, crushing a democratic campaign in Spain and a slave revolt in Italy led by the legendary and heroic figure of Spartacus (a heroic figure who could have been conceptualized as an authentic leader; see Chapter 9, "Authentic leadership"). The *lex Manilia* law was to further extend Pompey's dictatorial powers over Asia Minor, Armenia and Syria. Pompey remained a popular figure, who was able to command personal loyalty from his troops.

This period of Pompey's rule was characterized by a period of great excess, where power-seeking individuals regularly hosted free spectacles for the people of Rome, such as gladiator fights and circus performances. Acting as patrician for these types of events was perceived to offer the greatest route to personal power and wealth for individuals, where popular votes tended to be given to those charismatic leaders that led armies into battle against foreign opponents, returning victorious to an admiring public (Chapter 6, "Charismatic leadership"). The continual emergence of the personalized charismatic leader and the destructive effects that he/she wages on society (Chapter 10, "Destructive leadership") is effectively conceptualized later in the book, as is an explanation of the susceptibility of followers to collude and aid such a destructive personality. The success of fraudulent, egoistic leaders such as Allen Stanford and Bernie Madoff provide just two examples among a swathe of modern business leaders who made great promises of wealth and fortune to investors as a means of perpetuating their own powerful and extravagant lifestyles.

These individuals would cement their popularity by sponsoring grand, luxurious free events such as gladiatorial shows for the people of Rome, and ever more bloody military battles to cement their heroic status. The original founding values of Rome – self-discipline and simplicity (Chapter 2, "Trait theories") – had clearly eroded, and the Empire was damaged severely by the infighting of these individuals who eventually turned on each other to mete out bloody civil wars in their thirst for power. It is interesting that modern academic studies of leadership have turned towards the study of the need for authenticity (Chapter 9, "Authentic leadership"), and a return to such values.

IDEA IN BRIEF

Leadership of Sparta

Leadership of the powerful and militaristic city state of Sparta was based on the concept of the survival of the fittest. From the ages of 7 to 60 years of age, Spartan males lived communally in military barracks and engaged in a life of fighting. Young Spartan women were required to train alongside the males, in order that they would produce healthy offspring. The backbone of Spartan life was one of order and obedience, where land and goods were distributed communally and equally, where each man was guaranteed a minimum wage upon which he could live, and where each man enjoyed equal status before the law. Alongside Athens, Sparta was the most powerful city-state in the pan-Hellenic world.

Perhaps the most famous of Roman military commanders is Julius Caesar, an engaging strategist and orator, whose intelligence, charisma (Chapter 6, "Charismatic leadership") and military success, combined with great ambition (Chapter 2, "Trait theories" and Chapter 3, "Skills theories"), cemented his success as undisputed ruler of the Roman Empire and (following his defeat of Pompey) the entire Eastern Mediterranean. Initially, Caesar contributed much to the social fabric of Rome, encouraging the educated liberal classes (such as doctors and teachers) to return to Rome, developing public libraries, providing free food to the poor, rebuilding Rome's infrastructure and taking good care of his armies. Caesar even demonstrated an impressively even-handed approach in allowing old senatorial enemies to retain their former positions of power upon his victorious return after his defeat of Pompey (Chapter 8, "Emotional intelligence"). However, his eventual demise can be attributed to vanity and ego – he installed himself as a living God, building a temple where Romans could worship him (Chapter 10, "Destructive leadership"). While retaining popularity with many Romans, as many as 60 senators were directly and physically involved in his murder.[14]

Caesar was succeeded by his only heir, Augustus, who rejected the titles and luxuries that had led to so much trouble for Caesar, and instead, successfully and dependably, secured the stability of the Empire. Although he reverted to the old edicts that law and stability took precedence over personal liberty, he did also safeguard the important principles that political power should be undertaken in the interests of the Roman people, that government should remain a shared responsibility among those who had been elected and that no man should be above the law. One of the central facets of these principles was his replacing the old system of corrupt provincial administration with an efficient and fair civil service. He also made it possible for individuals to be voted into the Senate on the basis of merit and personal integrity (Chapter 2, "Trait theories"), replacing the older, more nepotistic system of access via lineage (i.e. based on one's class and ancestry).

Augustus was a steadfast, intelligent man, showing little pretension or interest in the luxuries that could have been afforded to him because of his position. A fascinating modern example of such modesty is embodied by Warren Buffett, a man with a net worth of $50 billion, who still lives in the same modest family home that he purchased in 1957 for $31,500.

While Augustus did not possess the charisma of his father, he did possess humility and a great vision for Rome (Chapter 9, "Authentic leadership"). These qualities added to his popularity, possibly because they represented a moral integrity and authenticity that represented a return to the *mos maiorum* (old ways) of his Roman ancestors. It is the great corporate visionaries (Jeff Bezos, Steve Jobs, Bill Gates) who remain the most successful, and the concept of vision remains central to modern studies of leadership, most notably in the context of transformational and charismatic leadership. Ultimately, Augustus contributed notably to the development and strength of the Roman Empire, retaining his interest in promoting moral values and doing what he could to benefit his people (Chapter 7, "Transformational leadership"). In the face of great power and popularity, he did not become corrupt, nor did he bow to the temptations of wealth and privilege (Chapter 4, "Behavioural theories") and, as a result, remained popular to his death.

The actions of Donald Woods, Steve Biko, Winston Churchill, Barack Obama, Warren Buffett and the many other inspirational leaders profiled in the pages of this book offer reassurance that the potential for principled leadership does not reside only in the footnotes of history, in the form of Augustus and his compatriots. It also has the potential to exist in equal measure in today's boardrooms and corridors of power, in the actions of corporate visionaries and philanthropists, and in the actions of the world's great leaders who have the courage to stand firm against injustices.

CHAPTER 1 QUIZ

1   Stogdill (1974, p. 259) commented succinctly that "there are almost as many definitions of leadership as there are persons who have attempted to define the concept". Find the definition that you find most explanatory and explain why you feel this person is most equipped to comment upon leadership.

2   When did the academic study of management begin, and with what theory?

3   Identify the major leadership/management theories, in chronological order, that emerged within the field of management studies over the last 100 years.

4   When did leadership theory move away from an exclusively 'leader-centric' approach?

5   Which theories include the articulation of a vision as a central element?

6   How can you separate a 'good' leadership theory from a 'bad' one?

7   Which leadership theory has a 'dark side'?

8   When did leadership begin to emerge as a field of study in its own right (as opposed to being studied as part of management studies)?

9   Why do you think that political and corporate leaders fail, repeatedly, to learn the lessons of the past?

10 What do you think are the most important traits, skills or attributes that a leader can possess?

Notes

1   Quote taken from an interview conducted for this book, which appears in the expert insight "Changing lives" at the end of this chapter.

2   Marcus Aurelius (2004). *Meditations*, Book Seven. Harmondsworth, UK: Penguin Classics, p. 49.

3   "Leadership", *Collins English Dictionary – Complete and Unabridged 10th Edition*. Available at: http://dictionary.reference.com/browse/leadership [Accessed 24 February 2012].

4   Quote taken from Marcus Aurelius (2004), *Meditations*, Book Seven, p. 49.

5   "Never give in", quote taken from a speech delivered by Winston Churchill on 29 October 1941 at Harrow School, England.

6   Part of a speech delivered by Jesse Jackson: Rainbow Coalition Speech, Democratic National Convention Address, delivered on 18 July 1984 in San Francisco, California.

7   Delivered as part of Barack Obama's 2013 Inaugural Address, 21 January 2013.

8   This statement is taken from a letter written by Abraham Lincoln to A.G. Hodges, entitled "If slavery is not wrong, nothing is wrong".

9   Ralph Waldo Emerson, "The American scholar", taken from an oration delivered before the Phi Beta Kappa Society at Cambridge, Massachusetts, 31 August 1837.

10   This quotation appears in Homespun Wisdom from the Oracle of Omaha. *Business Week Online*, 5 July 1999. Available at: www.businessweek.com/1999/99_27/b3636006.htm [Accessed 3 February 2013].

11   This quotation is likely a modern paraphrasing of a longer passage from Thucydides' *History of the Peloponnesian War*, II.43.3.

12   Burke, E. (1770). *Thoughts on the Cause of the Present Discontents*. 3rd ed. London: J. Dodsley in the Pall-Mall, p. 106.

13   This expert insight originally appeared in the 1st Edition of this book; the organizational profile/overview has accordingly been updated for the 2nd Edition.

14   Caesar was actually the nephew of Marius, who suffered at the hands of Sulla, eventually fleeing into exile during Sulla's purging of the liberal elite of Roman society.

References

Lipman-Blumen, J. (2005). Toxic Leadership: When Grand Illusions Masquerade as Noble Visions. *Leader to Leader*, 35(36), pp. 29–36.

Salovey, P. and Mayer, J.D. (1990). Emotional Intelligence. *Imagination, Cognition, and Personality*, 9, pp. 185–211.

Stogdill, R.M. (1974). *Handbook of Leadership: A Survey of Theory and Research*. New York: Free Press.

Other resources

See PowerPoint slides on the companion website at www.routledge.com/9780367374822.

2

TRAIT THEORIES

"With power comes a lot of responsibility."
— *Bassma El-Amir Riley, former Head Trader at Deutsche Bank*[1]

On 29 October 1941, Winston Churchill was to make one of his most indomitable speeches, addressing the pupils of Harrow School with his powerful call to: "never give in – never, never, never, in nothing great or small, large or petty, never give in except to convictions of honour and good sense. Never yield to force; never yield to the apparently overwhelming might of the enemy".[2] It is not an overstatement to say that Churchill's powers of oratory played a decisive role in mobilizing the strength of the Allies in the heroic fight against Hitler's Third Reich, and that his great self-belief, military strategizing and powers of leadership made him a great man of history – a man who led his country to victory in one of its darkest hours. Churchill is a powerful figure with which to open our consideration of leadership theory, not least because he remains an ultimately complex, oft-debated leadership figure. Churchill was responsible for serious transgressions which should not be ignored; he was also, of course, responsible for spearheading the fight back against the Third Reich – the greatest evil that the modern world has ever known. As such, he constitutes a worthy figure with which to begin the case studies of this chapter, reminding us that the task of exemplifying leadership remains a nuanced and complex task. It is with Churchill's historic words in mind that we begin our journey, one that will traverse the diverse landscape of leadership theory over the chapters that follow. We begin with the presentation of trait theory, an approach that claims its foundations in the 'Great Man' theory of leadership.

Structure of the chapter

This chapter seeks first to introduce the history of trait theory. The chapter then critically conceptualizes the key traits that have been theorized to constitute those of the Great Man or great leader by grouping traits into sub-domains (physiological, cognitive and personality traits). The chapter then progresses towards a consideration of the ways in which traits might be robustly measured, before engaging the reader with an expert insight written by the Head of Government Bonds & Repo at a leading global universal investment bank ("The role of personality traits in leadership success"). A case study of Winston Churchill ("Winston Churchill: born leader?") also provides a lively and challenging foundation upon which readers can argue the key points of trait theory and stake their position in the 'born or made' debate.[3]

Introduction: the Great Man theory

For over a century, scholars have attempted to answer the question of what characterizes a leader and sets them apart from a non-leader, or an ineffective leader. Thomas Carlyle effectively opened the floor to the modern study of trait theory with his conceptualization of the 'Great Men' who had shaped history (Carlyle, 1907; Galton and Eysenck, 1869), and many scholars have subsequently picked up the baton in an attempt to discover 'heritable traits' that might differentiate leaders from non-leaders. The Great Man theory later became known as the 'trait approach', as a wide range of modern-day scholars sought to conduct research into the traits that set apart great leaders from ineffectual ones.

Of course, the study of great men in history is not, in itself, new; one can regard the great myth of the hero, legendary figure or leader in antiquity across a myriad of cultures (for example, Ancient Greece, Rome and Babylon), via the observations of great philosophers (Aristotle, Socrates), politicians (Renaissance authors such as Machiavelli) and even within the realm of sport (e.g. quarterback Colin Kaepernick, whose decision to kneel in protest at racial inequality within the US during a San Francisco 49ers game in 2012 inspired the impactful #TakeAKnee protest). Leadership trait studies enjoyed a surge of popularity in the early part of the twentieth century, but declined in popularity in later years, largely due to critiques of the approach (see "Critiques of trait theory" later in this chapter). However, the trait approach has recently enjoyed a renewed surge in interest, largely due to the emergence and popularity of 'new leadership school' theories such as charismatic and transformational leadership (see Chapters 6 and 7). This renewed interest has been characterized by a multidisciplinary focus that now centres upon the role of neurological brain functioning, gender, intelligence, physiognomy (the appearance of the face of a leader) and other physical traits in leadership.

This chapter now divides a presentation and discussion of trait research into seven subheadings: personality traits; neurological traits; cognitive traits; gender and leadership; emotional intelligence and leadership; physiognomy; and power.

Personality traits

Stogdill's pivotal 1948 study of 124 trait studies (conducted between 1904 and 1947) concluded that there could be no claims made as to the universality of personality traits exhibited by leaders that could definitively separate them from non-leaders across a range of different situations. Instead, he concluded that situational variables would largely affect the ability of an individual to emerge as a leader. He did, however, identify eight personality traits that differentiated leaders from non-leaders: intelligence, alertness, insight, responsibility, initiative, persistence, self-confidence and sociability. A subsequent 1959 study conducted by Mann compared in excess of 1,400 trait studies of leadership in small groups. Mann concluded, similarly, that specific personality traits differentiated leaders from non-leaders, with his study identifying the traits of *intelligence, masculinity, adjustment, dominance, extraversion* and *conservatism*. It should be noted that both Mann (1959) and Stogdill (1948) are characteristic of their time, in that they demonstrate a Western hegemonic interpretation of constructs such as *conservatism* within their studies, an approach that renders generalizations of their findings potentially problematic to non-individualistic cultures. The trait of *masculinity* identified by Mann (1959) also betrayed the cultural norms surrounding the absence of women in the workplace during the 1950s. Nevertheless, the studies formed a solid foundation upon which the future study of leadership traits could be based. A subsequent study by Lord *et al.* (1986), who utilized a meta-analytic approach[4] to study trait research, similarly identified *intelligence, masculinity* and *dominance* as key leadership traits.

In a follow-up study conducted in 1974 (with data taken from 163 studies conducted between 1948 and 1970), Stogdill modified his claims regarding the prominence of situational factors as a key determinant of leadership, and instead posited that it was a mix of personality factors, in addition to situational factors, that constituted key determinants of leadership. Leadership research conducted within the field of leadership studies has largely continued to focus on the existence and prevalence of specific personality traits that may differentiate an effective leader from an ineffective one.

The Big Five

Much modern research into the existence of personality traits within the study of trait theory is based on the 'Big Five' personality dimensions (Goldberg, 1981) – *neuroticism/emotional stability, extraversion, agreeableness, conscientiousness* and *openness to experience* – with extraversion linked most strongly to the emergence of leadership (Judge *et al.*, 2002). The 'Big Five' represent personality at a low level of abstraction (i.e. conceptualizing personality in a very general way), with each of the five traits encapsulating a more specific and detailed range of personality characteristics.

Hoffman *et al.* (2011), for example, cite a relationship between leadership and the traits of *achievement motivation, energy, dominance, honesty/integrity, self-confidence, creativity* and *charisma*. Lord *et al.* (1986) identified a relationship between leadership effectiveness and the traits of *dominance, extraversion* and *adjustment*, a theory supported by Scott Derue *et al.* (2011) who reported a particularly significant predictive relationship between effective leadership and the traits of *conscientiousness, extraversion* and *agreeableness*. Adjustment, or the ability to adapt, has actually emerged from a wide range of academic studies as a necessary trait for leadership to occur, and is linked to the ability of the leader to self-monitor and to be flexible (Bass, 1990). Bridges identifies "transferring skills" – higher order skills that enable graduates to "select, adapt, adjust and apply his (or her) skills to different situations, across different social contexts and perhaps similarly across different cognitive domains" (Bridges, 1993, p. 50), while Hinchliffe (2002) discusses the need for graduates to deal effectively with a complex, unpredictable world – an ability that arguably requires the attainment of a sophisticated level of metacognition and critical awareness. Personality traits of *extraversion* and *openness* (themselves related to the elicitation of effective leadership) are also related to intelligence (Judge *et al.*, 2002), with the trait of *adjustment* seen to be positively mediated by neurological traits such as neurological coherence (Cacioppo *et al.*, 2008).

Neurological traits

Turkheimer (2000, p. 160) theorizes that "everything is heritable". This statement tells us that personality, and therefore personality traits, are, to an extent, inherited. One might observe, for example, that intelligence, itself considered heritable to an extent, has been positively linked to effective leadership (Judge *et al.*, 2004). This leads us neatly to a consideration of neurological traits – a partially heritable construct that plays its part in the 'nature versus nurture' debate, and which also raises the question of the necessary neurological traits that a leader must possess in order for specific personality traits and behaviours to be exhibited.

Neurological traits: brain chemistry

Neuroscience identifies the role of brain chemistry in defining individual traits, behaviour and learning and, subsequently, as a potentially key contributor to leadership ability. For example, some research points to the fact that 30 per cent of the individual differences in leadership can be attributed to genetics (Arvey *et al.*, 2007). Bass and Bass (2009) recount how leadership trait research, constructs and theory only have the capacity to account for around 10 per cent of the variance in leadership outcomes. This has led to the recent emergence of the use of neuroscience in various fields, such as neuro-finance and neuro-economics (the study of the role of neuroscience in economic decision making), and in the role of neurology in risk-taking behaviour.

Neurological traits: serotonin

Brain chemistry has emerged as a physiological trait associated with effective leadership. Specifically, the presence of serotonin in the brain (Cawthorn, 1996) determines the ability to regulate one's emotions (a key element of emotional intelligence, which is also related to effective leadership).[5] The absence of serotonin and the presence of cortisol (when heightened in the presence of stress) can disrupt performance and negatively impact leadership performance. The fields of political physiology and evolutionary science provide elucidating insights into one reason why we never seem to learn from history: evolutionarily speaking, we have not substantively changed since the days of cavemen, yet we now inhabit an artificial world for which we are poorly physiologically and neurologically designed. Further, we no longer exist in the small communities for which we were created but in nations of millions. We are simply not hardwired to rationally conceptualize the way in which one vote might affect millions of others we will never meet, which is why we so often fall foul of propaganda-based, emotional political appeals.

An individual who possesses a high level of serotonin is likely to moderate stress more effectively, which is likely, in turn, to exert a positive effect on decision making (Cawthorn, 1996), while genetic levels of dopamine has been observed to moderate voting preferences. Serotonin exerts an effect on emotional intelligence by increasing feelings of happiness and optimism, with a concomitant effect of enhancing the individual's ability to deal with stress. These neurological observations add an intriguing layer to discussions surrounding the role of emotional intelligence in leadership, which will be explored further in Chapter 8.

DISCUSSION STARTER

Testosterone and financial traders

Coates and Herbert (2008) studied the role of the endocrine system in financial risk taking in their study of male financial traders who actively traded in the City of London. They observed that a trader's morning testosterone levels significantly predicted the profitability of the trader throughout that day, and that testosterone levels were higher on days when the trader made more profit than their one-month daily average.

They also observed that levels of the stress hormone cortisol would rise with: (a) the variance of the traders trading results (but not, interestingly, when a loss occurred) and (b) the volatility of the market (where the greater the volatility, the greater the rise in cortisol). The authors also observed that the long-term effects of acutely raised testosterone and cortisol (mostly prevalent during times of marked market volatility) could lead to a compromised ability of the trader to engage in rational choice when making trades. This can be attributed to the fact that testosterone has rewarding and addictive properties, leading to androgenic priming and increased (possibly irrational) risk taking in consequent events. The over-activation of various regions of the brain, caused by acutely raised steroid levels, was also observed to lead to irrational behaviour. Long-term elevation of cortisol can cause debilitating emotional and cognitive effects, such as a weakened ability to cope with stress and a tendency to perceive risks and stressors where none exist, compromising one's ability to effectively manage risk.

Start the discussion: How might neurological factors affect one's ability to perform effectively in the workplace?

Neurological traits: endogenous steroids (testosterone and cortisol)

Endogenous steroids – testosterone and cortisol – are produced naturally by the body, and both possess cognitive and behavioural effects. Cortisol is known as the 'stress hormone' as levels of the hormone increase when we face a stressful situation. Long-term exposure to elevated cortisol levels has been shown to exert a negative effect on mood. Testosterone exerts a significant effect on behaviour, and excessive levels are known to disrupt emotional regulation, leading to mood swings, irrational judgement, anger and aggression.

Cognitive traits

Early work surrounding trait theory (Mann, 1959) identified the role of intelligence as one of the greatest traits of leadership. Intelligence, as measured by standardized IQ (intelligence quotient) testing, measures the quotient of an individual against the general population.

DISCUSSION STARTER

The role of IQ in presidential elections

In his study of US Presidents, Simonton (2006, pp. 511–512) reports that the impact of general intelligence can be witnessed at five levels of specificity:

1 at the level at which general intelligence is closely associated with ability to cope with the complexity of modern life
2 as the most important predictor of job performance across a wide range of occupations
3 as a positive correlate with leadership performance
4 the importance of such correlations with the needs of political leadership
5 that intelligence has a positive correlation with the performance of US Presidents, being the only measured trait to correlate positively and consistently with all measures of Presidential greatness.

Interestingly, some research has demonstrated a positive relationship between intelligence and the Big Five personality dimensions; for example, "openness to experience", which has been correlated strongly to "intellectual brilliance" in a study of 42 US Presidents (Simonton, 2006). Simonton (2006) also found that intellectual brilliance is correlated strongly with presidential success, but that, interestingly, highly intelligent Presidents were much less likely to win an election by a landslide (Simonton, 1987). George Bush was found to exhibit the lowest score for "openness", the second lowest score for "IQ" and the third lowest "intellectual brilliance" score among all twentieth-century US Presidents measured by the study (Simonton, 1987). His integrative complexity score was also notably lower than other US Presidents. Low scorers on integrative complexity measures are unlikely to be able to appreciate different perspectives, meaning that the individual is likely to feel relatively comfortable executing decisions that are based only on their own point of view. Recent analyses of President Trump's writing style level indicated the level of a fifth grader.[6]

Start the discussion: Identify critiques of Simonton's study, particularly with regard to the comments made about President Trump.

The role of intelligence in leadership continues to be well documented, correlating positively with leadership performance (Bass, 1990; Judge *et al.*, 2004), professional and personal success (including financial income), higher levels of education and as a universally desired characteristic of leaders (Den Hartog *et al.*, 1999). Cognitive ability also allows an individual to intellectually approach a problem from a myriad of different standpoints, allowing the development of a more strategic and robust approach to decision making.

Gender and leadership

Gender appears to mediate the behaviours and personality of leaders. For example, women are perceived as being more considerate of the needs of others, and of the needs of the organization, whereas males are perceived as more self-interested and power-orientated. Interestingly, however, such gender differences seem to be based only on perceptions, rather than actual observable differences (Eagly and Karua, 2002). This might stem from the importance attributed by followers to leaders' physical traits, where masculinity and maturity of appearance are perceived as being more powerful than feminine traits. Attractiveness is a positive predictor of leadership success, although the relationship between success and attractiveness has interestingly been shown to be inverse in the case of females (Heilman and Stopeck, 1985).

Emotional intelligence and leadership

Many authors have already established a link between emotional intelligence and neurology. For example, Morse (2006), suggests that the articulation of a vision is affected by limbic system activity, and Paulus *et al.* (2003) believe that the cortex may help to mediate regulation of risk and to affect behaviours in anticipation of emotional responses such as fear. Research also indicates that right frontal brain dysfunction predisposes an individual to poor social skills, poor emotional regulation and poor self-awareness (Salloway *et al.*, 2001), and that frontal cortex activity affects moral judgement (Knabb *et al.*, 2009). The role of emotional intelligence in leadership is considered at length in Chapter 8, so will not be subject to further consideration here.

Physiognomy

Physical attractiveness or the appearance of the face ('physiognomy') has emerged forcefully in the leadership literature as a trait that is strongly significantly related to a follower's perceptions of a leader. Cherulnik *et al.* (1990) report that followers are more likely to respond favourably to a leader who possesses traits of physical attractiveness and maturity, and much leadership research supports this observation.

Studies of physiognomy in perceptions of leadership have emerged with particular strength in the field of political science, with many studies reporting that physical attractiveness leads to greater political success (Sigelman *et al.*, 1986) and career success in a range of professions (Hamermesh, 2006; Hosoda *et al.*, 2003; Mobius and Rosenblat, 2006), and that 'attractive' individuals experience better treatment in general (Dion *et al.*, 1972; Griffin and Langlois, 2006). For example, Martin (1978) asked research subjects to rate photographs of Australian political candidates according to their 'gut reaction' of the candidate. Ratings carried strong predictive power of the actual performance of those candidates on election day. Similarly, Todorov *et al.* (2005) and Ballew and Todorov (2007) asked students to view photographic images of US House, Senate and Gubernatorial[7] candidates, and to rate candidates according to their impressiveness across various dimensions such as competence, leadership, intelligence, honesty, charisma and likeability. The ratings given by the students – based only on physical appearance – correlated strongly with the outcomes of the actual elections. Banducci *et al.* (2008) conducted a similar study in Britain, asking research subjects to rate British political candidates in terms of perceived personality traits (such as trustworthiness, empathy and competence). Again, ratings carried strong predictive power as to who actually won the elections, as did a Finnish study by Poutvaara *et al.* (2009), a study of American candidates (Lawson *et al.*, 2010) and an American study of ratings of Canadian political candidates (Rule and Ambady, 2010). Recent advancements in political physiology suggest a biological basis for charisma that might partly explain this perceived role of attractiveness in political success (explored in greater depth in Chapter 6, "Charismatic leadership").

Rule and Ambady's (2010) study asked research subjects to compare photographs of Fortune 500[8] CEOs, and to rate each CEO in terms of how successful they perceived them to be as a leader. Findings also positively predicted the actual success of the CEOs, measured by how much profit they made. In all cases, raters inferred positive personality traits in respect of those political candidates who were deemed more physically attractive than others. Traits included higher perceived levels of power, intelligence, honesty and trustworthiness (Rule and Ambady, 2010). Interestingly, ratings given by children and adults were surprisingly consistent across studies.

Such observations are at once insightful and worrying – insightful for those who wish to develop winning strategies for political candidates, and worrying for those who fear the impact of such voter decision-making stratagems on the efficacy of the democratic process. This chapter has identified general intelligence as the only positive, consistent predictor of presidential greatness, yet it is certainly possible to argue on the basis of academic evidence that it is physical attractiveness (including perceptions of charisma) – and not intelligence – that is most likely to propel a candidate to office.

Power

An individual's need for power, or *power motivation*, emerges as a necessary trait within the literature (McClelland and Burnham, 1976) as a precursor to the pursuit of leadership. McClelland and Burnham reported that leaders in large, hierarchical organizations are motivated to lead by their need for *authority and power*, *achievement* and *affiliation*, with leaders who demonstrate a high power motivation emerging as the most effective. There are two types of power motivation: self-serving *personalized power*, which has been linked to depraved behaviour (Winter, 2002), aggressiveness, extreme risk taking, impulsive and anti-social behaviour (Magee and Langner, 2008), and the socially-focused *socialized power* that is associated with pro-social behaviour and, often, the selection of pro-social professions such as teaching. McClelland's Theory of Needs is discussed in greater detail later in the book (Chapters 4 and 6) alongside theories of narcissism, so will not be elucidated upon further here.

In the earlier work of French and Raven (1959), the type of power held by a leader can be further conceptualized in five ways: *reward power* (the power to reward followers for their actions); *coercive power* (the power to punish followers for their actions); *expert power* (power based on expert knowledge); *legitimate power* (power deriving from a hierarchical position, such as CEO or Head of Marketing); and *referent power* (power based on respect for the leader). Consider the following examples:

- Steven Hawking demonstrates great **expert power**, popularizing quantum physics in seminal works such as *A Brief History of Time*.
- Donald Trump is a heavy user of **coercive power**, as he uses his legitimate position of power as President of the US to directly vilify, target and insult individuals who displease him.
- Corporate CEOs such as Jamie Dimon possess high **legitimate power**, as their position affords them a formal seniority that must be recognized by subordinates and colleagues.

- Any manager who is able to award financial remuneration (e.g. a bonus) possesses strong **reward power** over his subordinates.

- Greta Thunberg possesses strong **referent power**, as she holds no legitimate position of authority, is only 17 years old (at the time of writing), yet commands great loyalty and respect from followers. Her Fridays for Future protests inspired a generation and, to date, she has achieved incredible feats; leading the largest climate strike in history, addressing the United Nations, meeting the Pope, facing down national leaders, holding powerful adults to account, being named Time Person of the Year 2019 and addressing national parliaments. Thunberg was nominated for the Nobel Peace Prize in March 2019.

DISCUSSION STARTER

Allen Stanford

In March 2012, tycoon Allen Stanford was convicted of multiple counts of fraud. At one time, Stanford had been one of the richest men in the US, with an estimated personal net worth of $1.2 billion. For 22 years, Stanford had engineered investment scams involving billions of dollars and an estimated 17,000 investors became victims of his fraudulent activities. His income helped to finance a lavish personal lifestyle that saw his acquisition of yachts, a fleet of private jets and high-value sponsorship of cricket tournaments. Stanford's level of fraud was so great that it counts as one of the largest cases of fraud in US history, second only to Bernie Madoff, who received a 150-year sentence for his $50 billion Ponzi scheme.

Start the discussion: What kind of power motivation does Allen Stanford exhibit? Can you think of any modern political and/or corporate examples that exhibit the same kind of power?

Measuring leadership traits

While readers are encouraged to explore a wide range of personality traits in their own research, it is nevertheless important to use instruments that are valid, reliable and generalizable. For example, an instrument should exhibit adequate construct validity.[9]

In terms of measuring traits, a number of measures exist. These mostly centre on the measurement of the Big Five personality traits. The majority of personality trait instruments that possess adequate construct validity constitute Big Five trait measures. These include:

- the NEO PI-R, a 240-item inventory; the NEO-FFI (Five-Factor Index); and the NEO-FFI, a 60-item version of the NEO PI-R (Costa and McCrae, 1992)

- the Big Five Inventory (BFI; John *et al.*, 1991)
- the 100-item Trait Descriptive Adjectives (TDA; Goldberg, 1992)
- the Big Five Inventory (BFI), a 44-item self-report measure (John *et al.*, 1991).

While the use of the Myers–Briggs Type Indicator remains popular among the corporate sector (both in terms of consulting and recruitment), it demonstrates relatively low empirical validity to support such extensive use (Carlson, 1985). As a result, its role is perhaps better situated as an effective illustrative tool and facilitator of broader discussion around concepts of teamwork and leadership.

Critiques of trait theory

Critiques of trait theory abound. For example, the approach has been branded as "too simplistic" (Conger and Kanungo, 1998, p. 38) and as unsystematic and lacking in theoretical integration (Avolio, 2007; Bennis, 1959; Hoffman *et al.*, 2011; Zaccaro, 2007). Zaccaro (2007) further critiques the use of narrow categories in the investigation of traits (such as via the use of the Big Five model), and Scott Derue *et al.* (2011) criticizes the continual development of new leadership theories in the absence of any explicit comparison or falsification of existing theories.

Neurological studies discussed in this chapter point to the role of endogenous steroids (testosterone and cortisol) in decision making in financial markets. However, other factors should be taken into consideration in addition to neurological traits in a financial markets context. For example, the intersection of traders' self-interest, a tendency for the traders' peer group to exhibit a high need for personalized power, and the remuneration structure of the financial institution within which they work (financial markets traders usually receive a commission at the point of trade, regardless of how risky the trade is or how poorly the financial vehicle might perform in the future). All of these factors might exert a potentially cumulative effect on traders' tendency to undertake increasingly risky decisions. These critiques underscore the importance of weighing neurological factors alongside the situational variables within which they occur.

Reporting of personality traits is often done using self-reporting measures; and the bias associated with self-reporting of leadership traits can notably affect the reliability of data (Donaldson and Grant-Vallone, 2002). Indeed, one might theorize that, while one can observe successful leaders, CEOs, politicians and executives, and measure their traits via self-reporting, we cannot ascertain how extensively genetics may influence their thoughts and actions, how great a gap exists between the leader's self-perception and reality or whether the leader is telling the truth in their answers.

Social anthropologists theorize that the traits that may have led to adaptive success for our ancestors (such as the ability to physically dominate in a fight) might now be somewhat redundant in the modern world, where our environments now demand different adaptive abilities such as refined manners (Van Vugt *et al.*, 2008). This is a salient point and may explain why voters still continue to respond intuitively and favourably to candidates on the basis of certain physical traits – perhaps a throwback to earlier times when physical strength was a necessary trait – as opposed to cognitive and personality traits such as intellectual openness.

It has also been argued that *motives* – such as ambition and a high need for power – are greater motivators for action and behaviour in a leader than traits (Hoffman *et al.*, 2011), and that it is instead behaviours, which arguably can be developed via training and feedback, that might provide the greatest predictor of leadership success (Day, 2000; Scott Derue *et al.*, 2011). The use of training and feedback in leadership development is considered in greater detail in Chapter 3, "Skills theories".

 **Expert insight**

The role of personality traits in leadership success

This expert insight is provided by Bassma El Amir-Riley, formerly Head of Trading for Government Bonds & Repo at a leading global universal investment bank, a role that involved managing a team of six (male) traders. El Amir-Riley remains one of the only women in UK investment banking to have headed up a trading desk.

❝Traders are by nature strong personalities. My management style is of a laissez-faire nature and I lead by example. I include the senior traders in most of my decision-making process as I find this conducive to a more efficient and happy working environment. I take part in all aspects of our job to encourage hard work from the other members of the desk. I do, however, ensure my authority is firm and I make it clear that targets are there to be met. Empathy and being a hard worker have made my job of managing a team of traders a success.

Innate traits: the role of gender in leadership

Due to the nature of the business being so male dominated it was a challenge for me as a woman to manage six men and to establish my authority. A man would not have faced the same difficulties given the trading environment. Men on the trading floor are not accustomed to working with women, let alone reporting to one. However, having said this, once I earned the respect of my peers, I believe I have succeeded more than a man would have, given the lack of women in this type of job.

By nature, it is my belief that men and women are different, so it is logical that their management styles would be different. In general, women have a more emotional aspect to managing which often works in their favour and of course can also be to their detriment. I also believe that women in leadership roles have to work harder than men to reach the same level. Having said this, I do feel that gender is now taking up a more important role than it deserves.

Everyone is all too aware of gender issues and, if anything, women are now given a fairer chance than men to improve statistics for firms.

Many women do not enjoy trading, the hours nor the working environment. However, the few women that work as traders in general have the same ability and desire to perform as well as their male peers. As they are a minority, they tend to want to outperform the average trader and prove themselves more. Having said this, the nature of women does mean that they are not as comfortable with huge risk as a man would be.

Personality traits of traders

Traders are, for the most part, selfish individuals. They are trained to perform as sole employees and are remunerated for their financial efforts only. Many employers would lead you to believe that traders are compensated for their teamwork or other non-financial objectives. In reality, traders work for their bonus, which is solely and directly linked to their profit and loss.

Leadership of traders is generally very black and white; i.e. completely P&L [profit and loss] driven. Traders are not trained to, nor expected to, have high morals, nor are they expected or required to help others. They are generally highly intelligent, quantitative individuals who are motivated by the financial benefits of their jobs. They are not expected to be team players either. Their management does not take the time to get to know them and rarely do they spend time on the desk. I believe this is changing due to the financial crisis[10] and the pressure on banks from a gender and race perspective.

The long hours and banking culture require dedication and generally most traders do not stop working when they leave work. The markets are open until late and traders generally check them several times during the evening and read any news that is relevant in the evenings and early in the mornings on the way in, e.g. reading news from the Asian markets before the London markets open. This job clearly requires a very strong work ethic. In terms of gender, there are few females in the trading world in general. The trading environment is highly aggressive and competitive. The hours are extremely long, and the commitment required is high, so mothers may struggle with this aspect of the job. Many women may not enjoy working in this kind of environment. Having said this, there is a large number of female sales employees who sit on the trading floor. They still need to keep abreast of the markets but perhaps not to the same extent as traders.

The role of skills vs traits

Are skills and qualifications as important as traits? It is certainly true that a degree is necessary to gain access to a trading role at our bank. However, through my years of trading what I have observed is that the most educated of traders are not necessarily the most successful. Mathematical ability is definitely a prerequisite. Being able to build spreadsheets for pricing is also extremely important. Another non-tangible skill is the confidence and courage to put risk on [take risky decisions]. Having the intelligence or ideas alone does not necessarily mean the trader can handle the pressure of having risk on. Discipline is another skill needed. The hardest decision is to close a losing trade and not let the position go too far against you.[11]

Personality traits of the leader

For me, as a leader, in terms of my motivation to lead, I would say that I enjoy the feeling of power, to an extent [this answer was given in response to being asked to identify power, achievement or affiliation as her primary motivational driver as a leader]. With power comes a lot of responsibility for others – not to mention hard work and long hours. I would never allow this desire for power to change my nature nor step on others' toes to achieve this. The need for affiliation is also high, as for me it is important to work in a comfortable and friendly environment and earn the respect of my peers. Finally, I am competitive by nature and I do not believe in holding a powerful position without setting myself high targets and achieving them.

I am a very strong-willed and competitive person and it is imperative to me to be extremely successful in my career. Perhaps being a woman in such a male-dominated environment gives me extra impetus to be motivated. When I do anything in life, I always give it my all and this has certainly helped me in my career. I set myself realistic goals that are higher than my colleagues' targets and ensure that I achieve them. None of this would be possible without hard work.

My advice for graduates: educate yourself to the highest possible level, work as hard as you can, help others as much as possible, be empathetic and pleasant to your peers no matter what their position is, and do not stand on anyone's toes for your own gain.**"**

Questions

1   What personality traits does El Amir-Riley identify in this expert insight as being crucial to her leadership success? How well do these correlate with the academic literature discussed in this chapter?
2   Discuss the role of neurological traits in the elicitation of effective performance of El Amir-Riley and her team in this expert insight.
3   Consider the key challenges faced by El Amir-Riley as a result of gender.
4   In what ways does this expert insight a) strengthen and b) challenge the assumptions and theories made by academic traits theorists?
5   El Amir-Riley voices an interesting idea that ethics are important (via her recommendations that one should not step on another's toes to succeed). The centrality of ethics and morals to leadership effectiveness emerges with force in

later chapters (Chapter 7, "Transformational leadership" and Chapter 9, "Authentic Leadership"). Theorize why acting in an ethical way improves organizational productivity and effectiveness.

Summary

The 'Great Man' theory of leadership paved the way for an extensive consideration of the personality traits associated with great leadership throughout the twentieth century. While the trait approach has waned in popularity over the decades, it again rose to prominence around the start of the twenty-first century, with advances in medical science, political physiology and neuro-finance allowing for the consideration of neurological, genetic and cognitive traits in environments as diverse as finance, politics and education. The development of personality trait instruments that demonstrate high construct validity allow researchers to add meaningfully to research within this field. Although criticism of the field exists, it is likely that trait research will continue to remain in a position of prominence in leadership research, due in part to the associated emergence of the 'new leadership school' (transformational, charismatic and authentic leadership) that considers traits such as vision and charisma in the elicitation of highly effective leadership.

Case study: Winston Churchill – born leader?

Winston Churchill, a former British prime minister, was a legendary orator and writer who successfully fought Adolf Hitler's Third Reich, against seemingly insurmountable odds, safeguarding the future of his country and inspiring a generation to pull together in the hardest of times against the worst of enemies.

Winston Churchill was the son of Lord Randolph Churchill, a member of the British Parliament, and his American heiress mother, Jennie Jerome. A strong maternal influence remained throughout his life in the form of his nanny, Elizabeth Everest. Born in 1874 at his grandfather's stately pile, Blenheim Palace, the young Churchill undoubtedly experienced a life of wealth, influence and privilege during his formative years. He attended Harrow School, where he was introduced to the study of military tactics. A relatively average but popular scholar, Churchill graduated into the Royal Military College at Sandhurst in 1893, where he was to graduate in the upper echelons of his class and receive a commission as cavalry officer. Serving in India and the Sudan, Churchill was to combine his role as officer with a fledgling career as a war correspondent, receiving his first commission as a writer for the *Daily Graphic*, then for other publications such as the *Morning Post*. During this period he also wrote two books based on his experiences in combat entitled *The Story of the Malakand Field Force* (1898) and *The River War* (1899). In 1899, Churchill was to act as war correspondent for the *Morning Post* during the Boer War in South Africa, where he was captured, escaping after a month in captivity. This experience formed the basis of another book – *London to Ladysmith via Pretoria*, published in 1900.

Churchill's experiences in combat inspired in him an interest in politics, a goal that he achieved in his mid-twenties. Campaigning successfully against a backdrop of familial parliamentary history, military experience and authorial success, Churchill became an MP and became known quickly for his commanding and energetic oratory. Migrating from the Tory Party to the Liberal Party in 1904, Churchill quickly gained a significant level of power as Under-Secretary of State at the Colonial Office, then President of the Board of Trade (a Cabinet position) and, later, Home Secretary. In 1911, Churchill was made First Lord of the Admiralty, giving him responsibility for the leadership of the Royal Navy. Already aware of the growing militaristic threat of Germany, he was to become significantly involved in military affairs. As the leader of the disastrous Dardanelles campaign in Turkey in 1915 that led to widespread British casualties, Churchill shouldered the blame for its failure and was subsequently to disappear from British politics for some time. His expulsion from political life came as a great blow, and during the ensuing years Churchill took up painting as a means of escaping the deep depression that affected him.

Two years later, in 1917, Churchill re-entered politics, when he was offered the post of Minister of Munitions, and then in 1918 Secretary of State for War and Air. He later progressed to Secretary of State for the Colonies but experienced varied success, losing his seat as an MP shortly after. Returning to the Conservative Party in 1924, Churchill regained a seat as MP, quickly ascending to the position of Chancellor of the Exchequer in the new Conservative government that same year, a position he was to hold for five years before Labour ousted the Tories from power for the next decade. A prolific writer, Churchill was also to pen the six-volume World War I treatise *The World Crisis* in the 1920s, in addition to his autobiography, *My Early Life*, published in 1930.

As the dark spectre of war with Nazi Germany loomed, Churchill continued to speak out against the growing militaristic threat of Germany and openly attacked the then British Prime Minister Neville Chamberlain's strategy of acquiescence and appeasement against Hitler – a strategy that was to appear futile and ineffective following Hitler's invasion of Poland in 1939. Shortly after the invasion, Churchill was again given the post of First Lord of the Admiralty. When Hitler attacked France on 10 May 1940, Prime Minister Chamberlain stepped down and King George IV appointed Churchill as prime minister. His famous 'Blood, toil, tears and sweat' speech was delivered shortly after in the House of Commons. His impressive and moving oratory was to prove a necessary tool for motivating his party and the people of Britain in what then appeared to be an almost insurmountable fight against the most evil of enemies.

A talented and tactical statesman, Churchill quickly entered discussions with both the US and Soviet Union regarding an alliance against Nazi Germany. He was to take many difficult strategic decisions, such as the sinking of the French fleet at the port of Mers-el-Kébir outside Oran, Algeria, in 1940. Churchill had won the backing of his War Cabinet to sink the fleet as a means of preventing it from falling into Germany's hands – a move that tragically led to the deaths of 1,297 French soldiers, but which transmitted a clear message of strength to Hitler that England would continue to fight and never acquiesce. He is widely credited as one of the most defining forces of leadership that enabled the Allies to achieve victory over Germany in World War II.

Although a powerful force in times of crisis, the British public initially rejected Churchill as a peacetime leader. He was, in fact, to become prime minister a second time, in 1951, and in the intervening period lectured and wrote prolifically. His works included a second six-volume wartime classic, *The Second World War* (1948–1953). In his final retirement, Churchill continued to write, finishing his four-volume *A History of the English Speaking Peoples* (1956–1958). He also continued to give speeches and to paint.

Made Knight of the Garter by Queen Elizabeth II in 1953, Sir Winston Churchill went on to win the Nobel Prize in Literature. He remained an MP until the year before his death (1965). A prolific force in politics, military strategy and literature, the world owes much to his knowledge, courage and leadership.

The spirit of Churchill was invoked in the United Kingdom's recent 'Brexit' campaign, with Boris Johnson and Project Leave's campaigns appealing to nostalgic nationalistic sentiment. Churchill, however, would likely have been aghast at the idea of leaving the European Union; in fact, he was one of its founders. In a rousing speech made in 1948 at the Hague, to the Congress of Europe, Churchill stated passionately that "We cannot aim at anything less than the Union of Europe as a whole, and we look forward with confidence to the day when that Union will be achieved".[12] It was a dream of European unity that Churchill had, in fact, treasured and foreseen for many years.

Questions

1 In what ways does Churchill embody the eight personality traits of a leader, as identified by Stogdill (1948)?
2 Turkheimer (2000, p. 160) stated that "Everything is heritable". To what extent could Churchill's power of communication (both written and verbal) be considered incontrovertibly genetic, as opposed to learned behaviour?
3 Comment on Churchill's power motivation.
4 Stogdill (1974) argued that claims could not be made with respect to the universality of personality traits in a leader without also highlighting the important mediating effect of situational variables. Comment on this observation and discuss why it is so relevant in the case of Churchill.
5 Churchill remains a divisive figure with critiques surrounding his racist worldview – criticisms that remain greatly warranted and of significant concern, and which have risen to prominence within the public discourse during the George Floyd protests. Consider how this knowledge supports the idea that we should never deify our leaders and should instead be prepared to engage in a far more nuanced, intellectual and complex treatment of how we appraise leaders of the past and present.

CHAPTER 2 QUIZ

1 Identify the eight personality traits identified by a 1948 study to differentiate leaders from non-leaders.
2 Did Mann's 1959 study support or conflict with the findings of the study mentioned above?
3 Who first conceptualized the 'Great Man' of leadership?
4 What is Western hegemony, and why is it important to understand its impact on trait research?
5 List the 'Big Five' personality dimensions (Goldberg, 1981).
6 What is metacognition and why is it important to leadership?
7 Turkheimer (2000, p. 160) theorizes that "Everything is heritable". What does he mean by this?
8 To what has 30 per cent of individual differences in leadership been attributed?
9 How have endogenous steroids been observed to impact leadership?
10 The role of intelligence in leadership has been well documented. How is it theorized to impact leadership?
11 Provide a definition of physiognomy and identify three ways in which it is theorized to affect leadership.
12 Name two power theories and provide a brief definition of each.
13 Identify three ways of measuring leadership traits.
14 Why is self-reporting a potential issue in the measurement of leadership traits?
15 Explain trends in voting, as explained in Chapter 2, and consider the negative ramifications of these trends on the political process.

Notes

1 Quote taken from an interview with Bassma El-Amir Riley, conducted for this book. El-Amir Riley remains one of the only female traders to ever head a trading desk. The quote appears in the expert insight "The role of personality traits in leadership success" later in this chapter.
2 "Never give in," quote from a speech delivered by Winston Churchill on 29 October 1941 at Harrow School.
3 Are great leaders born or made? Such a question continues to stimulate great debate among academics and practitioners alike.
4 Meta-analysis is a method used in statistics, and involves the aggregation of results from a wide range of different studies that investigate the same concept.
5 The reader is directed to Chapter 8, "Emotional intelligence", for further consideration of this concept.
6 Kayam, O. (2018). The Readability and Simplicity of Donald Trump's Language. *Political Studies Review*, 16(1), pp. 73–88.
7 Gubernatorial – of, or relating to, a governor.
8 Fortune 500 is an annual list of the top 500 companies in the US ranked by revenue, as profiled by *Fortune* magazine.
9 Construct validity refers to the extent to which an instrument actually measures what it claims to measure.
10 This remark referenced the 2008 global financial crisis.
11 This phrase explains the ability to close a position that has lost you money, so that you limit overall losses. The temptation is to continue to trade to 'win' back what you have lost, but that is similar to gambling and can lead to even greater losses as a result.

12 Address given by Winston Churchill at the Congress of Europe in The Hague, 7 May 1948. *CVCE.eu.* Available at: www.cvce.eu/en/obj/address_given_by_winston_churchill_at_the_congress_of_europe_in_the_hague_7_may_1948-en-58118da1-af22-48c0-bc88-93cda974f42c.html.

References

Arvey, R.D., Zhang, Z., Avolio, B.J. and Kreuger, R.F. (2007). Developmental and Genetic Determinants of Leadership Role Occupancy among Women. *Journal of Applied Psychology*, 92(3), pp. 693–706.

Avolio, B.J. (2007). Promoting More Integrative Strategies for Leadership Theory-Building. *American Psychologist*, 62(1), pp. 25–33.

Ballew, C.C. and Todorov, A. (2007). Predicting Political Elections from Rapid and Unreflective Face Judgments. *Proceedings of the National Academy of Sciences*, 104(46), pp. 17948–17953.

Banducci, S.A., Karp, J.A., Thrasher, M. and Rallings, C. (2008). Ballot Photographs as Clues in Low-Information Elections. *Political Psychology*, 29(6), pp. 903–917.

Bass, B.M. (1990). *Bass & Stogdill's Handbook of Leadership: Theory, Research, and Managerial Applications.* 3rd ed. New York: Free Press.

Bass, B.M. and Bass, R. (2009). *Bass Handbook of Leadership: Theory, Research and Managerial Applications.* 4th ed. New York: Free Press.

Bennis, W.G. (1959). *Leadership Theory and Administrative Behavior: The Problem of Authority.* Boston, MA: Boston University Human Relations Center.

Bridges, D. (1993). Transferable Skills: A Philosophical Perspective. *Studies in Higher Education*, 18(1), pp. 43–51.

Cacioppo, J.T., Berntson, G.G. and Nusbaum, H.C. (2008). Neuroimaging as a New Tool in the Toolbox of Psychological Science. *Current Directions in Psychological Science*, 17(2), pp. 62–67.

Carlson, J.G. (1985). Recent Assessments of the Myers–Briggs Type Indicator. *Journal of Personality Assessment*, 49(4), pp. 356–365.

Carlyle, T. (1907). *On Heroes, Hero Worship and the Heroic in History.* Boston, MA: Houghton Mifflin.

Cawthorn, D. (1996). Leadership: The Great Man Theory Revisited. *Business Horizons*, 39, pp. 1–4.

Cherulnik, P.D., Turns, L.C. and Wilderman, S.K. (1990). Physical Appearance and Leadership – Exploring the Role of Appearance-Based Attribution in Leader Emergence. *Journal of Applied Social Psychology*, 20(18), pp. 1530–1539.

Coates, J.M. and Herbert, J. (2008). Endogenous Steroids and Financial Risk Taking on a London Trading Floor. *Proceedings of the National Academy of Sciences*, 105(16), pp. 6167–6172.

Conger, J.A. and Kanungo, R.N. (1998). *Charismatic Leadership in Organizations.* Thousand Oaks, CA: Sage.

Costa, P.T. and McCrae, R.R. (1992). *NEO Personality Inventory (NEO PI-R) and NEO Five-Factor Inventory (NEO-FFI).* Odessa, FL: Psychological Assessment Resources.

Day, D.V. (2000). Leadership Development: A Review in Context. *Leadership Quarterly*, 11(4), pp. 581–613.

Den Hartog, D.N., House, R.J., Hanges, P.J., Ruiz-Quintanilla, S.A. and Dorfman, P.W. (1999). Culture-Specific and Cross-Culturally Generalizable Implicit Leadership Theories: A Longitudinal Investigation. *Leadership Quarterly*, 10(2), pp. 219–256.

Dion, K., Berscheid, E. and Walster, E. (1972). What is Beautiful is Good. *Journal of Personality and Social Psychology*, 24, pp. 285–290.

Donaldson, S. and Grant-Vallone, E. (2002). Understanding Self-Report Bias in Organizational Behavior Research. *Journal of Business and Psychology*, 17(2) (December), pp. 245–260.

Eagly, A.H. and Karua, S.J. (2002). Role Congruity Theory of Prejudice Toward Female Leaders. *Psychological Review*, 109, pp. 573–598.

French, J.R.P. and Raven, B. (1959). The Bases of Social Power. In D. Cartwright (ed.), *Studies in Social Power*. Ann Arbor, MI: University of Michigan Press, pp. 150–167.

Galton, F. and Eysenck, H.J. (1869). *Hereditary Genius*. London: Macmillan.

Goldberg, L.R. (1981). Language and Individual Differences: The Search for Universals in Personality Lexicons. In L. Wheeler (ed.), *Review of Personality and Social Psychology* (Vol. 2). Beverly Hills, CA: Sage, pp. 141–165.

Goldberg, L.R. (1992). The Development of Markers for the Big-Five Factor Structure. *Psychological Assessment*, 4(1), pp. 26–42.

Griffin, A.M. and Langlois, J.H. (2006). Stereotype Directionality and Attractiveness Stereotyping: Is Beautiful Good or is Ugly Bad? *Social Cognition*, 24(2), pp. 187–206.

Hamermesh, D.S. (2006). Changing Looks and Changing "Discrimination": The Beauty of Economics. *Economics Letters*, 93(3), pp. 405–412.

Heilman, M.E. and Stopeck, M.H. (1985). Attractiveness and Corporate Success: Different Causal Attributions for Males and Females. *Journal of Applied Psychology*, 70(2), pp. 379–388.

Hinchliffe, G. (2002). Situating Skills. *Journal of Philosophy and Education*, 36(2), pp. 187–205.

Hoffman, B., Woehr, D., Maldagen-Youngjohn, R. and Lyons, B. (2011). Great Man or Great Myth? A Quantitative Review of the Relationship between Individual Differences and Leader Effectiveness. *Journal of Occupational and Organizational Psychology*, 84(2), pp. 347–381.

Hosoda, M., Stone-Romero, E.F. and Coats, G. (2003). The Effects of Physical Attractiveness on Job-Related Outcomes: A Meta-Analysis of Experimental Studies. *Personnel Psychology*, 56(2), pp. 431–462.

John, O.P., Donahue, E.M. and Kentle, R.L. (1991). *The Big Five Inventory: Versions 4a and 54*. Technical report, Institute of Personality and Social Research, University of California, Berkeley, CA.

Judge, T., Bono, J., Ilies, R. and Gerhardt, M. (2002). Personality and Leadership: A Qualitative and Quantitative Review. *Journal of Applied Psychology*, 87(3), pp. 765–780.

Judge, T.A., Colbert, A.E. and Ilies, R. (2004). Intelligence and Leadership. A Quantitative Review and Test of Theoretical Propositions. *Journal of Applied Psychology*, 89(4), pp. 542–552.

Knabb, J.J., Welsh, R.K., Ziebell, J.G. and Reimer, K.S. (2009). Neuroscience, Moral Reasoning, and the Law. *Behavioural Sciences and the Law*, 27(2), pp. 219–236.

Lawson, C., Lenz, G.S., Baker, A. and Myers, M. (2010). Looking Like a Winner: Candidate Appearances and Electoral Success in New Democracies. *World Politics*, 62(4) (October), pp. 561–593.

Lord, R.G., DeVader, C.L. and Alliger, G.M. (1986). A Meta-Analysis of the Relation between Personality Traits and Leadership Perceptions: An Application of Validity Generalization Procedures. *Journal of Applied Psychology*, 71(3), pp. 402–410.

McClelland, D.C. and Burnham, D.H. (1976). Power is the Great Motivator. *Harvard Business Review*, 54(2), pp. 100–110.

Magee, J.C. and Langner, C.A. (2008). How Personalized and Socialized Power Motivation Facilitate Antisocial and Pro-social Decision-Making. *Journal of Research in Personality*, 42, pp. 1547–1559.

Mann, R.D. (1959). A Review of the Relationship Between Personality and Performance in Small Groups. *Psychological Bulletin*, 56(4), pp. 241–270.

Martin, D.S. (1978). Person Perception and Real-Life Electoral Behaviour. *Australian Journal of Psychology*, 30(3), pp. 255–262.

Mobius, M.M. and Rosenblat, T.S. (2006). Why Beauty Matters. *American Economic Review*, 96(1), pp. 222–235.

Morse, G. (2006). Decisions and Desire. *Harvard Business Review*, 84(1), pp. 42–51.

Paulus, M.P., Rogalsky, C. and Simmons, A. (2003). Increased Activation in the Right Insula during Risk-Taking Decision Making Is Related to Harm Avoidance and Neuroticism. *Neuroimage*, 19(4), pp. 1439–1448.

Poutvaara, P., Jordahl, H. and Berggren, N. (2009). Faces of Politicians: Babyfacedness Predicts Inferred Competence but Not Electoral Success. *Journal of Experimental Social Psychology*, 45(5), pp. 1132–1135.

Rule, N. and Ambady, N. (2010). First Impressions of the Face: Predicting Success. *Social and Personality Psychology Compass*, 4(8), pp. 506–516.

Salloway, S.P., Malloy, P.F. and Duffy, J.D. (2001). *The Frontal Lobes and Neuropsychiatric Illness*. Washington, DC: American Psychiatric Publishing.

Scott Derue, D., Nahrgang, J., Wellman, N. and Humphrey, S.E. (2011). Trait and Behavioural Theories of Leadership: An Integration and Meta-Analytic Test of Their Relative Validity. *Personnel Psychology*, 64(1), pp. 7–52.

Sigelman, C.K., Sigelman, L., Thomas, D.B. and Ribich, F.D. (1986). Gender, Physical Attractiveness, and Electability: An Experimental Investigation of Voter Biases. *Journal of Social Applied Psychology*, 16(3), pp. 229–248.

Simonton, D.K. (1987). *Why Presidents Succeed: A Political Psychology of Leadership*. New Haven, CT: Yale University Press.

Simonton, D.K. (2006). Presidential IQ, Openness, Intellectual Brilliance, and Leadership: Estimates and Correlations for 42 US Chief Executives. *Political Psychology*, 27(4), pp. 511–526.

Stogdill, R.M. (1948). Personal Factors Associated with Leadership: A Survey of the Literature. *Journal of Psychology*, 25(1), pp. 35–71.

Stogdill, R.M. (1974). *Handbook of Leadership: A Survey of Theory and Research*. New York: Free Press.

Todorov, A., Mandisodza, A.N., Goren, A. and Hall, C.C. (2005). Inferences of Competence from Faces Predict Election Outcomes. *Science*, 308(10), pp. 1623–1626.

Turkheimer, E. (2000). Three Laws of Behavior Genetics and What They Mean. *Current Directions in Psychological Science*, 9(5), pp. 160–164.

Van Vugt, M., Hogan, R. and Kaiser, R. (2008). Leadership, Followership, and Evolution: Some Lessons from the Past. *American Psychologist*, 63(3), pp. 182–196.

Winter, D.G. (2002). Motivation and Political Leadership. In O. Feldman and L.O. Valenty (eds.), *Political Leadership for the New Century: Personality and Behavior among American Leaders*. Westport, CT: Greenwood, pp. 25–47.

Zaccaro, S.J. (2007). Trait-Based Perspectives of Leadership. *American Psychologist*, 62(1), pp. 6–16.

Other resources

See PowerPoint slides on the companion website at www.routledge.com/9780367374822.

3

SKILLS THEORIES

"No one gets a free pass to success – it is a lot of hard work and paying your dues."
– Paige Arnof-Fenn, CEO of Mavens & Moguls[1]

Are great leaders born or made? The purpose of this chapter is to counter the claims of Great Man and trait theorists that they are *born*, and to argue instead that leaders can, to some extent, be *made*. Certainly, notable skills theorists, such as Katz (1955) and Mumford *et al.* (2000), argue that leadership is a *skill* that can be learned, as opposed to an *innate set of traits* (as defined by trait theory). Certainly, the notable emergence and growth of the executive coaching industry, worth an estimated $3,500 per hour (Coutu and Kauffman, 2009) points to an incontrovertible belief in the potential for leadership to be taught as a skill.

The debate is certainly a compelling one. Take Nancy Pelosi, for example. Pelosi is the first woman in the history of the US to hold the position of Speaker of the US House of Representatives, and she remains the highest-ranking female official in the history of the US. At the time of writing she is serving her seventeenth term as a Congresswoman. Pelosi is famously spiritual, an outspoken critic of the Iraq War and an instrumental figure in the passing of many momentous bills such as the Affordable Care Act and the Dodd–Frank Wall Street Reform and Consumer Protection Act.

Nancy was the youngest of seven children, the daughter and sister of prominent Democratic politicians (both her father and her brother Thomas were Mayors of Baltimore). Pelosi attended a Catholic all-girls school before pursuing a BA in Political Science, then interned for Democratic Senator Daniel Brewster. By that time Nancy Pelosi had a great deal of campaign experience for her age, having helped her father at numerous campaign events. Pelosi is intelligent, led by her values and strong; she has faced abuse many times, particularly since the 2016 US Presidential elections when she received many sick, obscene telephone, text and email messages that prompted her to warn other fellow politicians not to let family members – and particularly their children – answer their phone or open their email.

A now historic image of Pelosi ripping up the State of the Union address given by Donald Trump in February 2020 hit headlines around the world, as did Trump's many personal attacks on Pelosi following that address. In Pelosi's words,

> I tore up a manifesto of mistruths. It was necessary to get the attention of the American people to say, "This is not true. And this is how it affects you." And I don't need any lessons from anyone, especially the President of the United States, about dignity.[2]

Pelosi is without doubt a dignified, principled individual – extending her hand to shake Trump's before the State of the Union address only to have him ignore her. Pelosi also remarked that Trump's address reflected a state of mind that had absolutely no contact with reality.

To what extent are Pelosi's historic achievements facilitated by the skills that she has learnt (e.g. via attaining her qualifications), the experience that she has attained (e.g. as a Congresswoman), environmental influences (e.g. a political Italian-American family), or via her innate traits (e.g. integrity, courage, a value-driven approach to her political work)? The purpose of this chapter is to explore these issues to contest the Great Man Theory and to help you form your own theory-driven answers to this most debated and fascinating of questions.

Structure of the chapter

This chapter sets out to: (1) review skills theories of leadership and (2) provide an academic critique of the efficacy of the executive coaching industry, a sector that seeks to capitalize on the notion that leadership skills can be taught. Critiques of skills theory are provided alongside a discussion on how leadership skills can be measured. The expert insight for this chapter profiles Mavens & Moguls CEO and Harvard alum Paige Arnof-Fenn. A case study of hedge fund magnate Philip Falcone ("Harbinger of fortune") provides an opportunity to relate theory to practice. An end-of-chapter quiz concludes the chapter.

Introduction

The skills approach initially emerged during the 1950s, largely as a result of the theorizations of Robert Katz (1955). Katz argued that both executives and educators recognized the importance of developing leadership, but that little consensus existed with regard to what actually made a leader effective. At the time, approaches to leadership generally centred upon identifying the traits possessed by successful leaders. Katz argued that it might instead be more effective to identify what successful leaders *do* (i.e. demonstrate the skills that they have for delegation and problem solving), as opposed to what they *are* (i.e. traits, such as intelligence).

Three skills approach

Katz (1955) developed a skills-based model that argued that successful leadership depended upon the possession of *technical*, *human* and *conceptual* skills:

- *Technical skill*: specialist knowledge, and the ability to undertake specialist tasks that relate to a particular discipline (e.g. the ability of a cardiologist to perform open heart surgery).
- *Human skill*: the ability to work effectively as part of, and lead, a group (e.g. as the manager of a marketing department). A leader with good human skills will be self-aware, aware of the feelings and perceptions of others, cognizant of the way in which they need to lead in order to foster feelings of trust, security and productivity in their team, and knowledgeable about how to interact with their team in order to produce the best results.
- *Conceptual skill*: the ability to see the 'big picture' and to conceptually understand how various functions of an organization or a project interact with, and exert effects upon, each other.

Katz (1955) argued that human skills are important at every level, but that technical skills are most important at lower levels of management (for example, within the context of a junior manager who supervises minimum wage employees in the kitchen of a McDonald's outlet). He argued that the ascension of the leader to upper echelons of management required a shifting emphasis from technical to conceptual skills. Certainly this explains why many companies have a CEO who has successfully moved from one industry to another – Edward Whitacre Jr., who enjoyed a brief tenure as Chairman and CEO of General Motors after a successful career at AT&T and SBC,[3] provides one such example.

It was not until early in the twenty-first century that the skills movement enjoyed a resurgence of interest. Fleishman *et al.* (1991) and Mumford *et al.* (2000) recognized the complex nature of leading in organizations, referring to the need for leaders to engage in complex social problem solving. Marshall-Mies *et al.* (2000, p. 137) argued that organizational problems possess four distinct characteristics:

1. Problems emerge in dynamic environments and require that problems are solved within an environment characterized by uncertainty.
2. Organizations are complex, ambiguous environments, leading to the emergence of problems that are generally ill-defined.
3. The dynamic nature of the organizational environment means that the parameters of problems are often unfamiliar to the leader.
4. Solutions identified by the leader need to be implemented in a complex organizational environment where many factors exist concurrently to facilitate and constrain the effective implementation of the solution.

IDEA IN BRIEF

Evolution of trading

In 2010, Moscow TV reported on a Russian chimpanzee named Lusha that outperformed 94 per cent of Russia's investment funds by investing £21,000 in 8 companies out of a possible choice of 30. Russian Finance Editor Oleg Anisimov commented that, "She did better than almost the whole of the rest of the market." Pavel Trunin, Head of Monetary Policy at the Institute for the Economy in Transition in Moscow remarked that, "It shows that financial knowledge does not play a great role in giving forecasts to how the market will change. It is usually a matter of more or less successful guessing. And the monkey got lucky."[4]

Leadership skills model

Mumford *et al.* (2000) recognized the complexity of leadership by developing a Capability Model of Leadership that focuses on five elements: *individual attributes*, which lead to the development of *competencies*, which in turn lead to effective *leadership outcomes, career experiences* and *environmental influences* (Figure 3.1). Presentation of the model is followed by a more detailed discussion of each of the elements.

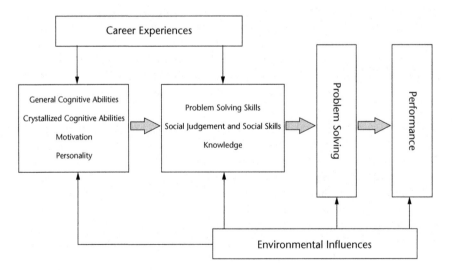

FIGURE 3.1 Influence of leader characteristics on leader performance.

Source: Mumford *et al.* (2000, p. 35).

Individual attributes

The individual attributes of a leader are those skills and traits that pre-empt the development of *leadership competencies*. Individual attributes constitute: *general cognitive ability* (intelligence); *crystallized cognitive ability* (intelligence that is developed as a result of experience and which enhances social judgement, conceptual ability and problem-solving skills); *motivation* (the motivation to lead, to exert influence over others and to advance the goals of the organization) and *personality* (a tolerance for ambiguity, owing to the complex nature of organizations, openness, confidence and curiosity).

Competencies

The competencies of *problem solving*, *social judgement* and *knowledge* lead to the elicitation of effective leadership. These are predetermined largely by the *individual attributes* of a leader (as identified above).

- *Problem-solving skills.* Due to the complex nature of organizations, leaders must possess the ability to solve problems, regardless of how novel, ill-defined or complex they are.
- *Social judgement skills* (which could be colloquially referred to as 'people skills') require an understanding of the complexity of the work environment and the way in which the interests of different stakeholders need to be balanced in the implementation of a solution. This requires an understanding of social dynamics and organizational politics, and rests principally on four elements: perspective taking (empathy and sensitivity to the perspectives of others); social perceptiveness (what people will do when faced with proposed changes); behavioural flexibility; and social performance (the ability to persuade, communicate a vision, mediate conflict, lessen resistance to change, provide support and direction via coaching and mentoring) (Mumford *et al.*, 2000).
- *Knowledge skills* refer to the ability of the leader to identify and organize relevant knowledge into an appropriately complex and sophisticated mental schema that allows complex problem solving and the application of solutions to take place.

Leadership outcomes

Outcomes of leadership include the ability to recognize and solve complex problems, and the elicitation of high levels of performance within a leadership role.

Career experiences

The model identifies the integral role of career experience in maximizing the skill acquisition and elicitation of the leader, illustrating how leadership traits alone (for example, a high IQ) are not sufficient for leadership success to occur: "leaders are not born, nor are they made; instead, their inherent potentials are shaped by experiences enabling them to develop the capabilities needed to solve significant social problems" (Mumford *et al.* 2000, p. 24; see also Erikson, 1959; Lewis and Jacobs, 1992). Katz similarly observes the necessary intersection of skills with traits in order that a leader can realize their potential:

> We talk of "born leaders", "born executives", "born salesmen". It is undoubtedly true that certain people, naturally or innately, possess greater aptitude or ability in certain skills ... But research in psychology and physiology would also indicate, first, that those having strong aptitudes and abilities can improve their skill through practice and training, and, secondly, that even those lacking the natural ability can improve their performance and effectiveness.
>
> *(Katz, 1955, p. 40)*

Environmental influences

It is critical that a leader possesses the cognitive ability to appreciate the complexities of the environment in which they operate in order to undertake the most effective leadership possible – a particularly complex task when one considers the skills, traits, experiences and other factors that contribute to cognition and performance. An example can be taken from the field of cognitive resource theory (Fielder and Garcia, 1987), which states that a leader is less likely to effectively apply their cognitive capabilities when faced with high levels of stress – a common characteristic of modern organizations. As organizations are complex, pressurized, political environments, it is likely that the leader will often face this challenge.

IDEA IN BRIEF

Better a leap in the dark than assisted suicide[5]

The 2013 Italian elections saw four key figures standing for the country's highest position of office. The first, Mario Monti, served as technocratic Prime Minister of Italy from 2011–2013.[6] Monti's team were responsible for the implementation of a series of sensible and strategically sound initiatives (such as cutting pensions and curbing budget deficits) that had restored a meaningful level of confidence to the markets, and which had rescued the country from falling off a metaphorical economic cliff. The second was Silvio Berlusconi who, at the time of the election, was appealing a one-year conviction for tax fraud (he received a second one-year prison term shortly after the election, this time for an illegal wire-tap). Beppe Grillo ostensibly provided a comedic element – a comedian running for parliament as a leader of a party called the Five Star Movement (M5S). Finally, Pier Luigi Bersani, head of the centre-left Democratic Party coalition, represented a potentially formidable and familiar figure.

The election came at a tumultuous and critical time, both for Italy and for the Eurozone. Italy was in desperate need of parliamentary reform; experiencing rising labour costs, falling productivity and rising unemployment, where the inability to secure market growth meant that Italy was unable to service its debt. Despite this, electoral turnout was relatively low compared to previous Italian national elections. Beppe Grillo received 25.6 per cent of the vote as head of the M5S (making it the country's most-voted-for single party). Berlusconi won 29.2 per cent, with Bersani's Democratic Party coalition emerging with 29.5 per cent. Monti, the man largely identifiable as rescuer of Italy's finances, received a paltry 10 per cent of the vote. In quite literal terms, a quarter of Italy's voters had chosen a comedian to run their country, rejecting the only candidate with a strong and competent history of successful economic reform. Berlusconi went on to form Forza Italia six months later, which was overtaken in 2018 as Italy's largest centre-right coalition party member by Lega Nord.

A further example can be taken from the observation that leaders, and organizations, do not exist in a vacuum. Consider the challenges faced, for example, by the leaders of the European Union and Project Remain voters and politicians during Brexit negotiations, by military forces operating in Syria at the time of the Trump Administration's sudden withdrawal from the region, or by the owners of fisheries located within the Gulf of Mexico at the time of the Deepwater Horizon oil spill in April 2010. The skills theories of leadership consequently open our eyes to the need to deconstruct leadership via recognition of the complex environment within which it exists.

Developing leadership skills

> The battle of Waterloo was won on the playing fields of Eton.
>
> *Duke of Wellington*[7]

Wellington's words speak volumes about the attitudes, beliefs and values of the culture of the English public school system, and of the belief that structured sport developed leadership ability in students who would go on to become the future military and political leaders of the British Empire (a belief that has emerged subsequently across a wide range of environments, including sports,[8] military,[9] academic[10] and corporate environments[11]).[12] This idea that sports coaching – or the process of coaching itself – can develop leaders lies at the core of the executive coaching industry.

Leadership and executive coaching

Over recent years, the leadership and management field has been characterized by a proliferation in leadership development methods, most notably leadership training courses that are characterized by classroom-based (for example, leadership seminars) and activity-based (for example, white-water rafting and adventure-based) interventions, both of which use coaching as a means of developing performance. Perhaps the most popular and notable management intervention of recent years is the use of 360-degree feedback (Atwater and Waldman, 1998), which involves the elicitation of feedback from all directions – superiors, peers and subordinates – in addition to the provision of self-ratings of leadership (Figure 3.2). Comparing the variability in ratings between groups (for example, a variance in how a leader rates themselves, as compared to how their subordinates rate them) can provide a multifaceted and additive view of both (1) perceptions of leadership and (2) actual leadership ability.

Executive coaching involves the use of practical, goal-focused forms of one-on-one learning which lead to (positive) changes in behaviour (Hall *et al.*, 1999). Executive coaching interventions tend to be short term – a quality that invites criticism, given that recent research has identified the need for coaching interventions to be both ongoing and developmental if they are to achieve positive change (VanVelsor and McCauley, 2004).

While the academic field of leadership has grown in stature over recent years, the executive coaching field has made similar strides in its popularity and growth. This growth has not yet, however, been matched by a concurrent growth in the use of peer-reviewed, empirical research upon which its practice and claims are based. For example, Spence and Oades (2011) reported that, while over 400 coaching-related publications have appeared in behavioural science and business

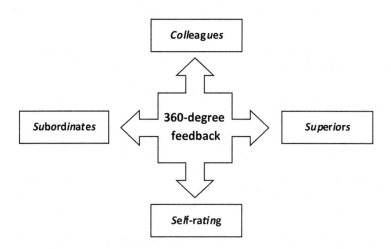

FIGURE 3.2 360-degree feedback.

databases since 2005, the majority of these constitute reviews, opinion pieces and surveys. Very few substantive academic studies exist. Similarly, it has been observed by some that the coaching field appears to be characterized by a level of methodological disparity:

> I'm aware of no research that has followed coached executives over long periods; most of the evidence around effectiveness remains anecdotal. My sense is that the positive stories outnumber the negative ones – but as the industry matures, coaching firms will need to be able to demonstrate how they bring about change, as well as offer a clear methodology for measuring results.
>
> *(Charan, 2009, p. 93)*

A lack of theoretical gravitas in the field of leadership and executive coaching raises a number of issues. The first issue relates to a lack of universality in how the concepts of *leadership* and *leadership success* are defined. The second is related to the substantive nature of leadership coaching interventions that are not based on substantive theory (and thus cannot provide evidence of their effectiveness). Coaching originated in sport; often, coaches know their athletes extremely well, develop a deep, ongoing relationship with them, and utilize extensive feedback systems, training logs and performance-based indicators. Businesses simply cannot mirror such a detailed approach so may fall at the first hurdle when it comes to the efficacy of a coaching intervention. The third relates to a similar disparity in the way in which leadership interventions are measured. Without an empirically valid means of measuring the impact, or Return on Investment (ROI) of leadership education, the potential value of the training interventions is itself compromised (Kincaid and Gordick, 2003). A concomitant lack of systematic evaluation of the impact of leadership training by the corporations that participate in it might lead to a failure to fully understand its impacts. To this end, Avolio *et al.* (2010) argue for the use of RODI (Return on Leadership Development Investment) in the assessment of the efficacy of any leadership training courses, using Cascio's ROI methodology.

Defining leadership

How is *leadership* defined within the leadership training sector? For example, is leadership a skill, behaviour or trait, and is a coaching intervention designed to develop the *leader* or the practice of *leadership*?

When one identifies a leader, we are taught in leadership and management education to seek to emulate their qualities or practices: "managers are people who do the thing right and leaders are people who do the right thing" (Bennis and Nanus, 1985, p. 21). However, it is not clear upon what basis leadership success is measured. Take the example of Jamie Dimon, CEO of JPMorgan Chase & Co. Dimon is a charismatic leader who demonstrates intelligence, dedication to his role and the ability to challenge the status quo, making risky trading decisions that led to great financial gain for the bank. He undoubtedly possesses both legitimate and referent power over his employees. However, trading losses have raised questions regarding Dimon's efficacy as a leader. For example, despite trader Bruno Iksil (the 'London whale') and JPMorgan Chief Investment Officer Ina Drew ultimately being held responsible for a $6.2 billion trading loss in 2012, as Dimon was the man in charge at that time he bore ultimate accountability for the mistake. Thus, if "leaders are people who do the right thing" (Bennis and Nanus, 1985, p. 21), how does one quantify what the right thing is, and who should take responsibility for it? And is there a temporal element to this consideration? Before the 2012 $6.2 billion loss, Dimon was hailed as a great leader; afterwards, he was still the same man, executing the same role competently, but many (in the immediate aftermath of the loss) viewed his leadership skills differently as a result.

Seven years on, those perceptions have, again, shifted. WeWork founder Adam Neumann was quickly hailed as a visionary, but became perhaps the most fleeting $billionaire in history. Similarly, a generation sought to mimic tech maverick Mark Zuckerberg, before his role in hosting US election propaganda led to his vilification by many as one of the most dangerous anti-democratic forces prevalent in society. Elizabeth Holmes, CEO of Theranos, adopted Steve Jobs' iconic black turtleneck and, for a time, managed to situate herself as a mystical, enigmatic $billionaire visionary before being deposed as a fraud. Ultimately, it should not be forgotten that many CEOs, once lauded as great leaders, have subsequently experienced great failure, and even jail terms and bankruptcy (for example, Allen Stanford, who recently received a 110-year prison sentence for the fraudulent use of $7 billion of investor funds, or the historic failing of the Enron board profiled in Chapter 9).

One might also consider the case of Bernie Madoff. Madoff was the President of the Board of Directors for the NASDAQ stock exchange, and managed billions of dollars under the auspices of his Wall Street firm Bernard L. Madoff Investment Securities LLC. Madoff consistently produced positive returns for his investors over a long period of time, despite volatile market conditions, and in doing so consistently outperformed other funds. He counted Steven Spielberg and the owner of the New York Mets among his many clients, possessed great legitimate power and was greatly admired. Madoff would, of course, be subsequently jailed for operating the largest Ponzi scheme in history.

Differentiating management and leadership

Do coaching interventions seek to develop managers or leaders? Barker comments that

> Leadership training that emphasizes a set of definable and learnable skills and abilities can only be defended if leadership and management are defined in the same way. This is a view of leadership as excellent management or, as some would put it, as a function of management.

> *(Barker, 1997, p. 357)*

If the ultimate aim of corporate leadership training is to help managers achieve corporate goals more effectively, then the goal of the leadership training is actually to enhance management ability not leadership and to maintain a status quo in order to consistently achieve adherence to the cultural norms, values and goals of the company. Further observations of the cultural norms of a company also encourage the consideration of cultural complexity, and raises the question of whether external, short-term coaching interventions can really lead to substantive, transformative outcomes. Schein (1982, p. 5) comments that "neither culture nor leadership, when one examines each closely, can really be understood by itself", suggesting that an intricate knowledge of, and appreciation for, the complexities of a specific organizational culture is required if meaningful improvements in leadership are to be made.[13] If the short-term intervention focuses on the development of a technical skill with the concurrent development of consciousness of one's expert power within the context of the utilization of that skill, this seems a logical way of developing leadership. Conversely, a generic 'how to be a better leader' course seems, empirically, to represent a waste of resources.

Measuring leadership skills

Questions have been raised regarding the transferability of problem-solving capabilities from one environment to another (Zaccaro et al., 1991). A lack of valid and reliable instruments with which we can effectively measure leadership skills is also a concern as, without these, it is problematic to understand the level to which leadership skills have been improved by leadership skills training. Furthermore, Ericsson and Charness (1994) argue that it typically takes seven to ten years for an individual to attain the skills needed to perform effectively at the top level of their field. This undermines the claims of leadership development programmes that seek to develop leadership skills via the implementation of short-term interventions such as workshops or team-building events. Given that a great deal of contention surrounds our ability to even agree what leadership is, or how one should measure it, we can at least conclude that any short-term intervention needs to: (1) be extremely focused on technical skills development, outcomes, and impact measurement; (2) be delivered in the context of the traits, skills and experiences of each individual; (3) meet the goals of the team and organization; and (4) identify whether it is, in fact, leadership or management that the organization is seeking to develop.

Summary

Skills theories of leadership do not appear to diametrically oppose the trait approach. Instead, they argue for an identification and understanding of the skills necessary for effective leadership to occur. The words of John F. Kennedy reflect the idea that "leadership and learning are indispensable to each other",[14] a sentiment reflected in the academic theories contained within this chapter.

 **Expert insight**

Mavens & Moguls

Mavens & Moguls is a global strategic marketing consulting firm run by CEO and founder Paige Arnof-Fenn. Previously profiled in The New York Times and The Washington Post, Mavens & Moguls has been profiled as a Harvard Business Review case study ("Creating a new business model")[15] and continues to expand across the globe, working with diverse companies from start-ups to Fortune 500 corporations. Paige Arnof-Fenn continues to extend the Mavens & Moguls brand across the globe. In this expert insight, Paige offers us a great insight into her journey so far.

An accidental entrepreneur

"I did not plan on starting a company. I always wanted to go work for a large multi-national business and become a Fortune 500 CEO. I subsequently started my career on Wall Street in the '80s and enjoyed a successful career in the world of corporate America at companies like Procter & Gamble and Coca-Cola. I also worked at three different start-ups as their Head of Marketing.

I became an entrepreneur and took the leap right after 9/11 when the company I worked for cut their marketing. At that time, I had nothing to lose. I still joke that I am an accidental entrepreneur, but I am so glad that I hit out on my own. Being an entrepreneur provides me a platform to do work I truly enjoy, with and for people I respect. I get to set my priorities, I have time to travel and hang out with my inner circle and I find time to work out every day.

Enjoy the journey

It has been a journey to get here but I am lucky to have found it. I love the autonomy and the flexibility and the fact that I know every day the impact that I have on my business. When I worked at big companies I always felt the ball would roll with or without me, that if I got hit by a bus someone new would be in my office right away. Now my DNA is in everything we do, and I can trace every decision and sale to something I did or a decision I made. That is such an incredibly gratifying and fulfilling feeling.

What's in a name?

When I started the firm I jokingly referred to the women as the Marketing Mavens & the guys as the Marketing Moguls and for short I called them Mavens & Moguls as a working name but never expected it would stick. I conducted a lot of research with prospective clients, referrers, media and so on, and tested around 100 names. To my great delight and surprise, Mavens & Moguls emerged a clear winner! The name has helped us be memorable and stand out from the pack.

Ultimately, names contribute to your brand and, in our case, I think that our name has been a major plus. Maven is Yiddish for expert and a Mogul is someone of rank, power or distinction in a specified area. I like the alliteration and I think it sets us apart from other consulting firms. It shows a little personality and attitude and implies we do not take ourselves too seriously. Would you rather hire 'Strategic Marketing Solutions' or Mavens & Moguls? We are the 'not your father's Oldsmobile' of marketing firms. If nothing else our name is a great conversation starter and getting into a conversation is sometimes all it takes.

What makes a leader?

You need thick skin, a strong work ethic and a good sense of humour because it is a tough job where the hours are long, a lot of people tell you no (investors, board, customers) and it can be lonely at times. You also have to be a magnet for great talent to be able to build a strong team. For me, the most important qualities for effective leaders are:

- A strong moral compass – you cannot compromise on ethics and values.
- Being a good communicator – having the ability to rally the troops and keep them on the critical path.
- Having the smarts – you need to be technically competent and you also need to work hard to earn the respect of your team.
- Being in possession of a great sense humour and being fun to work with – this is a bonus on top of the other key attributes.

The main difference in terms of leadership competencies required for corporate and entrepreneurial environments is that in a corporate environment you need strong political skills to thrive whereas as an entrepreneur, you are the most invested in the vision and results of the company. The buck always stops with you and you have to be okay with that.

To practice effective leadership, you need to learn to focus and to say no, and to create a vision and plan for a team to achieve something together that none of them could accomplish alone. When done well, it is incredibly inspiring and motivating to be part of that kind of experience.

People are drawn to great leaders because they want to contribute to something larger and more meaningful where they have real impact that matters. The power is when the mission and vision transcend the product or service they are selling. It takes effort and a commitment to excellence to continually improve as you move up the ladder and especially when you get to lead.

I think it is true, also, that the best leaders are respected but not always popular. They need to be tough at times and make hard decisions that not everyone will like or agree with. It comes with the territory. Buy a dog if unconditional love is what you're after – don't chase it at work!

You will never work harder

You will never work harder or more than you do as an entrepreneur! But, because it is for your vision and dream, you will never love another job more. People who start businesses thinking it is less work will be disappointed. There is always more you can be doing to build your business and your brand, so it is hard to switch off. I think that Instagram and other social media can create an impression that entrepreneurship is easy. If you followed me around for a few days you'd realise that it is certainly not as glamorous as it looks! I worked really hard for 20 years before starting my business, so I laugh at people who thought I was an overnight sensation.

Higher quality mistakes

I think many people believe CEO's have the answer and are confident in their decisions most of the time. People also believe that they never screwed up or failed in their career. Another one I have heard is that the leader had a lot of lucky breaks. In my experience, none of these things are true. Leaders often need to make decisions with partial information and data so are not always confident they are making the right decisions. In truth, every leader I know has plenty of war stories of times they got knocked around or screwed up or even got fired. They learned from each setback and moved forward.

The truth is you always learn more from failures and the next time you just get to make higher quality mistakes as you move up the ladder! No one gets a free pass to success – it is a lot of hard work and paying your dues. The harder you work the luckier you get by making your luck and spotting opportunities along the way.

Finding your niche

I do not think I could ever go back to a corporate role. I am so much happier and more productive as an entrepreneur than I ever was working for others. It is all about controlling your calendar. I no longer try to squeeze in more meetings or hit multiple events at night. As an entrepreneur, I can be selective. Less really is more. I've chosen quality over quantity. It sounds trivial, but it is true. I created a platform to do work that I enjoy and that I feel energized by.

Sometimes you need to break the rules

In my corporate life I was always trying to bend, break and change the rules.

Now, as an entrepreneur, I realize this life is a much better fit for my personality and aspirations. I feel I have found my purpose because I used to work all the time and life was passing me by. I got raises and promotions in my corporate roles, but I was all work and no play, and I did not feel fulfilled. Since starting my business I have joined boards and volunteered at several organizations. I am a mentor to the next generation of leaders and have helped build a very successful anti-bullying program that >100,000 middle school aged kids have participated in. As a marketing consultant, I write articles, contribute to books and speak at events to share my experience and lessons learned.

The truth is when you are doing work you love and enjoy the money will come. I do not miss the steady pay check at all – but I admit that it was great having a tech help desk for computer problems and a corporate jet while it lasted!

What I wish I'd known

What I wish I'd known when I was graduating from university:

1   **Be patient.** It really is a marathon not a sprint, so do not set arbitrary goals like being named 30 under 30, or 40 under 40,[16] because it may take you longer than Mark Zuckerberg to hit your stride! And that's okay. Most people take many detours on their career path before finding their true calling. Don't be disappointed if you get to 40 and are still exploring, because the journey really is a great adventure – so enjoy it!

2   **Fail fast.** Don't be scared to fail, just learn from every bump in the road so you make better mistakes next time. That is where you learn the most! You learn to do by doing. Course correct and pivot along the way – it makes for a fun career path.

3   **Keep learning.** Finishing school is not the end of your education. You will be a student for the rest of your life so never stop learning new things. Your education is just getting started – be a sponge for knowledge & enjoy the learning process.

Like most entrepreneurs, I am working harder and longer than ever yet I have never been happier. Working for yourself and building a business you started is incredibly rewarding and gratifying. It has been a lot of fun – and that, to me, is a real mark of success. I also knew I had made it as an entrepreneur when Harvard wrote two case studies on my business a few years after I had founded it!''

Find out more

- Mavens & Moguls website: www.mavensandmoguls.com

Questions

1 Apply Katz's (1955) Three Skills Model to this expert insight, discussing the key roles and interactions of technical, human and conceptual skills required in the achievement of Paige's success as an entrepreneur.
2 Referring to the Capability Model of Leadership (Mumford *et al.*, 2000), identify the way in which individual attributes and competencies led to the emergence of effective leadership outcomes in this expert insight.
3 The Capability Model theorizes the role of career experiences and environmental influences in effective leadership. What environmental influences facilitated or constrained the elicitation of effective leadership in this expert insight?
4 Paige remarks that she was an "accidental entrepreneur" and that failing is a means of learning. Why is learning to cope with failure – "failing fast", as Paige puts it – such an important skill?

Case study: harbinger of fortune

This case study profiles former Harvard hockey star and Kidder Peabody trader Philip Falcone. He was once lauded as a financial genius for multi-billion dollar trades in subprime debt, but then criticized heavily for subsequent unprofitable investments in LightSquared, which subsequently entered bankruptcy and led to Falcone being sued by the US Securities and Exchange Commission (SEC).[17] A 1990 acquisition of AAB Manufacturing had, in fact, formed Falcone's first bankruptcy experience, but his subsequent founding of the hedge fund Harbinger Capital Partners in 2008 proved to be incredibly successful. Harbinger rose quickly to prominence as one of the most successful and powerful hedge funds in the world, leveraging Falcone's ability to take on risk, investing in troubled companies (including Fortescue Metals and General Chemicals) and adopting large positions against subprime mortgage securities in 2006. Those positions led to a cool $11 billion profit – an amazing 116 per cent return on investments following the 2008 subprime mortgage crisis. By 2011, Harbinger boasted $26 billion AUM (assets under management). By now a billionaire, Falcone became known for his lavish lifestyle, purchasing a $49 million mansion and appearing on the cover of *Business Week* as one of Wall Street's brightest stars.

Falcone's propensity for risk led to his decision to acquire LightSquared, in 2010, for around $1 billion. A visionary company, LightSquared boldly aimed to develop a national 4G mobile network using innovative satellite technology. The company initially secured approval – and a multi-billion dollar grant – from the FCC (Federal Communications Commission) in January 2011. As part of the approval conditions, the FCC required LightSquared to commit to the construction of a network that would be capable of reaching 100 million consumers by 2012, and 260 million by 2015. This aggressive growth strategy would allow LightSquared to compete aggressively with existing major mobile providers such as AT&T and promised the delivery of broadband services to US citizens in rural and remote areas, to boost competition among mobile providers, to create jobs and to generate a highly lucrative return for Harbinger Capital and its investors.

Despite the early promises of FCC regulation and investment, in early 2012 Harbinger's good fortunes began to unravel. Following fears over the potential interference of the technology with GPS navigation equipment (vital to the US Defense Department's national defence strategy), the FCC withdrew its support. Around the same time, a group of Harbinger investors quickly began legal action against the fund, citing irresponsible use of investor funds in the funding of the LightSquared project.

Amid growing troubles from the FCC, the US Defense Department and Harbinger investors, Harbinger's AUM rapidly spiralled downward, reaching $4 billion by early 2012, the same year that LightSquared filed for bankruptcy protection. Falcone's problems grew exponentially when, in June 2012, the SEC filed fraud charges against Falcone and Harbinger Capital Partners LLC. According to the SEC, "illicit conduct that included misappropriation of client assets, market manipulation, and betraying clients' provided the basis for the charges."[18]

These charges prompted SEC's Director of Enforcement Robert Khuzami to remark that, "Today's charges read like the final exam in a graduate school course in how to operate a hedge fund unlawfully."[19]

Questions

1   In Ancient Rome, *censors* were appointed in an attempt to provide a moral compass and a level of regulation in a society that had become increasingly reckless and indulgent. Is there a comparison to be made between the failings of these censors and the power of other regulatory agencies (e.g. the FCC) in this case study?
2   Identify the personality traits that you feel have led to Falcone's success. Were the same traits also responsible for his failures?
3   In 2007, Falcone was hailed as a hero of Wall Street, but by 2012, he faced significant professional difficulties. What does this tell you about the transience of leadership success, and what it might mean for how we define a leader as a 'success'?
4   Consider the role of situational variables (for example, economic factors, government legislation) in determining the success (or failure) of a leader.
5   Does Falcone exhibit a high need for personal or socialized power?

CHAPTER 3 QUIZ

1   John F. Kennedy said that "leadership and learning are indispensable to one another". What did he mean by this?
2   Name two leading skills theorists.
3   Identify the three skills in Katz's (1955) 'Three Skills Model'.

4 Identify the four distinct characteristics that organizational problems possess (Marshall-Mies *et al.*, 2000).
5 List the five elements of Mumford *et al.*'s (2000) Capability Model of Leadership.
6 According to cognitive resource theory, when is a leader less likely to effectively apply their cognitive capabilities?
7 What is 360-degree feedback and why is it effective?
8 On what grounds can executive coaching and leadership programmes be criticized?
9 Identify Spence and Oades' (2011) critiques of leadership-based publications.
10 Schein (1982, p. 5) comments that "neither culture nor leadership, when one examines each closely, can really be understood by itself". What does he mean by this, and why is this an important consideration in the delivery of leadership programmes?
11 How can leadership skills be measured?
12 Identify what 'successful' leadership means to you and defend your choice.

Notes

1 Quoted as part of an interview for this book, which appears in the expert insight "Mavens & Moguls" later in this chapter.
2 Byrd, H. (6 February 2020). Nancy Pelosi Defends Tearing Up the State of the Union Address. *CNN.com*. Available at: https://edition.cnn.com/2020/02/06/politics/nancy-pelosi-state-of-the-union-reaction/index.html.
3 SBC – the Southwestern Bell Corporation – acquired telecommunications giant AT&T in 2005.
4 Find out more: www.thisismoney.co.uk/money/investing/article-1687043/Chimps-portfolio-beats-94-of-Russian-bankers.html#ixzz1mwMeOCPR.
5 Beppe Grillo's 2013 campaign slogan.
6 A technocracy is an ideological system of governance where those in charge are selected on the basis of their expertise in a given area of responsibility.
7 This quote, popularized in modern literature, is actually likely to be a misquote; it is more likely to have been "There grows the stuff that won Waterloo", a remark made by Wellington at an Eton cricket match. Nevertheless, it remains an inspiring, and much used quote that eloquently speaks of the role of sport in the development of character.
8 Dobosz and Beaty (1999); Goldberg and Chandler (1991); Pascarella and Smart (1991); Snyder and Spreitzer (1992).
9 Dvir, T., Eden, D., Avolio, B.J. and Shamir, B. (2002). Impact of Transformational Leadership in Follower Development and Performance: A Field Experiment. *Academy of Management Journal*, 45, pp. 735–744.
10 Graustrom (1986); Ryan (1989); Savin-Williams (1979).
11 McClelland and Boyatzis (1982).
12 Many notable critiques of the over-representation of English public school attendees among British parliamentarians continue to exist, and remain central to government-focused discourse surrounding the concept of equity and diversity in politics.
13 The mediating effect of culture is considered at greater length later in Chapter 5, "Situational theories".
14 Speech prepared for delivery by John F. Kennedy in Dallas on the day of his assassination, 22 November 1963.

15 Hart, M.M., Lieb, K.J. and Winston, V.W. (2004). Mavens & Moguls: Creating a New Business Model. *Harvard Business Review.*
16 '30 under 30 and 40 under 40' refer to industry lists that the trade press often compiles of the most promising young practitioners in their respective field, as moderated by age; '30 under 30', for example, might refer to the 30 best lawyers under the age of 30. Lists are usually compiled annually.
17 For more information, consult the official SEC website: www.sec.gov/news/press/2012/2012-122.htm.
18 *CNS* (28 June 2012). Hedge Fund Boss Swiped $113m Unlawfully, SEC Says. Available at: www.courthousenews.com/hedge-fund-boss-swiped113-million-sec-says/.
19 Ibid.

References

Atwater, L. and Waldman, D. (1998). 360 Degree Feedback and Leadership Development. *Leadership Quarterly*, 9, pp. 421–426.

Avolio, B.J., Avey, J.B. and Quisenberry, D. (2010). Estimating Return on Leadership Development Investment. *Leadership Quarterly*, 21(4) (August), pp. 633–644.

Barker, R.A. (1997). How Can We Train Leaders if We Do Not Know What Leadership Is? *Human Relations*, 50(4), pp. 343–362.

Bennis, W. and Nanus, B. (1985). *Leaders: The Strategies for Taking Charge.* New York: Harper & Row.

Cascio, W.F. and Boudreau, J.W. (2008). *Investing in People: Financial Impact of Human Resource Initiatives.* Upper Saddle River, NJ: FT Press.

Charan, R. (2009). What the Experts Say: The Coaching Industry: A Work in Progress. In Diane Coutu and Carol Kauffman, (eds.), What Can Coaches Do for You? Harvard Business Review Research Report, January, p. 93.

Coutu, D. and Kauffman, C. (2009). HBR Research Report: What Can Coaches Do for You? *Harvard Business Review*, 87(1), p. 91.

Dobosz, R.P. and Beaty, L.A. (1999). The Relationship between Athletic Participation and High School Students' Leadership Ability. *Adolescence*, 34(133), pp. 215–220.

Dvir, T. (1988). *The Impact of Transformational Leadership Training on Follower Development and Performance, a Field Experiment.* Doctoral Dissertation, Tel Aviv University.

Ericsson, K.A. and Charness, W. (1994). Expert Performance: Its Structure and Acquisition. *American Psychologist*, 49(8), pp. 725–747.

Erikson, E.H. (1959). *Identity and the Life Cycle* (Psychological Issues Series). New York: International Universities Press.

Fielder, F.E. and Garcia, J.E. (1987). *New Approaches to Effective Leadership: Cognitive Resources and Organizational Performance.* New York: Wiley.

Fleishman, E.A., Mumford, M.D., Zaccaro, S.J., Levin, K.Y., Korotkin, A.L. and Hein, M.B. (1991). Taxonomic Efforts in the Description of Leadership Behaviour: A Synthesis and Functional Interpretation. *Leadership Quarterly*, 2(4), pp. 245–287.

Goldberg, A. and Chandler, T. (1991). The Role of Athletics: The Social World of High School Adolescents. *Youth & Society*, 21(2), pp. 238–250.

Graustrom, K. (1986). Interactional Dynamics between Teenage Leaders and Followers in the Classroom. *Journal of School Psychology*, 24, pp. 335–341.

Hall, D., Otazo, K. and Hollenbeck, G. (1999). Behind Closed Doors: What Really Happens in Executive Coaching? *Organizational Dynamics* 29 (Winter), pp. 39–53.

Katz, R.L. (1955). Skills of an Effective Administrator. *Harvard Business Review* 1 (January–February), pp. 33–42.

Kincaid, S.B. and Gordick, D. (2003). The Return on Investment of Leadership Development: Differentiating Our Discipline. *Consulting Psychology Journal: Practice and Research*, 55(1), pp. 47–57.

Lewis, P. and Jacobs, T.O. (1992). Individual Differences in Strategic Leadership Capacity: A Constructive/Developmental View. In R.L. Phillips and J.G. Hunt (eds.), *Strategic Leadership: A Multi-Organizational-Level Perspective*. Westport, CT: Quorum Books, pp. 121–137.

McClelland, D.C. and Boyatzis, R.E. (1982). The Leadership Motive Pattern and Long-Term Success in Management. *Journal of Applied Psychology*, 67(6), pp. 737–743.

Marshall-Mies, J.C., Fleishman, E.A., Martin, J.A., Zaccaro, S.J., Baughman, W.A. and McGee, M.L. (2000). Development and Evaluation of Cognitive and Metacognitive Measures for Predicting Leadership Potential. *Leadership Quarterly*, 11(1), pp. 135–153.

Mumford, M.D., Zaccaro, S.J., Harding, F.D., Jacobs, T.O. and Fleishman, E.A. (2000) Leadership Skills for a Changing World: Solving Complex Social Problems. *Leadership Quarterly*, 11(1), pp. 11–35.

Pascarella, E.T. and Smart, J.C. (1991). Impact of Intercollegiate Athletic Participation for African-American and Caucasian Men: Some Further Evidence. *Journal of College Student Development*, 32, pp. 123–133.

Ryan, F. (1989). Participation in Intercollegiate Athletics: Affective Outcomes. *Journal of College Student Development*, 39(2), pp. 122–128.

Savin-Williams, R.C. (1979). Dominance Hierarchies in Groups of Early Adolescents. *Child Development*, 50, pp. 923–935.

Schein, E.H. (1982). Increasing Organisational Effectiveness through Better Human Resource Planning and Development. In R. Katz, *Career Issues in Human Resource Management*. Englewood Cliffs, NJ: Prentice Hall.

Snyder, E. and Spreitzer, E. (1992). Social Psychological Concomitants of Adolescents' Role Identities as Scholars and Athletes: A Longitudinal Analysis. *Youth and Society*, 23, pp. 507–522.

Spence, G.B. and Oades, L.G. (2011). Coaching with Self-Determination in Mind: Using Theory to Advance Evidence-Based Coaching Practice. *International Journal of Evidence Based Coaching and Mentoring*, 9(2), pp. 37–55.

VanVelsor, E. and McCauley, C.D. (2004). Our View of Leadership Development. In C.D. McCauley and E. VanVelsor (eds.), *The Center for Creative Leadership Handbook of Leadership Development*. 2nd ed. San Francisco, CA: Jossey-Bass, pp. 1–22.

Zaccaro, S.J., Foti, R.J. and Kenny, D.A. (1991). Self-Monitoring and Trait-Based Variance in Leadership: An Investigation of Leader Flexibility across Multiple Group Situations. *Journal of Applied Psychology*, 76(2), pp. 308–315.

Other resources

See PowerPoint slides on the companion website at www.routledge.com/9780367374822.

4

BEHAVIOURAL THEORIES

"Concepts, such as loyalty to your co-workers and your employer, a pleasant work environment, etc. tend to be relegated to the sidelines."

— *MD, leading investment bank*[1]

One of the most eloquent, motivational and moving lectures of recent years was delivered by Randy Pausch, a professor at Carnegie Mellon University. The lecture, entitled "Last lecture: Achieving your childhood dreams",[2] was delivered by Pausch on 18 September 2007, shortly before he lost his life to pancreatic cancer. The lecture was turned into a *New York Times* bestselling book, and has since been translated into 48 languages. At the time of writing, the video[3] of his lecture had been viewed almost fifteen million times on YouTube. Pausch's style, rapport, passion and vision provide a noteworthy exemplar of motivation in action and readers are subsequently directed to either the video or his lecture for further elucidation.

Randy Pausch's "Last lecture" serves as a compelling example of how a leader can influence the behaviour of followers by motivating and inspiring them. Such a skill is compelling for the leadership scholar, as it has been proven that more motivated employees and followers are more likely to be productive and efficient and less likely to leave the organization or movement, while also becoming more likely to contribute positively to organizational goals. The study of the role of motivation in leadership falls under the auspices of the behavioural management (also known as the human relations) approach, which subsequently forms the focus of this chapter.

Introduction

The early twentieth century study of management was dominated by scientific and classical approaches. These approaches assumed that employees were essentially tools of work, from whom maximal productivity could be expediently extracted via close supervision, and by the threat of punishment if targets were not met. No effort was made to invest in resources or programmes that would enhance motivation or satisfaction among workers, as it was not yet understood that such factors positively affected productivity. Famous management theorists of the time included Henry Ford, who pioneered the production line approach to manufacturing, and the time and motion studies conducted by the Gilbreths.[4] These studies reflected the dominant managerial concerns of the day, which were based around manufacturing industries, and reflected the need for organizations to extract maximum work from a factory line of employees in the shortest possible time to retain a competitive advantage. Of course, today's organizational environment is characterized by a great deal more complexity, where forces such as globalization, terrorism, networked communications and widespread technological advances arguably require a far more sophisticated approach to the management of employees and followers, with the retention of talent, the ability to innovate and the ability to react quickly to change remaining key managerial foci.

Structure of the chapter

This chapter introduces the reader to the history of behavioural theories of leadership. The chapter initially focuses on the prevalence of classical and scientific management approaches where approaches to organizational productivity generally focused on treating employees as if they were machines, using time and motion studies and other scientific techniques to extract the maximum possible exertion and productivity from them. The chapter then briefly outlines the surprising outcome of the Hawthorne Studies (the *Hawthorne Effect*) that identified the motivational effect that occurred when employees felt that their managers were taking an interest in them. This precedes a more detailed consideration of motivational theories, specifically *content* and *process* theories. The former constitutes Maslow's Hierarchy of Needs, ERG (Existence, Relatedness and Growth) Theory, Herzberg's Two-Factor Theory and McClelland's Needs Motivation Theory, while the latter includes Vroom's Expectancy Theory, House's Path–Goal Theory, Adams' Equity Theory and Locke's Goal Theory. The emphasis on motivational (as opposed to classical or scientific) theories within this chapter is justified, given the ongoing relevance of motivational theories to the leader and, specifically, the way in which motivational techniques can be used to engender performance beyond expectations in both oneself and one's employees.

The chapter then identifies key critiques of motivational theories of leadership, before identifying ways in which motivational theories can be measured. The expert insight for this chapter is provided by Andrew Barnes, CEO and co-founder of the not-for-profit 4-Day Week project and board member of the Wellness Research Institute at the University of Oxford ("4-Day Week"). This precedes a case study entitled "Tragedy at Longhua". A quiz completes the chapter.

The behaviourist approach

The history of the behavioural approach begins largely with the *Hawthorne Studies*. These studies were conducted by Elton Mayo between 1929 and 1932 in Chicago, at the Hawthorne Works of the Western Electric Company. The objective of the first of Mayo's two studies was to determine the relationship between lighting levels and employee productivity. Theorists were surprised to note that employee productivity actually increased significantly as lighting levels decreased. Performance only declined when the employees were no longer able to see what they were doing sufficiently to carry out their tasks. Further experiments a number of years later, this time conducted by Mayo and a colleague, F.J. Roethlisberger, involved the supervision of five female bank employees who were awarded special privileges, such as the right to take rest periods and enjoy free lunches. A significant increase in productivity was also observed within this group. In the first study, working conditions had been diminished and, in the second, improved – yet significant increases in productivity were observed in both cases. How could this be explained?

The researchers concluded that the significant increase in productivity observed across both groups was attributable to the intensive attention paid by the researchers (who had essentially adopted the position of supervisors) to the employees. This attention positively affected motivation and, as a result, productivity. This effect became known as the *Hawthorne Effect*. The studies greatly influenced management theory, as they identified the potential impact of human relations (in this case, the relationship between managers and their subordinates) on the motivation and, sub-sequently, the productivity of the workforce. This led to the emergence of studies of motivation in management, a concept that subsequently dominates discussions throughout the remainder of this chapter. These began with a drive to understand the role of the satisfaction of employee *needs* on performance.

During the 1960s, *needs* theories were largely supplanted by *goals*-based cognitive approaches to the study of motivation. The early part of this chapter presents the dominant *need*- and *goal*-based theories of motivation, discussed as *content* and *process* theories. The 1970s witnessed an emerging focus on the concept of *intrinsic motivation*, with Deci (1975) proposing that internally motivated behaviours are based on the needs of individuals to feel *competent* and *self-determined*. This led to the development of *Self-Determination Theory*. The aforementioned theories and approaches consequently form the basis for discussion in the next section of this chapter.

Theories of motivation

> We are still masters of our fate. We are still captains of our souls.
> *Winston Churchill*[5]

Motivational theory – which recognizes the role of human behaviours, values and needs in motivation – can be broadly separated into two types: *content* and *process*

TABLE 4.1 Content and process theories

Content theories	Process theories
Maslow's Hierarchy of Needs	Vroom's Expectancy Theory
ERG Theory	House's Path–Goal Theory
Herzberg's Two-Factor Theory	Adam's Equity Theory
McClelland's Needs Motivation Theory	Locke's Goal Theory

theories of motivation (Table 4.1). Content theory focuses on the *intrinsic* factors that exert power over an individual's behaviour (for example, the need for recognition), whereas process theories explain the *external* factors that influence one's behaviour (such as an employee's perception that a manager is treating them unfairly by giving them fewer opportunities and lower pay than his/her colleagues).

Content theories

Content theories constitute Maslow's Hierarchy of Needs, ERG Theory, Herzberg's Two-Factor (Motivation–Hygiene) Theory, and McClelland's Needs Motivation Theory. *Maslow's Hierarchy of Needs* was developed by Abraham Maslow in 1943, and is based on the fundamental idea that each of us is born with a complete, and somewhat unique, set of needs, and that the satisfaction of these needs, which leads to our personal growth, requires an environment conducive to their healthy expression (Maslow, 1970).

Maslow's Hierarchy theorizes the existence of five needs that must be satisfied in ascending hierarchical order and argues that, if needs are met, then high levels of motivation (and, subsequently) performance will occur. These needs are: *physiological* (air, water, food, clothing and shelter); *safety* (physical, environmental and emotional safety); *love and belongingness* (the need to belong); *self-esteem* (to feel good about and value oneself); and *self-actualization* (achieving one's true potential). According to the theory, *lower order* (physiological and safety) needs (also referred to as *deficiency needs*) must be met most urgently. Maslow argued that the presence of lower order needs are not motivators in themselves, but act as de-motivating influences if they are not present. We are thus motivated to prioritize satisfaction of these needs before we are able to progress to the pursuance and realization of *higher order* needs (love and belongingness, self-esteem and self-actualization, also referred to as *being needs*).

IDEA IN BRIEF

Chasing self-actualization

For examples of Maslow's theory in action, one can observe the phenomenon of successful business leaders who pursue extreme sports and activities in their spare time – thrill-seeking activities, which require the deliberate denial of lower order needs as a means of seeking self-actualization. Examples include Jean-Philippe Blochet, a successful hedge fund manager who completed the Marathon des Sables (a 243-kilometre foot race across the Sahara desert),[6] or Micron CEO Steve Appleton, who often spent his free time stunt piloting (Appleton sadly lost his life in a plane crash in 2012).

Maslow's Hierarchy has been criticized for applying a Western homogenization to the concept of motivation, as it reflects the ethos of an individualistic Western culture, and not that of an Eastern collectivist society (a criticism which the reader might consider applying to a number of other theories in this book). As stated by Hofstede (1984, p. 396), "the ordering of Maslow's hierarchy represents a value choice – Maslow's value choice. This choice was based on his mid-20th Century US middle class values." Hofstede refers to the subjectivity and bias of the theorist and the danger of attempting to generalize their findings to wider social groups; he also states that "management, as the word is presently used, is an American invention" (Hofstede, 1993, p. 81). Maslow's Hierarchy has also been criticized from a business and management perspective for being a theory of human development, as opposed to a theory that specifically considers employee motivation.

Some of the criticisms of Maslow's Hierarchy were addressed by *ERG Theory* (Alderfer, 1967, 1969). ERG Theory is a motivational construct that seeks to understand the intrinsic factors that cause an individual to act (i.e. what motivates an employee to act in the way that they do?). It extended the work of Maslow by seeking to combine empirical research on needs theory with Maslow's Hierarchy, thereby addressing the theoretical limitations of Maslow's work. ERG Theory subsequently simplified Maslow's five motivational needs into three separate elements: *existence* (physiological and safety needs), *relatedness* (the need for meaningful interpersonal relationships) and *growth* (the human need for personal development and actualization) (Figure 4.1).

ERG Theory possesses a greater degree of empirical validity than Maslow's Hierarchy (Luthans, 1998; Robbins, 1998) and recognizes the complexity of the motivational process in that multiple needs can and should, in some circumstances, be satisfied simultaneously.

Maslow's theory also inspired the work of Frederick Herzberg's (1968) *Two-Factor Theory*. Herzberg's Motivation–Hygiene factor theory, developed in 1959, remains one of the most recognized and widely utilized theories used to investigate and explain the relationship between motivation and job satisfaction (Figure 4.2).

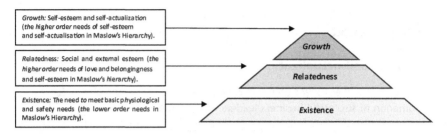

FIGURE 4.1 The relationship between Maslow's Hierarchy and ERG Theory.

FIGURE 4.2 Hygiene and motivator factors.

Herzberg's (1968) Two-Factor Theory identifies two sets of factors that mediate the relationship between job satisfaction and job performance in organizations.

The first set of factors is known as 'satisfiers' or 'motivators'. These factors cause job satisfaction to occur when an employee's need for them is satiated. Motivators are typically recognized as intrinsic to the individual – for example, achievement of personal goals, an inherent enjoyment of the task at hand, or of the challenge associated with the role, or with a particular task. Herzberg theorized that employees would find motivational factors to be intrinsically rewarding as they would meet psychological needs of *recognition* (receiving appropriate praise for their accomplishments), a *sense of achievement, growth and opportunities for promotion, responsibility* and *meaningfulness* in one's work.

The second factor in the model is referred to as '*dissatisfiers*' or '*hygiene factors*'. Hygiene factors cause the employee to experience dissatisfaction in his/her job when the work environment is deficient in them, although, critically, their presence does not provide a motivating effect. Consider the case of a sales team based in an office in Mumbai. The office has sufficient air conditioning, lighting, desks and technological facilities (e.g. photocopiers, PCs) for the sales associates to perform their roles and for all responsibilities to be performed correctly by the employees. These facilities are not considered to be motivators, yet in their absence they become hygiene factors. If the same sales team is provided with membership of a local gym that has a swimming pool and tennis courts, then this would be considered a motivator.

Hygiene factors are only dissatisfiers if they are absent, but they do not have the power to motivate simply by being present – for example, heating (Jaafar *et al.*, 2006). Motivational factors are the most important of the two, because they directly affect a person's motivational drive to achieve a high level of performance within the job or task they have been set (Nelson and Quick, 2003). Thus, hygiene factors provide support for *motivators* but do not directly affect a person's motivation to work; they only influence the extent, in the case of their absence, to which the employee experiences discontent.

In 1976, the *Harvard Business Review* (HBR) published what is now considered an HBR classic, "Power is the Great Motivator" (McClelland & Burnham, 2003). The article introduced the *Motivation Needs Theory* that argues that managers can be classified into three groups: managers with a dominant need for *affiliation*, managers with a dominant need for *achievement* and managers with a dominant need for *power* (Figure 4.3). McClelland's theory is an empirical theory of personality that assumes that needs are *learned*, as opposed to being *innate*, and that need strengths will vary as a result of the social context that created them.

Affiliative managers need people to like them more than they need to get things done. Their need to win the external approval of others leads to a self-serving interest to gain popularity, which ultimately compromises their authority. A manager who exhibits a dominant need for affiliation is subsequently most likely to exhibit the least effective performance among the three motivational groups.

Managers with a dominant need for *achievement* are competitive, goal-orientated individuals who prioritize achievement of their own personal goals over those of the organization. Achievement-orientated managers seek positive reinforcement and feedback from their superiors and peers, and seek recognition (for example, sales awards, a promotion or bonus) for their accomplishments.

Managers with a high need for *power* (otherwise known as *institutional* managers) exhibit a high need to make an impact, to influence the people around them and to seek power through influencing others. These empire builders are willing to sacrifice personal goals for those of the team, possess a clear sense of justice and are interested in helping others. They tend to engender high levels of morale and employ a coaching style of management. They also possess smaller egos than achievement-motivated managers as well as greater emotional maturity. These managers are also the most likely to achieve high levels of performance. McClelland and Burnham (2003) specify that a manager's *power motivation* can be either *socialized* or *personalized* and that this need for power must be socialized in order to lead to

FIGURE 4.3 Motivation Needs Theory.

Source: Ryan and Deci (2000).

positive outcomes. The institutional power manager who possesses a socialized power motivation is therefore characterized as one who possesses high levels of *referent power*, as opposed to the *coercive* and *legitimate* power upon which *personalized power* managers and managers with a dominant need for *achievement* are more likely to rely.

Process theories

Whereas content theories focus on *intrinsic* factors that affect motivation (such as the drive to satisfy the need to self-actualize), process theories adopt a different focus, and seek to explain how behaviour is influenced by *external* factors (such as the need to be treated fairly and equitably, or by the financial value that one attributes to the outcome of a project or work task). Dominant process theories that form the basis of discussion in this chapter are *Adams' Equity Theory, Vroom's Expectancy-Value Theory, House's Path–Goal Theory* and *Locke's Goal Theory*.

Equity Theory (Adams, 1963, 1965) identifies the key role of perceptions of equitable treatment as a motivating force, where employees strive for an equitable balance between their personal *inputs* to the organization (for example, loyalty to the organization, hard work, enthusiasm and skill), and the *outputs* that are generated as a result of their actions (for example, a salary that they feel is commensurate with their abilities and contribution to the company). Adams (1963, p. 427) theorized that employees will perceive unfairness in the workplace if they feel that their efforts are being rewarded less than other employees: "the presence of inequity will motivate a person to achieve equity or reduce inequity, and the strength of motivation to do so will vary directly with the amount of inequity." Equity Theory has received theoretical support within the academic literature, and displays empirical validity (Chen *et al.*, 1998; Chen *et al.*, 2002; Miles *et al.*, 1994; Scheer *et al.*, 2003).

Equity Theory suggests that employees display a natural tendency to compare themselves to other social referents, such as workplace colleagues or their Master of Business Administration (MBA) classmates. An employee who perceives a high level of equity within an organization is likely to display greater *organizational commitment* (the strength with which the employee identifies with and involves themselves in a particular organization) – most notably, *affective commitment* (the emotional attachment that the employee feels towards the company) and *continuance commitment* (high continuance commitment leads to a low likelihood of leaving the company). This is because the personal needs and values that they hold in association with fairness and equity have been satisfied. However, it is important that the rewards that they receive in exchange for their work are rewards that hold a high level of value for them (as stated by Adams, 1963), and it is a challenge for the leader to identify what rewards hold value for each individual employee, as this might differ significantly among the workforce. As Adams (1963, p. 427) questions, "Is the frequently used practice of giving a man a prestigeful title an effective substitute for greater monetary outcomes?".

A process theory of motivation known as *Expectancy-Value Theory* provides a theoretical structure for calculating the perceived *valence* of a reward, as perceived by an employee, which will determine the extent to which they will exert effort towards the realization of a particular task.

Brockner *et al.* (1992) identify work effort as the result of the incentive structure facing employees. This assumes that employees are rational economic agents, who regard work effort as a form of cost, and seek to conserve energy.

Expectancy-Value, or *VIE (Valence, Instrumentality, Expectancy), Theory* (Vroom, 1964), the third process theory discussed, provides a cognitive-motivational view of leadership. This implies that behaviour is a result of cognitive processes, and that individuals are capable of calculating the costs and benefits to themselves regarding potential courses of action. Van den Broeck *et al.* (2009, p. 300) define expectancy theory thus: an "individuals' motivation to strive for or choose a particular goal is regarded as a (multiplicative) function of their expectancies to successfully attain this goal and the subjective valence the individual ascribes to that goal."

VIE is calculated using the formula shown in Figure 4.4. This can be most effectively illustrated via the use of an example. A trader working in the financial markets will be motivated to execute a high volume of trades if he/she is remunerated financially by a commission awarded to him/her at the point of trade. A high motivation to attain the financial bonus is likely to lead to the trader attempting to execute a high volume of trades and to work long hours. Thus, we can see that expectancy theory offers a rational, economic view of motivation and of the role that it plays in determining human behaviour.

Expectancy theory can be criticized on grounds of universality, i.e. that it applies only to some individuals, and not to others (Landy and Becker, 1987). It is also criticized for its difficulty in practical application (Benkhoff, 1997), including measurements of performance.

If we refer back, for example, to our trader, he/she might choose to engage in far riskier trades than that which could be considered rational, and which may compromise the long-term stability of the organization as a result of his/her motivation

Valence of outcome x Expectancy = Instrumentality = Motivation Force

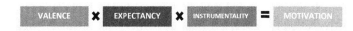

Expectancy: E -> P. The belief of the person that her/his effort (E) will result in attainment of desired performance (P) goals;

Instrumentality: P -> R. The belief of the person that she/he will receive a reward (R) if the performance (P) expectation is met;

Valence: The value of the reward according to the person.

FIGURE 4.4 Calculating VIE.

Source: Vroom (1964).

to maximize the size of their bonus. Certainly, the 'point of trade' bonus culture in investment banking has been identified as a causal factor in the practice of risky decision making and trading of toxic debts that contributed to the global meltdown of markets in 2008. This indicates that rationality cannot automatically be assumed to form the basis of a leader's or an employee's actions.

Building on the work of Vroom (1964), House developed his 1971 *Path–Goal Theory of leadership effectiveness*. The foundations of the theory are built on the notion that leaders behave in such a way as to remove obstacles that obstruct subordinates' satisfaction and performance. A dyadic theory of supervision, Path–Goal Theory relates to the day-to-day quality of the relationship between leader and subordinate, and concerns the way in which the behaviour of a manager mediates the motivation of his employees. As stated by House (1971, p. 324),

> the motivational function of the leader consists of increasing personal payoffs to subordinates for work-goal attainment and making the path to these payoffs easier to travel by clarifying it, reducing roadblocks and pitfalls, and increasing the opportunities for personal satisfaction en route.

The concept of role ambiguity (a failure to clarify the specificities of an employee's role) has been linked to toxic leadership (Alvesson and Sveningsson, 2003; see Chapter 10, "Destructive leadership").

The original 1971 Path–Goal Theory identified two distinct classes of leader behaviour: *path–goal* clarifying behaviour, and behaviour directed towards the *satisfaction of employee needs* – a concept extended by House and Mitchell (1974) to encapsulate four distinct behaviours:

1   *Directive path–goal clarifying leader behaviour*, which is based on the provision of a clear structure for subordinates. Consider the case of an investment banking consultancy which has been hired by Standard Bank to implement a global risk management solution. The project manager high in path–goal clarifying behaviour would provide a clear project plan for their team, making the roles and responsibilities of each team member explicit. They would provide deadlines and hold regular meetings, ensuring that the lines of communication between themselves, their team and the client were always open, in order to facilitate timely sharing of information. A healthy psychological environment would be facilitated for the IT team, as each employee would know exactly what was required of them. They would know who to approach with specific issues or questions, and they would also be protected from project creep via the creation and dissemination of a clear contractual agreement between consultancy and client that clearly outlined the limits of the work to be undertaken.
2   *Supportive leader behaviour* involves the leader taking an interest in the psychological well-being, needs and preferences of subordinates via the provision of a supportive and healthy work environment. An example of a company with a culturally supportive strategy is Hilton, which was recently placed first on the

2019 Forbes 4.3 million employee survey-based "100 Best Companies to Work For" list.

3   *Participative leader behaviour* involves the engagement of subordinates in decision-making activity, and in the seeking of subordinate feedback to enhance the overall operations of the team, department or organization. Outcomes of participative behaviour include greater employee autonomy and a greater alignment of employee goals with those of the organization.

4   *Achievement-oriented behaviour* encourages performance excellence via a structured approach of goal-setting, feedback and a demonstrated belief, by the leader, in the ability of his subordinates. An example of such a leader is John Wooden, famed for his inspirational yet calm approach towards development of his athletes. Under Wooden, University of California, Los Angeles secured ten National Collegiate Athletic Association (NCAA) national championships over a 12-year period.

The theory was further reformulated as the path–goal theory of unit leadership (House, 1996). The reformulated theory addressed empirical critiques of the original theory and extended its focus considerably. Key extensions of the theory included the effects of a leader's behaviour on the ability of his subordinates to perform effectively, and the effects of the leader on his/her overall team/unit, not only on the individual. A compelling legacy of Path–Goal Theory was the development of House's 1976 theory of charismatic leadership (House, 1977), a theory also notably influenced by the work of McClelland (which forms the focus of Chapter 6, "Charismatic leadership").

IDEA IN BRIEF

When money is the only motivational driver

The MD (Managing Director) of a global investment bank shares with us some anonymised, and valuable, insights into the way in which banks and other financial institutions still rely heavily on one external motivational driver – money – to motivate employees.

"Most people who work in investment banks are there for the money. Of course, working in an investment bank can also be very rewarding in other ways – for example, the intellectual stimulation of complex projects, influence, etc., but – by and large – money always matters. Certainly more than in it does in other industries.

On the one hand, this is probably somewhat understandable, as most work undertaken within an investment bank revolves around (sometimes substantial, but always considerable) financial sums. Our whole reason for being is to trade, and make, money. On the other hand, however, it is an industry where money appears to be the main motivational driver for people's career decisions, whilst other concepts, such as loyalty to your co-workers and your employer, a pleasant work environment, etc. tend to be relegated to the sidelines, as they are considered to be far less important – or sometimes even non-existent. This might also be (at least partially) due to the fact that job security in this industry is very low and banks tend to hire and fire quite aggressively when market conditions depreciate. These factors create a situation where the focus on money as the key driver is somewhat natural, as one cannot necessarily count on their next pay cheque.

Equally, due to the high-pressured environment of investment banking, it is quite rare to see people in their fifties (and certainly not in their sixties) working in an investment bank. An investment banker's 'shelf-life' is certainly shorter than in most other careers. Interestingly, the same could probably be said for a high-achieving athlete, but in sport there are clearly other non-money-related aspects at work that act as key motivational drivers, and which, arguably, create a far more positive culture as a result."

Path–Goal Theory is grounded in expectancy theory and recognizes the fact that people will be more focused and motivated if they believe they are *capable* of high performance, that their *effort* will result in *desired outcomes* and that their work is *worthwhile*. According to path–goal theory, leaders *motivate* followers to accomplish identified objectives by *clarifying the paths* to performance and goal achievement and by *removing obstacles* that stand in the way of achievement of high levels of performance and realization of desired objectives (House, 1996). A related theory, *Goal Theory* (Locke, 1968) recognizes the central role of *goals* in the motivational process. Goal Theory posits that high levels of employee motivation and performance will be elicited if the manager sets specific goals that are challenging but achievable, and if effective feedback on performance is provided.

Regulation determination of motivation in employees

The fullest representations of humanity show people to be curious, vital, and self-motivated. At their best, they are agentic, and inspired, striving to learn; extend themselves, master new skills; and apply their talents responsibly ... Yet it is also clear that the human spirit can be diminished or crushed.

(Ryan and Deci, 2000, p. 68)

Self-Determination Theory (SDT) constitutes an empirically grounded approach to the study of human motivation and personality (Ryan *et al.*, 1997), and identifies the extent to which behaviours are *externally* motivated or *internally* motivated. The theory has received substantial empirical validation and provides a manager with a means of identifying the importance of balancing extrinsic motivators (such as a bonus) with intrinsic motivators (for example, challenging an employee with a difficult yet stimulating project that allows them to master new skills) in order to elicit maximum productivity and high levels of performance.

SDT claims that an individual's level of motivation can range from *amotivated* to *intrinsically motivated* (see Figure 4.5).

According to the self-determination continuum, intrinsically motivated employees experience higher levels of satisfaction with, and commitment to, their job, possess greater psychological well-being and elicit improved levels of performance (Vansteenkiste *et al.*, 2007). Conversely, employees who require, or are subject to, high extrinsic motivation (and who exhibit low intrinsic motivation), are more likely to experience a negative impact on their mental well-being, physical health, vitality and self-actualization. A reliance on extrinsic motivators such as bonuses, for example, is also negatively related to the development of affect intrinsic motivation (Deci and Ryan, 2000; Kasser and Ryan, 1996; Sheldon *et al.*, 2004). Thus, SDT informs us of the value of developing high levels of self-determined and self-regulated intrinsic motivational behaviours in both ourselves and our employees, and also explains the mechanisms by which motivation is self-determined (Ryan *et al.*, 1997).

How can managers increase intrinsic motivation in their teams, or in themselves? According to SDT, *intrinsic motivation* occurs as a result of the *internalization* of organizational values into one's own existing system of beliefs and values (Deci and Ryan, 2000), which occurs when three key psychological needs – for *competence*, *autonomy* and *relatedness* – are satisfied.

- *Competence* – this relates to the psychological need to feel competent at one's job or career, or in the task that one is currently undertaking. When goals are mastered, social-contextual factors, such as feedback, communication and rewards, heighten both feelings of *competence* and feelings of self-efficacy towards the desired behaviour (Ryan and Deci, 2000). Deci (1971) found that provision of unexpected positive feedback increased an individual's intrinsically motivated drive to complete the task, meaning that their need for competence was satisfied. Conversely, provision of negative feedback led to a diminished sense of intrinsic motivation by undermining feelings of competence (Vallerand and Reid, 1984).
- *Autonomy* – this relates to volition, voluntarism or the desire to self-organize experience and behaviour and to have activity concordant with one's integrated sense of self (Deci and Ryan, 2000, p. 231). A high degree of autonomy is considered essential to the development of intrinsic motivation, itself positively related to performance and feelings of well-being. It is essential that managers do not habitually reward intrinsically motivated behaviours with external rewards, such as bonuses, as this undermines the power of intrinsic motivation, and subsequently compromises autonomy (Deci, 1971). If employees are afforded greater autonomy and choice, this is likely to increase their intrinsic motivation (Zuckerman *et al.*, 1978).
- *Relatedness* – this need relates to the human need to interact with, be connected to and experience feelings of caring for others (Baumeister and Leary,

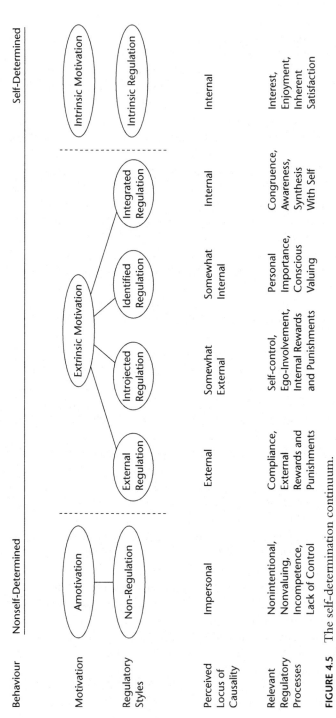

FIGURE 4.5   The self-determination continuum.
Source: Ryan and Deci (2000).

1995). Deci and Ryan (2000) theorize that intrinsic motivation is more likely to develop in an environment where the individual feels secure, and where needs of relatedness are met. Examples include the camaraderie of the *Daily Dispatch* journalistic staff under Donald Woods' editorship (see Chapter 7 case study).

According to SDT, one can theorize that business leaders who seek to facilitate *internalization* and *integration* of organizational values, and who seek to foster a climate where the facilitation of intrinsic motivation is encouraged, will be more likely to develop a workforce that exhibits high levels of performance and that seeks to contribute effectively to organizational goals. An example of the facilitation of *competence* is the provision of high-quality feedback by a country manager to his regional executives in order to encourage their feelings of competence (Reeve and Deci, 1996).

Measuring motivation

Students who wish to research SDT using psychometric instruments are advised to visit the official SDT website at www.psych.rochester.edu/SDT/questionnaires. php, where a range of free access instruments are available. ERG Theory can be measured using an instrument developed by Alderfer (1967) or via the use of more recent instruments designed to measure employee motivation (e.g. Wiley, 1997).

Critiques of motivational theories

The causal relationship between needs satisfaction and workplace performance has been questioned (Luthans, 1998) on the basis that employee satisfaction does not automatically result in improved performance. Needs theories have also been criticized for a lack of empirical validity.

The universality of the *valence* attributed to a particular task may differ tremendously between employees, suggesting that it is difficult to identify generic motivational strategies that might appeal equally to all. For example, whereas one employee might value the assignation of additional responsibility, another might balk at this offer, preferring the idea of a financial bonus or other perk. It is not yet understood how one type of reward (for example, a bonus) affects individual needs (e.g. self-esteem), and whether fulfilment of one need (e.g. self-esteem) over another (e.g. relatedness) might exert a stronger causal power over performance.[7] Needs theories thus assume some level of psychological uniformity among work teams, a generalization that might not be accurate.

Deci and Ryan (2000, p. 233) define intrinsic motivated activities as those that "are freely engaged out of interest without the necessity of separable consequences and, to be maintained, they require satisfaction of the needs for autonomy and competence". Will a manager motivated highly by achievement (according to McClelland's Needs Theory) display consistently high levels of performance? Or is his/her ability to perform mediated by other environmental factors? These factors warrant further investigation so that our understanding of the phenomenon is elucidated and clarified.

Summary

Actively disengaged employees cost the US up to $550 billion annually in lost productivity.

CNBC, 2013[8]

Despite a long history of behavioural studies of motivation in management and leadership, Lussier and Achua's (2004) research betrays an ongoing difficulty among leaders in demonstrating the ability to effectively motivate employees. This suggests a potential chasm between motivational theory and the ability to practise it.

Benkhoff (1997) attributes this partly to the inability of organizations to appropriately measure and evaluate performance, and partly to the complexity of organizations, that makes it impossible for one organization to copy the approach of a more successful one. Another response might be to question whether leaders possess sufficient knowledge of motivational theories to understand how best to motivate employees. Scholars might further question the cultural relevance and limitations of dominant motivational theories: "most management literature on motivation is psychologically oriented and is based on psychological models developed and tested almost exclusively in the United States" (Fatehi, 1996. P. 165).

The need to adopt a less leader-centric view, and to recognize the impact of the situation on the leadership process, leads us to the consideration of *situational and contingency* theories of leadership, which subsequently form the basis for discussion in the next chapter.

 **Expert insight**

The 4 day week – turning orthodoxy on its head

This expert insight chronicles the work of Andrew Barnes, 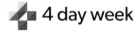 *CEO of Perpetual Guardian and co-founder of the 4 Day Week Global Foundation. Andrew's experiences in trialling a 4-day week made headlines around the world, preceding a similar successful recent trial by Microsoft Japan. As a Board member of the Wellness Research Centre at the University of Oxford, Andrew continues to spearhead investment and research into the productivity and motivation benefits of a 4-day week. A brief background to the concept precedes a Q&A with Andrew.*

Background

Microsoft recently trialled a 4-day work week in Japan, reporting a 40 per cent jump in productivity and increased efficiency in meetings, with employees who participated in the trial also reporting greater levels of balance and happiness. The trial involved the entire 2,300-person workforce at Microsoft Japan being given Fridays off for five weeks in a row. As part of the trial, the company also agreed to partly subsidise family vacations. CEO Takuya Hirano attributed the impressive upswing in productivity to the fact that employees were more well rested. Environmentally, the trial worked effectively too – employees used 23 per cent less electricity and printed 59 per cent less paper during the 4-day weeks, when compared to a regular 5-day format.

As CEO of Perpetual Guardian, Andrew Barnes trialled a 4-day work week in 2018 within his company. The trial ran over a two-month period, involving 240 employees. Staff stress levels fell, employees reported a better work–life balance and employees were more focused. These findings mirrored those of a recent Harvard study that found that shorter working days increased productivity. More information about the 4-day work week concept can be found at www.4dayweek.com.

Q. How did you first come up with the idea to focus on the 4-day work week concept?

I was sitting on a plane reading an *Economist* magazine article which talked about how low productivity in the workplace was, and I wondered if this was the case in my business. This led me to think that if we could improve productivity, I could then reward our staff with time off.

Q. Do you face a lot of resistance from organizations or do you feel that many CEOs and executive boards are open to trialling the idea?

In my experience business leaders fall into two categories, those who like the idea but are not sure how they would make it work, and those who have no idea how to make it work, so immediately dismiss the idea. The old saying, "Whether you think you can, or whether you think you can't, you are right", is very much applicable here. It's about giving it a go! In general, since we started this journey, we have been met with interest and enthusiasm – so much so that we developed a white paper to share our research results and provide a guideline on how to implement a trial, which has been downloaded by thousands of people.

Q. The 4-day work week approach is based strongly on empirical research. Could you please tell us about the in-house research that you use as a foundation of the approach and explain why research-based evidence is so important in promoting the concept?

We decided early that having external research as well as in-house data would be important for giving the leadership and board the independent evidence as to whether what we were doing was working. The data doesn't lie – our independent researchers undertook quantitative and qualitative research that tells a compelling story. What we have learned following the global interest is that there is a need for a larger body of research which will allow businesses interested in the 4-day work week to go ahead with its implementation. It also allows them to plug into this global system and movement for change so that they can feel part of a wider international movement, with the ability to compare their results to others.

Q. The 4-day work week concept clashes with orthodox managerial productivity-focused approaches. Do you think that some companies are just too ingrained in the 5-day culture to change?

Yes, I do. Evidence shows that we are not fully productive for all the time we are at work. There are many reasons for this, mostly to do with the way our days are structured. Worse still, businesses often ask their staff to find ways to be more productive without providing any incentive. Staff read this as 'do more with less', which is obviously demotivating. Without incentive employees might find some ways to be more productive, but when you give staff a true, genuine benefit, such as time off, they will search high and low for the ways they can find productivity hacks. The results of numerous studies, including our own, show this to be clearly the case.

Q. As a culture we seem to suffer from what Harvard Business School professor Ashley Whillans refers to as "time poverty". Do you think that the 4-day work week approach is the best way of addressing this concern?

In short, yes. The research that Ashley and her fellow researchers have conducted in this area is significant to understanding the value of time in our lives, not just for our well-being, but also financially. The consequences of us being time poor are real and play out every day all around the world. The ability to have more time away from work and to use that time to benefit yourself, your family and society is at the core of what we advocate. The focus on productivity makes it 'safe' for business and the economy to feel that they can take this step. Also, we can no longer ignore the environmental benefits of lower energy consumption linked to less time on site and that needs to be taken more seriously as a benefit than it is now.

Q. Does the concept work better in some industries or levels of seniority than others?

There will always be some industries, businesses and teams within those businesses where a 4-day work week will be easier to roll out than others. Some of those constraints will be external and hard for a company to mediate, but much of it ultimately depends on how capable, prepared and willing a business leader is to make changes that do not just benefit the business, but their employees and our society, economy and environment too. We ensured that our trial was staff-led, so that our staff felt empowered to create productivity solutions that worked for their individual and team style of work.

Q. Your work has led you to become a board member of the Oxford University Wellbeing Research Centre. What does this entail?

We are very proud of our association with the research aspect of our trial. This made us realize there is much work to be done, so when the Director of the Centre approached us about not only being on the Board – but also funding a research fellow – we were very happy to be involved. We hope to work alongside Laura Giurge – The Barnes Research Fellow – to continue to research and understand further the economics of wellbeing in the workplace. Laura is part of an international group of researchers (including Ashley Whillans) who share knowledge that together creates a larger whole. We think that, ultimately, the 4-day work week concept holds a great deal of promise not only for individual employees, but for society, the economy and the environment as a whole.

Find out more

- Paul, K. (4 November 2019). Microsoft Japan Tested a Four-Day Work Week and Productivity Jumped by 40%. *The Guardian*. Available at: www.theguardian.com/technology/2019/nov/04/microsoft-japan-four-day-work-week-productivity.
- Wellbeing Research Centre, University of Oxford: https://wellbeing.hmc.ox.ac.uk/home.

Questions

1   With reference to Herzberg's Two-Factor Theory, identify how a 4-day work week model effectively addresses hygiene factors and motivating factors.
2   How might the studies performed by Microsoft, and by Perpetual Guardian, reinforce concepts that underpin the theoretical assumptions of the Hawthorne Effect?
3   Apply SDT Theory to this expert insight to explain why reducing the number of days spent at work can effectively lead to an increase in productivity.

Case study: tragedy at Longhua

In 2010, an unprecedented wave of suicides occurred at the Foxconn's Longhua factory,[9] shining a light on the working conditions within that plant. At that time, Foxconn were responsible for fulfilling almost all of Apple Inc.'s manufacturing orders, in addition to fulfilment of contracts for Dell, Sony and Hewlett Packard. A number of suicides and attempted suicides at the Longhua factory were to lead to the tragic loss of 14 young lives. It is thought that unrelenting pressure to deliver orders – in the context of a reduced workforce – placed unrelenting pressure on those who worked at the factory.

A report by British newspaper the *Daily Telegraph* attributed suicides and employee burnout to conditions within the factory itself, as opposed to being attributable to personal or other problems. The undercover newspaper investigation cited poor management as a contributory factor, a style of management that relied on strategies such as a no-talking rule on the factory floor, combined with low wages and high levels of overtime. Foxconn countered such claims by referencing the free provision of swimming pools, tennis courts, chess, calligraphy, mountain climbing and fishing clubs for workers. The suicides were referred to by the late Apple CEO Steve Jobs as "troubling" – although he stated that the Foxconn suicide rate was still considerably below the national average of China or the US.

Foxconn responded to the suicides by employing counsellors and installing safety nets around their buildings. However, in January 2012, the company was again hit with the threat of suicide, with a group of around 150 employees threatening to leap from the roof of the factory if Foxconn did not address their grave concerns over working conditions. Controversies reignited in 2018 when Foxconn opened a Wisconsin-based manufacturing base, promising 13,000 jobs, receiving billions of dollars in US government incentives and basking in the glow of the deep praise of President Trump. The jobs did not materialize, mirroring similar situations in India in 2015 and Brazil in 2011 where promises of billions of dollars in investments failed to materialize. Further, Wisconsin Legislative Fiscal Bureau also reported that Wisconsin would not recoup the costs of the deal with Foxconn until 2042, at the earliest. According to Bloomberg, outgoing Foxconn chairman Terry Gou, the richest man in Taiwan, is famed for his reputation for punishing underperforming managers by requiring them to stand for long periods in meetings, and is widely regarded as an aggressive negotiator.

In 2017, a *Financial Times* special report detailed the plight of Foxconn workers, reporting the case of interns and school-aged students who were forced to work 11-hour days at the plant, and that the iPhone X had been assembled with illegal student labour.[10] In 2018, the apparent suicide of employee Li Ming, 31, at a Foxconn site in Zhengzhou, China, reignited serious concerns over working conditions at the company. In December 2019, the colloquially-named 'iPhone city' Foxconn plant in Zhengzhou experienced protests when hundreds of temporary workers flooded the streets to protest against the non-payment of wages. The protests were shut down quickly; the plant can manufacture up to half a million iPhones in a day, particularly when a new model is launched, so the company would have sustained major financial losses even if only one day of production was disrupted. It remains to be seen how the impact of manufacturing closures caused by the COVID-19 pandemic impacts Foxconn profits and overall working conditions at the firm.

Questions

1   Recent concerns (Q1 [first quarter] 2020) over US–China trade wars and the COVID-19 pandemic have shaken the financial markets and threatened production capacity. Discuss the way in which economic factors external to a company such as Foxconn can threaten employee motivation, and how companies can respond positively to these threats.

2   Identify the hygiene factors present in the managerial approach outlined in this Foxconn/Longhua-focused case study.

3   Motivational Theory clearly identifies the positive impact that motivational approaches have on employee turnover, satisfaction and productivity. Why, then, did Foxconn seemingly disregard such theories, and instead base their managerial approach on a scientific management approach?

4   Self-Determination Theory (SDT) identifies the need for employees to be intrinsically motivated, and that relying only on external motivating factors (such as financial bonuses or perks such as swimming pools) can actually be detrimental to the psychological well-being of the employee. Apply this concept to this case study.

5   Foxconn have attempted to provide perks to motivate workers, yet these perks seem to act more as hygiene factors than motivational factors. Discuss possible reasons for this.

6   With reference to Maslow's Hierarchy, discuss the importance of meeting the safety and emotional needs of workers before seeking to provide perks and other motivators.

7   Why did the words of the late business icon Steve Jobs, as referenced in this case study (referring to suicide rates) raise deep concern over fears that productivity was being placed ahead of employee well-being?

CHAPTER 4 QUIZ

1   Why were the scientific and classical approaches so dominant in the earlier part of the twentieth century?

2   Outline the structure and purpose of the Hawthorne Studies and explain what the Hawthorne Effect is.

3   How did observation of the Hawthorne Effect lead to the emergence of the study of needs in management theory?

4   Identify the two categories of Motivational Theory, and name three dominant theories in each category.

5   What are deficiency needs?

6   Describe each level of Maslow's Hierarchy of Needs, referring to a relevant example in your answer (e.g. failure to meet the safety needs of workers in the 2010 Deepwater Horizon oil spill).

7   Identify critiques of Maslow's Hierarchy of Needs.

8   Critiques of Maslow's Hierarchy of Needs led to the development of which theory?

9   Explain Herzberg's Two-Factor Theory and provide examples for each factor, referring to the Foxconn case study in your answer.

10   Identify the three dominant needs that can be observed in a manager, according to McClelland and Burnham (2003).

11   Which need leads to the least, and most, successful outcomes?

12   Differentiate a personalized, from a socialized, need for power.

13   Provide an overview of Equity Theory.

14   In Expectancy-Value Theory, what is the role of valence?

15   Why is reliance on external motivating factors potentially detrimental to the well-being of an employee (Deci and Ryan, 2000; Kasser and Ryan, 1996; Sheldon *et al.*, 2004)?

Notes

1 The quote appears later in this chapter in the idea in brief "When money is the only motivational driver", based on an interview conducted for this book.
2 Available at: www.ted.com/talks/randy_pausch_really_achieving_your_childhood_dreams.
3 Ibid.
4 Scientific management is often referred to as Taylorism, after Frederick Winslow Taylor, the man largely responsible for the creation of scientific management. Frank and Lillian Gilbreth worked with Taylor on many studies, creating methods of measuring worker productivity. Many of these approaches remain popular in the present day.
5 Speech made to the House of Commons on 13 May 1940.
6 Official website of the Marathon des Sables: www.darbaroud.com.
7 Recent advancements in behavioural finance, neuro-finance and political physiology might provide some elucidation as to whether genetic, neurological factors might play a role in needs and motivation determination.
8 As reported in Americans Hate Their Jobs, Even with Office Perks, *CNBC Online*. Available at: www.cnbc.com/id/100835261 [Accessed 15 October 2013].
9 Foxconn is a Taiwanese multinational electronics contract manufacturer and the largest provider of electronics manufacturing services in the world.
10 Yang, Y. (21 November 2017). Apple's iPhone X Assembled by Illegal Student Labour. *Financial Times*. Available at: www.ft.com/content/7cb56786-cda1-11e7-b781-794ce08b24dc.

References

Adams, J. (1963). Towards an Understanding of Inequity. *Journal of Abnormal and Social Psychology*, 67(5), pp. 422–436.

Adams, J.S. (1965). Inequity in Social Exchange. In L. Berkowitz (ed.), *Advances in Experimental Social Psychology* (Vol. 2). New York: Academic Press, pp. 267–299.

Alderfer, C.P. (1967). Convergent and Discriminant Validation of Satisfaction and Desire Measures by Interviews and Questionnaires. *Journal of Applied Psychology*, 51(6), pp. 509–520.

Alderfer, C.P. (1969). An Empirical Test of a New Theory of Human Needs. *Organizational Behaviour and Human Performance*, 4(2), pp. 142–175.

Alvesson, M. and Sveningsson, S. (2003). Good Visions, Bad Micro-Management and Ugly Ambiguity: Contradictions of (Non-)Leadership in a Knowledge-Intensive Organization. *Organization Studies*, 24(6), pp. 961–988.

Baumeister, R. and Leary, M.R. (1995). The Need to Belong: Desire for Interpersonal Attachments as a Fundamental Human Motivation. *Psychological Bulletin*, 117(3), pp. 497–529.

Benkhoff, B. (1997). Ignoring Commitment Is Costly: New Approaches Establish the Missing Link between Commitment and Performance. *Human Relations*, 50(6), pp. 701–726.

Brockner, J., Grover, S., Reed, T.F. and Dewitt, R.L. (1992). Layoffs, Job Insecurity, and Survivors' Work Effort: Evidence of an Inverted-U Relationship. *Academy of Management Journal*, 35(2), pp. 413–425.

Chen, C.C., Meindl, J.R. and Hui, H. (1998). Deciding on Equity or Parity: A Test of Situational, Cultural and Individual Factors. *Journal of Organizational Behavior*, 19(2), pp. 115–129.

Chen, C.C., Choi, J. and Chi, S. (2002). Making Justice Sense of Local Expatriate Compensation Disparity: Mitigating by Local Referents, Ideological Explanations, and International Sensitivity in China–Foreign Joint Ventures. *Academy of Management Journal*, 43(4), pp. 807–817.

Deci, E.L. (1971). Effects of Externally Mediated Rewards on Intrinsic Motivation. *Journal of Personality and Social Psychology*, 18(1), pp. 105–115.

Deci, E.L. (1975). *Intrinsic Motivation*. New York: Plenum.

Deci, E.L. and Ryan, R.M. (2000). The "What" and "Why" of Goal Pursuits: Human Needs and the Self-Determination of Behavior. *Psychological Inquiry*, 11(4), pp. 227–268.

Fatehi, K. (1996). *International Management: A Cross-Cultural and Functional Perspective*. Upper Saddle River, NJ: Prentice Hall.

Herzberg, F. (1966). *Work and the Nature of Man*. Cleveland, OH: World Publishing Company.

Herzberg, F. (1968). One More Time: How Do You Motivate Employees? *Harvard Business Review*, 46, pp. 53–62.

Hofstede, G. (1984). *Culture's Consequences: International Differences in Work-Related Values*. Beverly Hills, CA: Sage.

Hofstede, G. (1993). Cultural Constraints in Management Theories. *Academy of Management Executive*, 7(1), pp. 81–94.

House, R.J. (1971). A Path–Goal Theory of Leader Effectiveness. *Administrative Science Quarterly*, 16, pp. 321–388.

House, R.J. (1977). A 1976 Theory of Charismatic Leadership. In J.G. Hunt and L.L. Larson (eds.), *Leadership: The Cutting Edge*. Carbondale, IL: Southern Illinois University Press, pp. 189–207.

House, R.J. (1996). Path–Goal Theory of Leadership: Lessons, Legacy, and a Reformulated Theory. *Leadership Quarterly*, 7(3), pp. 323–352.

House, R.J. and Mitchell, T.R. (1974). Path–Goal Theory of Leadership. *Journal of Contemporary Business*, 3, pp. 1–97.

Jaafar, M., Ramayah, T. and Zainal, Z. (2006). Work Satisfaction and Work Performance: How Project Managers in Malaysia Perceived It? In *Academy of World Business, Marketing and Management Development Conference Proceedings*. Paris: AWBMAMD, 2(113) (July).

Kasser, T. and Ryan, R.M. (1996). Further Examining the American Dream: Differential Correlates of Intrinsic and Extrinsic Goals. *Personality & Social Psychology Bulletin*, 22, pp. 80–87.

Landy, F.J. and Becker, W.S. (1987). Motivation Theory Reconsidered. *Research in Organizational Behavior*, 9, pp. 1–38.

Locke, E.A. (1968). Toward a Theory of Task Motivation and Incentives. *Organizational Behaviour and Human Performance*, 3(2), pp. 157–189.

Lussier, R. and Achua, C. (2004). *Leadership: Theory, Application, and Skill Development*. Eagan, MN: Thomson-West.

Luthans, F. (1998). *Organizational Behavior*. Singapore: McGraw-Hill.

McClelland, D.C. and Burnham, D.H. (2003). Power Is the Great Motivator. *Best of HBR Motivating People* (January), pp. 117–126. [Reprinted from Harvard Business Review (1976)].

Maslow, A.H. (1970). *Motivation and Personality*. New York: Harper & Row.

Miles, E., Hatfield, J.D. and Huseman, R.C. (1994). Equity Sensitivity and Outcome Importance. *Journal of Organizational Behavior*, 15(7), pp. 585–596.

Nelson, D.L. and Quick, J.C. (2003). *Organizational Behaviour: Foundation, Realities and Challenges*. 4th ed. Mason, OH: Thomson South-Western.

Obama, B. (2012). Coaching My Girls. *Newsweek* (2 and 9 July, double issue), pp. 16–17.

Pausch, R. (2007). Last Lecture: Achieving Your Childhood Dreams. Speech delivered at Carnegie Mellon University, 18 September 2007.

Reeve, J. and Deci, E. L. (1996). Elements within the Competitive Situation That Affect Intrinsic Motivation. *Personality and Social Psychology Bulletin*, 22, pp. 24–33.

Robbins, S.P. (1998). *Organizational Behavior: Concepts, Controversies, Applications*. Upper Saddle River, NJ: Prentice-Hall.

Ryan, R.M. and Deci, E.L. (2000). Self-Determination Theory and the Facilitation of Intrinsic Motivation, Social Development, and Well-Being. *American Psychologist*, 55(1), pp. 68–78.

Ryan, R.M., Kuhl, J. and Deci, E.L. (1997). Nature and Autonomy: Organizational View of Social and Neurobiological Aspects of Self-Regulation in Behaviour and Development. *Development and Pathopsychology*, 9, pp. 701–728.

Scheer, L., Kumar, N. and Steenkamp, J.E.M. (2003). Reactions to Perceived Inequity in US and Dutch Interorganizational Relationships. *Academy of Management Journal*, 46(3), pp. 303–316.

Sheldon, K., Ryan, R., Deci, E. and Kasser, T. (2004). The Independent Effects of Goal Contents and Motives on Well-Being: It's Both What You Pursue and Why You Pursue It. *Personality and Social Psychology Bulletin*, 30(4), pp. 475–486.

Vallerand, R.J. and Reid, G. (1984). On the Causal Effects of Perceived Competence on Intrinsic Motivation: A Test of Cognitive Evaluation Theory. *Journal of Sport Psychology*, 6, pp. 94–102.

Van den Broeck, A., Vansteenkiste, M., Lens, W. and de Witte, H. (2009). Unemployed Individuals' Work Values and Job Flexibility: An Explanation from Expectancy-Value Theory and Self-Determination Theory. *Applied Psychology: An International Review*, 59(2), pp. 296–317.

Vansteenkiste, M., Neyrinck, B., Niemiec, C., Soenens, B., De Witte, H. and Van den Broeck, A. (2007). On the Relations among Work Value Orientations, Psychological Need Satisfaction, and Job Outcomes: A Self-Determination Theory Approach. *Journal of Occupational and Organizational Psychology*, 80, pp. 251–277.

Vroom, V.H. (1964). *Work and Motivation*. New York: Wiley.

Wiley, C. (1997). What Motivates Employees According to over 40 Years of Motivation Surveys. *International Journal of Manpower*, 18(3), pp. 263–281.

Zuckerman, M., Porac, J., Lathin, D., Smith, R. and Deci, E.L. (1978). On the Importance of Self-Determination for Intrinsically Motivated Behaviour. *Personality and Social Psychology Bulletin*, 4, pp. 443–446.

Other resources

See PowerPoint slides on the companion website at www.routledge.com/9780367374822.

5

SITUATIONAL THEORIES

"… we didn't know much about them – they were away from people, kind of Gods."

– *Dr. Desislava Stoyanova*[1]

Upon which physical, cognitive and other assailable traits, skills and characteristics is great leadership based? Maybe the question should not rest at all with a consideration of such traits, skills and characteristics, but with a more methodological question. Is the assumption that successful leadership depends solely on the ability of the leader a flawed one? Certainly, over the course of history great political leaders and strategists have ruminated upon such a concept. Niccolo Machiavelli (1882, p. 132), for example, noted that "whoever desires constant success must change his conduct with the times". This suggests that the dynamic nature of the environment in which the leader operates plays a decisive role in their success – and it is not (as previous theories would have us believe) a function of simply the traits or skills of the leader that will ultimately cause them to succeed or fail.

Consider the recent example of Mario Monti, an academic and former prominent European Union (EU) civil servant. Faced with burgeoning debt and imminent economic collapse, the Italian Government took the unprecedented step of appointing – rather than voting in – Monti as Prime Minister in 2011, effectively forming a technocratic, as opposed to a democratic, Italian Government that served for two years, until 2013. The appointment of Monti was a response to the imminent crisis that had accompanied Silvio Berlusconi's exit from government alongside a landslide of economic problems; these included a public debt of 120 per cent gross domestic product (GDP) and a bond yield of 6 per cent that had severely undermined investor confidence and placed the country at risk of an exit from the Eurozone. Prime Minister Monti immediately assembled a team of policy experts to assist him, and put into place a raft of economic measures that were designed to stem the tide of economic disaster facing the country. These measures included a cut in pensions, reform of Italian labour laws and increases in taxation levels.

While it is undoubtedly true that Monti's intelligence, knowledge and skill as an economist undoubtedly formed the basis for his appointment at the helm of Italy's government, it also clearly demonstrates the need for a specific type of leader (in this case, a highly skilled economist) whose style of governance (in this case, technocratic) is *contingent* on the situation. In this sense, situational variables (a weakened economy, political malfeasance) dictated the choice of the most appropriate leader for that situation.[2] This chapter moves from leader-centric theories to consider exactly those theories that examine the impact of the situation – as in Monti's Italy – as mediators of the success of the leader.

Structure of the chapter

This chapter introduces the reader to situational and contingency theories of leadership and focuses on three key theories: Fiedler's (1967) Theory of Contingency Leadership, Hersey and Blanchard's (1982) Situational Leadership Theory (SLT) and LMX (Leader–Member Exchange Theory). Critiques of the aforementioned theories precede a consideration of the ways in which situational theories can be measured. The expert insight for this chapter profiles Bulgarian-born Dr. Desislava Stoyanova, who provides a compelling first-hand account of consumerism before and after the fall of Communism ("From the Iron Curtain to Coca-Cola HQ"). This precedes a case study titled "Casino banking". An end-of-chapter quiz concludes the chapter.

Situational and contingency theories of leadership

Fiedler's contingency leadership theory

The contingency model of leadership effectiveness was developed by Fiedler in 1967. It is a model that has received great empirical attention in the decades following its inception. The contingency model predicts that a leader's effectiveness is based on whether their *motivational orientation*, or style (either *task* or *relationship* oriented), is 'in-match' with their *situational control* (the level to which he/she is able to control the team, as measured by the quality of the leader–member relationship, the level of task structure that he/she has created and the nature and strength of his/her position power).

According to the model, an *in-match* leader would be: (1) one whose task orientation is high, and whose situational control is either high or low, or (2) one whose relationship orientation is high, and whose situational control is moderate (Figure 5.1).

With reference to Fiedler's contingency theory, the aforementioned example that opened this chapter is a relevant one, as it demonstrates key facets of the theory – most notably that Monti had been selected on the basis that his expertise met the

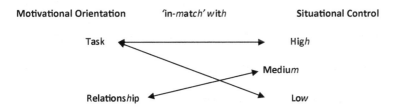

FIGURE 5.1 The extent to which a leader is 'in-match'.

immediate needs of the situation, combining his high *task orientation* with high *situational control*. In terms of the latter, one can observe that his *position power* (Prime Minister of Italy) was high, his *task structure* was extremely clear and the *leader–member* relationship between him and his team appeared to be of a very high quality. The predictive validity of Fiedler's contingency model is strong, suggesting that the application of this theory to Monti's case would have led to the elicitation of effective task-related outcomes. Monti did, in fact, implement successful economic reforms in terms of lowering the public debt and increasing investor confidence. It is worth noting, however, that the leader of a technocracy is not necessarily likely to develop a strong or meaningful relationship with followers. The implications of this are that such a leader might fare badly in any pursuant democratic election, despite their relative task-related success. It is subsequently of interest to note, in the light of such implications, that Monti won only 10 per cent of the electoral vote in Italy's 2013 elections, trailing far behind Beppe Grillo, a comedian with no political experience, and Berlusconi, a man convicted of multiple criminal offences (a concept explored further in Chapter 6, "Charismatic Leadership").

There is empirical evidence (Ayman and Chemers, 1991; Giffort and Ayman, 1989; Rice, 1981) that team member satisfaction levels were highest when leaders were found to be 'in-match', and that levels of stress and illness were higher among 'out-of-match' leaders (Chemers *et al.*, 1985). To understand the 'in-match' concept further, the two key predictors of effectiveness (motivational orientation and situational control) are described in detail below.

Motivational orientation

The motivational orientation, or style, of the leader refers to the level to which they are task oriented or relationship oriented. A leader who possesses a dominant task orientation is one who possesses a high personal investment in the accomplishment of a specific task (for example, an Olympic heptathlete), and who ultimately values this accomplishment more highly than the negotiation and development of personal relationships with subordinates, teammates or colleagues. A leader who displays dominance in relationship orientation is one who is more focused on the support, development and maintenance of positive relationships with team members and who values this over task accomplishment.

Situational control

Fiedler (1978) defines situational control (the second predictor of effectiveness) as the leader's sense of influence and control that is afforded by the situation. This influence and control is, in turn, affected by three specific components, listed here in chronological order of importance (as theorized by the model): (1) the strength and quality of the leader–member relationship; (2) the task structure provided by the leader; and (3) the position power held by the leader.

1 *Leader–member relationship* – this relates to the degree of cohesiveness in the work team, and the level of support that team members have for the leader. A low level of support for the leader is destructive, as a leader would, in this instance, require that his/her energy be expended in controlling the group, as opposed to engaging meaningfully in productive tasks. A high level of respect for the leader is most desirable within this context. This can be measured using the Leader–Member Relation (LMR) Scale (Fiedler *et al.*, 1976) which demonstrates good internal reliability and strong construct validity.
2 *Task structure* – the extent to which a leader is able to confidently and clearly communicate the activities, roles and responsibilities of a team and its individual members. This ability rests on the knowledge, wisdom, technical acuity and experience of the leader. A leader high in task structure is able to offer predictability, confidence and a sense of security to their team, thereby enhancing productivity and effectiveness. The Task Structure Rating (TSR) Scale (Fiedler *et al.*, 1976) was developed to measure task structure, but it is also possible for task structure to be assessed via empirical observation.
3 *Position power* – the administrative authority possessed by the leader that affords him/her power to reward or punish subordinates.

Fiedler's (1978) theorization of the components of situational control display interesting parallels with the concept of *legitimate power* (position power), *expert power* (task structure) and *referent power* (leader–member relationship) that were discussed earlier in this book under the auspices of French and Raven's (1959) five bases of power theory (Chapter 2, "Trait theories").

Hersey and Blanchard's Situational Leadership Theory (SLT)

The concept of situational leadership first emerged in Reddin's (1967) 3-Dimensional Management Style Theory, which highlighted the importance of matching a manager's style to the needs of a particular situation in order to be effective. Reddin identified the extent to which a manager was *task oriented* (task structuring) or *relationship oriented* (high emotional support and interaction), and argued that the needs of the situation would dictate the degree to which the manager should adopt either style. The task–person approach dominated leadership research for a significant period before the advent of values-based leadership.

Hersey and Blanchard (1969) extended the concept of matching managerial style to the needs of each unique situation by proposing a *life cycle* of leadership. SLT holds that the differing preferences that employees hold for their leaders are mediated by their job maturity and the life cycle of their career. The life cycle indicates that an employee entering the first phase of their career life cycle will display a strong preference for a task-oriented leader – or, in other words, a leader who is most focused on providing the structure, order, clear delineation of rules and responsibilities, and instructions necessary for the employee to effectively engage with their role. As the employee's career reaches maturity, their own level of expertise, wisdom, experience and clear understanding of the rules, regulations and instructions of complex tasks will negate the need for such clear *task* direction from their leader. They will instead, at this point, display a strong preference for a leader with high *relationship* orientation.

In accordance with the life cycle, there is subsequently a need for a leader to adopt either a *task-* or *relationship*-oriented style, depending on how mature their subordinates are. These theorizations provided the framework for Hersey and Blanchard's Situational Leadership Theory (SLT) (1982).

SLT (Hersey and Blanchard, 1982) stipulates the need to match the style of the leader (either task or relationship oriented) to the psychological and job maturity level of the employee. This prescriptive matching process is situated on a *prescriptive curve* that allows the leader to identify the correct interaction of leadership style with employee maturation. SLT further details an optimal combination of leader style and follower maturity (otherwise referred to as self-direction) as:

- The use of a 'telling' style of leadership (i.e. close supervision and a high level of direction) for followers who possess little to no maturity, using a task-oriented managerial style. Blanchard (2007) stipulates that this type of follower is a beginner who displays enthusiasm, high commitment to the organization, but low competence.
- The use of a 'selling' style of leadership for followers who possess some maturity within their role. This follower may begin to display disillusionment in the learning process, hence the need to coach and 'sell'. He/she will also display low to moderate competence, in addition to low commitment (Blanchard, 2007).
- The use of a 'participating' style of leadership (i.e. use of greater relationship orientation and less task orientation by the leader) for followers who display a moderately high level of maturity. This individual will possess high competence but his/her commitment will be variable (Blanchard, 2007).
- The use of a 'delegating' style of leadership (very little supervision and high relationship orientation) for followers who display a high level of maturity. This type of follower will display a high level of commitment, competence and self-directive behaviour, so will value a low support, low directive style of leadership (Blanchard, 2007). Readers will recall Deci and Ryan's Self-Determination Theory (introduced in Chapter 4, "Behavioural theories"),

which identifies a correlation between the level of self-determination and motivation of an individual. This style appears to possess similarities to the conceptualization of self-direction presented in the SLT model.

SLT-II[3] replaces the terms 'telling–selling–participating–delegating' with 'directing–coaching–supporting–delegating' and renames the prescriptive curve as the performance curve. The four levels of maturity in SLT are renamed the four levels of development in SLT-II, and renamed again as the four levels of readiness in subsequent adaptations of the model.

Although Hersey and Blanchard's (1982) SLT has undergone significant revision over time, academics remain circumspect about its empirical credentials. While strengths of the model include its easily understood, intuitive appeal and prescriptive nature, questions persist regarding its validity, reliability and predictive power (Graeff, 1983; Thompson and Vecchio, 2009; Yukl, 2006). Such concerns have persisted, despite the inception of newer versions of the model, namely SLT-II, that sought to answer these empirical critiques:

> In the absence of more substantial research findings … those who instruct others within leadership training programs should, as a matter of professional honesty, advise their trainees that SLT still lacks a strong empirical grounding, and that its alluring character should not substitute for the absence of empirical substantiation.
>
> *(Thompson and Vecchio, 2009, p. 846)*

Hersey *et al.* (1996) recognize this limitation themselves, commenting that SLT is not a theory, but a practical model that is intended to be used by managers, salespersons, teachers or parents. Nevertheless (or perhaps because of this), SLT remains one of the most widely recognized and most frequently used leadership theories in the field of management and leadership consulting and practice.

Leader–Member Exchange (LMX) Theory

LMX Theory is a relationship-based exchange theory of leadership. It posits that the effectiveness of a leader is contingent on the quality of the relationship (exchange) that exists between a leader and his/her followers, and argues that a leader not only acts as a source of influence for followers, but that followers are able to exert a reciprocal effect on the leader if the quality of the relationship is high enough. This approach marks a separation from many earlier leadership theories that are *leader-centric*, instead positioning the *relationship* (or exchange) between leader and subordinate as central to the understanding of how the leadership process works.

LMX Theory thus concentrates on the relationship between a follower and a leader, and explores how this relationship contributes to organizational effectiveness. The theory argues that a leader (manager) needs to establish a high-quality mature relationship with employees – a relationship which could also be conceptualized as a partnership – in order for truly effective leadership to occur.

The origins of LMX Theory actually lie in the development of its precursor – Vertical Dyad Linkage (VDL) Theory (Dansereau *et al.*, 1975), in the 1970s – which theorized that effective leaders develop a differentiated leadership style with different subordinates and colleagues within their work unit, using a traditional *vertical* model of leadership. A unique vertical dyad was theorized to exist between each employee and the leader, thus conceptualizing the leader's interaction with the work group as one that consisted of a series of vertical dyads. At this stage, VDL Theory identified the existence of both an *in-group* (a well-developed relationship between employee and leader, characterized by extra responsibilities and high-quality interactions) and an *out-group* (those employees whose relationship with the leader are restricted only to those interactions bound by contractual obligation). Dansereau *et al.* (1975) argued that a number of variables such as personality governed the in- or out-group status of an employee within a work unit, and that those employees enjoying in-group status could expect greater involvement and influence, and would also contribute above and beyond what is contractually expected of them.

LMX Theory challenged popular conceptualizations of the day that supported the idea of an 'average' leadership style (a concept that emerged from the Ohio State and Michigan leadership studies). If one compares VDL and LMX theories, one can observe that VDL identified the nature of relationships that exist within the workplace, with LMX seeking to identify how these relationships develop and how they impact upon the organization within which they exist (Figure 5.2).

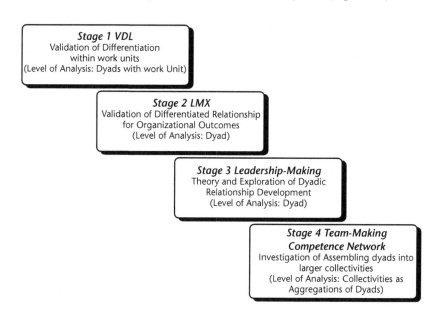

FIGURE 5.2 LMX (Leader–Member Exchange) Theory.

Source: Graen and Uhl-Bien (1995, p. 237).

Leader-making identifies a number of 'dyads' that describe the strength of a relationship between subordinate and manager – from the initial phase 1 (*stranger*) stage (low-quality leadership, with limited social interaction based solely on contractual requirements), to the phase 2 (*acquaintance*) stage (involving a more involved relationship than that of the stranger, but with limited incremental influence), to the most influential and effective, phase 3, which is characterized by the existence of a mature *partnership* between leader and follower. Movement from phase 1 to phase 2 is characterized by the initiation of an act that could lead to an improved social exchange (originated by either follower or leader), such as the offer to take on extra responsibility by the follower, or by the leader's willingness to offer new challenges to the employee. It is on the basis of the outcomes of such exchanges that movement between phases may or may not occur.

A mature relationship is one of reciprocity, where high-quality social exchange, trust, respect, support and loyalty occur. Such a relationship is empowering for both leader and follower and empirical studies have identified positive outcomes for leaders, followers, work groups and organizations, such as lower employee turnover, greater employee empowerment and a greater incidence of promotions (Graen and Uhl-Bien, 1995).

Factors affecting the quality of leader–follower relationships

While an appreciation of the existence of 'in-groups' and 'out-groups' within the workplace (Dansereau *et al.*, 1975) can inform our understanding of leadership dynamics, it does not provide elucidation on the specific reasons as to why certain employees are more likely to enter either group. Similarly, it is often unclear as to why certain leaders find that their *leader–member control* (Fiedler, 1967) might be consistently low. Although poor leadership can be attributable to a myriad of factors, it would, nevertheless, be remiss not to consider the effect of diversity on recruitment and promotion, workplace relationships and general assimilation into the culture of an organization.

Diversity: the impact of culture

Culture, as defined by Schein (1992, p. 12), can be viewed as "a pattern of basic assumptions that the group learned as it solved its problems of external adaptation and internal integration", where the group can be considered to be a company (e.g. Google) or a department (for example, an international marketing department), and where the assumptions can be represented by cultural norms (e.g. that working from home promotes a more positive and motivated working culture). Hofstede (2001) identifies five cultural dimensions: individualism–collectivism (IC), power distance, uncertainty avoidance, masculinity and long-term orientation. He argues that managers who work in collectivist societies (e.g. China) are more likely to use a directive style that encourages conformity, whereas Western individualistic cultures display a preference for participative leadership. This suggests that the quality of the leader–follower relationship, and the leader's situational control, might be mediated by cultural variables (for example, the race, culture or national identity of a leader or follower), particularly if it differs notably from that of their team. Interestingly, however, the GLOBE project (House *et al.*, 2004) reported that notable similarities emerged across cultures, with inspirational and team-oriented attributes viewed globally as attributes of an effective leader. Paris *et al.* (2009) also reported that female managers preferred a participative, team-oriented leadership style more than their male counterparts.

Diversity: the impact of gender

Interestingly, the existence of diversity and leadership as two distinct and, frequently, unrelated fields of research have been described as a *"troubling intellectual segregation"* (Eagly and Chin, 2010, p. 216; emphasis added). What effect, for example, does gender exert on the way in which a leader is accepted by her team?

Referring to the '*in-group*' phenomenon (first conceptualized by VDL Theory; Dansereau *et al.*, 1975), it could reasonably be suggested that a leader who differs considerably in cultural terms from her staff might face some resistance (whether conscious or unconscious) upon her promotion. For example, a young Hispanic woman might be less likely to be promoted in an environment where white, older males constitute the majority – and, if she is promoted, she may experience both hostile and benevolent sexism (Bass *et al.*, 1996) as a result. She may experience pressure to conform to a masculine leadership prototype (Gardiner and Tiggemann, 1999), although – somewhat ironically – controlled experiments have shown that female managers who behave in culturally masculine ways tend to receive more negative evaluations as a result (Eagly *et al.*, 1992). For an example, one might look to President Donald Trump's recent characterization of the Speaker of the US House of Representatives, Nancy Pelosi, as an "unhinged" third-rate politician, during a meeting, on 16 October 2019, that immediately followed an overwhelming 354–60 vote on a non-binding resolution that criticized the President's sudden withdrawal of troops from Syria.

Adopting a longer-term perspective, Pelosi's presence within the team may be beneficial, as her different cultural experiences and ideas may create opportunities to deter *groupthink* within the team (Baron, 2005). Findings of the GLOBE Project also report that women score higher on measures of charismatic/values-based leadership, and also of participative leadership, than some of their male counterparts (House *et al.*, 2004). Interestingly, a record number of women now serve in the US Congress following the 2018 US midterm elections, most of whom were voted in on an anti-Trump ticket, fighting back against perceived misogyny. The most famous of these elected Democratic officials – all women of colour – are now referred to as 'The Squad': Alexandria Ocasio-Cortez of New York, Rashida Tlaib of Michigan, Ayanna Pressley of Massachusetts and Ilhan Omar or Minnesota.

Although boardroom gender diversity has been positively related to improved overall corporate performance (EU, 2011), many European companies appear to have been slow to capitalize on these benefits. A European Commission report on gender balance in business leadership (EU, 2011, p. 9) reports that,

> More than 50 years after the signing of the Treaty of Rome, which affirmed the principle of equal pay for men and women for the same work of equal value, women across the EU earn 17.5% less on average than men and there has been no reduction of the gender pay gap in the last few years.

Furthermore, only 3 per cent of the largest publicly quoted companies are led by females and, in Luxembourg, Cyprus, Italy and Malta, only 5 per cent of board members are female. These disparities are attributed largely to the challenges of reconciling work, family and private life, an issue that emerges with particular strength in Eastern Europe (most notably Estonia, Hungary, Slovakia and the Czech Republic) and which has contributed to the assignation of EU boardroom quotas. It should be observed, however, that pay inequality is unlikely to be countered by legislation alone. For example, a recent EU report on gender equality highlighted the need for parents to share childcare more equally; while more households now have two main earners, the mother is still traditionally more likely to take on the bulk of childcare and domestic responsibilities.[4]

DISCUSSION STARTER

Gender inequity in Japan

In Japan's car industry, female managers remain significantly under-represented. For example, in 2018, only 8 per cent of executives in the top 20 motor vehicle and parts companies listed in the Fortune Global 500 were women, with 65 per cent of those reporting being tasked with lower-level assignments than male peers. Sixty-five per cent reported unwanted sexual advances, while 25 per cent reported feeling unsafe at work, according to figures released by Catalyst.[5]

Start the discussion: Why is the concept of quotas so contentious? And why have companies failed to meaningfully increase gender representation at executive and board level in recent years?

In addition to the melee of issues surrounding childbirth and the becoming a working mother, the *doble jornada* ('double working day') of the female manager has been found to act as a barrier to women, most significantly during their thirties (Chaturvedi *et al.*, 2012). This is impacted by the fact that this is also a time when gender inequity issues in the workplace (as characterized by factors such as differences in pay and other experiences of discrimination) also tend to rise to the fore (Schneer and Reitman, 1994). The emergence of women in junior and middle management roles is encouraging, yet women still remain a minority in senior managerial positions. Women continue to be under-represented in national parliaments, constituting an average of only 19 per cent of seats and 18 per cent of ministers (UNDP, 2011).

Returning to the concept of national culture, Sweden ranks number one on the Gender Inequality Index (according to UNDP, 2011), closely followed by the Netherlands, Finland, Denmark and Switzerland. Conversely, women in Arab States (UNDP, 2011) experience both unequal labour force participation and low educational attainment. In South Asia, women fall significantly behind their male counterparts in every dimension of the Gender Inequality Index, most significantly in education, national parliamentary representation and labour force participation. All of these factors ultimately affect women's access to the workplace and their ascension to positions of leadership.

The Multidimensional Poverty Index of the Human Development Report (2019)[6] reveals that two-thirds of multidimensionally poor people live in middle-income countries, and that half of the 1.3 billion multidimensionally poor people recorded are under the age of 18 (a third of that number are under the age of 10). How is an exceptional young leader in the deprived Aire Métropolitaine, Kolda or Kerala regions, for example, able to come anywhere close to realizing their leadership potential if their daily struggle to find clean water far supersedes the opportunity to attend school, study or pass exams? Similarly, limited access to education and prevailing high illiteracy rates in areas of high poverty disempowers the electorate from understanding political issues and being able to make meaningful voting decisions. The effects of poverty are clearly complex and multifaceted, affecting every area of one's life.

How to measure situational leadership

The motivational orientation of the leader in Fiedler's Contingency Leadership Theory is measured using the Least Preferred Co-Worker (LPC) Scale. The LPC Scale asks the leader to provide a rating for the chosen co-worker, in the context of how the co-worker has stood in the way of the leader accomplishing a particular task. The LPC Scale works by inferring a high task orientation, or style, to a leader who gives a particularly negative (low) rating to the co-worker in this context. The basis for this theorization is that the more task oriented the leader, the angrier and more embittered they will be when recalling the actions of the co-worker, thus providing the most negative rating. The LPC Scale has received some support (Fiedler and Garcia, 1987), but also extensive criticism, within the academic literature, most notably for its lack of face validity.

Hersey and Blanchard's Situational Leadership Theory (SLT) has been measured with a range of instruments, including the LEAD instrument, the Leader Behaviour Description Questionnaire (LBDQ-XII; Stogdill and Coons, 1957), items of the Job Description Index (JDI; Vecchio, 1987), a five-item scale developed by Liden and Graen (1980), a modified ten-Item Employee Readiness Scale (Fernandez and

Vecchio, 1997; Hersey and Blanchard, 1988) and an LMX measure (Scandura and Graen, 1984). The LEAD instrument has been criticized for possessing unknown psychometric properties (Graeff, 1983). SLT itself can be criticized for possessing little empirical support for its claims and for concerns over instrumentation used to test it (Thompson and Vecchio, 2009; Vecchio, 1987).

LMX theory uses the LMX-7 Questionnaire. The development of an instrument that measures the LMX construct has undergone continual and extensive re-evaluation over the last few decades. Development of an LMX instrument began with the development of a two-item scale (Dansereau *et al.*, 1975). The scale has subsequently undergone significant revision from a two-item to a four-, five-, seven- and ten-item version of the scale, with the seven-item version demonstrating the strongest construct validity.

Critiques of situational theories

Both Fiedler's Contingency Leadership Theory and LMX Theory have been criticized for a lack of explanatory power. Returning to the earlier example of Italian Prime Minister Mario Monti, Fiedler's theory explains well the successful interaction of Monti's high task motivation with his high situational control, but it cannot explain why Monti would be more successful in a situation of high or low (as opposed to moderate) situational control. Similarly, while LMX Theory identifies the existence and formation of high- and low-quality relationships between leaders and followers, it does not explain the mechanisms by which such a phenomenon occurs. LMX Theory development has also been criticized for a simultaneous development of multiple instruments of measurement, rendering results of LMX studies somewhat incomparable (for example, measurement of Negotiating Latitude (Dansereau *et al.*, 1975); or Leader–Boss Linking-Pin Quality (Graen *et al.*, 1977)).

Hersey and Blanchard's Situational Leadership Theory (SLT, SLT-I, SLT-II) has been criticized for a lack of internal theoretical coherence (Graeff, 1983), and lacks empirical support (Thompson and Vecchio, 2009), drawing into question its predictive accuracy (Vecchio, 1987) and making endorsements of its use in leadership training programmes somewhat circumspect (Thompson and Vecchio, 2009; Vecchio, 1987).

Situational variables have been found to both predict (Mumford *et al.*, 2007) and influence (Brown and Trevino, 2006) ethical decision making, partly owing to the detrimental mediating effect of stress on cognitive decision-making processes, and also because of the significant pressure on the leader to perform consistently to a high level. Aberrances between the leader's actions and personal values, as a result of such pressure, may lead to interpersonal conflict and even greater stress and compromised decision making by the leader (Levinson, 1986). Such aberrances might, however, exist subconsciously in a leader, and might also represent one of a tranche of factors upon which leadership success is contingent. Such complexities of leadership might prove somewhat confounding to the situational leadership scholar and might also prove problematic to its predictive efficacy.

Summary

Situational and contingency theories of leadership move away from earlier leader-centric conceptualizations of leadership to consider the key role of the situation and the follower in the leadership process. Contingency leadership (Fiedler, 1967) argues that the motivational orientation of the leader should be 'in-match' with their situational control, while Hersey and Blanchard's Situational Leadership Theory argues for the efficacy of matching one's leadership style to the role maturity of one's employees. LMX Theory further illustrates the potentially reciprocal effect of the leader–subordinate relationship, further emphasizing the concept of leadership as a process that requires the interaction of the leader, the follower and the environment for successful leadership to occur.

The power that both situational variables and followers exert on the leadership process can be extreme and was, in fact, conceptualized as such by Max Weber as a key determinant of the success of a charismatic leader. Weber's theory, alongside other theories of charismatic leadership, offers a significant and elucidating extension to the arguments presented within this chapter and are thus discussed at length in the next chapter ("Charismatic leadership").

 **Expert insight**

From the Iron Curtain to Coca-Cola HQ

Dr. Desislava Stoyanova recounts her experiences of growing up under Communism, and the way in which a move to a free market economy has affected both her own experiences and those of foreign companies wishing to do business in Bulgaria. Her views are preceded by the provision of a brief overview of reasons behind the emerging popularity of Bulgaria as a destination for some of the world's biggest companies. The purpose of this expert insight is to recognize a paradigm shift that occurred as a result of the emergence of situational theories of leadership. This represented a move away from leader-centrism to a more critical appreciation of the role of the follower and the situation in determining the success of, and style adopted by, a leader.

In 2013, Coca-Cola Enterprises established a Finance Shared Service Centre in Sofia, the capital of Bulgaria. The Centre employs around 150 people, a strategic move designed to centralize Coca-Cola's enterprises in the region. Given that Bulgaria was, at the time, one of the poorest nations in the EU, one might have initially questioned its choice as a European centre of operations. The motivation of the firm lay in lower taxes, simpler tax laws and lower employee wages that companies were at the time subject to, compared to other EU countries. Interestingly, the country also has the third lowest government debt and currently ranks a fair 61 of the 183 in the World Bank's Ease of Doing Business Index.[7]

A severe and austere climate in neighbouring Greece in recent years further contributed to the allure of Bulgaria, with corporate and personal income tax rates in Bulgaria the lowest in the EU. Many Greek firms have moved operations to Bulgaria as a result. Never-theless, the stark economic conditions within the EU and the instability of Greek-owned Bulgarian banks threaten stability for investors, as the threat of economic contagion from its Greek neighbours continues to loom large.

"'I am still relatively young, but during this short period of my lifetime, I have witnessed so many changes that my country has been through, that some-times I feel like I have lived a lot longer …

I was born in Bulgaria, in 1977, during the Communist regime. When I was a little girl I don't remember people talking much about money or careers. Maybe because more or less all of us were living the same lives, apart from the really big guys who worked in the government and ruled the country who were, of course, very different from the rest of us. But we didn't know much about them – they were away from people, kind of Gods.

As for all the rest of us – we were people who didn't have many rights. We were not really free (we were not allowed to travel freely, we couldn't listen to foreign radio stations or watch foreign TV apart from some special Russian pro-grammes, broadcast by Bulgarian TV), yet we had enough to be satisfied with our lives. We were living sort of 'under a glass lid', but this type of closed life had lots of positives. That is why, nowadays, there are many people who go back into their memories with nostalgia.

Today, almost all Bulgarian people own a property – a house or an apart-ment, or both, and all this was acquired during the Communist regime. At that time, no one had ever heard of unemployment, because during Communism everybody had to work – it was a must. Even if someone didn't want to work, he was forced by the state. High school education was compulsory and abso-lutely free, healthcare was excellent, life was very calm and there was almost no crime.

We had never heard of shopping as a hobby – it was impossible, simply because the diversity of goods in shops that we have today didn't exist. So we were used to buying only the necessary items that we needed. Imagine a country where only a few (basically domestic) brands of shoes, clothes and cosmetics existed, and that is how it was. So, all of us had pretty much the same stuff. It doesn't sound too good, but on the other hand we had less reason to envy each other than we do today.

For all Bulgarian children of Communism, some things were considered a real luxury. Few of us, for example, had ever seen or eaten bananas or raisins! Amazing, isn't it? Bananas were a rare good, possible to find in shops only around Christmas time, but don't think buying them was easy. Our parents had to queue in a line for hours. And it was not only the bananas!

A can of Coke or a chocolate egg were something extraordinary – a touch to the Western world. Indeed, we were enchanted not only by the taste of these foods, but by their colourful shiny wrappers. The food industry in Bulgaria was owned by the State (like all the other industries). There were standards for all types of foods – cheese, bread, sausages, chocolate, etc. – and the result was that everywhere in the country one could buy the same food at the same price. (I have to say that food in Bulgaria at that time was very high quality – unlike today!) That, of course, meant no private producers, no rivalry, no commercials, no attractive wrappers. But, whatever the wrapper, the customer would buy it, just because he didn't have [a] choice between different producers.

On 10 November 1989, Bulgaria ended Communist rule. In the years that followed, the changes in the political structure of the country brought many economic changes. The open market brought diversity in goods, private producers appeared, imports of consumer items swelled, and the State no longer controlled prices. Bananas, chocolate eggs, jeans and cassette and video recorders – all those items that were previously so desirable and hard to attain – entered our shops in abundance. They were now accessible to everyone who could buy them.

I remember when McDonald's restaurants opened up in Sofia, and it was a huge thing! Despite the fact that the prices there were high (and they still are!), many people used to go there, maybe because we hadn't had any fast food restaurants in Bulgaria before. As a result, they easily gained popularity. Later on, other popular fast food brands like KFC and Dunkin' Donuts also opened restaurants.

Nevertheless, in the first few years after Communism, the ambience of the country (shops, restaurants, cafes, hotels) remained almost the same for quite some time. Later on, slowly, big brands appeared, opening their own shops in the capital – in Sofia – and in other big cities – Plovdiv, Varna and Bourgas. During the 1990s, still not so many fashion brands were presented at the Bulgarian market and the culture of shopping for the Bulgarian consumer was still very low. We didn't have shopping malls. We hadn't heard of the concept of sales, and we didn't ask for samples in the cosmetic shops.

When brands did enter the Bulgarian market, I would even say that some of the fashion brands treated the Bulgarian customer as a second-hand customer.

Lots of famous brands (Mango, Adidas, etc.) used to import goods into Bulgaria – not the actual collections, but clothes that had been left in their brand outlets for a few seasons. It is at least a perception that they kind of used Bulgaria as a 'dustbin' – a last chance to sell something that in Europe they would otherwise throw away, but the Bulgarians would buy them, relying only on the fact that they were buying a brand label. The truth is that in the 1990s (especially the early 1990s) Bulgarian people had not so much information, despite that we already had European TV, press, radio stations, etc. The internet was available to only a few people and online information was not so easy and quick to access as it is nowadays. But, anyway, these brands weren't very successful during the first years on the Bulgarian market for [a] few reasons that can be summarised:

- the fact that the Bulgarian economy was in a serious crisis and people had little disposable income
- lots of goods (of poor quality) were imported from Turkey and because they were cheaper people preferred buying them
- the first shopping malls appeared in Sofia in 2006; and this was a crucial moment for the Bulgarian market as it improved the offering of goods in shops, and enhanced the shopping culture of the Bulgarian consumer, creating the concept of shopping as a hobby or leisure pastime.

People started to be more demanding, they learned how to spend their money in a smart way – waiting for sales, trying to look for the best price – the variety was out there and the brands now had to strive for customers' attention. Communism, the lack of choice and the queues were not only gone, they were forgotten, by those who have been through them. For the younger generations that were born after 1989, all these sound like a bad joke …

Now [in 2013], in the big cities of Bulgaria you can find everything that you would find in European big cities as well. Unfortunately, this is not the situation in the countryside. Lots of people there are unemployed; many of them left Bulgaria and went to work in Spain, Italy, Greece and other European countries. There are no malls there. People are hardly able to pay their bills, so they don't care about brands – they just care about survival. We could say that the standard of living in the big cities and in the small villages in the country is very different.

In some ways, maybe, Bulgaria is a European India – a country with almost no middle class, a few very rich people and a majority of poor people. There are the contrasts of the Mercedes and the carts on the streets, shopping malls and shiny cafes in the big cities and misery in the small villages, plastic surgery clinics and people who can't afford [to buy] even simple medicines.

I hope that the Bulgarian politicians will work harder to make Bulgaria more attractive for foreign investors, through the development of appropriate laws and through ameliorating the infrastructure of the country. I wish that Bulgaria is chosen by investors because it offers good conditions – not only because Greece or another Balkan country is going through a deep crisis. I [hope] that investors are not stuck to the idea of opening outlets and investing in Sofia only, because the rate of unemployment in the countryside is very high and it can be overcome only with the help of business investments.

I would love to see the moment where the label 'post-Communist country' will be forgotten by the Western business company, when they would consider the labour of Bulgarian people equal to those of all the other Europeans. This label is [given] to other post-Communist countries as well and it has affected the whole Eastern market. There are companies that follow double standards – they produce a high-quality product for the Western Europe market yet provide products with lower comparable quality for the Eastern European market. I believe that this is not what a united Europe should be. Ultimately, I hope that more investments come to Bulgaria in the next few years, because the only way that the country can develop and follow European standards is through decreasing unemployment and reinvesting revenue to stimulate the Bulgarian economy.**''**

Questions

1 Entering a post–Communist Bulgarian market offered McDonald's and other global brands the potential for significant profit. However, entering a post–Communist Bulgaria would also have posed significant challenges to foreign investors (e.g. US investors), who had up to that point been accustomed only to operating in a free market economy. Identify what these challenges might be, making specific reference to how they might impact the situational control (Fiedler, 1967) of an investor seeking to enter the market.
2 How might an investor specifically seek to enhance their position power via the acquisition of a domestic agent?

Case study: casino banking

The wildly speculative activities of financial institutions that contributed decisively to the 2008 global financial crisis sparked the term 'casino banking' – "the practice whereby a commercial bank engages in unduly speculative or risky financial activities with the aim of achieving high profits" (*Oxford Dictionaries*). However, there is one market where the intersection of real estate, casinos and banking continues to attract not only investors, but the potential for real profit without the threat of wild speculation and without a toxic CDO (collateralized debt obligation) in sight. As major players in the residential and casino sector now count Deutsche Bank, JPMorgan, Paulson, Apollo, TPG, Ladder Capital Finance Holdings LLLP and Goldman Sachs among their ranks, Las Vegas has become, quite literally, the home of casino banking. This case study introduces the reader to the way in which major firms in the financial sector have played their hand – to varying effect – to become major players in the world of Las Vegas gaming.

Hedge funds: the new landlords?

The post-subprime crash Las Vegas residential property market (post-2008) offered the potential for lucrative returns for investors. Five years after the crash, early 2013 figures reflected a spike in house foreclosures caused by the inability of many sub-prime mortgage holders to meet their repayments. This subsequent fall in home ownership led to a sharp rise in rental demand which hedge funds, in particular, had been quick to recognize. Many larger funds capitalized on the value of this distressed asset. The upshot? The new reality for many current Las Vegas residents is that their new landlord might, conceivably, be a hedge fund manager.

Hedge fund manager John Paulson, for example, recently acquired a $17 million, 875-acre investment in undeveloped residential land on the Las Vegas Lake resort in

Henderson, Nevada, alongside the acquisition of several other Las Vegas area acquisitions. These acquisitions were made via the deployment of the Paulson Real Estate Recovery Fund, a private equity vehicle for Paulson & Co which also included a $12.37 million share stake in legendary Vegas casino Caesars. Paulson was by no means the first investor to recognize the potential of the area. Transcontinental Corp. became the first large-scale real estate investor to commence development of a 3,600-acre project in the 1990s that was designed to attract wealthy second-home owners and retirees to an upscale residential area of beautiful homes, golf courses, resorts and a small casino. While, at one point, big names like Ritz-Carlton were attracted to the project, Transcontinental defaulted on a $540 million Credit Suisse loan in 2008. The hotel eventually opened as the Dolce Hotels and Resorts owned Ravella at Lake Las Vegas. In Vegas, one can observe that it is not only individuals who hit the tables that end up going bust with startling regularity, but investors, too.

Carrington Investment Partners, founded by Bruce Rose (a major player in the subprime mortgage-backed security market) offers another example. Carrington recently invested in the Las Vegas real estate market as a means of profiting from the high foreclosure-to-rental trend that now characterizes the Las Vegas residential property market. A few years after the 2008 crisis, Carrington Investment Partners acquired thousands of family home properties to the value of almost $500 million, with the intention of converting them to rental properties – a move also made by Sam Zell and Apollo Investment Management.

Both the lower-cost and more upscale residential markets in Las Vegas have been affected by an upswing in foreclosures, stalling in property purchase and an associated boom in renting. The MGM Resorts International Group, for example, was forced to discount a remaining unsold 427 units located at its Veer Towers within its $8.5 billion City Centre complex (a joint venture with Dubai World) as a bulk purchase for the total of $119 million (approximately $278,000 per unit from the original $500,000 price tag, or $300 per square foot). The discounted sale, made to Ladder Capital Finance Holdings LLLP in 2013, reflected concerns at the time that the Las Vegas luxury real estate market continued to remain depressed, but that it would nevertheless represent a significant longer-term value investment. Altogether MGM and Dubai World absorbed a $700 million write-down via its sale of the City Centre units.

Casino bankers: a metaphor becomes reality

Acquisition of Las Vegas commercial real estate by financial institutions has also been prolific, with Las Vegas casinos now demonstrating significant ownership stakes by investment banks and hedge funds.

Perhaps the biggest – and certainly the highest profile – financial markets player in Las Vegas at the moment is Deutsche Bank. Following a 2008 foreclosure on a $760 million construction loan to the Cosmopolitan project that originated in 2003 (originally made to developer Ian Bruce Eichner), and a $5.4 billion leveraged buyout of Station Casinos, Inc., Deutsche Bank became the outright owner of the Cosmopolitan, with Deutsche Bank executives acquiring gaming licences from Nevada casino regulators. Deutsche Bank also hold a financial stake in the Fontainebleu and Caesars, making them, at that time, a prolific casino presence both on the strip and in local gaming markets.[8]

The Cosmopolitan hotel is one of the most extravagant on the strip, counting major players such as the Bellagio and Wynn Las Vegas among its direct competitors. Holder of a 25 per cent stake in Station Casinos with a further credit extension of $3.9 billion to the Cosmopolitan, this brings Deutsche Bank's Las Vegas investment to a figure in the region of $4.6 billion.[9] Deutsche Bank went on to sell the Cosmopolitan to hedge fund Blackstone in 2014 for $1.73 billion, who are now looking to sell following a $500 million refurbishment.

Station Casinos represents the largest operator in the Las Vegas local gaming market and remains one of the most heavily leveraged companies in the gaming industry (it is also part-owned by JPMorgan and borrowed a further $310 million from Jefferies and Goldman Sachs). The debt financing for the management-led buyout consisted mainly of a $2.5 billion CMBS (commercial mortgage backed security) loan from Deutsche Bank and JPMorgan. Deutsche Bank recently faced claims of knowingly perpetuating unsafe working conditions for Station Casinos staff, according to a human rights watchdog.[10]

The new Station Casinos LLC, part owned by the family of the original founder (who took a $200 million minority stake) went on to sign a 25-year management contract with Fertitta Entertainment LLC to manage and operate its casinos on a fee basis. A proposed $2.45 billion offer for Station Casinos after its Chapter 11 filing from Boyd Gaming Corp. was rejected, partly on the basis that acquisition of assets by Boyd would lead to an increased risk of unionization. Deutsche Bank's credit exposure to Station Casinos stood at approximately $1.16 billion at that point.

Such acquisitions have not been, of course, without their risks, as evidenced by the post-2008 crash failure of the $2.9 billion Fontainebleu Las Vegas casino resort development project. Partly pushed into bankruptcy by the implosion of Lehman Brothers – alongside other problems such as overrun costs and a sluggish economy – Fontainebleu saw massive losses shouldered by a number of lenders and investment funds. These investors, led by Brigade Leveraged Capital Structures Fund Ltd, subsequently engaged in a legal battle to recoup damages. Deutsche Bank also invested in Fontainebleu and as a result faced many problems over the ensuing years – a ruptured aquifer that sat below the development, for example, multiple redesigns, delays and lawsuits from buyers and agents.[11]

The outlook for the 2020 Las Vegas real-estate market seems unclear; while some commentators are confident that the sector will remain strong, economic and financial indicators point to the threat of a US market bubble/market correction, an ongoing threat of trade wars, the political impact of impeachment and the impact of the COVID-19 pandemic on Chinese production. Baccarat profits are already down in early 2020 due to the absence of Asian high-rollers, as a result of the Coronavirus pandemic, according to the Las Vegas Review Journal.

Meanwhile, Deutsche Bank recorded major overall losses for 2019, mostly due to a failed merger, profit warnings, a cumulative $18 billion in fines originating from the

2008 financial crisis and ongoing investigations (e.g. a recent criminal investigation into multiple allegations of money laundering).

Questions

1 As stated in the case study, John Paulson acquired a significant stake in Henderson, Las Vegas via the Paulson Real Estate Recovery Fund. Apply Fiedler's model to explain how Paulson can be considered 'in-match' in terms of both his motivational orientation and his situational control, and why this allows him to profit from a volatile market where others have notably lost large sums.

2 According to situational theory, situational variables have been found to predict and influence ethical decision making. Relate this to the current money laundering investigations into Deutsche Bank (you may need to research the bases of these charges if you are not already familiar with them) and comment on how these external political factors may have influenced Deutsche Bank's ethical decision making.

CHAPTER 5 QUIZ

1 What are the key predictions made by Fiedler's (1967) contingency model?

2 Explain how Mario Monti's motivational orientation and situational control contributed to his success as Prime Minister of Italy's technocratic government.

3 Previous leadership theories have focused on a leader-centric approach (i.e. that leadership success is contingent only on the presence of certain traits, skills or other qualities of the leader). Explain – with reference to the success of Berlusconi and Grillo in the Italian national elections of 2013 – why such an approach may be criticized, and why the consideration of leadership as a process (i.e. one that requires the successful interaction of leader, situation and follower) might, instead, prove more effective.

4 What is the role of position power in Fiedler's theory?

5 Provide an overview of Hersey and Blanchard's Situational Leadership Theory.

6 The original SLT model proposed by Hersey and Blanchard identifies four positions on a prescriptive curve. What are they?

7 What position on the prescriptive curve would be most relevant for adoption by a manager working with a team of: (i) college interns taking part in an IBM summer programme; (ii) IT analysts working on a highly- pressurized client project; and (iii) a highly-skilled sales team who are working on the bid for a £10 million sales contract that would not only allow them to generate significant revenue for the company, but which would also allow them to expand their brand globally.

8 LMX Theory is a relationship-based exchange theory of leadership. What does this mean?

9 Discuss the importance of the 'in-group' phenomenon, both in terms of how it can help, and hinder, an employee.

10 A strength of LMX Theory is that it challenged popular conceptualizations of its day that supported the idea of an 'average' leadership style. Discuss why the notion of an 'average' style is flawed.

11 Identify difficulties associated with the measurement of situational leadership.

12 What difficulties might arise in the use of situational and contingency theories to predict leadership behaviour?

Notes

1 Quoted in an interview for this book with Dr. Desislava Stoyanova, as part of the expert insight "From the Iron Curtain to Coca-Cola HQ" that appears later in this chapter.

2 That Monti stood for office in the 2013 elections and received only 9 per cent of the vote (trailing far behind Grillo, a comedian, and Berlusconi, who had recently been sentenced for fraud) raises interesting questions, which will be revisited later in the book (see Chapter 6, "Charismatic leadership").

3 SLT-II is the second version of the original model.

4 EU (2019). *Report on Equality between Men and Women in the EU*. Available at: https://ec.europa.eu/info/sites/info/files/aid_development_cooperation_fundamental_rights/annual_report_ge_2019_en.pdf.

5 Catalyst Research (2020). *Women in the Automotive Industry*. Available at: www.catalyst.org/research/women-in-the-automotive-industry/.

6 *The 2019 Global Multidimensional Poverty Index*, a UN Human Development Report, can be downloaded from the United Nations Development Programme website: http://hdr.undp.org/en/2019-MPI.

7 World Bank Ease of Doing Business Index 2019 – more information can be found via the World Bank website: www.doingbusiness.org/rankings.

8 Berzon, A. (2 October 2011). Casino Giants Struggle against Volatile Credit Markets. *Wall Street Journal*. Available at: http://online.wsj.com/article/SB10001424052970204138204576605932867592882.html.

9 Sieroty, C. (4 October 2011). G2E 2011: Cosmopolitan Said to Represent Future of Gaming. *Las Vegas Review-Journal*. Available at: www.lvrj.com/business/cosmopolitan-said-to-represent-future-of-gaming-131102793.html.

10 Business and Human Rights Resource Center (June 2016). Facing Finance. Available at: www.business-humanrights.org/sites/default/files/documents/BHRRC%20Rejoinder%20-%2027062016%20-%20EN.pdf.

11 Jinks, B and Keehner, J. (16 November 2009). Deutsche Bank Drowning in Vegas on Costliest Bank-Owned Casino. *Bloomberg*. Available at: www.bloomberg.com/apps/news?pid=newsarchive&sid=apdCk2i8v.tI.

References

Ayman, R. and Chemers, M.M. (1991). The Effect of Leadership Match on Subordinate Satisfaction in Mexican Organizations: Some Moderating Influences of Self-Monitoring. *Applied Psychology: An International Review*, 40(3), pp. 299–314.

Baron, R.S. (2005). So Right It's Wrong: Groupthink and the Ubiquitous Nature of Making. *Advances in Experimental Social Psychology*, 37, pp. 219–253.

Bass, B.M., Avolio, B.J. and Atwater, L. (1996). The Transformational and Transactional Leadership of Men and Women. *Applied Psychology: An International Review*, 45(1), pp. 5–34.

Blanchard, K.H. (2007). *Leading at a Higher Level*. Upper Saddle River, NJ: Prentice-Hall.

Brown, M.E. and Trevino, L.K. (2006). Ethical Leadership: A Review and Future Directions. *Leadership Quarterly*, 17(6), pp. 595–616.

Chaturvedi, S., Zyphur, M.J., Arvey, R.D. and Avolio, B.J. (2012). The Heritability of Emergent Leadership: Age and Gender as Moderating Factors. *Leadership Quarterly*, 23(2), pp. 219–232.

Chemers, M.M., Hays, R.B., Rhodewalt, F. and Wysocki, J. (1985). A Person–Environment Analysis of Job Stress: A Contingency Model Explanation. *Journal of Personality and Social Psychology*, 49(3), pp. 628–635.

Dansereau, F., Graen, G. and Haga, W.J. (1975). A Vertical Dyad Linkage Approach to Leadership within Formal organisations: A Longitudinal Investigation of the Role-Making Process. *Organisational Behaviour and Human Performance*, 13(1), pp. 46–78.

Eagly, A.H. and Chin, J.L. (2010). Diversity and Leadership in a Changing World. *American Psychologist*, 65(3), pp. 216–224.

Eagly, A.H., Makhijani, M.G. and Klonsky, B.G. (1992). Gender and the Evaluation of Leaders: A Meta-Analysis. *Psychological Bulletin*, 11(1), pp. 3–22.

EU (2011). *EU Report on Progress on Equality between Women and Men in 2011: The Gender Balance in Business Leadership*. Luxembourg: Publications Office of the European Union.

Fernandez, C.F. and Vecchio, R.P. (1997). Situational Leadership Theory Revisited: A Test of an Across-Jobs Perspective. *Leadership Quarterly*, 8(1), pp. 67–84.

Fiedler, F.E. (1967). *A Theory of Leadership Effectiveness*. New York: McGraw-Hill.

Fiedler, F.E. (1978). The Contingency Model and the Dynamics of the Leadership Process. In L. Berkowitz (ed.), *Advances in Experimental Social Psychology* (Vol. 11). New York: Academic Press, pp. 59–96

Fiedler, F.E. and Garcia, J.E. (1987). *New Approaches to Leadership: Cognitive Resources and Organisational Performance*. New York: Wiley.

Fiedler, F.E., Chemers, M.M. and Mahar, L. (1976). *Improving Leadership Effectiveness: The Leader Match Concept*. New York: Wiley.

French, J.R. and Raven, B. (1959). The Bases of Social Power. In D. Cartwright (ed.), *Studies in Social Power*. Ann Arbor, MI: Institute for Social Research, University of Michigan, pp. 150–167.

Gardiner, M. and Tiggemann, M. (1999). Gender Differences in Leadership Style, Job Stress, and Mental Health in Male- and Female-Dominated Industries. *Journal of Occupational and Organisational Psychology*, 72(3), pp. 301–315.

Giffort, D.W. and Ayman, R. (1989). Contingency Model and Subordinate Satisfaction: Mental Health Organizations. Paper presented at Academy of Management Annual Conference, Anaheim, CA.

Graeff, C.L. (1983). The Situational Leadership Theory: A Critical View. *Academy of Management Review*, 8(2), pp. 285–291.

Graen, G.B. and Uhl-Bien, M. (1995). Relationship-Based Approach to Leadership: Development of Leader–Member Exchange (LMX) Theory of Leadership over 25 Years: Applying a Multi-domain Perspective. *Leadership Quarterly*, 6(2), pp. 219–247.

Graen, G., Cashman, J.F., Ginsburgh, S. and Schiemann, W. (1977). Effect of Linking Pin-Quality upon the Quality of Working Life of Lower Participants: A Longitudinal Investigation of the Managerial Understructure. *Administration Science Quarterly*, 22(2), pp. 491–504.

Hersey, P. and Blanchard, K.H. (1969). Life-Cycle Theory of Leadership. *Training and Development Journal*, 23(2), pp. 26–34.

Hersey, P. and Blanchard, K.H. (1982). *Management of Organization Behavior: Utilizing Human Resources*. 4th ed. Englewood Cliffs, NJ: Prentice-Hall.

Hersey, P. and Blanchard, K. (1988). *Management of Organizational Behavior: Utilizing Human Resources*. 5th ed. Englewood Cliffs, NJ: Prentice-Hall.

Hersey, P., Blanchard, K.H. and Johnson, D.E. (1996). *Management of Organizational Behavior: Utilizing Human Resources*. Upper Saddle River, NJ: Prentice-Hall.

Hofstede, G. (2001). *Culture's Consequences: Comparing Values, Behaviours, Institutions, and Organizations across Nations*. 2nd ed. Thousand Oaks, CA: Sage.

House, R.J., Hanges, P.J., Javidan, M., Dorfman, P.W. and Gupta, V. (2004). *Culture, Leadership and Organisations: The GLOBE Study of 62 Societies*. Thousand Oaks, CA: Sage.

Levinson, D.J. (1986). A Conception of Adult Development. *American Psychologist*, 41(1), pp. 3–13.

Liden, R.C. and Graen, G. (1980). Generalizability of the Vertical Dyad Linkage Model of Leadership. *Academy of Management Journal*, 23, pp. 451–465.

Machiavelli, N. (1882). *The Historical, Political, and Diplomatic Writings of Niccolo Machiavelli* (trans. Christian E. Detmold). Boston, MA: J. R. Osgood and Company.

Mumford, T.V., Campion, M.A. and Morgeson, F.P. (2007). The Leadership Skills Strataplex: Leadership Skills Requirements across Organizational Levels. *Leadership Quarterly*, 18(2), pp. 154–166.

Oxford Dictionaries. Available online at: http://oxforddictionaries.com/definition/english/casino-banking.

Paris, L.D., Howell, J.P., Dorfman, P.W. and Hanges, P.J. (2009). Preferred Leadership Prototypes of Male and Female Leaders in 27 Countries. *Journal of International Business Studies*, 40, pp. 1396–1405.

Reddin, W.J. (1967). The 3-D Management Style Theory. *Training and Development Journal*, 21(4), pp. 8–17.

Rice, W.R. (1981). Leader LPC and Follower Satisfaction: A Review. *Organizational Behavior and Human Performance*, 28, pp. 1–25.

Scandura, T.A. and Graen, G.B. (1984). Moderating Effects of Initial Leader–Member Exchange Status on the Effects of a Leadership Intervention. *Journal of Applied Psychology*, 64, pp. 428–436.

Schein, E.H. (1992). *Organizational Culture and Leadership*. 2nd ed. San Francisco, CA: Jossey-Bass.

Schneer, J.A. and Reitman, F. (1994). The Importance of Gender in Mid-Career: A Longitudinal Study of MBAs. *Journal of Organisational Behaviour*, 15(3), pp. 199–207.

Stogdill, R.M. and Coons, A. E. (1957). *Leader Behavior: Its Description and Measurement*. Columbus, OH: Bureau of Business Research, The Ohio State University.

Thompson, G. and Vecchio, R.P. (2009). Situational Leadership Theory: A Test of Three Versions. *Leadership Quarterly*, 20(5), pp. 837–848.

UNDP (2011). *Human Development Report 2011. Sustainability and Equity: A Better Future for All*. United Nations Development Programme. Available at: http://hdr.undp.org/en/content/human-development-report-2011.

Vecchio, R.P. (1987). Situational Leadership Theory: An Examination of a Prescriptive Theory. *Journal of Applied Psychology*, 72(3), pp. 444–451.

Weber, M. (1924 [1947]). *The Theory of Social and Economic Organisations* (trans. T. Parsons). New York: Free Press.

Yukl, G. (2006). *Leadership in Organizations*. 6th ed. Upper Saddle River, NJ: Pearson-Prentice Hall.

Other resources

See PowerPoint slides on the companion website at www.routledge.com/9780367374822.

6

CHARISMATIC LEADERSHIP

> *"Sometimes CEO's lie outright, which might be why we have seen a lot of multi-billion-dollar fines levied by the SEC[1] recently."*
>
> *– MD, leading investment bank[2]*

Despite never having held a position of political leadership, Mario Monti, former Prime Minister of Italy's technocratic government,[3] was credited with rescuing his country from the brink of economic collapse during his tenure as Prime Minister from 2011–2013. Monti remains widely recognized across Europe as the safest pair of hands during that period, with which Italy was guided into a more prosperous situation. From theoretical discussions undertaken in the previous chapter, his success as a leader can be readily explained via the use of Path–Goal Theory (House, 1971) – or, in other words, by his ability to enable Italy to achieve its *goal* of greater economic prosperity by removing obstructions (e.g. a public debt of 120 per cent GDP) from its *path*. His presence at the nation's political helm remains particularly valuable, given the ongoing precipitous nature of the European economy.

Monti was, however, completely trounced at the 2013 Italian national elections. The reason for this failure lay, in large part, to his inability to match the charismatic rhetoric, seductive promises and emotional appeal of his two less qualified (but far more popular) rivals, Silvio Berlusconi and Beppe Grillo. While neither could match Monti's track record of fiscal success or economic brilliance, they were nevertheless able to make far superior gains in popularity, via their ability to connect emotionally with the electorate, and to use rhetoric accordingly to secure votes. These heavily emotive, social media fuelled campaigns were early forebears of the populist social media fuelled tsunami of populism that has swept across Western Europe in the intervening years, and that we now see characterized by the Trump campaign, Project Leave and British Prime Minister Boris Johnson in Great Britain,

Italy's far-right League Party, the Alternative for Germany Party, Vikto Orbáns Fidesz Party in Hungary and by Narendra Modi and the Bharatiya Janata Party in India.

In recent years, the ability of political consultants and parties to connect emotionally with an electorate has become far more scientific, with charisma now observed to be a potentially biological phenomenon (Zehndorfer, 2019). Moreover, social media enable the kind of emotional relationship inherent in a charismatic leader–follower relationship to be magnified to extreme levels, often with extremely damaging consequences. For example, neurological studies inform us that we process data emotionally, not rationally (e.g. De Martino *et. al.*, 2006). In the field of political physiology, there has been much interest in the use of emotion in politics, particularly in recent years, where the emotional targeting of voters, and the recasting of politics as a form of entertainment, has been a major focus of analysis. To leadership scholars, such studies are interesting, as there is no greater legitimate authority when it comes to leadership than a country's Prime Minister or President.

Cambridge Analytica, a political consulting firm, used the specialist military psychological operational expertise of their parent company, Strategic Communications Laboratories (SCL), to achieve great wins for their clients. They recently formed the focus of an undercover documentary titled, "Data, Democracy and Dirty Tricks", broadcast by Channel 4 in the UK.[4] As Cambridge Analytica's Managing Director Mark Turnbull stated, it is no good relying on facts to win in politics: you need, instead, to whip up as much emotion as you can – mostly fear – to win voters over to your side.

> The two fundamental human drivers when it comes to taking information on board effectively are hopes and fears, and many of those are unspoken and even unconscious – you didn't know that was a fear until you saw something that just evoked that reaction from you … our job is to get, is to drop the bucket further down the well than anybody else to understand what are those really deep-seated, underlying fears, concerns. It's no good fighting an election campaign on the facts, because actually it's all about emotion.[5]

The populist, emotive campaigns run by Cambridge Analytica focused on whipping up fear and anger, using social media algorithms, micro-targeting and clickbait to win over voters. A knowledge of voters' physiological reactions benefited them enormously; if a voter sees a fearful video online, for example, their brain processes it emotionally, 'switching off' the rational area of the brain as an automatic survival response. This meant that fear- and anger-based campaigns lowered the ability and motivation of voters to question the data that they were bring presented with, which made them easier to manipulate.

Interestingly, one of the most powerful legacies of Path–Goal Theory (House, 1971) remains its foundational influence upon the subsequent development of House's 1976 theory of charismatic leadership (House, 1977), a theory that draws inspiration from McClelland's Three Needs Theory (discussed in Chapter 2, "Trait theories"), and which recognizes the vital role of charisma in the leadership process.

Charismatic leadership theory extends the scope of Path–Goal Theory by illustrating that it is not only the facilitation of the follower's goal by the leader that is important. It is also vital that the leader articulates a vision of such strength, with such charisma and passion, that followers are strongly motivated and driven to achieve their goal. The theory of charismatic leadership (House, 1977) formed one of a new coterie of leadership studies, referred to henceforth as *values-based* leadership (Bass, 1985, 1998; Bass and Avolio, 1994; Deluga, 2001; Den Hartog *et al.*, 1999; House and Howell, 1992; Trice and Beyer, 1986, Yukl, 1998).

The importance of charisma to organizational theory is particularly relevant, due to its potential impact on organizational productivity and profitability. Charisma has been shown to: be related positively to leader effectiveness (Lowe *et al.*, 1996), perceived organizational performance (Agle *et al.*, 2006; Lowe *et al.*, 1996) and perceived and actual organizational performance (Wilderom *et al.*, 2012); be a predictor of actual effectiveness (Howell and Avolio, 1993); enhance the motivation and performance of followers in the achievement of a goal (House, 1977; Smith, 1992); and be a positive agentic force of organizational change (Bass and Avolio, 1993).

Charismatic leadership is, however, by definition, a transitory and unstable phenomenon (Weber, 1924), and charismatic leaders are capable of both ethical and unethical leadership (Howell and Avolio, 1992). Consequently, much theoretical work in the field of charismatic leadership centres upon the differentiation of the personalized (self-serving) from the socialized (egalitarian) charismatic leader (Bass, 1988; House and Howell, 1992), the ramifications of which carry important significance for both organizational success and societal well-being. An understanding of this complexity is, subsequently, considered of value to the leadership scholar and features prominently in this chapter.

Structure of the chapter

This chapter opens with a brief history of charismatic leadership. First, the Weberian conceptualization of charisma *in statu nascendi* is introduced. The emergence of charisma in organizational theory is then discussed. The key role of the articulation of a vision by the charismatic leader pre-empts an overview of the *dark side* of charisma, alerting the reader to the idea that charisma can be utilized effectively by both the *personalized* (self-serving) and *socialized* (altruistic) charismatic leader. Methods of measuring charisma are then presented alongside a consideration of key criticisms of the theory. An expert insight profiling the Managing Director of a leading investment bank tells us what happens "When leadership fails", while a case study of legendary investor and pro-Democracy philanthropist George Soros ("George Soros – in defence of an open society") allows the reader to apply theory to practice.

A history of charismatic leadership

Charismatic leadership was first conceptualized by the sociologist Max Weber in 1924. He remarked that,

> Charisma is self-determined and sets its own limits. Its bearer seizes the task for which he is destined and demands that others obey and follow him by virtue of his mission. If those to whom he feels sent do not recognize him, his claim collapses; if they recognize it, he is their master as long as he "proves" himself.
>
> *(Weber, 1924, p. 1113)*

The instability of charisma is discussed at length in both sociological and neo-charismatic approaches to the conceptualization of charisma in leadership. Weber considers charisma to exist only *"in statu nascendi"* (Weber, 1924, p. 1121), in other words, in a state of formation. Once a period of revolution passes, the inevitable routinization of charisma, and the institutionalization and bureaucratization that accompany it, can lead to disillusionment as the emotional bond between leader and follower dissipates. One might consider the example of the left-wing Nicaraguan Sandinista leader Daniel Ortega, who rose to prominence after leading his country to revolution and through a civil war. Despite initially sweeping to power on this wave of great revolutionary activity, Ortega was voted out in 1990. He was to make a political comeback in the November 2006 elections against a backdrop of great economic and financial difficulties that had detrimentally affected Nicaragua and led to wide-scale poverty and unemployment.

Charisma and uncertainty

Charisma is a process that requires the necessary interaction between a leader, a follower and a situation in order to emerge (Deluga, 2001; Shamir, 1995; Weber, 1924). Charismatic leadership was reported to be most successful in times of uncertainty (Shamir *et al.*, 1993; Trice and Beyer, 1986), as the vision and direction of the charismatic leader appears to create a source of psychological comfort for followers (Bass, 1985; Conger and Kanungo, 1998). As Scott (1981, p. 33) opines, charisma constitutes "an unusual form of normative social structure that emerges in times of crisis, when people look to charismatic individuals who are 'perceived as possessing extraordinary gifts of spirit and mind' to lead them through the crisis with 'radical reorganizations'".

Yammarino and Bass (1991) similarly reported that charismatic leader traits are more likely to emerge in weak, rather than strong, situations. Weak situations were characterized by a lack of norms, rules, guides, incentives and prior learning with respect to the enactment of normatively appropriate behaviours. The work of early organizational theorists identified the necessary interaction of leader, follower and social structure in order for effective leadership to occur (Eisenstadt, 1968; Merton, 1975; Selznik, 1949; Weber, 1968).

Klein and House (1995, p. 185) similarly note that *crisis breeds charisma*. A leader must be in possession of a radical and novel solution to the crisis, and must continually seek out tests to demonstrate their charisma. Trice and Beyer (1986) describe charismatic leaders as people who are exceptionally gifted, and who are most likely to emerge in times of crisis when they are able to offer a radical solution to followers, to use their charisma to attract followers, and to be in a position to validate the belief that followers have in them through achieving repeated success. The leader may have to resort to the use of force to sustain their hold on power (as was the case in Castro's post-revolutionary Cuba, or Mugabe's Zimbabwe); for, when success deserts the charismatic leader, so does their authority (Turner, 2003). As stated by Beetham (1977, p. 176):

> It is useless, anti-historical and anti-scientific to hope that dictators, having happily initiated their political work, will abdicate at the height of their power, since abdication is an act of weakness … The charismatic leader does not abdicate, not even when the water reaches to his throat. Precisely in his readiness to die lies one element of his force and his triumph.

IDEA IN BRIEF

Charisma and uncertainty

Waldman *et al.* (2001) used data from 48 Fortune 500 companies to assess the potential of charismatic and transactional leadership as predictors of financial performance. They observed that, while charismatic leadership was in itself a predictor of improved performance, this only occurred in situations of uncertainty.

Weber's theorizations on charisma are covered at length in the seminal work *Economy and Society* (Weber, 1968), to which leadership scholars are directed for further analysis. The chapter now turns to a consideration of the impact and role of charisma in organizations.

Charisma in organizations

It was not until the 1970s that charismatic leadership rose to prominence within the field of organizational and management studies, forming part of a new coterie of *values-based* leadership theories (Bass, 1985, 1998; Bass and Avolio, 1994; Deluga, 2001; Den Hartog *et al.*, 1999; House and Howell, 1992; Trice and Beyer, 1986; Yukl, 1998).

Studies of charisma in leadership in the management literature, often referred to as the *neo-charismatic* paradigm, includes, and is represented most notably by, House's

1976 Theory of Charismatic Leadership (House, 1977) and by work undertaken by Bass (1985, 1998) and Burns (1978) in conceptualizations of transformational leadership – of which charisma (referred to in this context as *idealized influence* – is a requisite part (more of this later in Chapter 7, "Transformational leadership").

House's (1977) Theory of Charismatic Leadership characterized the charismatic leader as a person who possesses strong verbal ability (charismatic rhetoric), high self-confidence, a high *n-pow* need (need for influence/power) and an exceptional conviction in the morality of their beliefs (House and Howell, 1992). The manner in which a leader employs charisma – ethical or unethical – is determined by whether the individual's 'power motivation' (need for power) is primarily *personalized* or *socialized* (McClelland and Burnham, 1976, p. 103). Personalized leaders were conceptualized as authoritarian, exploitative, self-aggrandizing and orientated towards win–lose problem solving and conflict resolution, whereas socialized leaders were egalitarian, non-exploitative, altruistic and orientated towards win–win problem solving and conflict resolution.

House and Shamir (1993, p. 86) define charismatic leadership as:

> an interaction between leader and followers [during or after a crisis situation] that results in 1) making the followers' self-esteem contingent on the vision and mission articulated by the leader, 2) a strong internalization of the leader's values and goals by the followers, 3) a strong person or moral … commitment to these values and goals, and 4) a willingness on the part of the followers to transcend their self-interests for the sake of the collective.

Klein and House (1995) also report that settings where a desire for moral leadership is aroused are conducive to the development of charisma.

The migration of the concept of charisma to the field of organizational studies is not without its critics (Conger, 1993; Steyrer, 1998). Steyrer (1998, p. 809) commented that "the limitation of the 'New Leadership Approach' to the dimension of 'prophetic charisma', for which the articulation of a vision is a constitutive element, is a very limited view of the phenomenon indeed".

The articulation of a vision

House and Howell (1992, p. 82) identified charismatic leadership theory as that which "emphasises symbolic leader behaviour, visionary and inspirational ability, nonverbal communication, appeal to ideological values, intellectual stimulation of followers by the leader, and leader expectations for follower self-sacrifice and for performance beyond expectations". Adopting a sociological view, Weber (1924) had earlier identified the use of rhetoric and the communication of a vision or mission as key strategies of the charismatic leader in the development of an emotional bond with, and subsequent power over, his/her followers.

The presence of a vision (Bennis and Nanus, 1985; Conger and Kanungo, 1987) also appears within the management literature as the most commonly emphasized behaviour possessed by the charismatic leader, and is central to the concept of charisma (Bryman, 1992). Values-based leadership posits the importance of a passionate articulation of a vision in order to command great commitment and performance beyond expectations from followers (House, 1996; House and Shamir, 1993), in such a way that the followers' self-worth becomes contingent on their ability to contribute successfully to the leader's vision and mission (Bass and Avolio, 1994; House and Shamir, 1993).

As discussed earlier, the power of charismatic rhetoric has been shown to be particularly strong in conditions of uncertainty, and where negative feelings such as fear of persecution are present (Burns, 1978; House, 1977, 1996; House et al., 1991; Weber, 1924). Followers are highly motivated to make personal sacrifices to contribute to the vision or mission that has been ascribed by the leader, and to also experience a strong sense of identification with the leader (House, 1996).

Giampetro-Meyer et al. (1998) believe that a tremendously strong vision is required in successful leadership and that the leader needs to demonstrate an absolute commitment to, and conviction in, this vision in order to succeed. Charismatic leadership scholars have consistently asserted that vision creation, articulation and communication are the most important factors in predicting leadership effectiveness (Bass, 1990; Bycio et al., 1995; Simons, 1999). For example, the charismatic leader was reported to successfully "obtain success by vividly articulating a transcendent goal which clarifies or specifies a mission for followers and which communicates values that have ideological significance for them" (House, 1977 p. 189).

House and Howell (1992) identify the articulation of an ideological vision as one of the causes of successful outcomes for charismatic leaders. They also identify the tendency for goals to be distal, as opposed to proximate, in nature, and for the leader to act as a role model, via the communication of high expectations of their followers, and by the demonstration of behaviours that selectively arouse the motivations for power, achievement and affiliation. De Vries et al. (1999) further identify impression management, articulation of an appealing vision, communication of high expectations and expression of confidence as characteristic of the charismatic leader. Podsakoff et al. (1990) further argue that the trust, respect, vision and high performance expectations generated by a charismatic leader pushes subordinates to perform beyond expectations and accept organizational change.

Shamir et al. (1993, 1994) similarly discuss the use of charismatic rhetoric in the reference to history and tradition, emphasis of a collective identity, reinforcement of a collective efficacy and the communication of a vision, or hope, for a better future as common foundations of speeches of this nature.

DISCUSSION STARTER

The Hitler effect

History offers countless examples of the use of charismatic rhetoric in the communication of the leader's vision or mission, by the psychopathic, the ignominious and the egalitarian. For example, Hitler's rise to power as leader of the National Socialist Party (NSP) was strengthened significantly by his delivery of an emotional and charismatic speech broadcast to a German domestic audience on 19 February 1933. Goebbels first rallied the live audience in a vitriolic, forceful address before Hitler invoked the powerful combination of mission and religious discourse in a speech that was delivered with the appearance of a level of humility, the wearing of a military uniform and familiar greeting of *Volksgenossen*[6] (Eatwell, 2006) and the use of charismatic rhetoric (Weber, 1924) to establish a bond between himself and his followers.

Start the discussion: Why do you think that religious and militaristic imagery and discourse can be so powerful in forming emotional bonds with followers?

The dark side of charisma

Eatwell (2006) argues that a charismatic personality is in possession of three traits: first, that the individual appears to be a missionary – a person with a vision; second, that they have established a symbiotic hierarchy (they appear to be both above and of the people); and third, that they demonize an enemy in a way that serves to heighten the feeling of an evil threat from which they can deliver followers. Demonization of an enemy carries tremendous potential for societal harm, as it effectively represents the high price that certain groups in society will pay in order for a charismatic leader to gain greater power and stronger rhetoric. A classic example is the demonization of Jews in Nazi Germany by Hitler's Third Reich.

The potential for the charismatic leader to exhibit charisma alongside negative, dictatorial behaviour has been referred to as the *Hitler Effect* (Jacobsen and House 2001), and the "shadow side" of charisma (Conger and Kanungo, quoted in Bass, 1985). The extent to which a charismatic leader can be considered ethical or amoral can be understood in terms of their power motivation and charisma as either *personalized* or *socialized* (De Vries *et al.*, 1999; House and Howell, 1992; Howell, 1988; Howell and Shamir, 2005; Rosenthal and Pittinsky, 2006). Socialized charismatic leaders possess ethical integrity, embody the values of their followers and go beyond their own self-interest for the good of the group. While both types engage in self-regulation of their behaviour, personalized charismatic leaders are more likely to do so in order to engage in image building, to seek to collect symbols of power and prestige and to be deceptive, argumentative and uncooperative (House and Howell,

1992). O'Connor *et al.* (1995) carried out a quantitative and qualitative analysis of leaders' biographies and historic documents and found that personalized leaders articulated a vision of an unsocialized world, and experienced childhood events that contributed to their belief that personal safety is achieved through domination. Conversely, socialized leaders demonstrated a belief that power is to be used as a method of empowering others, not as a method of dominance.

Both personalized and socialized charismatic leaders seek to appeal to the self-concept, self-esteem and self-worth of the follower (Shamir *et al.*, 1993; Shamir *et al.*, 1994). Howell & Shamir (2005) argue that followers who have low self-concept clarity are more likely to form relationships with a personalized charismatic leader, as their lack of personal insight leaves them open to the potential for manipulation. Additionally, the strong vision of the personalized charismatic leader offers appeal and meaning to the follower. Personalized leaders often have to resort to force and threats to sustain their leadership after the initial emotional appeal of their vision and strength of their charismatic rhetoric has diminished. In this way, personalized leaders mimic far more closely the qualities of a narcissistic leader (Deluga, 2001; House and Howell, 1992; Howell and Avolio, 1992; McClelland, 1975). These destructive tendencies largely discern the ethical from the amoral and as such warrant further discussion.

Maccoby (2000) suggests that many charismatic leaders are likely to be narcissists, overly sensitive to criticism, poor listeners, lacking in empathy and exhibiting both a distaste for mentoring and an intense desire to compete. He refers to the narcissist tendency as manifest in "people with an inordinately well-developed self-image, in which they take great pride and on which they reflect frequently" (Maccoby, 2000, p. 69). Such a concept deserves more attention in this chapter due to its prominence within the literature.

Narcissism and charisma

Many authors (Maccoby, 2000; Rosenthal and Pittinsky, 2006; Sankowsky, 1995) identify the key role of charisma in the rise of the narcissistic leader. Rosenthal and Pittinsky (2006) theorize that one might expect the narcissistic leader to be most successful in positions where charisma and extroversion are important (for example, during political campaigns), and in times of instability (as characterized by Weber's *in status nascendi*), where a radical change is demanded (for example, during times of political revolution). They are likely to abuse their charisma and to demand that followers shoulder the blame when they fail (Sankowsky, 1995). Perhaps unsurprisingly, Pinto and Larsen (2006) argue that the charismatization of politics should be recognized as posing a serious challenge to democracy.

Abuses of charisma by the narcissistic leader make such figures potentially threatening and dangerous. Kets de Vries and Miller (1997) claim that many historic leadership figures who could be described as tyrants are narcissists driven by a personalized, egotistical need for power and for the admiration of others. The interesting characteristic of a narcissist is that, while they appear prone to inflating their own ability or self-worth, and expect others to admire them in a similarly deferent way, the characteristics upon which such an inflated self-concept are based (for example, a belief in one's own superior intelligence over others) are not normally possessed. Narcissistic leaders are more at risk of micro-managing employees and of being abusive managers, lapses in judgement, making poor judgements with greater confidence than non-narcissists and are more likely to deceive, self-promote and intimidate others (Rosenthal and Pittinsky, 2006). An inflated sense of superiority over others also risks a hypersensitive and angry response (for example, during disagreements within a board meeting), which can lead to instability and conflict (Kernberg, 1989).

DISCUSSION STARTER

"Nothing hits harder than life" – Rocky Balboa

In March 2013, *Bloomberg Businessweek* ran an article on the brokerage John Thomas Financial, drawing parallels between the company and the fictional JT Marlin brokerage featured in the movie *Boiler Room*. According to the report, John Thomas brokers are greeted every morning by the sounds of the *Rocky* theme tune. The founder and CEO, Anastasios 'Tommy' Belesis, regularly delivers charismatic speeches to his employees about entering a "war zone", and employees are directed to the bathroom and provided with shaving equipment if they turn up looking less than perfectly shaven and coiffed. The atmosphere could reasonably be characterized as one of pressure, machismo and power.

The use of the *Rocky* theme is particularly ironic, given that Rocky (in *Rocky Balboa*, the final instalment of the *Rocky* franchise) inspires his son Robert to resign from his role as a trader as he felt that it made him value the wrong things in life. The *Rocky* movies remain the archetypal underdog story, where family values, humility, self-belief and tenacity ultimately triumph over the transient and less valuable pursuit of wealth, status and power.

The company subsequently became the focus of a FINRA (Financial Industry Regulatory Authority) investigation and was subsequently closed down in 2015 amidst multiple regulatory violations.[7]

Start the discussion: Discuss the nature of power motivation and charisma within the working culture of John Thomas Financial.

How to measure charismatic leadership

The measurement of charisma is an interesting concept. Can one really measure such an elusive quality? Certainly, it is possible to argue in the affirmative, but measurement depends on: (1) the provision of a sound conceptual definition of charisma, and (2) whether there is an empirically robust instrument available to measure it in accordance with that definition. The MLQ (Multi-Factor Leadership Questionnaire) Form 5x measures charisma in addition to other *full range leadership* behaviours, with charisma conceptualized as both *attributed* and *behavioural* (this is discussed in greater depth in Chapter 7, "Transformational leadership"). A 360-degree instrument, the MLQ Form 5x measures self- and other-ratings of percep-tions of charisma in a leader. The instrument is discussed at length in the following chapter, so will not be subject to further discussion here.

Another relevant instrument is the California Personality Inventory Dominance Scale (CPI), which measures an individual's *n-pow*, or need for power, including their pro-social assertiveness. This provides valuable insight into the extent to which an individual's motivation for power is either personalized or socialized (McClelland, 1975). McClelland (1985) reported an association of n-pow with raised levels of adrenalin, dopamine and endorphins (see Chapter 2, "Trait theories"), and identified a high n-pow, in conjunction with low affiliative need and a high activity inhibition, as factors that predisposed effective leadership. House and Howell (1992) describe a high affiliative need as characteristic of a highly pro-social need to do good for others, and a low affiliative need as characteristic of the need for personal power, with the latter gaining empirical support as a predictor of leader effectiveness (House *et al.*, 1991; McClelland and Boyatzis, 1982; McClelland and Burnham, 1976).

Measures of dominance (a trait relevant to the 'dark side' of charismatic leadership) that possess empirical support include the Narcissistic Personality Inventory (NPI) (Raskin and Hall, 1979), and the Machiavellianism Scale (Christie and Geis, 1970).

Criticisms of charismatic leadership

Charismatic leadership as a theory is amoral. That is, the theory recognizes that charisma can exist in equal measure in a leader who is altruistic (Mahatma Gandhi) or psychopathic (Adolf Hitler). As Eatwell (2006, p. 277 states, "Turning to cha-risma, it is clearly naive to adopt a 'great man' view of history in which one person explains everything. Having said this, no Hitler, no Holocaust." Such a concept raises difficult moral questions when exploring the practical use and application of charisma in organizations. It is also difficult to differentiate whether charisma could be considered a trait, a skill or a characteristic, and there is also currently a lack of research relating to the extent to which charisma might be innate or learned.

While this is not, arguably, a criticism of the theory per se, it can raise a valid criticism of the way in which charisma is viewed as a commodity. If recruiters, organizations and voters are easily seduced by charisma, for example, and do not understand the differentiation between socialized and personalized motives, this may result in the hiring of a leader who is reckless and ineffectual, or to the election of a politician who is self-serving and narcissistic. Conversely, followers may become disillusioned by the self-serving actions and mistruths of personalized charismatic leaders to such an extent that they are unable to recognize a truly egal-itarian charismatic leader when faced with one.

It ultimately lies within the ability of an organization or individual to differentiate the self-serving aggrandizer from the socially additive leader, if the power of charisma is to be truly exploited.

Summary

The seemingly enigmatic, powerful and heroic nature of the charismatic leader is at once feared, and respected, for it is within charisma itself that the power to coerce, manipulate or empower lies. Characterized by instability, the charismatic leadership process carries the potential for either great organizational success or financial ruin. The fundamental concern for organizations is this: while charisma offers the most seductive form of leadership, it is certainly not the most effective.

Critically, however, it is possible that charisma can lead to performance beyond expectations – but only in the presence of other *transformational* behaviours. The theory of *transformational leadership* (Bass, 1985; Burns, 1978) subsequently forms the focus of the next chapter.

 **Expert insight**

When leadership fails

This expert insight has been written by the Head of Distressed Debt at a leading financial institution. He has requested anonymity due to the sensitivity of the subject under discussion.

"I have been working with distressed and highly leveraged businesses for over ten years now and what is interesting, from my perspective, is that certain leadership characteristics seem to reoccur when one is dealing with financially overstretched balance sheets and companies.

Let me, first of all, briefly provide more background about what I mean when I speak about 'distressed and highly leveraged' businesses. Simplistically speaking, companies, when viewed from a financial perspective, tend to fall into three broad categories:

1   Good companies with good balance sheets, i.e. strategically well-positioned companies with attractive products in a growing or at least a stable market, with vast financial resources and flexibility (e.g. Apple Inc., known as an iconic innovator, possesses almost no borrowings and is sitting on a $140 billion cash pile).

2   Good companies with bad balance sheets, i.e. strategically well-positioned companies, who are nevertheless financially constrained by their lack of financial resources. An example of this is traditional private equity companies who tend to finance their acquisitions with a lot of borrowings.

3   Bad companies with bad balance sheets. These companies are typically in a difficult situation, as they tend to have strategic problems. For example, they may be struggling to compete against a very strong rival company who is taking market share from them. This tends to result in negative profitability issues, for example, because they are then forced to sell their less attractive products at a discount. If this situation continues for too long without adequate strategic intervention from management, the profitability issue ultimately becomes also a liquidity problem – i.e. the company's cost base is not shrinking in line with their products. This lowers profitability to a critical level, where ultimately the company runs out of money.

Each scenario requires a very different kind of leader with different leadership qualities and talents. A very charismatic CEO with superior industry insights and relationships, for example, would be beneficial to a good company with a good balance sheet (Type 1 company) but not necessarily ideal if the company is facing financial constraints (Type 2 company) or, even worse, is not only financially constrained but also strategically challenged (Type 3 company). This basic, yet essential, dynamic is important to understand, as most companies go through stages (from good to bad, to – sometimes – ugly) in their existence and their leaders have to adapt to each stage or, alternatively, admit that they do not possess the required skills for the next stage and leave and make room for more appropriate candidates. In reality, though, it is difficult for a leader to let go in such circumstances, especially if they have been with the company for a long time. Equally, they sometimes don't want to let go of their corporate perks, from cars, to private jets, to helicopters and to yachts, which are, surprisingly (or maybe not surprisingly!), quite common features of the distressed situations that I and my team analyse.

Sometimes, in my line of work, one also comes across individuals/leaders who are not telling the truth, sometimes by hiding certain things from the financial community (the proverbial 'skeletons in the closet'), in the form of missing assets or incremental liabilities. Sometimes, the truth is distorted by the leadership of a distressed company, in the form of understating bad financial performance or overstating good financial performance, whichever would create a benefit to the company. Sometimes CEO's lie outright, which might be why we have seen a lot of multi-billion-dollar fines levied by the SEC recently.

In these instances, it is not uncommon to come across very autocratic leadership styles, where the leader at the top of an organization is very charismatic, has a very strong grip on his (sometimes quite inexperienced and easily impressed) employees, typically has an opportunistic and flexible approach to getting things done and is not limited by a strong moral compass. "

Questions

1   According to the leader interviewed above, what personality traits could be considered common among the leaders of unsuccessful (distressed) companies?
2   The MD interviewed notes that different scenarios may require a different type of leader. Identify different economic, social and political scenarios that offer excellent examples of this idea.
3   Why do you think that the acquisition of materialistic symbols of success, such as private jets and yachts, might be prevalent among leaders of distressed companies?
4   The final statement of this expert insight is that a distressed leader is not 'limited by a strong moral compass'. What does this mean in the long term for company profits and employee well-being? Use real-life examples to support your answer(s).

Case study: George Soros – in defence of an open society

George Soros, 89, is one of the most successful hedge fund managers in the world. Over the course of a long career in finance, he has amassed a fortune so vast that he has been able to donate more than $32 billion to charitable causes, meaning that he is now one of most prolific philanthropists of the modern age. Yet among some circles, Soros remains one of the most deeply reviled figures in modern history.

Born György Schwartz in Hungary in 1930, Soros's life was, from the outset, marred and shaped by anti-Semitism – a spectre of bigotry that has followed him throughout his life and which he continues to fight against today. When Schwartz was a small boy, his father renamed him George Soros to make him sound more Hungarian as a means of avoiding anti-Semitic bigotry and discrimination. The Soros family's assumed identities saved them from deportation to concentration camps during World War II.

George Soros is now as well known for his development of the Open Society Foundations (a form of political resistance against authoritarian regimes via philanthropy) as he is for investing. Soros's concept of an open society first began to take shape during his tenure as a student at the London School of Economics, where he studied the work of philosopher Karl Popper in regard to open and closed societies. It was a philosophical approach that informed not only his philanthropy and his world-view, but also his investing.

Because of the success of his work, Soros frequently became a target for physical and verbal intimidation, mockery and vicious personal attacks on his character by the alt-right.[8] Recently, for example, a pipe bomb was mailed to his home.

Powerful enemies

While Soros's status as an extremely powerful pro-democratic voice has earned him many enemies, his ethnic status as a wealthy, powerful Jewish man has marked him out specifically by many alt-right, far right and authoritarian groups, including President Donald Trump and members of his family and administration. Anti-Semitism remains the most heavily utilized 'dog whistle' technique of populist right wing campaigns, and it is common to see demeaning cartoons of Soros with a comedically large nose and other grotesquely over-inflated 'Jewish' features shared on social media. It is a phenomenon that harks back to pre-World War II Germany, when pamphlets distributed in anti-Jew campaigns by the German state under Hitler during the 1930s were used to scapegoat, mock and invoke fear and anger towards Jews.

Soros also counts the Chinese Government, Macedonia, Russia, the Trump Administration and Hungarian Prime Minister Viktor Orbán among many powerful enemies who have, at one time or another, systematically targeted him. What remains particularly ironic about Orbán's targeting is that, in 1989, Soros awarded Orbán a grant to further his studies in Britain. Around 20 years later, he donated a further $1 million to Orbán's government to be used in environmental assistance programmes.

Demonization of a name

Just as the word 'liberal' has been demonized in modern US populist campaigns, so too has the name 'Soros' become synonymous with a raft of ugly ideas that are easily shared across social media without the author of the post having explicitly stated bigoted, anti-Semitic or extreme views. Recently, Trump's lawyer, Rudy Giuliani, retweeted a comment accusing Soros of being the Antichrist, calling for his assets to be frozen. Another example, among a tidal wave of retweeted insults and propaganda, is Donald Trump Jr. retweeting a post by US comedienne Roseanne Barr that claimed that Soros was a Nazi. Soros, now in his eighties, continues to fight back. It remains a sad truth that Soros has faced this kind of attack his entire life. It is laudable that he has remained steadfast in providing a pro-democracy voice against the most powerful of opponents, and has, as a result, become admired as one of the greatest pro-democracy role models alive today.

Supporting change

At one time, US Republicans enthusiastically supported Soros. Politically independent, Soros was an admirer of former President Ronald Reagan's anti-Communist stance and was in, turn, admired by many anti-Communist Republicans who viewed him as a fellow freedom fighter.

Times have, of course, now changed. George Soros has never been more targeted by authoritarian figures and as always, he will continue to fight.

Find out more

- Walker, Shaun (22 June 2017). "A Useful Punching Bag": Why Hungary's Viktor Orbán Has Turned On George Soros. Available at: www.theguardian.com/world/2017/jun/22/hungary-viktor-orban-george-soros.

- Dalio, Ray (26 March 2017). The Developed World Populism Index. Available at: http://time-price-research-astrofin.blogspot.com/2017/03/the-developed-world-populism-index-ray.html.
- Open Society Foundations website: www.opensocietyfoundations.org/.

Questions

1 Research the background of George Soros and comment on his leadership traits and skills.
2 Earlier in the chapter, the concept of a charismatic leader having to resort to the use of force, propaganda and coercion to sustain their hold on power was discussed ("when success deserts the charismatic leader, so does his authority"; Turner, 2003, p. 14). Find examples within your country of studies of political leaders who are demonstrating this kind of behaviour.
3 How does the targeting of Soros ably illustrate the use of scapegoats in right-wing charismatic political rhetoric?
4 Soros has a great charisma of office, and charisma related to his expert power. Identify three other leaders with Soros's kind of (socialized) power and charisma, and three that characterise the 'dark' (personalized power-based) form of charisma.

CHAPTER 6 QUIZ

1 Define *in statu nascendi* and explain its relevance to theories of charisma.
2 Why has much work in this field concentrated on differentiating the personalized from the socialized charismatic leader?
3 Provide examples of a *personalized* charismatic leader, taken from: (i) religion, (ii) business and (iii) politics.
4 Provide examples of a *socialized* charismatic leader, taken from: (i) religion, (ii) business and (iii) politics.
5 The power of charismatic rhetoric has been shown to be particularly powerful under which specific condition?
6 Charismatic leadership could be considered a process that requires the necessary interaction of which three specific elements?
7 Could charisma be considered both a trait and a skill?
8 What are the most effective methods of measuring charisma?
9 Why is the presence of a vision crucial in the elicitation of charismatic leadership?
10 Shamir *et al.* (1993, 1994) discuss the use of charismatic rhetoric in reference to history and tradition, emphasis of a collective identity, reinforcement of a collective efficacy and the communication of a vision, or hope for a better future, as common foundations of charismatic speeches. Identify a specific speech (for example, Barack Obama's 2008 Presidential inauguration speech) that contains all of these elements.

Notes

1 SEC is the US Securities and Exchanges Commission.
2 Quote appears in the expert insight in this chapter, "When leadership fails', based on an interview with the Managing Director of a leading investment bank, conducted for this book.
3 Monti served as Prime Minister from 16 November 2011 to 21 December 2012.
4 *Channel 4 News* (19 March 2018). Data, Democracy and Dirty Tricks. Available at: www.channel4.com/news/data-democracy-and-dirty-tricks-cambridge-analytica-uncovered-investigation-expose.
5 As broadcast in the undercover investigation, Data, Democracy and Dirty Tricks.
6 In the context of Nazismm, this term relates to being a comrade or member of the German Volksgemeinschaft, an idealized people's community with no barriers or conflict, consisting only of Aryan members.
7 *SEC News Digest* (22 March 2013). SEC Charges Hedge Fund Manager and Brokerage CEO with Fraud. Available at: www.sec.gov/news/digest/2013/dig032213.htm.
8 Alt-right is an abbreviation of 'alternative right', a white nationalist movement with a global presence.

References

Agle, B.R., Nagarajan, N.J., Sonnenfeld, J.A. and Srinivasan, D. (2006). Does CEO Charisma Matter? An Empirical Analysis of the Relationships among Organizational Performance, Environmental Uncertainty, and Top Management Team Perceptions of CEO Charisma. *Academy of Management Journal*, 49(1), pp. 161–174.

Bass, B.M. (1985). *Leadership and Performance Beyond Expectations*. New York: Free Press.

Bass, B.M. (1988). Evolving Perspectives on Charismatic Leadership. In J.A. Conger and R.N. Kanungo (eds.), *Charismatic Leadership: The Elusive Factor in Organisational Effectiveness*. San Francisco, CA: Jossey-Bass, pp. 40–77.

Bass, B.M. (1990). Editorial: Transformational Leaders Are Not Necessarily Participative. *Leadership Quarterly*, 1, p. vii.

Bass, B.M. (1998). *Transformational Leadership: Industrial, Military, and Educational Impact*. Mahwah, NJ: Lawrence Erlbaum Associates.

Bass, B.M. and Avolio, B.J. (1993). Transformational Leadership: A Response to Critiques. In M.M. Chemers and R. Ayman (eds.), *Leadership Theory and Research: Perspectives and Directions*. San Diego, CA: Academic Press, pp. 49–80.

Bass, B.M. and Avolio, B.J. (1994). *Improving Organisational Effectiveness through Transformational Leadership*. Thousand Oaks, CA: Sage.

Beetham, D. (1977). From Socialism to Fascism: The Relation between Theory and Practice in the Work of Robert Michels. *Political Studies*, 25(1), pp. 161–181.

Bennis, W. and Nanus, B. (1985). *Leaders: The Strategies for Taking Charge*. New York: Harper & Row.

Bryman, A. (1992). *Charisma and Leadership in Organisations*. London: Sage.

Burns, J.M. (1978). *Leadership*. New York: Harper & Row.

Bycio, P., Hackett, R.D. and Allen, J.S. (1995). Further Assessment of Bass's Conceptualisation of Transactional and Transformational Leadership. *Journal of Applied Psychology*, 80(4), pp. 468–478.

Christie, R. and Geis, F.L. (1970). *Studies in Machiavellianism*. New York: Academic Press.

Conger, J. (1993). Max Weber's Conceptualisation of Charismatic Authority: Its Influence on Organisational Research. *Leadership Quarterly*, 4(3/4), pp. 277–288.

Conger, J. and Kanungo, R.N. (1987). Towards a Behavioural Theory of Charismatic Leadership in Organisations. *Academy of Management Review*, 12, pp. 637–647.

Conger, J.J. and Kanungo, R.N. (1998). *Charismatic Leadership in Organisations*. New York: Sage.

De Martino, B., Kumaran, D., Seymour, B., Dolan, R.J. (2006). Frames, Biases and Rational Decision-Making in the Human Brain. *Science*, 313(5787), pp. 684–687.

De Vries, R.E., Roe, R.A. and Taillieu, T.C.B. (1999). On Charisma and Need for Leadership. *European Journal of Work and Organisational Psychology*, 8(1), pp. 109–133.

Deluga, R.J. (2001). American Presidential Machiavellianism: Implications for Charismatic Leadership and Rated Performance. *Leadership Quarterly*, 12, pp. 339–363.

Den Hartog, D.N., House, R.J., Hanges, P.J., Ruiz-Quintanilla, S.A., Dorfman, P.U., Ashkanasy, N.M. and Falkus, S.A. (1999). Culture Specific and Cross-Culturally Generalisable Implicit Leadership Theories: Are the Attributes of Charismatic/Transformational Leadership Universally Endorsed? *Leadership Quarterly*, 10(2), pp. 219–256.

Eatwell, R. (2006). Explaining Fascism and Ethnic Cleansing: The Three Dimensions of Charisma and the Four Dark Sides of Nationalism. *Political Studies Review*, 4(3), pp. 263–278.

Eisenstadt, S.N. (1968). Charisma and Institution Building. In M. Weber and S.N. Eisenstadt (eds.) *Max Weber and Institution Building*. Chicago, IL: University of Chicago Press, pp. ix–lvi.

Giampetro-Meyer, A., Brown, T., Browne, M.N. and Kubasek, N. (1998). Do We Really Need More Leaders in Business? *Journal of Business Ethics*, 17(15), pp. 1727–1736.

House, R.J. (1971). A Path–Goal Theory of Leader Effectiveness. *Administrative Science Quarterly*, 16, pp. 312–338.

House, R.J. (1977). A 1976 Theory of Charismatic Leadership. In J.G. Hunt and L.L. Larson (eds.), *Leadership: The Cutting Edge*. Carbondale, IL: Southern Illinois University Press, pp. 189–207.

House, R.J. (1996). Path-Goal Theory of Leadership: Lessons, Legacy, and a Reformulated Theory. *Leadership Quarterly*, 7(3), pp. 323–352.

House, R.J. and Howell, J.M. (1992). Personality and Charismatic Leadership. *Leadership Quarterly*, 3(2), pp. 81–109.

House, R.J. and Shamir, B. (1993). Toward the Integration of Charismatic, Transformational, Inspirational and Visionary Theories of Leadership. In M. Chemmers and R. Ayman (eds.), *Leadership Theory and Research Perspectives and Directions*. New York: Academic Press, pp. 81–107.

House, R.J., Spangler, W. and Woycke, J. (1991). Personality and Charisma in the US Presidency: A Psychological Theory of Leader Effectiveness. *Administrative Science Quarterly*, 36(3), pp. 364–396.

Howell, J.M. (1988). Two Faces of Charisma: Socialised and Personalised Leadership in Organisations. In J.A. Conger, R.N. Kanungo and Associates (eds.), *Charismatic Leadership: The Elusive Factor in Organisational Effectiveness*. San Francisco, CA: Jossey-Bass, pp. 213–236.

Howell, J.M. and Avolio, B.J. (1992). The Ethics of Charismatic Leadership: Submission or Liberation. *Academy of Management Executive*, 6(2), pp. 43–54.

Howell, J.M. and Avolio, B.J. (1993). Transformational Leadership, Transactional Leadership, Locus of Control, and Support for Innovation: Key Predictors of Consolidated-Business-Unit Performance. *Journal of Applied Psychology*, 78(6), pp. 891–902.

Howell, J.M. and Shamir, B. (2005). The Role of Followers in the Charismatic Leadership Process: Relationships and their Consequences. *Academy of Management Review*, 30(1), pp. 96–112.

Jacobsen, C. and House, R.J. (2001). Dynamics of Charismatic Leadership: A Process Theory, Simulation Model, and Tests. *Leadership Quarterly*, 12, pp. 75–112.

Kernberg, O. (1989). *Severe Personality Disorders*. New Haven, CT: Yale University Press.

Kets de Vries, M.F.R. and Miller, D. (1997). Narcissism and Leadership: An Object Relations Perspective. In R.P. Vecchio (ed.), *Leadership: Understanding the Dynamics of Power and Influence in Organisations*. Notre-Dame, IN: University of Notre Dame Press, pp. 194–214.

Klein, K.G. and House, R.J. (1995). On Fire: Charismatic Leadership and Levels of Analysis. *Leadership Quarterly*, 6(2), pp. 183–198.

Lowe, K.B., Kroek, K.G. and Sivasubramaniam, N. (1996). Effective Correlates of Transformational and Transactional Leadership: A Meta-Analytic Review of the MLQ Literature. *Leadership Quarterly*, 7(3), pp. 385–425.

McClelland, D.C. (1975). *Power: The Inner Experience*. New York: Irvington Publishers.

McClelland, D.C. (1985). *Human Motivation*. Chicago, IL: Scott, Foresman.

McClelland, D.C. and Boyatzis, R.E. (1982). Leadership Motive Patterns and Long-Term Success in Management. *Journal of Applied Psychology*, 67(6), pp. 737–743.

McClelland, D.C. and Burnham, D. (1976). Power is the Great Motivator. *Harvard Business Review*, 25 (March–April), pp. 159–166.

Maccoby, M. (2000). Narcissistic Leaders: The Incredible Pros, the Inevitable Cons. *Harvard Business Review*, 78(1), pp. 68–77.

Merton, R.K. (1975). Bureaucratic Structure and Personality. In R.K. Merton (ed.), *Social Theory and Social Structure*. Glencoe, IL: Free Press, pp. 195–206.

O'Connor, J.A., Mumford, M.D., Clifton, T.C., Gessner, T.E. and Connelly, M.S. (1995). Charismatic Leadership and Destructiveness: A Historimetric Study. *Leadership Quarterly*, 6, pp. 529–555.

Pinto, A.C. and Larsen, S.U. (2006). Conclusion: Fascism, Dictators and Charisma. *Totalitarian Movements and Political Religions*, 7(2) (June), pp. 251–257.

Podsakoff, P.M., MacKenzie, R.H., Morman, R.H. and Fetter, R. (1990). Transformational Leader Behaviours and Their Effects on Followers' Trust in Leader, Satisfaction, and Organisational Citizenship Behaviours. *Leadership Quarterly*, 1(2), pp. 107–143.

Raskin, R. and Hall, C.S. (1979). A Narcissistic Personality Inventory. *Psychological Reports*, 45(2), p. 590.

Rosenthal, S.A. and Pittinsky, T.L. (2006). Narcissistic Leadership. *Leadership Quarterly*, 17(6), pp. 617–633.

Sankowsky, D. (1995). The Charismatic Leader as Narcissist: Understanding the Abuse of Power. *Organisational Dynamics*, 23(4), pp. 57–71.

Scott, W.R. (1981). *Organizations: Rational, Natural, and Open Systems*. Englewood Cliffs, NJ: Prentice-Hall.

Selznik, P. (1949). *TVA and the Grassroots*. Berkeley, CA: University of California Press.

Shamir, B. (1995). Social Distance and Charisma: Theoretical Notes and an Explanatory Study. *Leadership Quarterly*, 6(1), pp. 19–47.

Shamir, B., House, R.J. and Arthur, M. (1993). The Motivational Effects of Charismatic Leadership: A Self Concept Based Theory. *Organisation Science*, 4(1), pp. 577–594.

Shamir, B., Arthur, M.B. and House, R.J. (1994). The Rhetoric of Charismatic Leadership: A Theoretical Extension, a Case Study, and Implications for Research. *Leadership Quarterly*, 5(4), pp. 25–42.

Simons, T.L. (1999). Behavioral Integrity as a Critical Ingredient for Transformational Leadership. *Journal of Organizational Change Management*, 12(2), pp. 89–104.

Smith, T.S. (1992). *Strong Interaction*. Chicago, IL: University of Chicago Press.

Steyrer, J. (1998). Charisma and the Archetypes of Leadership. *Organisation Studies*, 19(5), pp. 807–828.

Trice, H.M. and Beyer, M. (1986). Charisma and its Routinisation in Two Social Movement Organisations. In B.M. Staw and L.L. Cummings (eds.), *Research in Organisational Behavior* (Vol. 8). Greenwich, CT: JAI Press, pp. 113–164.

Turner, S. (2003). Charisma Reconsidered. *Journal of Classical Sociology*, 3(1), pp. 5–26.

Waldman, D.A., Ramirez, G.G., House, R.J. and Puranam, P. (2001). Does Leadership Matter? CEO Attributes and Profitability under Conditions of Perceived Environmental Uncertainty. *Academy of Management Journal*, 44(1), pp. 134–143.

Weber, M. (1924). *The Theory of Social and Economic Organization* (trans. T. Parsons). New York: Free Press.

Weber, M. (1968). *Economy and Society* (ed. G. Roth and K. Wittich). New York: Bedminster Press.

Wilderom, C.P.M., van den Berg, P.T. and Wiersma, U.J. (2012). A Longitudinal Study of the Effects of Charismatic Leadership and Organisational Culture on Objective and Perceived Corporate Performance. *Leadership Quarterly*, 23(5), pp. 835–848.

Yammarino, F.J. and Bass, B.M. (1991). Persona and Situation Views of Leadership: A Multiple Level of Analysis Approach. *Leadership Quarterly*, 2(21), pp. 121–129.

Yukl, G.J. (1998). *Leadership in Organisations*. Englewood Cliffs, NJ: Prentice-Hall.

Zehndorfer, E. (2019). *Evolution, Politics and Charisma: Why Do Populists Win?* New York: Routledge.

7

TRANSFORMATIONAL LEADERSHIP

"We are honouring humanity in the ugliest of behaviours."

– *CEO Sammy Rangel*[1]

Charismatic leaders possess great power to influence others, but, as evidenced in the previous chapter charisma is, by its very definition, transient in nature, existent only *in statu nascendi* (Weber, 1924) and perpetually in danger of routinization. Where charisma exists, great danger may also accompany it, due to the higher propensity for risk taking, the collection of symbols of power and prestige, and the exploitation and subjugation of others that is so frequently characteristic of the amoral personalized charismatic leader.

One only needs to consider the case of the charismatic, yet ultimately ethically bankrupt organizational ethos of Enron, or of the seductive promises and ultimately calamitous losses of the Stanford Financial Group, for clear and compelling examples of such a phenomenon.

Organizations and industries that have aggressively valued the pursuit of profit, personal gain and a reliance on the coterie of the charismatic over all other things (fictionalized effectively in *Boiler Room* and represented ostensibly by the real-life examples of Bernard L. Madoff Investment Securities LLC and Michael Eugene Kelly's Universal Leases fraud) have often fallen on their sword. They have, ironically, lost billions of dollars through ensuing market instability (for example, the once lauded but short-lived Bailey Coates Cromwell Fund), become subject to Government investigations (Goldman Sachs), resulted in the loss of personal liberty (Allen Stanford) and even forced up the age of retirement for a generation as a consequence of diminished pension funds following the 2008 global financial crisis.

While powerfully seductive, charisma alone cannot guarantee any real level of long-term stability or profitability for an individual or organization. When combined with other transformational leadership behaviours, however, research tells a fascinating story; it is a combination that leads, in fact, to the direct empowerment of others and to the elicitation of performance beyond expectations.

Structure of the chapter

This chapter first introduces the reader to a history of transformational leadership (TL), which precedes an overview of the empirical bases upon which claims of the effectiveness of TL within organizations are based. The four individual transformational behaviours that constitute TL – *charisma* (referred to as *idealized influence* within the context of this theory), *inspirational motivation, individual consideration* and *intellectual stimulation* – are presented alongside an explanation of how specific *transactional behaviours* augment the impact of TL *(full range leadership)*. The Multi-Factor Leadership Questionnaire Form 5x, the most valid means of measuring TL, is discussed before the chapter concludes with a case study and an expert insight that allow the reader to critically apply theory to practice.

The expert insight for this chapter is provided by CEO and co-founder of Life After Hate, Sammy Rangel, while a case study of Donald Woods ("Sikhahlela Indoda Yamadoda"), former Editor of the South African anti-apartheid newspaper the *Daily Dispatch*, demonstrates the true power of transformational leadership. A quiz concludes the chapter.

History of transformational leadership

Over the last 20 years, much of the leadership research that has been conducted has concentrated on defining the characteristics and outcomes of transformational and charismatic leadership (Bass, 1985, 1996a; Bennis and Nanus, 1985; Tichy and Devanna, 1990). The academic Bernard Bass introduced transformational leadership to organizational settings (Avolio *et al.*, 1995; Bass, 1985) and, subsequently, the concept of transformational leadership has been subject to substantial theoretical consideration and empirical investigation and support (Avolio *et al.*, 1999; Bass, 1999; Lowe *et al.*, 1996). Transformational leadership is dominant in its presence throughout the literature, and has been linked to positive subordinate, executive, managerial and leadership outcomes across a diverse range of cultures and settings (Avolio & Howell, 1992; Avolio & Yammarino, 2002; Barling *et al.*, 1996; Bass, 1998; Bryman, 1992; Bycio *et al.*, 1995; Gardner and Cleavenger, 1998; Hater and Bass, 1988; Kelloway *et al.*, 2000; Lowe *et al.*, 1996; Pillai *et al.*, 1999; Podsakoff *et al.*, 1996; Ross and Offermann, 1997; Shamir *et al.*, 1998; Sosik and Godshalk, 2000).

Transformational leadership has been linked with employee attitudes such as affective commitment to the organization (Barling *et al.*, 1996; Bycio *et al.*, 1995), a sense of fairness within the organization (Pillai *et al.*, 1999), trust in the leader (Pillai *et al.*, 1999; Podsakoff *et al.*, 1996), enhanced satisfaction with both the job (Hater and Bass, 1988) and the leader (Hater and Bass, 1988) and lower levels of both job (Sosik and Godshalk, 2000) and role stress (Podsakoff *et al.*, 1996).

Moderate to strong links between aspects of transformational leadership and work performance were reported by Lowe *et al.* (1996). Bryman (1992) and Gardner and Cleavenger (1998) found that transformational leadership produces desirable outcomes in terms of subordinate satisfaction and assessment of the leader's skills, due to the latter's ability to communicate with followers on an individual level.

Shamir *et al.* (1993, p. 577) claimed that "transformational leaders cause followers to become highly committed to the leader's mission, to make significant personal sacrifices in the interests of the mission, and to perform above and beyond the call of duty". Similarly, Kouzes and Posner (1992, p. 481) opine that: "Transformational leadership creates a circle of relationships and bonds which enriches all those connected together. Justice is served when such a state exists."

While a number of theorists have contributed to the field of transformational leadership (Bennis and Nanus, 1985; Tichy and Devanna, 1986, 1990), the version of the theory that has, undoubtedly, produced the most extensive research is that of Bernard Bass (1985, 1996a), based on the earlier work of Burns (1978). Bass's model conceptualizes four behaviours, often referred to as the *four I's* of transformational leadership. Later in the chapter, the reader will be introduced to the concept of *transactional* leadership and to the augmentation effect that occurs when certain transactional and transformational behaviours, as conceptualized by Bass (1985, 1996a), interact. This interaction is more fully explored within the confines of the *full range leadership* theory, which will also be considered later in the chapter.

First, however, it is necessary to present the *four I's* of transformational leadership (Bass, 1985, 1996a).

The *four I's* of transformational leadership

Transformational leadership constitutes four separate behaviours: (1) charisma (or idealized influence); (2) inspirational motivation; (3) individual consideration; and (4) intellectual stimulation. Each of the four behaviours is explained below.

Idealized influence

The first transformational behaviour to be discussed is *charisma*. As stated by Bass (1985, p. 31), "charisma is a necessary ingredient of transformational leadership, but by itself it is not sufficient to account for the transformational process." Although the terms 'charisma' and 'transformational leadership' are sometimes used interchangeably in the leadership literature (Lievens *et al.*, 1997), a clear distinction can be drawn between them, with charisma forming a necessary sub-dimension of transformational leadership (Bass, 1985; Bass and Avolio, 1993). As a sub-dimension of transformational leadership, charisma has been referred to as *idealized influence* and *attributed behaviour* (Lievens *et al.*, 1997).

As discussed in the previous chapter, charismatic leadership (Conger and Kanungo, 1987; House, 1977; Shamir, 1991) is the name given to leadership that is based upon the emotional bonds between followers and leaders. Charisma was defined as "an awe-inspiring personality" (Stewart *et al.*, 1994, p. 96). Due to the extensive discussion of charisma in the previous chapter, it will not be elaborated upon further here.

Two points, however, remain to be made. First, those charismatic and transformational leaders who exhibit significantly higher preferences for ethical moral reasoning were found to be more successful (Gillespie and Mann, 2000); and, second, both the charisma that is *attributed* to the leader, in addition to the charisma that is actually evidenced by the leader (*behavioural*), are subject to measurement using the Multi-Factor Leadership Questionnaire Form 5x (discussed later in the chapter in the section "How to measure transformational leadership").

Inspirational motivation

The second transformational behaviour to be discussed – inspirational motivation – is a behaviour that leads followers' interests away from the self and towards the needs of the group, that is, "influencing their followers to put the organisation before their own self-interests" (Carlson and Perrewe, 1995 p. 829). Greta Thunberg is such an inspirational role model because she inspires people to focus on something far greater than themselves, and she is not afraid to be emotional and passionate in her rhetoric. Even small details – the way that she refuses to dress smartly for high-profile events – make her charismatic appeal feel genuine as it underscores the revolutionary, non-conformist nature of her message. As Jones (2002, p. 271) states, "In communicating the vision and strategy, leaders also need to exhibit emotive aspects of themselves, which will inspire everyone to follow."

Chanoch and House (2001) acknowledge that transformational leaders have very high levels of referent power and some of that power comes from the need to influence others. The roles of power and motivation in leadership have been discussed at length in earlier chapters (Chapter 4, "Behavioural theories" and Chapter 6, "Charismatic leadership") and will also provide the basis for further discussion in the context of other value-based theories of leadership (Chapter 9, "Authentic leadership"), so will not be subject to further discussion here.

Individual consideration

Individual consideration, the third transformational behaviour to be discussed, relates to the ability to empathize with individual followers, and to tailor one's leadership style to their needs. A sales manager might understand, for example, that salesperson A responds best to high performance targets, as they feel that it reflects positively on the confidence that the manager holds in them. Salesperson B, however, might view continually increasing targets as unacceptable pressure, instead responding most favourably to the formal assignment of more responsibility (such as taking on a new project) within their professional role.

Intellectual stimulation

Intellectual stimulation is a transformational behaviour that relates to the leader's ability to stimulate followers to be more curious and creative in their thinking and problem solving (Doherty and Danylchuk, 1996; Weese, 1994). Rick Pitino, a highly successful National Collegiate Athletic Association (NCAA) and National Basketball Association (NBA) coach, explained how he encouraged risk taking in individual players as a means of enhancing performance: "I let the players be creative, take chances and showcase their skill. I told them to just go out there and have fun. I gave them the freedom to take risks, because I didn't punish them for failure' (Pitino, cited in McNutt and Wright, 1995, p. 28). Bass (1990) echoes Pitino in his call for the development of organizational policy that seeks to support the maverick who is willing to take unpopular decisions and who knows when it is time to reject conventional wisdom or accepted organizational policy.

Transactional leadership

As stated by Bass (1990, p. 23), "Most experimental research, unfortunately, has focused on transactional leadership, whereas the real movers and shakers of the world are transformational." In the ensuing years, many scholars have, thankfully, answered Bass's call for greater research into transformational behaviours, leading to an extensive body of empirical research that has progressed the field of transformational leadership studies significantly.

There are three key transactional behaviours: *contingent reward, management by exception (active)* and *management by exception (passive)* behaviours. *Contingent reward* behaviour can be conceptualized as a series of exchanges and bargains between manager and subordinate (Boehnke *et al.*, 2003). Contingent reward behaviour involves the leader interacting with subordinates by rewarding efforts contractually, telling them what to do to gain rewards, punishing undesired action and giving extra feedback and promotions for good work (Lievens *et al.*, 1997). For example, a Head of Marketing at IBM might promote a Marketing Assistant to Marketing Executive based on their ability to attain and exceed performance targets (i.e. a *reward* offered by the manager – in this case, a promotion – is *contingent* on the subordinate's ability to consistently meet performance targets). A consistent honouring of agreements, as is the case with a contingent reward relationship, was found to contribute to the high levels of trust and respect associated with transformational leaders (Shamir *et al.*, 1993).

While *contingent reward* behaviour can lead to positive outcomes, *management by exception* behaviours are generally regarded as negative and demotivating to subordinates. *Management by exception* involves a manager paying close attention to the deviations, mistakes or irregularities of his/her team, often via the proactive use of micro-managerial approaches (*management by exception – active*), or by intervening reactively – i.e. only when problems and mistakes have already occurred (*management by exception – passive*) (Bass, 1985; Burns, 1978). Interestingly, *contingent reward* behaviour can augment the effectiveness of transformational leadership; a concept explored further in the context of *full range leadership*.

The full range model of leadership

Transformational leadership was first distinguished from transactional leadership by Downton (1973). However, it was the work of Burns (1978) that first drew attention to the ideas associated with transformational leadership (Leithwood *et al.*, 1996). Bass (1985) operationalized the work of Burns (1978) by developing a model of transformational and transactional leadership, referred to more recently as the *full range leadership model* (Bass, 1985). The purpose of this model was to build on the work of the theorists of the *new leadership school*, who contended that an individual could be both manager and leader (Kotter, 1990; Yukl, 1994) and that these concepts were interdependent (Soucie, 1994).

In studies of transformational leadership, the transactional behaviour of contingent reward often correlated highly and positively with transformational behaviours (Bass and Avolio, 1999; Bycio *et al.*, 1995; Wofford *et al.*, 1998). This was explained by the fact that transformational and contingent reward behaviours both involve active and constructive leadership (Avolio and Bass, 1995; Bass and Avolio, 1993, 1994).

Avolio (1999) stated that a base of certain transactional behaviours, augmented by transformational leadership, will maximize positive leadership outcomes (Avolio *et al.*, 1999; Bass & Avolio, 1997). This interaction is conceptualized as the 'augmentation effect' (Bass, 1985) and forms the basis of the 'full range model of leadership' which is summarized in Table 7.1.

The 'full range model of leadership' provides a version of transformational leadership theory that has since generated the most confirmatory and replication

TABLE 7.1 Transformational and transactional behaviours

Transformational leadership	Transactional leadership
Charisma: provides vision and sense of mission, instils pride, gains respect and trust	*Contingent reward:* contracts exchange of rewards for efforts, promises rewards for good performance, recognizes accomplishments
Inspiration: communicates high expectations, uses symbols to focus efforts, expresses important purposes in simple ways	*Management by exception – active:* watches and searches for deviations from rules and standards, takes corrective action
Intellectual stimulation: promotes intelligence, rationality and careful problem solving	*Management by exception – passive:* intervenes only if standards are not met
Individualized consideration: gives personal attention, treats each employee individually, coaches and advises	*Laissez faire:* abdicates responsibilities, avoids making decisions

research (Avolio *et al.*, 1995; Bass, 1985, 1996a). The full range model incorporates the four transformational behaviours, in addition to the transactional behaviours of *management by exception (active* and *passive)* and *contingent reward*, alongside *laissez-faire* (non-leadership) behaviour and outcomes of leadership (*satisfaction, extra effort* and *effectiveness).*

Authentic transformational leadership

Bass and Steidlmeier (1999) argue that, for a leader to be authentically transformational (and, therefore, to produce effective organizational outcomes), their leadership must possess a moral foundation. Bass and Steidlmeier's (1999) authentic transformational leadership theoretical framework extended the work of Burns' (1978) and Bass's (1985) seminal work in the area of transformational leadership. It theorizes that moral leaders act as agents of change by transforming and empowering followers who become more moral and more effective as leaders in their own right. It is certainly true that recent corporate failures (such as those endemic within the investment banking and hedge fund sectors), political economic catastrophes (Berlusconi's handling of Italy's national debt) and environmental disasters (the Deepwater Horizon oil spill of 2010) have led to highly ineffectual and, in many cases, calamitous outcomes and that these can subsequently be categorized inimitably as failures of leadership. One can argue a strong case for an absence of morality as a key factor is such failures.

Zhu *et al.* (2011) identify three types of values that are relevant to authentic leadership: (1) moral values (for example, kindness and altruism); (2) modal values (such as honesty, integrity, trustworthiness, reliability and accountability); and (3) end values (which include security, justice, equality and community). Authentic transformational leaders are ultimately considered to be those who are moral, and who employ their morality to empower and transform others. They confront ethical challenges in a moral way, inspiring their followers as a moral and authentic role model and, in so doing, transform their followers to question and potentially reassess their own moral beliefs. The concept of authenticity in leadership is discussed in further depth later in the book (Chapter 9, "Authentic leadership"), so will not be considered further here.

Transformational leadership and emotional intelligence

Emotional intelligence (EI), itself theorized to positively contribute to the elicitation of skills identified as valuable in a manager, leader or employee (Bass 1990; Caruso *et al.*, 2002; Dubinsky *et al.*, 1995; Goleman, 1998; Lusch and Serpkeuci, 1990), has also been linked to the elicitation of transformational leadership (Ashforth and Humphrey, 1995; Ashkanasy and Tse, 2000; Barling *et al.*, 2000; Sosik and Megerian, 1999). Correlations between EI and transformational leadership will be discussed at length later in the book (Chapter 8, "Emotional intelligence"), so will not be considered further here.

Teaching transformational leadership

Can transformational leadership be taught? Empirical studies conducted across military (Dvir *et al.* 2002), academic (Graustrom, 1986; Ryan, 1989; Savin-Williams, 1979), sport (Dobosz and Beaty, 1999; Goldberg and Chandler, 1991; Pascarella and Smart, 1991; Snyder and Spreitzer, 1992) corporate (Barling *et al.*, 1996; Geyer and Steyrer, 1998; McClelland and Boyatzis, 1982) and healthcare environments (Morales and Molero, 1995) appear to positively support this theory. For example, an increase in role self-efficacy has been identified (Parker, 1998) as one way in which tailored training can lead to improvements in transformational leadership.

McClelland and Boyatzis (1982) reported positive outcomes relating to an improved sense of responsibility, organizational clarity, team spirit and number of rewards received as a result of tailored training. Similarly, Barling *et al.* (1996) reported a positive increase in all transformational behaviours, particularly intellectual stimulation, following tailored training.

How to measure transformational leadership

The Multi-Factor Leadership Questionnaire (MLQ) is a 360-degree instrument that has been developed to measure full range leadership (Avolio *et al.*, 1999; Bass, 1985; Den Hartog *et al.*, 1997). The MLQ measures transformational, transactional and laissez-faire leadership behaviours. References to other leadership questionnaires are extremely limited; in most cases instruments are discussed only once in the literature – e.g. the Revised NEO Personality Inventory (Costa and McCrae, 1992); the California Psychological Inventory (Gough, 1987); the Leadership Behaviour Questionnaire.[2]

DISCUSSION STARTER

Can charisma be measured?

Red Auerbach (Auerbach & Webber, 1987, p. 85) once said: "I don't believe in statistics. There are too many factors that can't be measured. You can't measure a ballplayer's heart, his ability to perform in the clutch, his willingness to sacrifice his offence or to play strong defence." Interestingly, however, it is now possible to measure charisma, alongside other transformational behaviours, using the MLQ Form 5x (see "How to measure transformational leadership" above).

Start the discussion: Do you believe that charisma can be measured?

The MLQ was originally based on Burns' (1978) description of transforming leadership and measures charisma, inspirational motivation, intellectual stimulation, individualized consideration, contingent reward, management-by-exception and laissez-faire leadership behaviours. There is consensus among scholars that leadership measures generally lack construct validity (Bycio *et al.*, 1995; Carless, 1998; Den Hartog *et al.*, 1997), and that the MLQ remains one of the only instruments to demonstrate stringent testing, analyses and revisions. Many critiques and comprehensive analyses of the MLQ have been performed, leading to subsequent revisions (Bass, 1985; Bass and Avolio, 1990, 1993, 1994; Bryman, 1992; Bycio *et al.*, 1995; Den Hartog *et al.*, 1997; House and Podsakoff, 1994; Hunt, 1991; Waldman *et al.*, 1990) and stringent tests of the underlying factor structure of the instrument (Bollen, 1989). Confirmatory factor analysis was used to test the original MLQ proposed by Bass (1985), which indicated that MLQ research is the most useful instrument for measuring transformational leadership, when combined with other research procedures, such as interviews.

Lowe *et al.* (1996) performed 33 independent empirical studies using the MLQ and identified a strong positive correlation between all components of transformational leadership and both objective and subjective measures of performance. Transformational leaders were found to generate higher commitment from followers in studies when measured by the MLQ (Bass, 1999). Geyer and Steyrer (1998) used the MLQ to measure transformational ratings of Austrian bank managers and reported transformational behaviour elicitation to be a positive predictor of long-term market share and customer satisfaction. Dvir *et al.* (2002) reported that transformational leadership in platoon leaders, as rated by superiors, subordinates and platoon leaders themselves, was positively correlated with effective leadership in near-combat situations. Howell and Avolio (1993) reported that the transformational ability of department supervisors in a large Canadian financial institution, as measured by the MLQ, successfully predicted consolidated departmental performance. The relationship between transformational leadership and performance was also observed in a broad range of additional studies, including studies in diverse cultural settings such as managers in a Chinese state enterprise (Davis *et al.*, 1997), Polish and Dutch managers (Den Hartog *et al.*, 1997) and supervisors on North Sea oil platforms (Carnegie, 1995).

Interestingly, it has been claimed that as much as 59 per cent of the variation in transformational leadership dimensions is attributable to heredity (i.e. genetics) (Johnson *et al.*, 1998).

Critiques of transformational leadership

The transformational leadership behaviours discussed here were considered to be universally applicable to all cultures and organizational settings, despite their North American conception (Bass, 1996b, p. 731): "Although the model of transformational and transactional leadership may have needs for adjustments and fine-tunings as we move across cultures, particularly into non-Western, overall, it holds up as having a lot of universal potential."

However, it is possible that culture mediates perceptions of leadership (Den Hartog *et al.*, 1999, in Ardichvili and Kuchinke, 2002). Dominant leadership theories, such as transformational and charismatic leadership, are North American constructs and reflect Western ideology. Subsequently, they emphasize individualism over collectivism and articulate a hedonistic, rather than altruistic, motivation and democratic value orientation (Ardichvili, 2001). Cross-cultural research has shown that many cultures do not share the same cultural assumptions (Den Hartog *et al.*, 1997). Jung *et al.* (1995, in Ardichvili, 2001) hypothesize that transformational leadership is more effective in individualist cultures than in collectivist cultures. For example, Elenkov (1998) performed a comparative study of US and Russian managers, and found that US managers were more individualistic than Russian managers. US managers also displayed a lower power distance (tolerance of inequality in business and social relationships) and lower uncertainty avoidance than their Russian counterparts. Ardichvili *et al.* (1998) identified a preference by Russian managers to make decisions individually – without consultation with managers or subordinates – and to exhibit a preference for autocratic management. Interestingly, a high level of paternalism was also observed to exist between Russian managers and their subordinates (Trompenaars, 1993).

It is possible, however, that transformational leadership might possess universal appeal. For example, Den Hartog *et al.*, 1999, in Ardichvili and Kuchinke, 2002) studied leadership in 62 cultures and found that, while different cultural groups were likely to have different conceptions of what leadership entailed, all positively associated transformational leadership behaviours with outstanding leadership.

Summary

As discussed earlier in the chapter, Bass and Steidlmeier's (1999) authentic transformational leadership theoretical framework extended the work of Burns' (1978) and Bass's (1985) seminal work in the area of transformational leadership, theorizing that, for a leader to be authentically transformational (and, therefore, to produce effective organizational outcomes), their leadership must possess a distinctly moral foundation. This focus on morality, and on the need for a leader whose actions were driven by their own morally sound values and principles, heralded the arrival of a new field of leadership research: *authentic leadership*. The concept of authenticity in leadership subsequently forms the focus of discussion later in the book (Chapter 9, "Authentic leadership"). First, however, it is necessary to revisit the theoretical field of emotional intelligence in greater depth (see Chapter 8, "Emotional intelligence"), not only due to its theorized relationship to leadership, but also because of its foundational influence on aspects of authentic leadership.

Expert insight

This expert insight chronicles the work of  Sammy Rangel, co-founder and CEO of Life After Hate, an organisation that exists to help individuals leave violent far-right groups and reintegrate positively into society. Life After Hate has successfully lowered recidivism rates amongst ex-prisoners, rehabilitated hundreds of former white supremacists and successfully challenged social media based hate speech. Having recently raised over $1 million via crowdfunding, the organization remains the only one of its kind to actively rehabilitate white supremacists and alt-right extremists in the US. Sammy is the author of FourBears: The Myths of Forgiveness and holds a master's degree in social work. Here he shares his insightful experience and valuable thoughts on Life After Hate – an organization that captures the very essence of what transformational leadership seeks to achieve.

"The motivation for Life After Hate started at a summit in Ireland against violent extremism. We work with 'formers' – people who have left extremist groups. Formers Anonymous is something that I created personally, bringing in best practice from the clinical field alongside strength-based approaches. I apply the concept of 'Formers' to the 12-step community where there is no space to address criminality, hatred or violence.

We have what is known as an 80–20 rule – you can spend 20 per cent of the conversation talking about the issues, but then you need to be spending 80 per cent of the time talking about solutions, strengths, etc. The best practice science behind that is what you spend your time talking about is what you crave for yourself.

I think that a problem that exists with older and existing models aimed at deradicalizing and rehabilitating people is that they spend a lot of time talking about problems. We are trying to reverse that – and we also try to remove language that can act as barriers for people to come to the table – religious connotations and language, for example.

Remarkable stories

I think that everyone that we help has a remarkable story. I remember cases where someone wanted to shoot up a mosque or church, kind of inspired by other similar events that had already happened in the country years ago, who ended up praying with the same people that they wanted to harm. These people ended up being accepted into the community they wanted to harm.

Then you get another real story about exiting extremist groups – which relates to someone I am working with now. This person has left an extremist group, but his community continues to condemn him (or what or who he used to be) – so much so, that it continues to impact his dealings in family court, in the emergency room, at his church and trying to access alcohol and drug services in his community. This community has basically tarred and feathered him. It's been a couple of years and he still can't make progress. Life after Hate can only do so much for you in the face of that. It's hard for that gentleman to make traction and a reminder that changing your life isn't always rainbows – you aren't always welcomed back with open arms.

Facing hostility

We face a lot of trouble from white supremacy groups. The first time I experienced it was with a white supremacy group based in Germany. That group took it upon themselves to do a 2-hour special on Life After Hate and they aired out all of our details, all of our pictures, all of our website info, and really acted with the intention to hopefully trigger someone into doing something to us.

The other members of Life After Hate (I'm not an ex-white supremacist but I do have a very similar trajectory and experience) are former members of white supremacy groups. Some have been out for more than 20 years, yet they're still daily named in those white supremacy circles. We have to turn over messages or screenshots where they are like 'Hey so-and-so will be at this university at 2 pm ... why don't one of you good chaps go and shake their hand and say hello?'. And you know, it's not shaking our hand that they're really coming for.

Fighting back

We get trolled a lot and don't really engage – we pass it on typically to law enforcement and they will log it and if there is something there that's enough they will follow up on it. The problem is, these groups are quite experienced in how to toe the line and get right up to the line without crossing it, while at the same time trying to trigger an event.

One of the significant differences between traditional gangs and white supremacy groups are that gangs are pretty localized – if you leave your neighbourhood you should be safe enough. But these white supremacy groups, they have international reach. They are an international problem. As a result, wherever we go as an organization, we are running into components of that same group who want to pass on the torch of hate to make sure we are never feeling too comfortable, regardless of where we are. So that is a real problem for us.

Can anyone be radicalized?

An older sociological belief was that the majority of people who commit crimes or engage in extremist activity have a broken home, a broken nuclear family, severe socio-economic issues, and so on. While that remains true in many cases, I believe that that model doesn't explain this extremist, radicalized group as it is today. Quite a few of our formers and co-founders were raised in privileged homes, for example, with highly educated parents, middle to upper class homes, what I'd consider wealthy.

So called alt-right groups (who are just white supremacists rebranding themselves) do a lot of recruiting from campuses. There are multiple groups following this same ideology, who demonstrate common factors around past experiences of trauma, abuse, neglect – but we also see a healthy model of people who don't fit that paradigm. You will be able to find markers, though. I remember a couple of brothers from Michigan who we really helped, and while they were with us, we were taking one of the brothers through a black neighbourhood – and he shared that he grew up there and he used to get beat up all the time. He was the white guy in the black neighbourhood – so you don't need to be a rocket scientist to see what started a fracture that in his case led to radicalism. If you look hard enough you can find the reasons.

But we can't afford to say they [radicalized individuals] are all poor, they're all broken – it's just not the case. There's not one way to answer how radicalization happens. I wish I could answer that. Everyone is scrambling for the way to create the recipe for fighting that. But I will say I think if there is an underlying component that contributes to this it is grievances. Like this young man from Michigan who grew up as a white male in a black neighbourhood, 'I got beat up all the time'. It's an unaddressed grievance.

Proximity matters

Proximity matters – if you remove yourself from a harmful environment you are now exposed to new environment, and that can leave you vulnerable. People who have similar unmet grievances and trauma often bond, and some might be radicalized already, and recruit their new friends. It can also happen organically – this sub-group say, 'Hey, we need to do something about this', and look for a solution and that can be engaging with extremist groups in some way. Social media has enabled that process a lot. Dylan Roof is a good example. He was the white supremacist who walked into a black church and started shooting. Dylan had never met another white supremacist, never been to a party, never been to a function, never been to a meeting where he chatted to one, never stood in an alley and smoked a cigarette with one. Nothing. His radicalization happened 100 per cent online.

On the internet the process of radicalization can happen in light speed compared to pre-internet days – what once took months or years can now take minutes or hours. You can consume content extremely fast. Take the 2016 US elections – it wasn't won by Republicans or Democrats but people that understood that they needed to start a kind of civil war (code for a race war). We had very high-ranking individuals in our Administration saying that if you stand for civil rights you are unAmerican – that civil rights were an attack to undermine American values. These kinds of things are what lead to radicalization. How can average Joe America defend against that kind of radicalization if they are completely blind and ignorant to the fact that it is happening?

One of the remarkable cases and a referral to us from the FBI was a young man whose father was in the police force. His dad was in the military and someone tagged him in a Black Lives Matter anti-police rally online, which led to other related videos popping up on his social feed. Then of course Blue Lives Matter pops up and he felt that Blue Lives Matter were really trying to protect his dad while Black Lives Matter were trying to kill his dad. Those were his words. The more he consumed Blue Lives Matter content, the stronger against Black Lives Matter he became. White lives versus black lives – that is what it ended up getting to in his head. Online, people actually thought this kid was a danger which is what bought the attention of the FBI to him (and why he was referred to us). But offline he was very mild, meek, isolated and an introverted kid. But he could have been triggered into taking action.

Just banter ...?

It starts out as banter. It doesn't start off as 'white supremacy' but with a comment – 'Man that's f**ked up, you know that happened to us too, that's BS [bulls**t], we're with you.' That kind of thing. Then, 'Hey we can do something about this.' You're there online as a radicalizer to hold a position, which is why online banter is so effective for engagement. The only person who loses out in that scenario is the person defending civil rights, because they don't get to take control of the conversation – they are always on the defence.

Addictive vs. criminal personalities

We see a lot of substance abuse – but caution your readers that this is not the only reason or way to be in these groups.

In Formers Anonymous we say that an addictive personality is different from a criminal personality. A very basic explanation: you could say that addiction personality lives in emotions and you could say that criminal personalities live in a cognitive state. I'm probably as an addict going to kill myself – but as a criminal personality I'm more likely to kill someone else. It's a very different energy. You can have a person who lives with both of those things but it's no longer two separate things when they combine – it becomes a third – a hybrid. And then what happens, when you bring those two kinds of personality together? You have this very intense human being who is capable of just about anything.

Addressing criminogenic needs

'Criminogenic needs' need to be addressed – because if you get someone sober who has a criminal personality, all you then have is a sober criminal. If you get someone stable on their medication, all you get is a criminal who is stable on their medication. An addict[ive] personality might separate from empathy out of shame – like, 'I'm not worthy to engage', or maybe they experience physiological motivations to feed a physical addiction that overrides their higher level cognitive functions (such as empathy). Compare that to the criminal personality – criminality involves a disregard for other human life – so criminal personalities just don't feel empathy. We have to understand these two groups separately.

Why don't people leave extremist groups?

Why don't people leave white supremacy groups when they realize it's a bad path to take? Well, why don't people lose the 5 pounds they've been trying to lose all year? We all maybe have a burning motivation to make a change but being able to actually see through that change is monumental. Monumental.

Our society is very judgemental. If you take my personal story and see what I did as a child, how violent and aggressive I became as a child, after people hear my story, the typical audience member says that they understand why I did what I did. That doesn't mean they say it was okay, or that what I did was justified. It means they understand the evolutionary process, that there were other forces at play. Sadly, our society doesn't want to admit that we play a part in creating this sub- culture of our community – but we all do.

Recidivism and reform

Here in the US we think that if you deal with drugs and alcohol then you deal with criminality. It's not that simple. In fact, I read a recent study where it shows that if you get someone stable on medication and sober and get them a job – the 'big 3' as these factors were formerly known [the goals of re-entry into mainstream society], it still doesn't move the needle on recidivism. Recidivism rates stay the same.

I've just been able to convince the State of Wisconsin that the state itself contributes to recidivism rates. In Wisconsin's previous re-entry programme, which were seen as successful, recidivism rates were 26 per cent in year one. By year three, recidivism rates went up to around 60 per cent – high, but still better than the state average. We hit a 6 per cent recidivism rate for the programme that I designed for them in years one, two and three of the programme. And we'd lowered the revocation rate for sex offenders by 75 per cent by the end of the three years, too. Those were the same men and women that society would say, 'If they wanted to change, they would change. They obviously don't want to.' We have all these reasons why we can justify why they fail – but until we say we play a part in the failure rate, we won't change it.

We do not concede, nor do we condemn

Life After Hate remains the one and only entity in America right now who is telling a white supremacist this is a safe place for you if you want to talk.

Everyone else is saying, 'Not in my town buddy – get the hell out.' Since Charlottesville alone, we've helped over 350 individuals. It's not that I think these
former white supremacists are victims. We create a space where we can address
specific issues. Life After Hate's unwritten position is we don't call people out,
we call people in. It's a very hard road to walk in the face of what we are
dealing with but it's really the secret sauce behind what we are doing. We are
honouring the humanity in even the ugliest of behaviours – there is a person
behind those behaviours. And what we ask ourselves is can we reach beyond
that behaviour and touch the person? That is what we try to do.

I think as an educator or family member, you don't need to concede but
you don't need to condemn either. We aren't conceding anything by listening
to these people. But we also don't feel the need to condemn them. What I'm
most proud of personally is the fact that my children see their dad fighting for
the civil rights for all people, including those who would condemn us. I think
ultimately the most important message is to recognize that no one is broken
beyond repair … with the right approach and the right spirit, just about anything becomes possible.

Honouring grievances

My violence was my voice because I lived in a world where no one listened. I
know that about myself now. I've been out of my gang well over 20 years now,
so I don't feel at risk of going back – but I can tell you that in the beginning,
[the early] days and months, I felt like that was the only alternative. Because
there's a lot of fear to change, a lot of uncertainty.

I mean, I had never been to a supermarket because I'd been incarcerated for
a long time. Aged 30, I went to a grocery store called Woodman's – it's like a
mall, a huge store, tens of thousands of square feet large, with 50 different
types of vegetables I'd never seen. I reached in for a vegetable that first day out
of prison and the water sprayed out of it and it scared the s–t out of me! While
I can laugh about it today, in that moment it was deeply concerning to me –
like, what else could be waiting to jump out at me? If I can't even deal with that
how will I cope with the big stuff?

People can get triggered, too. We see the elections, maybe shootings …
then the old thoughts pop up. But when they are surrounded by us, by Life
After Hate, we can tell them, it's not unusual for us to have those thoughts,
brother. It's okay. Just know that's not where you are at today. We can coach
people through that. People can reach out to us without judgement. We are
only here to talk and listen. We encourage them to reach out to us, and you
never know what can happen in the conversation, especially with people who
have been down that path and take a position of compassion and empathy as
a principle.

After Charlottesville, national media picked up our story, and publicized the
fact that the Trump Administration had reversed our funding. The media

spread the message that we were the only group in America trying to fight the issues that lay behind Charlottesville – and we went viral quickly thereafter. I think we raised almost $1 million in a couple of months.**''**

Find out more

- Life After Hate: www.lifeafterhate.org/.
- We Counter Hate: https://wecounterhate.com/.
- Enzinna, W. (July/August 2018). Inside the Radical, Uncomfortable Movement to Reform White Supremacists. *Mother Jones*. Available at: www.motherjones.com/ politics/2018/07/reform-white-supremacists-shane-johnson-life-after-hate/.

Questions

1   Apply the four transformational behaviours of full range leadership to this expert insight.
2   Revisit the theory in this chapter and find the following (referenced) quote: "Transformational leadership creates a circle of relationships and bonds which enriches all those connected together. Justice is served when such a state exists." Who was this attributed to and how do we see this quote in action in this expert insight?
3   Leadership is a dynamic process. How does the use of the term 'formers' by Life After Hate respect this dynamic quality?
4   Why is being judgemental a flawed approach and an abdication of our personal responsibility to contribute positively to society? What could we be doing instead that would be more productive?
5   What does Sammy's personal journey tell us about the potential for transformation?

Case study: "Sikhahlela Indoda Yamadoda"

Donald Woods, Editor of the *Daily Dispatch*, inspired his team to continue making their voice heard against the injustice of apartheid. He was to eventually risk his life in smuggling a manuscript across the South African border that told the real story about the death of his great friend, and political leader, Steve Biko, at the hands of the South African security police.

The Afrikaner Nationalists were voted into power in 1948, only three years after World War II had ended. The party had largely managed to consolidate support amongst Afrikaners by promising complete segregation of the races. Their victory was somewhat unexpected, snatching victory from the ruling United Party. Their use of the term *apartheid* (meaning *separatedness*) came to embody not only the key promise of their electoral campaign, but their identity as a governing party. The scars of apartheid – the legacy of the Afrikaner Nationalist Party – still remain. There were many great leaders that emerged during this period, all of whom demonstrated great courage and conviction in fighting the system. One such individual is Donald Woods, Editor of the *Daily Dispatch*.

Donald Woods CBE was born in East London, South Africa in 1933. A leading South African journalist and anti-apartheid activist, Woods died on 19 August 2001. His legacy, for both South Africa and the international community, remains a powerful, inspiring and memorable one. Donald Woods ultimately remains an inspiring figure for future generations of young leaders who believe in the role of journalism in holding those in power to account – and in the importance of fighting tirelessly against injustices, wherever they occur.

Woods: his early career

Woods stood out as a charismatic presence throughout his school and college career. He was once reprimanded by his teacher during a college debate for misusing his natural eloquence to manipulate the opinions of others – relying more readily on rhetoric than fact to make his point and win debates. A naturally intelligent and able communicator, Woods studied law at university – although his first choice, had there been a degree available at the time, would have been journalism.

Clearly a talented communicator, Woods had sought out an academic vocation that was to eloquently and intellectually inform his journalistic career, allowing him to fight state interference of the press with the force of his legal knowledge. In their first three years of governance, for example, the Afrikaner National Party passed the first of over 300 racial laws, beginning with the Prohibition of Mixed Marriages Act, the Immorality Act (making sexual contact with a person of another race a crime), the Population Registration Act (requiring racial classification of all South Africans as white, black, coloured or Asiatic), the Suppression of Communism Act (giving the state power to declare anyone a Communist if they attempted to challenge racial laws) and the Bantu Authorities Act (a means of forcing black South Africans back into tribalism, thus preventing them from participating in national politics). The laws that followed were designed to reach into, and subjugate, every area of life for black South Africans – the Bantu Education Act, for example, made it illegal to gain the same education as whites, and the Reservation of Separate Amenities Act essentially made it impossible for blacks to use the same public amenities (for example, toilets, park benches) as whites. The Criminal Law Amendment Act made it illegal for a South African of any race to oppose any of the laws.

Woods' training in law was to assist him extensively in his knowledge of criminal law, statute law and the law of defamation at a time when the Afrikaner Nationalists had begun to crack down hard on newspapers that they deemed to be troublemakers. In fact Woods was to initiate more than 20 defamation lawsuits against the Government, winning them all (and donating the proceeds from each victory to the Institute of Race Relations or to the Progressive Party). The Government had actually installed more than 20 statutes that governed what could or could not be published in the press – empowering them to close down publications, ban and jail editors without explanation.

Woods: his formative influences

While Woods admitted that his views on racial segregation, as a young man, were discriminatory and ignorant, they were to undergo a revolution based on his subsequent experiences and exposure to role models such as Harold Levy, one of Woods' law professors at the University of Cape Town.

One of their first exchanges within the lecture theatre appeared less than auspicious, but was, nonetheless, remarkably formative. Levy had asked Woods to state his opinion of the way in which racial issues should be approached in the Transkei region (where Woods grew up). Woods was to state a racist and ignorant answer (that blacks should be sent back to the reserves, and that it was no good educating them). Harold Levy initially challenged him, asking him if he really believed such a statement. Over the following months Woods became increasingly uneasy about his own comments, regarding Levy's apparent disinterest in reopening the topic as unnerving in his silence. Levy was to exert a profound effect on Woods, stimulating him to critically question his own beliefs. Woods was to become ashamed of his earlier comments and would go on to experience a revolution in his world-view.

Woods remembered reading a statement by Abraham Lincoln ("What is morally wrong can never be politically right") as another defining moment in the shaping of his political and ideological beliefs. Meeting a black student from the US also exerted a profound effect, forcing him to question the assumption of black inferiority in South Africa and to reason for the first time that the environmental factors caused by apartheid – and not biological factors – were responsible for the vast differences in sociological conditions (living conditions, literacy) observed between black and white South Africans. As the reader will realize by the end of this case study, it is incredible to note the ideological journey that Woods traversed – from socialized, conservative and racist to one of the strongest and intellectually reasoned anti-apartheid voices in South Africa.

By 1955, Woods had developed his own political ideas, having read voraciously on the topic of constitutional law as well as studying extensively the political systems of North America, Australia and Switzerland. While he briefly considered a foray into politics, he adopted a different approach when his letters and articles about the Federal Party (of which he was a member and supporter) started to receive support from the *Daily Dispatch*, which regularly published his contributions. This allowed him to reach a wide audience and was to pre-empt his integration into the *Dispatch* staff as a cub reporter.

Another formative experience came from his travels to London, England, in 1958, where he first experienced racial integration and saw white men undertaking menial jobs that in South Africa would have been reserved only for black South Africans. Woods also markedly honed his journalistic skills during his tenure in England, writing for a number of newspapers, which included Fleet Street experience as a sub-editor and later as Editor of the *Daily Herald*. He was to continue his working travels, which took him to Canada, but he returned to South Africa after news of the Sharpeville tragedy of 1960 had reached him. He felt a sense of urgency to return to his country.

By now an agent of change, Woods was a vociferous voice against apartheid and felt the need to make a difference. His interest in returning to the *Dispatch* was based largely on the paper's aggressive anti-Government stance.

The greatest influence on Donald Woods came ultimately in the form of Steve Biko, a young political activist who the Afrikaner Government viewed at the time as "the most dangerous man in the country". For most of his life, Woods had been able to function effectively as a voice against apartheid from 'within the system', but it was meeting Biko that ultimately changed both his modus operandi and forced him to become a voice operating from outside of the system. His introduction to Biko largely came in 1973 when he was made an honorary member of NUSAS (the National Union of South African Students). Previously a member, Biko had broken away from what he felt was ineffectual white liberalism to form the black-only SASO (South African Students Organisation). Woods' reaction to SASO was initially a negative one. He attacked SASO in his editorials – that is, until he came into contact with Dr. Mamphela Ramphele,[3] a black doctor who worked closely with Biko and whom Biko sent to set up a meeting with Woods. This was to lead to their first meeting (at the time Biko was already banned) and an elucidating conversation about black consciousness. Woods was to view Biko as a man with a remarkable gift of communication, and Biko subsequently sent a young black journalist, Mapetla Mohapi, to write a column for the *Dispatch* to cover what he termed the "Black Consciousness Beat".

Woods was well placed to inform Biko of his conversations with the then Defence Minister P.W. Botha who had banned Biko and who was later to become Prime Minister. Woods made a point of facilitating meetings between Biko and visiting members of state (for example, Senator Dick Clark, Chairman of the US Senate Foreign Relations Committee), as he believed it would keep Biko safe from extreme actions on the part of the South African security forces.

Woods: editor of the Daily Dispatch

As a reporter, Woods set out his stall early. A notably early example was an open letter to Prime Minister Dr Verwoerd (Woods was to write many 'open letters' in this style to Afrikaner Nationalist cabinet members during his journalistic career). This particular letter reminded Verwoerd of his Nazi sympathies and likened Hitler's master race ideology to the Afrikaner Nationals' policy of apartheid. Another example was an open 'letter to the editor' that Woods had written to the Editor of the *Dispatch*, after he felt that the Editor had written an uncharacteristically racist article about a singer, Miriam Makeba, and her United Nations activities. Despite having a family to support and a mortgage to pay, Woods continuously placed his job and reputation on the line in in order to maintain and follow his own moral compass. The case of Miriam Makeba would not be the first – or the last – time that he would risk the ire of the Afrikaner Nationalist government – sometimes even risking imprisonment - to support his ideological beliefs.

In February 1965, Donald Woods was appointed Editor of the *Daily Dispatch* at the relatively young age of 31. He had begun his journalistic career on the staff of newspapers in London, Wales and Canada before joining the *Daily Dispatch* as a reporter. Rising to sub-editor, his roles at the newspaper included that of political correspondent, columnist and then Deputy Editor before becoming Editor. He assembled a strong editorial team and from the beginning of his tenure displayed a strong ideological stance against the regime of apartheid that guided the anti-apartheid stance of the *Dispatch*. Woods integrated the newspaper, recruiting black journalists and featuring pictures and articles about black as well as white South Africans and made it a policy to run regular features on successful black Americans (e.g. Martin Luther King, Muhammad Ali). The *Dispatch* also ran a 'name and shame' campaign against shops that made black customers wait for white customers to be served first – a practice that led to phone threats and bomb threats against Woods and his staff.

Woods also spearheaded the growth and diversification of the *Dispatch* to include a wide range of different companies, partly as a means of hedging against financial threats to the newspaper itself (e.g. as a result of advertisers sympathetic to the Government's policies pulling out their ads in protest). His technological investments made the newspaper the first in Africa to be automated and to produce high quality colour pictures.

Donald Woods was to have private interviews with both Prime Minister Verwoerd and his replacement, Prime Minister Vorster. In his first meeting with Vorster he vociferously argued against apartheid and asked the Prime Minister how he could reconcile this racist policy with his Christian beliefs.

The culture at the *Dispatch* became one of principle, where the Chairman of the newspaper, Denis Ross-Thompson, once put his own job on the line to defend Woods' appointment as Editor. There were many strong minds and strong personalities on the team, including Terry Briceland, who helped to triple advertising revenue for the paper. At one point, Woods and two of his colleagues even bought houses on the same street, just a few hundred metres from each other, so close were their friendships.

Woods: banned journalist

By 1977, Woods' family had started to receive threats, due mostly to the aggressive stance that he, and his newspaper, had taken against the apartheid regime. Mapetla Mohapi was to die that year under police interrogation. Mapetla's tragic death was the twenty-third in custody since a jail-without-trial law was introduced. Closely after Mapetla's death, on 18 August 1977, Steve Biko was also jailed without trial (the fourth time, in his case). By 13 September that year, Biko had been killed in detention.

On 14 September, the *Daily Dispatch* ran the front page headline "Biko dies in detention", followed by the words "We salute a hero of the nation" in both English and in Xhosa ("Sikhahlela Indoda Yamadoda") alongside a colour picture of Biko.

On 16 September 1977, two days after the initial article, Woods' *Daily Dispatch* ran a lead article that strongly criticized the then Minister of Justice Jimmy Kruger over Biko's death. The editorial asked key questions about the coroner's report into

Biko's death. Woods was to accompany Biko's wife, Ntsiki Biko, to view his body alongside a staff photographer. It seemed clear from the first moment they viewed the body that the official story of a hunger strike was an incorrect one. The staff photographer took extensive photographs, making a number of copies and hiding them from the Security Police in a variety of locations. Woods spent more than an hour that evening sketching his impressions of the wounds that he had witnessed on Steve Biko's face.

By 19 October 1977, Woods was served with a five-year banning order under the Internal Security Act – a ban served to him at Johannesburg Airport. The order required him to stay within his home. The effect of Woods' ban on the staff of the *Daily Dispatch* could have been disastrous but, under the guidance of Deputy Editor George Farr, the Managing Director Terry Briceland, and in the hands of dedicated journalistic staff, the newspaper continued to operate with much efficiency. Straight after Woods' detention, the newspaper was to run with the story of their editor's ban. The ban was extensive in its conditions and, among other causes, it prevented Woods from writing anything, from entering any printing or publishing premises and from being in the presence of more than one person at any time. It was normal for a ban to be extended from the moment it ended, so this five-year ban was likely to be extended another five years after it had been completed. It was effectively a life sentence that was designed to deny Woods his right to write as well as his livelihood and power as a journalist.

It took ten days for Woods to begin to flout the ban, when he began work on a book about Steve Biko. He had already secured a publishing agreement with a London publisher and began writing in earnest. This was an extensive undertaking, and Woods had to write everything at night to avoid spot visits by the Security Police, who may have found him writing. The book contained a damning indictment of the South African Government and led to Woods and his family planning to flee from South Africa. Their plans were accelerated following a vicious attack on their 5-year-old daughter Mary. The Security Police were responsible for the attack, and had intercepted a gift of children's-size T-shirts (carrying the image of Steve Biko) that had been addressed to the Woods family. They had soaked the T-shirts in Ninhydrin (a chemical that causes burning when it comes into contact with skin) before sending them on to the Woods family in their original packaging.

Woods and his family were to escape across the Lesotho border – the plan was that Woods would travel disguised as a priest, while his wife Wendy, travelling with their children, would travel separately. The family would only reunite after they had safely crossed over the Lesotho border. They were eventually granted safe exile in Britain. Woods had not only achieved freedom from persecution for himself and his family, but had also smuggled out a manuscript detailing the true story behind Biko's death in detention. This story was to form the basis of the globally acclaimed film *Cry Freedom* and the book *Biko*. In a touching detail of his escape, Woods had been faced – at 4 am – with a flooded river that he needed to cross, and which stood in the way of him reaching Lesotho in time for a pre-arranged phone call with his wife Wendy that would have informed her of whether she should continue with her travel across the Lesotho border. He had almost run out of time when a man named Tami Vundla, who Woods had defended ten years earlier, recognized him and offered to drive him to the nearest bridge.

Woods was awarded several honorary doctorates and a CBE by Queen Elizabeth in 2000 in recognition for his services to human rights. Among his many other extensive accomplishments, Woods also became the first private citizen in history to be invited to address the United Nations Security Council. His view was that apartheid was an affront against all of humanity, and as such was logically the concern of all humanity.

Woods passed away on 19 August 2001. He remains one of the most respected voices in journalism for his talent, courage and ideologically driven actions. His editorship of the *Daily Dispatch* and his ability to lead his editorial team with vision, skill and integrity played a significant role in opening the eyes of the world to the horrors and injustice of apartheid and helped to shape the future course of a nation.

Find out more

- Biko, S. (2002). *I Write What I Like: Selected Writings* (ed. C.R. Aelred Stubbs). Chicago, IL: University of Chicago Press.
- Woods, D. (1981). *Asking for Trouble: Autobiography of a Banned Journalist.* New York: Atheneum.
- Woods, D. (1991). *Biko.* Revised 3rd ed. New York: Holt Paperbacks.

Questions

1 Donald Woods was, without doubt, a charismatic leader. Identify one of the earliest examples of his charismatic abilities given in this case study.
2 As stated by Bass (1985, p. 31) earlier in the chapter, "charisma is a necessary ingredient of transformational leadership, but by itself it is not sufficient to account for the transformational process." Why would Woods not have been able to use his charisma to transform others in his early pre-*Dispatch* days?
3 How did Woods demonstrate intellectual stimulation in his business affairs?
4 As Editor, how did Woods safeguard the *Dispatch* against threats while simultaneously retaining its outspoken anti-apartheid stance?
5 Woods demonstrated a conservative view with regard to his early Transkei comments to Harold Levy, and with his initial reaction to SASO – yet he radically changed his approach in both cases. What caused him to change his mind?
6 Woods is an authentic transformational leader. Why is he such an effective example of such a leader?
7 The importance of communicating a vision is important for the transformational leader. As quoted earlier in the chapter, "In communicating the vision and strategy, leaders also need to exhibit emotive aspects of themselves, which will inspire everyone to follow" (Jones, 2002, p. 271). How did Woods achieve this goal?

8   Donald Woods was a great leader. Was he born a great leader or was he made into the type of leader he became by virtue of his experiences? Refer to key examples within this case study to illustrate your point.

CHAPTER 7 QUIZ

1   Earlier in the chapter, it was stated that, "While seductive, charisma alone is clearly not enough to safeguard either long-term effectiveness or profitability for an individual or organization." Provide evidence from within the chapter that supports this statement.
2   Identify the *four I's* of transformational leadership.
3   What is the difference between attributed and behavioural charisma?
4   Provide a definition of transformational leadership.
5   Identify five positive outcomes of transformational leadership (e.g. lower employee turnover).
6   How can transformational leadership behaviours be measured?
7   According to this chapter, what is the key contention of the 'new leadership school'?
8   Name and define the three transactional behaviours.
9   What is the augmentation effect?
10   Which transactional behaviour is linked particularly positively with transformational behaviours?
11   Define full range leadership.
12   How did transformational leadership influence the development of authentic leadership (the focus of Chapter 9, "Authentic leadership")?
13   How might culture mediate perceptions of leadership?
14   Provide an example of a manager who demonstrated management by exception – passive behaviour – and identify how it detrimentally impacted the organization.
15   Provide an example of a situation where a leader clearly exhibits: (i) intellectual stimulation; (ii) contingent reward behaviour; (iii) individualized consideration; and (iv) inspirational motivation (each of the four examples must involve different leaders). For example, Barack Obama displayed intellectual stimulation in his innovative approach to fundraising during his first presidential campaign.

Notes

1 Quoted in an interview conducted for this book with the CEO of Life After Hate, Sammy Rangel, which appears in the expert insight "Life After Hate" that appears later in this chapter.
2 The Leader Behaviour Description Questionnaire (LBDQ) was developed by staff of the Personnel Research Board at The Ohio State University.
3 Dr. Ramphele remains a prominent political voice within South Africa.

References

Ardichvili, A. (2001). Leadership Styles of Russian Enterprise Managers. *The Effect of Transactional and Transformation Performance Improvement Quarterly*, 14(1), pp. 96–117.

Ardichvili, A. and Kuchinke, K.P. (2002). Leadership Styles and Cultural Values among Managers and Subordinates: A Comparative Study of Four Countries of the Former Soviet Union, Germany and the US. *Human Resource Development International*, 5(1), pp. 99–117.

Ardichvili, A., Cardozo, R.N. and Gasparishvili, A. (1998). Leadership Styles and Management Practices of Russian Entrepreneurs: Implications for Transferability of Western HRD Interventions. *Human Resource Development Quarterly*, 9(2), pp. 145–155.

Ashforth, B.E. and Humphrey, R.H. (1995). Emotion in the Workplace: A Reappraisal. *Human Relations*, 48(2), pp. 97–125.

Ashkanasy, N.M. and Tse, B. (2000). Transformational Leadership as Management of Emotion: A Conceptual Review. In N.M. Ashkanasy, C.E.J. Hartel and W.J. Zerbe (eds.), *Emotions in the Workplace*. Westport, CT: Quorum Books, pp. 221–235.

Auerbach, A. and Webber, A.M. (1987). Red Auerbach on Management. *Harvard Business Review*, 65 (March–April), pp. 84–91.

Avolio, B.J. (1999). *Full Leadership Development: Building the Vital Forces in Organisations*. Thousand Oaks, CA: Sage.

Avolio, B.J. and Bass, B.M. (1995). Individual Consideration Viewed at Multiple Levels of Analysis: A Multi-Level Framework for Identifying the Diffusion of Transformational Leadership. *Leadership Quarterly*, 6(2), pp. 199–218.

Avolio, B.J. and Howell, J.M. (1992). The Impact of Leader Behaviour and Leader Follower Personality Match on Satisfaction and Unit Performance. In K.E. Clarke, M.B. Clarke and D.R. Campbell (eds.), *Impact of Leadership*. Greensboro, NC: The Center for Creative Leadership.

Avolio, B.J. and Yammarino, F.J. (2002). *Transformational and Charismatic Leadership: The Road Ahead*. Oxford: Elsevier Science.

Avolio, B.J., Bass, B.M. and Jung, D.I. (1995). *Construct Validation and Norms for the Multifactor Leadership Questionnaire (MLQ-Form 5x)*. New York: Center for Leadership Studies, Binghamton University and State University of New York.

Avolio, B., Bass, D. and Jung, D.I. (1999). Re-examining the Components of Transformational and Transactional Leadership Using the Multifactor Leadership Questionnaire. *Journal of Occupational and Organizational Psychology*, 72(4), pp. 441–462.

Barling, J., Weber, T. and Kelloway, E.K. (1996). Effects of Transformational Leadership Training on Attitudinal and Financial Outcomes: A Field Experiment. *Journal of Applied Psychology*, 81(3), pp. 827–832.

Barling, J., Slater, F. and Kelloway, E.K. (2000). Transformational Leadership and Emotional Intelligence: An Exploratory Study. *Leadership and Organization Development Journal*, 21(6), pp. 157–161.

Bass, B.M. (1985). *Leadership and Performance Beyond Expectations*. New York: Free Press.

Bass, B. (1990). From Transactional to Transformational Leadership: Learning to Share the Vision. *Organizational Dynamics*, 18 (Winter), pp. 19–31.

Bass, B.M. (1996a). *A New Paradigm of Leadership: An Inquiry into Transformational Leadership*. Alexandria, VA: US Army Research Institute for the Behavioural and Social Sciences.

Bass, B.M. (1996b). Is There Universality in the Full Range Model of Leadership? *International Journal of Public Administration*, 19(6), pp. 731–761.

Bass, B.M. (1998). *Transformational Leadership: Industry, Military, and Educational Impact*. Mahwah, NJ: Lawrence Erlbaum Associates.

Bass, B.M. (1999). Two Decades of Research and Development in Transformational Leadership. *European Journal of Work and Organisational Psychology*, 8(1), pp. 9–32.

Bass, B.M. and Avolio, B.J. (1990). *Transformational Leadership Development: Manual for the Multifactor Leadership Questionnaire*. Palo Alto, CA: Consulting Psychologist Press.

Bass, B.M. and Avolio, B.J. (1993). Transformational Leadership: A Response to Critiques. In M.M. Chemmers and R. Ayman (eds.), *Leadership Theory & Research: Perspectives and Directions*. San Diego, CA: Academic Press, pp. 49–88.

Bass, B.M. and Avolio, B.J. (1994). *Improving Organizational Effectiveness through Transformational Leadership*. Thousand Oaks, CA: Sage.

Bass, B.M. and Avolio, B.J. (1997). *Full Range Leadership Development: Manual for the Multifactor Leadership Questionnaire*. Redwood City, CA: Mind Garden.

Bass, B.M. and Avolio, B.J. (1999). Re-examining the Components of Transformational and Transactional Leadership Using the Multifactor Leadership Questionnaire. *Journal of Occupational & Organizational Psychology*, 72(4), pp. 441–462.

Bass, B.M. and Steidlmeier, P. (1999). Ethics, Character, and Authentic Transformational Leadership Behavior. *Leadership Quarterly*, 10(2), pp. 181–217.

Bennis, W. and Nanus, B. (1985). *Leaders: The Strategies for Taking Charge*. New York: Harper & Row.

Boehnke, K., Bontis, N., DiStefano J.J. and DiStefano, A.C. (2003). Transformational Leadership: An Examination of Cross-National Differences and Similarities. *Leadership and Organization Development Journal*, 24(1), pp. 5–15.

Bollen, K.A. (1989). *Structural Equations with Latent Variables*. New York: Wiley.

Bryman, A. (1992). *Charisma and Leadership in Organisations*. London: Sage.

Burns, J.M. (1978). *Leadership*. New York: Harper & Row.

Bycio, P., Hackett, R.D. and Allen, J.S. (1995). Further Assessments of Bass's (1985) Conceptualization of Transactional and Transformational Leadership. *Journal of Applied Psychology*, 80(4), pp. 468–478.

Carless, S.A. (1998). Assessing the Discriminant Validity of the Transformational Leadership Behaviour as Measured by the MLQ. *Journal of Occupational and Organizational Psychology*, 71(4), pp. 353–358.

Carlson, D.S. and Perrewe, P.L. (1995). Institutionalisation of Organisational Ethics through Transformational Leadership. *Journal of Business Ethics*, 14(10), pp. 829–838.

Carnegie, D. (1995). *Performance of North Sea Offshore Platform Supervisors*. Doctoral Dissertation, Aberdeen University, Scotland.

Caruso, D.R., Mayer, J.D. and Salovey, P. (2002). Relation of an Ability Measure of Emotional Intelligence to Personality. *Journal of Personality Assessment*, 79(2), pp. 306–320.

Chanoch, J. and House, R. (2001). Dynamics of Charismatic Leadership: A Process Theory, Simulation Model, and Tests. *Leadership Quarterly*, 12(1), pp. 75–112.

Conger, J.A. and Kanungo, R.N. (1987). Towards a Behavioral Theory of Charismatic Leadership in Organizational Settings. *Academy of Management Review*, 12(4), pp. 637–647.

Costa, P. and McCrae, R. (1992). Four Ways Five Factors Are Basic. *Personality and Individual Differences*, 13, pp. 653–655.

Davis, D.D., Guaw, P., Luo, J. and Maahs, C.J. (1997). Need for Continuous Improvement, Organization Citizenship, Transformational Leadership, and Service Climate in a Chinese State Enterprise. Paper presented to the Society for Organizational and Industrial Psychology, St Louis, MO.

Den Hartog, D.N., Van Muijen, J.J. and Koopman, P.L. (1997). Transactional versus Transformational Leadership: An Analysis of the MLQ. *Journal of Occupational and Organizational Psychology*, 70(1), pp. 19–29.

Den Hartog, D.N., House, R.J., Hanges, P.J., Ruiz-Quintanilla, S.A., Dorfman, P.W., Abdalla, I.A., Adetoun, B.S., Aditya, R.N., Agourram, H., Akande, A., Akande, B.E., Akerblom, S., Altschul, C., Alvarez-Backus, E., Andrews, J., Arias, M.E., Arif, M. S., Ashkanasy, N.M., Asllani, A. … Zhou, J. (1999). Culture Specific and Cross-Culturally Generalizable Implicit Leadership Theories: Are Attributes of Charismatic/Transformational Leadership Universally Endorsed? *Leadership Quarterly*, 10(2), pp. 219–256.

Dobosz, R.P. and Beaty, L.A. (1999). The Relationship between Athletic Participation and High School Students' Leadership Ability. *Adolescence*, 34(133), pp. 215–220.

Doherty, A.J. and Danylchuk, K.E. (1996). Transformational and Transactional Leadership in Interuniversity Athletics Management. *Journal of Sport Management*, 10(3), pp. 292–309.

Downton, J.V. (1973). *Rebel Leadership: Commitment and Charisma in a Revolutionary Process.* New York: Free Press.

Dubinsky, A.J., Yammarino, F.J. and Jolson, M.A. (1995). An Examination of Linkages between Personal Characteristics and Dimensions of Transformational Leadership. *Journal of Business & Psychology*, 9, pp. 315–344.

Dvir, T., Eden, D., Avolio, B.J. and Shamir, B. (2002). Impact of Transformational Leadership on Follower Development and Performance: A Field Experiment. *Academy of Management Journal*, 45(4), pp. 735–744.

Elenkov, D. (1998). Can American Management Concepts Work in Russia? A Cross-Cultural Comparative Study. *California Management Review*, 40(4), pp. 133–156.

Gardner, W.L. and Cleavenger, D. (1998). The Impression Management Strategies Associated with Transformational Leadership at the World-Class Level: A Psychohistorical Assessment. *Management Communication Quarterly*, 12(1), pp. 3–41.

Geyer, A.L. and Steyrer, J. (1998). Transformational Leadership, Classical Leadership Dimensions and Performance Indicators in Savings Banks. *Leadership Quarterly*, 47, pp. 397–420.

Gillespie, N.A. and Mann, L. (2000). *The Building Blocks of Trust: The Role of Transformational Leadership and Shared Values in Predicting Team Members' Trust in their Leader.* Melbourne: Melbourne Business School, University of Melbourne.

Goldberg, A. and Chandler, T. (1991). The Role of Athletics: The Social World of High School Adolescents. *Youth & Society*, 21(2), pp. 238–250.

Goleman, D. (1998). *Working with Emotional Intelligence.* New York: Bantam.

Gough, H.G. (1987). *California Psychological Inventory Manual.* Palo Alto, CA: Consulting Psychologists Press.

Graustrom, K. (1986). Interactional Dynamics between Teen-Age Leaders and Followers in the Classroom. *Journal of School Psychology*, 24, pp. 335–341.

Hater, J.J. and Bass, B.M. (1988). Superiors' Evaluations and Subordinates Perceptions of Transformational and Transactional Leadership. *Journal of Applied Psychology*, 73(4), pp. 695–702.

House, R.J. (1977). A 1976 Theory of Charismatic Leadership. In J.G. Hunt and L.L. Larson (eds.), *Leadership: The Cutting Edge.* Carbondale, IL: Southern Illinois University Press, pp. 189–204.

House, R.J. and Podsakoff, P.M. (1994). Leadership Effectiveness and Future Research Direction. In G. Greenberg (ed.), *Organisational Behaviour: The State of the Science.* Hillsdale, NJ: Lawrence Erlbaum Associates, pp. 45–82.

Howell, J.M. and Avolio, B.J. (1993). Transformational Leadership, Transactional Leadership, Locus of Control, and Support for Innovation: Key Predictors of Consolidated Business Unit Performance. *Journal of Applied Psychology*, 78(6), pp. 891–902.

Hunt, J. (1991). *Leadership: A New Synthesis.* Thousand Oaks, CA: Sage.

Johnson, A.M., Vernon, P.A., McCarthy, J.M., Molso, M., Harris, J.A. and Jang, K.J. (1998). Nature vs Nurture: Are Leaders Born or Made? A Behavior Genetic Investigation of Leadership Style. *Twin Research*, 1, pp. 216–223.

Jones, G. (2002). Performance Excellence: A Personal Perspective on the Link between Sport and Business. *Journal of Applied Sport Psychology*, 14, pp. 268–281.

Jung, D.I., Bass, B.M. and Sosik, J.J. (1995). Bridging Leadership and Culture: A Theoretical Consideration of Transformational Leadership and Collectivistic Cultures. *Journal of Leadership Studies*, 2(4), pp. 3–18.

Kelloway, E.K., Barling, J. and Helleur, J. (2000). Enhancing Transformational Leadership: The Roles of Training and Feedback. *Leadership and Organizational Development Journal*, 21(3), pp. 145–148.

Kotter, J.P. (1990). What Leaders Really Do. *Harvard Business Review*, 90(3), pp. 103–111.

Kouzes, J.M. and Posner, B.Z. (1992). Ethical Leaders: An Essay about Being in Love. *Journal of Business Ethics*, 11 (5–6), pp. 479–484.

Leithwood, K., Tomlinson, D. and Genge, M. (1996). Transformational School Leadership. In K. Leithwood, J. Chapman, D. Corson, P. Hallinger and A. Hart (eds.), *International Handbook of Educational Leadership and Administration*. Dordrecht, The Netherlands: Kluwer Academic Publishers, pp. 785–840.

Lievens, F., Van Geit, P. and Coetsier, P. (1997). Identification of Transformational Leadership Qualities: An Examination of Potential Biases. *European Journal of Work and Organizational Psychology*, 6(4), pp. 415–430.

Lowe, K.B., Kroeck, K.G. and Sivasubramaniam, N. (1996). Effectiveness Correlates of Transformational and Transactional Leadership: A Meta-Analytic Review of the MLQ Literature. *Leadership Quarterly*, 7(3), pp. 385–425.

Lusch, R.F. and Serpkeuci, R.R. (1990). Personal Differences, Job Tension, Job Outcomes, and Store Performance: A Study of Retail Managers. *Journal of Marketing*, 54(1), pp. 85–101.

McClelland, D.C. and Boyatzis, R.E. (1982). Leadership Motive Patterns and Long-Term Success in Management. *Journal of Applied Psychology*, 67(9), pp. 737–743.

McNutt, R. and Wright, P.C. (1995). Coaching Your Employees: Applying Sports Analogies to Business. *Executive Development*, 8(11), pp. 27–32.

Morales, J.F. and Molero, F. (1995). Leadership in Two Types of Healthcare Organization. In J.M. Peiró, F. Prieto, J.L. Meliá and O. Luque (eds.), *Work and Organizational Psychology: European Contributions of the Nineties*. Hove, UK: Erlbaum, pp. 209–221.

Parker, S.K. (1998). Enhancing Role Breadth Self-Efficacy: The Roles of Job Enrichment and Other Organizational Interventions. *Journal of Applied Psychology*, 83(6), pp. 835–852.

Pascarella, E.T. and Smart, J.C. (1991). Impact of Intercollegiate Athletic Participation for African-American and Caucasian Men: Some Further Evidence. *Journal of College Student Development*, 32(2), pp. 123–130.

Pillai, R., Schreisheim, C.A. and Williams, E.S. (1999). Fairness Perceptions and Trust as Mediators for Transformational and Transactional Leadership – A Two Sample Study. *Journal of Management*, 25(6), pp. 897–933.

Podsakoff, P.M., MacKenzie, S.B. and Bommer, W.H. (1996). Transformational Leader Behaviors and Substitutes for Leadership as Determinants of Employee Satisfaction, Commitment, Trust, and Organizational Citizenship Behaviors. *Journal of Management*, 22(2), pp. 259–298.

Ross, S.M. and Offermann, L.R. (1997). Transformational Leaders: Measurement of Personality Attributes and Work Group Performance. *Personality and Social Science Bulletin*, 23(10), pp. 1078–1086.

Ryan, F. (1989). Participation in Intercollegiate Athletics: Affective Outcomes. *Journal of College Student Development*, 30(2), pp. 122–128.

Savin-Williams, R.C. (1979). Dominance Hierarchies in Groups of Early Adolescents. *Child Development*, 50, pp. 923–935.

Shamir, B. (1991). The Charismatic Leadership: Alternative Explanations and Predictions. *Leadership Quarterly*, 2(2), pp. 81–104.

Shamir, B., House, R.J. and Arthur, M.B. (1993). The Motivational Effects of Charismatic Leadership: A Self-Concept Based Theory. *Organisational Science*, 4(4), pp. 577–594.

Shamir, B., Zakay, E., Breinin, E. and Popper, M. (1998). Correlates of Charismatic Leader Behaviour in Military Units: Subordinates' Attitudes, Unit Characteristics, and Superiors' Appraisals of Leader Performance. *Academy of Management Journal*, 41(4), pp. 387–409.

Snyder, E. and Spreitzer, E. (1992). Scholars and Athletes. *Youth and Society*, 23, pp. 507–522.

Sosik, J.J. and Godshalk, V.M. (2000). Leadership Styles, Mentoring Functions and Job-Related Stress: A Conceptual Model and Preliminary Study. *Journal of Organizational Behaviour*, 12(4), pp. 365–390.

Sosik, J.J. and Megerian, L.E. (1999). Understanding Leader Emotional Intelligence and Performance: The Role of Self-Other Agreement on Transformational Leadership Perceptions. *Group and Organizational Management*, 24(3), pp. 367–390.

Soucie, D. (1994). Effective Managerial Leadership in Sport Organizations. *Journal of Sport Management*, 8(1), pp. 1–13.

Stewart, C.J., Smith, C.A. and Denton, R.E. (1994). *Persuasion and Social Movements*. 3rd ed. Long Grove, IL: Waveland Press.

Tichy, N.M. and Devanna, M.A. (1986). *The Transformational Leader*. New York: Wiley.

Tichy, N. and Devanna, M. (1990). *Transformational Leadership*. New York: Wiley.

Trompenaars, F. (1993). *Riding the Waves of Culture: Understanding Diversity in Business*. London: Economist Books.

Waldman, D.A., Bass, B.M. and Yammarino, F.J. (1990). Adding to Contingent Reward Behavior: The Augmenting Effect of Charismatic Leadership. *Group and Organizational Studies*, 15, pp. 381–394.

Weber, M. (1924). *The Theory of Social and Economic Organization* (trans. T. Parsons). New York: Free Press.

Weese, W.J. (1994). A Leadership Discussion with Dr Bernard Bass. *Journal of Sport Management*, 8(3), pp. 179–189.

Wofford, J.C., Goodwin, V.L. and Whittington, J.L. (1998). A Field Study of a Cognitive Approach to Understanding Transformational and Transactional Leadership. *Leadership Quarterly*, 9(1), pp. 55–84.

Yukl, G. (1994). *Leadership in Organizations*. Upper Saddle River, NJ: Prentice-Hall.

Zhu, W., Avolio, D., Riggio, R. and Sosik, J. (2011). The Effect of Authentic Transformational Leadership on Follower and Group Ethics. *Leadership Quarterly*, 22(5), pp. 801–817.

Other resources

See PowerPoint slides on the companion website at www.routledge.com/9780367374822.

8

EMOTIONAL INTELLIGENCE

> *"I learnt to fail fast – to be honest that I wasn't succeeding and move on quickly to a*
> *better strategy."*
> *– Lauren Grech, CEO of LLG Agency*[1]

The study of emotional intelligence (EI) in business appears at once seductive and full of promise. It remains a popular concept within the practitioner literature and has even led to claims of revolutionary activity – an "affective revolution" (Barsade *et al.*, 2003, p. 3) in the field of organizational behaviour. The words of JPMorgan Chase & Co. CEO Jamie Dimon echo the great interest held by the business community in the power of EI: "where people often fall short is on the EQ.[2] Emotional intelligence is critical".[3]

However, the use of EI in applied settings (for example, in the context of managerial training workshops) appears to be contentious. The concept has been referred to, for example, as "unethical and unconscionable" (Antonakis, 2004, cited in Antonakis *et al.*, 2009, p. 248), subject to questions over a lack of methodologically well-designed EI studies (Antonakis, 2004) and remains a target of critiques that note its over-reliance on self-reporting and non-empirical sources (such as anecdotes) to support its claims of efficacy. Mayer *et al.* (2008, p. 503) succinctly address these concerns by reflecting that "the apparent size of the field dwarfs what we recognize as relevant scientific research".

A certain irony arises in the idea that EI appears, as a construct, to elicit great emotion, with supporters on one side referring to EI as the *sine qua non* of leadership (Goleman, 1995) and detractors, on the other, referring to the "hyperbolic claims" made by some of its proponents (Antonakis *et al.*, 2009, p. 247).

It is subsequently of value for scholars of leadership to question the way in which EI is defined, why the concept is so contentiously debated and why it is perceived as valuable in the context of leadership.

Structure of the chapter

The chapter opens with an overview of competing definitions of EI, before briefly differentiating *trait* and *ability* approaches to the concept. Leading models are identified, before the chapter moves to a consideration of a relationship between EI and transformational and authentic leadership. Critiques of EI are then addressed and the methodological issues surrounding the measurement of EI are discussed. An engaging expert insight profiles Lauren Grech, CEO of LLG Agency, while a case study entitled "A tale of two visionaries" offers a compelling glimpse into the worlds of SoftBank and WeWork. Both precede an end-of-chapter quiz.

Defining emotional intelligence

Concordant with leadership, no universally accepted definition of what EI is actually exists. In addition to Goleman's earlier observation (EI as the *sine qua non* of leadership) Goleman (1995, p. 34) conceptualizes EI as a trait, defining it as "a set of abilities and attributes that enable accurate identification and monitoring of the self and other feelings and internal states, which is then used to guide cognition and behaviour".

Other dominant definitions of EI include the contention of Salovey and Mayer (1990, p. 189), that it is "the sub-set of social intelligence that involves the ability to monitor one's own and others' feelings and emotions, to discriminate among them and to use this information to guide one's thinking and actions". Conversely, Van Rooy and Viswesvaran (2004, p. 72) refer to EI as "the set of abilities (verbal and non-verbal) that enable a person to generate, recognize, express, understand and evaluate their own and others' emotions in order to guide thinking and action that successfully cope with environmental demands and pressures". EI has also been defined as "an instance of standard intelligence that can enrich the discussion of human capacities" (Mayer *et al.*, 2001, in Mayer *et al.*, 2008).

It is reasonable to state that the concept of EI has found a far more receptive audience amongst practitioners (for example, a manager wishing to enhance his ability to interact more effectively with his team) than it has among academics. This can be attributed to the fact that EI is an accessible concept. It is reasonably straightforward to apply to any workplace situation, and carries an appealing message of self-improvement. Such an appeal, however, has led to a glut of EI models, approaches and dialogues, with practitioners seeking to capitalize on a potentially lucrative market for EI training. This has resulted in a situation where the term 'emotional intelligence' has come to encompass such a broad array of models and approaches that it has been criticized for being "preposterously all-encompassing" (Locke, 2005, p. 428) and "no longer an intelligible concept" (Locke, 2005, p. 426). Indeed, Locke (2005, p. 428) questions the fundamental assumption that the abilities or traits included in different conceptual definitions of EI are actually 'intelligence', posing the rhetorical question, "What does EI … not include?".

A major academic critique lies in the fact that EI often appears to bear striking similarity to existing theoretical concepts – for example, aspects of self-leadership (see Chapter 11, "Self-leadership") and authentic leadership (see Chapter 9, "Authentic leadership") theories, and conceptualizations of EI as a trait that might make it more effectively studied within the context of trait theories (see Chapter 2, "Trait theories").

Despite these methodological concerns, however, some theoretical evidence does exist to support the concept that EI is positively related to transformational and authentic leadership.

Trait and ability models

EI can be considered as both a *trait* (Bar-On, 1997; Goleman, 1995) and as an *ability* (Salovey and Mayer, 1990). EI trait researchers consider EI to be an innate characteristic, whereas EI ability theorists cite its importance as a means of understanding and regulating emotions.

Trait models

Goleman (1995) first popularized the phrase 'emotional intelligence' within the world of business, in his bestselling book of the same name. In so doing, he popularized a concept that continues to influence the working practices of many business leaders, and which has spawned a wealth of EI-related books, training courses and educational materials.

Based on his research of the competency models used by 188 large companies, Goleman reported that EI was twice as important as technical skills and IQ in the emergence of excellent performance and, furthermore, that the impact of EI increased with seniority (Goleman, 1995, 1998). Goleman's model of EI identifies *self-awareness, self-regulation, motivation, empathy* and *social skill* as the five components of emotional intelligence at work; it remains perhaps the most widely recognized and utilized model of EI among the practitioner community.

Trait-based models encapsulate a wide range of personal characteristics, traits and capabilities such as self-confidence and motivation. In addition to Goleman's (1995) aforementioned model, other popular trait models include Bar-On's (1997) definition of EI. This model conceptualizes EI as a set of non-cognitive abilities, skills and personal characteristics that affect the way in which individuals cope with environmental demands and pressures (Day and Carroll, 2008). Trait approaches have traditionally formed the basis of extensive human resources (HR) activities in the recruitment, selection and retention of personnel.

In the consideration of traits and EI one can also return to the role of neurological traits in leadership that were discussed in Chapter 2 ("Trait theories"). Here, it was discussed that, for instance, the cortex may help to mediate regulation of risk and to affect behaviours in anticipation of emotional responses such as fear (Paulus *et al.*, 2001). It is also possible that right frontal brain dysfunction predisposes an individual to poor social skills, poor emotional regulation and poor self-awareness (Salloway *et al.*, 2001); that frontal cortex activity affects moral judgement (Knabb *et al.*, 2009); and that the endocrine system exerts an effect on the profitability, decision making and risk tolerance of city traders (Coates and Herbert, 2008).

It is also interesting to note that what one employee perceives as distressing – and, therefore, as a debilitating source of stress – might be perceived by another as a challenge. It is possible (as stated earlier in Chapter 2) that neurological and other antecedents mediate the individual's ability to display resilience (Bonanno, 2005), to self-regulate his/her own emotions and to assess the situation clearly in order to minimize perceived negative stress (McCauley, 1987).

IDEA IN BRIEF

Risk-taking and the teenage brain

Research shows us that the prefrontal cortex of a young person's brain (which governs logic and self-control) has not yet fully developed, unlike the amygdala, which sits at the heart of the limbic system (and powers emotions and impulsivity). A young person's tendency to seek out risks and immediate gratification is subsequently heightened at this age, which might in turn render them more vulnerable to emotional personal and political appeals.[4] This age group might, as a result, be more vulnerable to grooming and radicalizing influences; data indicates that 100 per cent of 18–29 year olds in the US use the internet, and much of this organized predatory behaviour has been observed to take place online.[5] According to the i-SAFE Foundation around 50 per cent of teens have been the victim of online bullying with around the same number having engaged in bullying behaviour. Yet only 1 in 10 tell their parents if they have been bullied.[6]

As stated by Kaiser,[7]

> The reward seeking system is becoming more easily aroused, particularly during early adolescence, which makes kids seek and go after rewards. The braking system is still developing very, very slowly and it's not fully mature until people are well into their 20's.

Many products aimed at young people target exactly these responses; the 'Like' Facebook button was designed, for example, to stimulate dopamine hits every time a 'Like' is achieved, making the user more hooked on the platform. Tech addiction has become a very real problem for young people who are by far the highest consumption group when it comes to social media and new networked technologies. This heavy social media use is partly blamed for historic levels of stress and anxiety among school- and college-aged young people.[8] There are also rising concerns that the neurological immaturity of the adolescent brain might even make some young people more vulnerable to radicalizing influences.

Find out more

• Tackling radicalisation facts and advice. Available at: www.internetmatters.org/issues/radicalisation/

Ability models

In contrast to trait models, proponents of the ability-based approach view EI as a cognitive ability. Perhaps the best-known ability model is Mayer and Salovey's (1997) Four-Branch Model of EI, which identifies *emotional perception, emotional facilitation, emotional understanding* and *emotional management* as the four key components of EI.

The ability-based approach has recently increased in popularity among HR and consulting practitioners, owing in part to concerns over the empirical robustness of trait-based measures. This concern can be attributed to the fact that measurement of EI as a trait can prove problematic, as it relies largely on self-reports. Self-reporting as a method of testing is notorious for susceptibility to faking by respondents. There is some evidence that cognitive, ability-based EI tests are more resistant to this kind of faking than non-cognitive trait-based tests. For example, a 2008 study (Day and Carroll, 2008) compared the incidence of faking in the use of the MSCEIT (Mayer–Salovey–Caruso EI Test; Mayer *et al.*, 2002), and the EQ-i (Bar-On, 1997), reporting that the EQ-i appeared more susceptible. If self-reported ability-based measures of EI are more reliable, this carries interesting ramifications for organizations that currently seek to measure EI within their recruitment and retention programmes. Nevertheless, the 133-item EQ-i has been subjected to extensive data collection, having been translated into more than 30 languages and completed by thousands of individuals across numerous countries (Bar-On, 2006).

EI and transformational leadership

As reported earlier in discussions (in Chapter 7) of transformational leadership, EI has been theorized to be positively related to skills identified as valuable in a manager, leader or employee (Barling *et al.*, 2000; Bass 1990; Caruso *et al.*, 2002; Dubinsky *et al.*, 1995; Goleman, 1998; Lusch and Serpkeuci, 1990; Mandell and Pherwani, 2003) and as an important topic for occupational psychology and HR management (Gardner, 1983; Goleman, 1995, 1998; Salovey and Mayer, 1990). EI has also been theorized to be positively related to transformational leadership (Ashforth and Humphrey, 1995; Ashkanasy and Tse, 2000; Barling *et al.*, 2000; Sosik and Megerian, 1999). Correlations between EI and transformational leadership have been reported (Sosik and Megerian, 1999), and a positive relationship between transformational leadership and emotions has been observed (Ashforth and Humphrey, 1995). Transformational leadership has even been referred to as management of emotion (Ashkanasy and Tse, 2000).

Some studies (Barling *et al.*, 2000; Palmer *et al.*, 2001) have suggested that EI pre-empts and facilitates transformational leadership (Goleman, 1995, 1998; Mayer and Salovey, 1997; Salovey and Mayer, 1990). For example, Duckett and Macfarlane (2003) measured transformational leadership and emotional intelligence in a study of retail managers and concluded that transformational leadership and EI were positive predictors of success. Barling *et al.* (2000) and Palmer *et al.* (2001) reported that leaders who scored highly in contingent reward behaviour also scored highly in EI. Furthermore, Gardner and Stough (2002) reported identification and understanding the emotions of others as the best predictor of charisma, individual consideration contingent reward, laissez faire and outcomes of transformational leadership (effectiveness, extra effort and satisfaction).

The emergence of emotion as an integral element of the charismatic leadership process is also fascinating. It appears that the emotional bond that is created between the charismatic leader and followers (principally via the use of charismatic rhetoric by the leader) heightens emotional arousal in the follower and speaks to their emotional needs (previously discussed at length in Chapter 6, "Charismatic leadership"). This may partly explain why charismatic leadership is successful in times of uncertainty (Shamir *et al.*, 1993; Trice and Beyer, 1986), when followers are most emotionally vulnerable. In this situation it is the vision and direction of the charismatic leader that provides a source of significant psychological comfort for followers (Bass, 1985; Conger and Kanungo, 1998) and assuages the fear and uncertainty that they are experiencing. It also increases feelings of happiness among followers (Erez *et al.*, 2008) via the effects of emotional contagion.

One study found that hopeful leaders positively affected feelings of resilience amongst organizational employees during traumatic periods (Norman *et al.*, 2005). Winston Churchill's wartime speeches bear striking testament to such a concept, in the sense that his great messages of hope kept the British nation optimistic and strong in the face of great adversity. The very act of being emotionally expressive appears to raise attributions of charisma to a leader (Bass, 1990) and encourages (a potentially reciprocal) emotional contagion between leader and followers (Reichard and Riggio, 2008). In this sense, EI appears to be positively related to charismatic leadership.

DISCUSSION STARTER

Lessons from the Oracle of Omaha

Affectionately referred to as the Oracle of Omaha, Warren Buffett is CEO of Berkshire Hathaway Holdings, a holding company considered to be the most profitable in the world.

Fortune magazine journalist Carol Loomis, a close personal friend of Buffett, cites the trait of rationality as his greatest strength; whereas most investors "get swept up by their emotions",[9] Buffett remains unmoved. Loomis's observation is, perhaps, unsurprising, given Buffett's own ideas on emotional intelligence: "Success in investing doesn't correlate with IQ once you're above the level of twenty-five. Once you have ordinary intelligence, what you need is the temperament to control the urges that get other people into trouble in investing."[10]

The value of emotional intelligence was similarly noted by charismatic leader Jamie Dimon, CEO of JPMorgan Chase & Co., who told Harvard Business School students in 2009,

> You all know about IQ and EQ. Your IQs are all high enough for all of you to be very successful, but where people often fall short is on the EQ. Emotional intelligence is critical. It's something you develop over time.[11]

Rationality is referred to by Loomis as a trait. The ability to be led by rationality, and to control one's emotions, is arguably a skill that can be developed over time, and which, according to Dimon, leads to far greater success than IQ alone. This suggests that the existence of both heritable traits (IQ) and learned skills (EQ) significantly impact success as a leader, and effectively situates EI into the *born or made* debate of leadership.

Start the discussion: How do rationality, EI and IQ intersect in the case of this discussion starter?

Emotional intelligence and authentic leadership

Similarities between authentic leadership and EI prevail, with EI exerting a significant foundational effect on the development of authentic leadership theory. For example, self-regulation is an ability that appears central to some theorizations of both EI and authentic leadership (e.g. Gardner *et al.*'s 2005 conceptual framework for authentic leader and follower development, discussed in Chapter 9, "Authentic leadership"). The ability to self-regulate requires a leader to possess the ability to self-regulate their emotions and to share their emotional feelings with followers as a means of demonstrating authenticity (Gardner *et al.*, 2005).

Authentic leaders are viewed by others as emotionally intelligent leaders (Klenke 2007, in Gardner *et al.*, 2005), and as individuals who self-regulate their emotional responses in divergent situations, subsequently acting in a way that promotes effective decision making. An example of this can be found in the 11 'Leadership Principles' of the US Marines, the first of which is to "Know yourself and seek self-improvement".[12] A US Marine will be called upon to engage in highly pressurized decision making in significantly diverse situations, an ability that requires self-awareness and self-regulation of one's emotions in order to develop a high tolerance for stress. It is interesting to note within this context that EI has been theorized to be positively related to one's tolerance for stress in testing circumstances (Wong and Law, 2002).

Critiques of emotional intelligence

While there is empirical support for the notion that EI and transformational leadership are related, not all theorists agree. Harms and Credé (2010), for example, cite Lindenbaum (2009) in their meta-analytic review of EI and transformational–transactional leadership, claiming that EI "thrives on hyperbolic claims on one hand, and empirical evidence to the contrary on the other" (Harms and Credé, 2010, p. 5). As discussed earlier in the chapter, disagreements exist with regard to what EI should encompass, and whether it should be considered as a trait or an ability.

The efficacy of using EI measures in the HR recruitment and selection process has been questioned due to a lack of research into their validity and utility (Day and Carroll, 2008), and the field is currently fragmented to the point where it is difficult to ascertain what exactly does, and does not, constitute EI. It has even been claimed that there is actually no such thing as emotional intelligence, but rather intelligence, which can be applied to emotions as it can be applied to other areas of life (Locke, 2005).

How to measure emotional intelligence

A criticism of EI also lies in the divergence and heterogeneity of EI measures –for example, the Mayer–Salovey–Caruso Emotional Intelligence Test (MSCEIT; Mayer et al., 2002), the Emotional Intelligence Inventory (EQ-i) (Bar-On, 1997) and the Emotional Competence Inventory (ECI) (Boyatzis et al., 2000). It has been suggested that there is inadequate evidence to support the use of the EQ-i as a selection device (Newsome et al., 2000), and all three have also been criticized on the grounds of validity and reliability.

Summary

In 1948, Stogdill identified (cognitive) intelligence as one of the traits that could separate leaders from non-leaders. His findings have received ongoing support within the managerial literature (Judge et al., 2004; Lowe et al., 1996; Mann, 1959) and it is clear that general intelligence emerges consistently as a trait that correlates positively with leadership performance (Bass, 1990; Judge et al., 2004), and as a trait that is universally desired within of leaders (Den Hartog et al., 1997). While intelligence has been debated regarding not only the nature, but also the number of intelligences that exist (Neisser et al., 1996), it remains clear that *emotional intelligence* remains at once flawed, yet popular. It remains to be seen whether this fascinating field of study is able to produce an empirical foundation strong enough to support its grandest of claims.

The next chapter discusses the emerging and fascinating field of *authentic leadership*, a theoretical area that owes much of its development to the study of emotions in leadership and performance.

 **Expert insight**

Redefining luxury

Lauren Grech is the co-founder of LLG Events. Recently voted Corporate and Incentive Travel's Most Influential Woman of 2019, Lauren is well-versed in the unpredictable, challenging but exciting world of start-ups. In this insightful and entertaining expert insight, Lauren shares the importance of learning the skills that she needed to build her business from the ground up.

 While she originally trained for a career in medicine, Lauren's passion for weddings truly took hold when she began planning her own wedding. This ultimately led her to co-found LLG with her husband Paul. The worldwide media reach of LLG now consists of 1,000+ media outlets and 4,000+ media contacts, with a global network reach of 1,800+ hotels, resorts and venues, 300+ vendors and 25+ tourism boards. LLG Agency works with leading tourism and hospitality brands to allow the sector to capitalize on a lucrative market – luxury and destination weddings. Lauren's story reminds us of the value of taking risks, working hard and following your dream.

The power of recognition

“It was such an incredible honour to start 2019 by being recognized in our industry for the work that we've been doing. To be globally acknowledged as a mover and shaker in my industry is indescribable. I've worked so hard over the past five years, so to receive this level of recognition is so validating to me. It continues to motivate me to work harder, each and every day.

 I co-founded LLG Events with my husband Paul and branded LLG as a husband-wife duo, which, at the time, was very new in our industry. We came up with the idea at my mom's kitchen table and worked our 40 hour a week jobs, then on top of that volunteered most Thursdays, Fridays, Saturdays and Sundays as wedding events staff (usually 32 hours a week or so) at the place where we got married so that we could shadow the maître d'. We worked every job going – bar, wait staff, assisting the bride, valet, bathroom attendant – to literally learn everything that we could. I knew that if we were going to be successful and respected, we needed to have that kind of on-the-ground exposure to every position.

Wedding renegades

We call ourselves 'The LLG Renegades'. I am the first to question the idea of what best practices in the industry should look like, whether we can ever move away from a commission-based model, how best we should accredit vendors in a digital marketplace, how to instil best practices into the company going forward, and so on. I address these questions head-on as an adjunct professor and curriculum builder for New York University's new Master of Science in

Event Management program – the first of its kind in the United States. In the lecture theatre as well as the office I am always challenging the norm.

As disruptors we do sometimes face resistance to change. We are challenging the way the event industry has operated for years, replacing what is a largely passive approach to events to a more direct model. For example, vendor referrals should not just be based on who you know but based on their performance level and business goals. Some things that may be obvious in other industries are still not so obvious in ours – it is an archaic industry and we are struggling to change the mindset.

From inspiration to innovation

One major issue that stood out for us immediately was a need for a uniform industry-wide accreditation system. Interestingly, there has never been any formal, accredited training established within the wedding and event industries as they now apply to hospitality and tourism, which often leads to such wide variations in service that it regularly leads to a confused clientele with no baseline knowledge of what to expect or who to entrust with their event investment. Not only are clients confused, but new vendors entering the industry also do not know how to price themselves, and have difficulty defining their value and knowing where to start. That is exactly where we come in, offering a system for an industry-wide, globally recognized event management standard and vendor accreditation for the luxury wedding market.

The true value of a team

After two years of trying to do it all on my own, I eventually matured through age, experience, and falling flat on my face. I finally realized that I had to start accepting other people's strengths if I wanted LLG to be a success. I had to learn to share the highs and ride the lows with loyal and trusted colleagues and not try to do everything on my own. When I opened myself up to learn from other people and listen to what others had to say, that is when I overcame adversity in my business.

The value of failing fast

I learnt to fail fast – to be honest that I wasn't succeeding and move on quickly to a better strategy. I learnt that I needed to have a way of measuring success or failure and I learnt the importance of testing the waters before making life-changing commitments. The decision to start your own company, for example, is a big leap of faith, so don't quit your job and lose your current revenue stream. Instead, begin by, say, volunteering in your industry of choice. That will allow you to ask yourself: 'Would I like to do this daily? Would I like to invest my time, money and resources in this? Is this an area I'm even skilled in?

Can I understand it?' Right there and then, you learn so much about yourself and the industry, the job or the idea that you're looking to pursue.

Learning to lead

One of the hardest lessons I had to learn in founding the company was the art of patience! Patience enables you to see the difference between short and long-term gains and creates a high level of self-control. A high level of self-control allows you to make fewer impulsive decisions or fewer emotionally-driven decisions and empowers you to make decisions without fear. But it wasn't a skill that I found came naturally to me.

As an up-and-coming entrepreneur, I wanted immediate success, fast clients, fast money, and to prove my worth and value. I was originally defining my success based on how others viewed me and my accomplishments – which was a mistake. Once I developed the art of being patient I was able to see a real difference between short- and long-term gains. I was able to redefine what success truly meant to me.

What I learnt from that experience was that success is driven by what fulfils you as an individual, not by the interpretation of your success by others. Do not put off your dreams or your goals because you do not fit into a specific definition of success. Create your own definition, make your own terms and do not allow anyone to stop you from achieving it!

Leadership requires management

To run a company successfully everyone needs at least basic knowledge in business management, marketing, taxes and sales and they need to be knowledgeable of the technical aspects of the industry. My early volunteering experience was invaluable in giving me those insights Understanding your industry and combining on-the-ground knowledge with technical skills and academic study is, in my view, essential for success.

My education has helped me develop a proper business model, enabled me to understand certain law documents or tax law by giving me the ability to think critically and analytically, and provided the tools necessary to analyse those documents thoroughly. My R&D skills taught me about extreme ownership and accountability, as well as proper time management skills, team building and the importance of deadlines and prioritization. I had to think critically, analytically and thoroughly about every problem, and that has helped me tremendously with LLG.

Leaders invest in their team

Being a CEO means you work for your team. You invest yourself in the people you hire. If making an employee succeed means that they need to work from home on a certain day, or they need to take extra time during their lunch break to workout but will make up the time later, you need to be flexible and try to accommodate those needs. Making an employee happy means that they are more likely to be productive and successful. This, in turn, will help you fulfil your personal and company goals faster.

Greatest memories

The coolest thing about LLG Agency is that I get to travel all around the world – Dubai, Abu Dhabi, Bora Bora, Maldives, Qatar, Greece, England, Switzerland and more. It continues to be an incredible journey and one that I am very grateful for.

I think the best memories so far, however, have come from our efforts to give back to the community via the LLG Gifted program. We've been nominated twice for the Forbes 30 Under 30 Social Entrepreneur list which is amazing.

Every year, we donate our planning and design services to a deserving couple to help them experience the wedding of their dreams. In the first year of the program, we worked with a couple, Marty and Lauren, who had weathered two back-to-back Category 5 hurricanes (Irma and Maria) in the US Virgin Islands. They lost everything material but hadn't lost their spirit – in fact, they took their engagement photos amongst the wreckage of St. John as a symbol of hope and went directly to work on rebuilding the Islands. We were able to gather 20+ elite wedding industry vendors from across the US to create a $135 K pro-bono three-day dream wedding that also brought multiple communities together and refocused media attention on the plight of the Islands to further their recovery. That wedding event attracted coverage from Good Morning America, Fox TV, ABC News, Brides and more, achieving a social media reach of over 70 million and a daily digital reach of over 14 million. **"**

Find out more

- Visit LLG Events at their official website: www.llgevents.com.

Questions

1   How did the CEO in this expert insight demonstrate excellent self-awareness and EI to turn around potential failures and succeed?
2   EI trait researchers consider EI to be an innate characteristic, whereas EI ability theorists cite its importance as a means of understanding and regulating emotions. Identify and discuss examples in this expert insight where the CEO had to work on developing a skill that didn't appear to be an innate characteristic for her.
3   With reference to theory, explain how this CEO is able to self-regulate her emotional responses in divergent situations, subsequently promoting effective decision making.

Case study: a tale of two visionaries

On 27 May 2017 SoftBank and the Public Investment Fund of Saudi Arabia (PIF), the kingdom's main sovereign wealth fund, partnered to create the SoftBank Vision Fund. With assets under management totalling $93 billion, the Vision Fund constituted the world's largest private equity fund.

For a brief period, SoftBank held the investment world in thrall, promising visionary tech investments on a vast scale. This gargantuan fund with seemingly limitless potential was run by Masayoshi Son, an investor viewed by many as a visionary and a genius on account of his success in transforming a $20 million investment in the Chinese firm Alibaba in 2000 into a $119 billion return.

Successes such as the 2018 sale of FlipKart Online Services Pvt Ltd. bolstered the SoftBank name further, with the latter earning the SoftBank Vision Fund an impressive $1.5 billion. However, it did not take long for the fortunes of the Vision Fund to fall away. The $21.6 billion that SoftBank paid for a controlling stake in Sprint in 2013, for example, has not translated into the impressive returns that many had hoped to see.

The pied piper of unicorns

Bloomberg Businessweek recently referred to SoftBank as "the pied piper of unicorns"[13] on account of its tendency to invest in highly charismatic, visionary (and virtually always male) CEOs with novel ideas and technologies.

From the outset, real estate company WeWork initially emerged as a shining star in a crowded start-up space, with the young, charismatic WeWork CEO Adam Neumann securing an awe-inducing, multi-billion-dollar investment from the Vision Fund only 28 minutes into a meeting with Son.

Much hyped, Neumann appeared to be a quintessential charismatic CEO, favouring bold predictions. Neumann spoke of bringing WeWork to Mars, that he would become the world's first trillionaire, that his descendants would be running WeWork in hundreds of years' time and that he would at some stage like to become president of the world. He created a visionary new school with the help of his wife, catering to ideals that he felt could not be found in existing academic institutions (the school has now closed).

Neumann certainly possessed the charisma to influence and persuade others to follow him, even if his vision or project was a risky one. The *New York Times*, for example, once ran a story that opened with an account of how Neumann took executives to the fifty-seventh floor of a skyscraper and climbed up to the ledge. They had all been drinking and standing on that ledge was dangerous – heavy wind or one clumsy step and they would have fallen to an instant, violent death. But Neumann invited them to take that risk with him, and they did, readily.

Neumann, in physical terms, is undoubtedly physically charismatic – tall, dark, striking in appearance with flowing brown hair and an overwhelming self-belief. He also had the eccentricities and magnetism that we often correlate with great charismatic visionaries – he often walked around the office barefoot, and organised wild parties and events for employees. Whether curated or natural, those eccentricities served for a time to bolster a kind of enigmatic appeal.

The downfall of WeWork

It didn't take long for cracks to emerge in the WeWork facade. Among a cascade of positive media, press calls and marketing junkets, details began to emerge that Neumann had leased real estate that he partly owned to WeWork, making millions of dollars in the process. Losses were clearly mounting; yet in the face of those losses, Neumann leased a Gulfstream jet and built a plunge pool and a sauna in his Manhattan office.

By October 2019, following a much-hyped IPO (Initial Public Offering) with a company valuation of $47 billion, Adam Neumann was forced to step down as CEO amid questions over the company's financing. At the time of writing, SoftBank had funnelled a further $8 billion into the company to keep it afloat. This second round of investment raised eyebrows as it equalled the entire valuation of WeWork Cos Inc. ($8 billion), and also included an additional $1.7 billion to buy out Neumann. This brings total SoftBank investments in WeWork to a total of around $18 billion, with Son and Neumann now intertwined as two charismatic visionaries intent on supporting the WeWork dream.

The dream that died?

Son and Neumann's shared dream seems to be dying off. WeWork's future liabilities to landlords, for a start, have been calculated at around $47 billion. For a company currently registering a loss of $2 billion per annum, many commentators questioned the legitimacy of SoftBank's decision to plough more funds into the real estate start-up. It does appear difficult to speculate as to how SoftBank will recoup the value of their 80 per cent share ownership in the company.

At the time of writing, SoftBank have written down a $5 billion loss on its WeWork and other high-profile investments. And S&P and Moody's ratings agencies have both rated SoftBank below investment grade. SoftBank currently holds a weighted average cost of debt of 3.7 per cent.

SoftBank has invested in a range of companies, and it would be premature to write off the success of the Fund. Nevertheless, some of SoftBank's other large-scale investments are struggling. For example, SoftBank has invested around $20 billion in total in ride-hailing services, many of which are struggling. Uber Technologies Inc., for instance, initially enjoyed huge success as a major disruptor and innovator in the taxi and mini cab space. A successful $82.4 billion IPO of Uber seemed to solidify SoftBank's early profile as a brilliantly visionary company (and of Uber as a game-changing disruptor), but Uber would soon hit a wall of legal, financial and PR problems. These difficulties recently led to a shareholder-led uprising (that included SoftBank) and the ousting of its CEO. Similarly, Didi Chuxing in China (a company that bought out Uber China) and Grab in South-East Asia are currently experiencing major downturns in revenue (incidentally, Didi Chuxing CEO Cheng Wei is former Vice-President of Alibaba's online payment service Alipay in which SoftBank currently hold a 26 per cent, $110 billion stake). Ola, India's SoftBank ride-hailing investment, recently delayed its IPO.

Fair.com, a flexible car ownership business currently valued at $1.2 billion (also a SoftBank investment), recently announced a 40 per cent staff layoff and the stepping down of CEO Tyler Painter. Brandless, another start-up backed by SoftBank has recently announced a round of layoffs and major board-level changes. Compass, a real estate business backed by SoftBank, recently lost three members of its board (the Chief Financial Officer, Chief Marketing Officer and Chief Technical Officer) whilst Wag, the dog-walking start-up which received a $300 million investment from Soft-Bank has recently experienced a major round of layoffs and board-level disruptions.

Son was recently quoted in a *Business Insider Singapore* article as saying that he had learned a valuable lesson about how a fondness for a charismatic individual could influence his investing judgement. "About loving Adam too much," he commented, "I learned a harsh lesson."[14]

You don't bring bad news to the cult leader

The cult of personality and the power of charisma feature prominently in the cases of WeWork and SoftBank, with esoteric, enigmatic figures firing up investors to make decisions that were not based on fundamental value but ever-rising euphoria. It is a phenomenon that inspired the Vanity Fair article "You Don't Bring Bad News to the Cult Leader".[15] SoftBank Group reported a 99 per cent fall in operating profit in Q1 (first quarter) of 2020.

Find out more

- Ren, S. (18 November 2019). SoftBank's Vision Fund Looks Like the Pied Piper of Unicorns. *Blomberg Businessweek*. Available at: www.bloomberg.com/news/articles/2019-11-18/most-of-SoftBank-s-vision-fund-unicorns-will-be-flops.

Questions

1   Comment why withstanding the seductive force of charisma requires excellent emotional intelligence, particularly when it comes to impulse, rational judgements and self-control.
2   Neumann referred to himself as a martyr and styled himself as a kind of Messiah figure. Comment on why this creates a more powerful emotional bond between leader and follower.
3   Son possessed far more legitimate and financial power than Neumann at the time of their first meeting, yet it only took Son a reported 28 minutes to pledge over $4 billion in that meeting. What does that tell us about the potentially dominant nature of referent power?

4   Son remarked that he learned a harsh lesson in "loving Adam too much". What can EI theory tell us about the conflicts that Son experienced in terms of rationally and intellectually evaluating WeWork's fundamental value, while also navigating the heady emotional feelings that he felt after spending such a short time with Neumann?

CHAPTER 8 QUIZ

1   Goleman (1995) referred to emotional intelligence as the *sine qua non* of leadership. What does he mean by this?
2   Statements such as Goleman's (above) have been referred to as "hyperbolic claims" by detractors of emotional intelligence. Upon what bases has such an accusation been made, and by whom?
3   Emotional intelligence can be defined as both a trait and an ability. Define the key conceptual difference that differentiates the consideration of emotional intelligence as a trait and as an ability.
4   How does emotional intelligence differ from general intelligence?
5   Mayer and Salovey's (1997) Four-Branch Model of emotional intelligence constitutes which four elements?
6   Identify three ways in which emotional intelligence has been theorized to be positively related to transformational leadership.
7   Identify the five components of Goleman's model of emotional intelligence.
8   Identify a potential conceptual link between emotional intelligence and authentic leadership.
9   Upon what basis are ability-based measures of emotional intelligence theorized to be a better choice for the assessment of employees than trait-based measures?
10   Upon what basis have measures of emotional intelligence generally been criticized?

Notes

1 Quote taken from an interview conducted for this book with CEO Lauren Grech for the expert insight "Redefining luxury" that appears later in this chapter.
2 EQ = emotional quotient (a measurement of an individual's emotional intelligence).
3 Taken from a speech by Jamie Dimon to the 2009 graduating class at Harvard Business School.
4 Arain, M., Haque, M., Johal, L., Mathur, P., Nel, W., Rais, A., Sandhu, R. and Sharma, S. (2013). Maturation of the Adolescent Brain. *Neuropsychiatric Disease and Treatment*, 9, pp. 449–461.
5 Clement, J. (18 June 2019). U.S. Internet Usage Penetration 2019, by Age Group Statista. Available at: www.statista.com/statistics/266587/percentage-of-internet-users-by-age-groups-in-the-us/.
6 *Bullying Statistics*. Available at: www.bullyingstatistics.org/content/cyber-bullying-statistics.html.

7 Kaiser, D. (14 November 2012). 6 Facts about Crime and the Adolescent Brain. *MPR News*. Available at: www.mprnews.org/story/2012/11/15/daily-circuit-juvenile-offenders-brain-development.

8 Schrobsdorff, S. (7 November 2016). Teen Depression and Anxiety: Why the Kids Are Not Alright. *Time Magazine*. Available at: https://time.com/magazine/us/4547305/november-7th-2016-vol-188-no-19-u-s/.

9 Jarvis, R. (20 January 2013). Just a Regular Billionaire. *CBS News*. Available at: www.cbsnews.com/video/just-a-regular-billionaire/.

10 Bianco, A. (5 July 1999). Homespun Wisdom from the "Oracle of Omaha". *Bloomberg*. Available at: www.bloomberg.com/news/articles/1999-07-05/homespun-wisdom-from-the-oracle-of-omaha.

11 Taken from a speech by Jamie Dimon to the 2009 graduating class at Harvard Business School.

12 Available at: www.marines.com/being-a-marine/leadership-principles.

13 Ren, S. (18 November 2019). SoftBank's Vision Fund Looks Like the Pied Piper of Unicorns. *Bloomberg Businessweek*. Available at: www.bloomberg.com/news/articles/2019-11-18/most-of-SoftBank-s-vision-fund-unicorns-will-be-flops.

14 Mohamed. T. (16 November 2019). The Last Person I Felt This with Was Jack Ma. *Business Insider Singapore*. Available at: www.businessinsider.sg/SoftBank-masayoshi-son-compared-wework-adam-neumann-alibaba-jack-ma-2019-11/.

15 Sherman, G. (Holiday, 2019). You Don't Bring Bad News to the Cult Leader. *Vanity Fair*. Available at: www.vanityfair.com/news/2019/11/inside-the-fall-of-wework.

References

Antonakis, J.J. (2004). On Why "Emotional Intelligence" Will Not Predict Leadership Effectiveness Beyond IQ or the "Big Five": An Extension and Rejoinder. *Organisational Analysis*, 12(2), pp. 171–182.

Antonakis, J., Ashkanasy, N.M. and Dasborough, M. (2009). Does Leadership Need Emotional Intelligence? *Leadership Quarterly*, 20(2), pp. 247–261.

Ashforth, B.E. and Humphrey, R.H. (1995). Emotions in the Workplace: A Reappraisal. *Human Relations*, 48(2), pp. 97–125.

Ashkanasy, N.M. and Tse, B. (2000). Transformational Leadership as Management of Emotion: A Conceptual Review. In N.M. Ashkanasy, C.E.J. Härtel and W.J. Zerbe (eds.), *Emotions in the Workplace: Research, Theory and Practice*. Westport, CT: Quorum Books, pp. 221–235.

Barling, J., Slater, F. and Kelloway, E.K. (2000). Transformational Leadership and Emotional Intelligence: An Exploratory Study. *Leadership & Organisational Development Journal*, 21(3), pp. 157–161.

Bar-On, R. (1997). *The Emotional Intelligence Inventory (EQ-i): Technical Manual*. Toronto: Multi-Health Systems.

Bar-On, R. (2006). The Bar-On Model of Emotional–Social Intelligence (ESI). *Psicothema*, 18, pp. 13–25.

Barsade, S.G., Brief, A.P. and Spataro, S.E. (2003). The Affective Revolution in Organisational Behaviour: The Emergence of a Paradigm. In J. Greenberg (ed.), *Organisational Behaviour: The State of the Science*. 2nd ed. Mahwah, NJ: Erlbaum, pp. 3–52.

Bass, B.M. (ed.) (1985). *Leadership and Performance Beyond Expectations*. New York: Free Press.

Bass, B.M. (ed.) (1990). *Bass & Stogdill's Handbook of Leadership*. New York: Free Press.

Bass, B.M. and Avolio, B.J. (2000). *Manual for the Multifactor Leadership Questionnaire*. Redwood City, CA: Mind Garden.

Bonanno, G.A. (2005). Resilience in the Face of Potential Trauma. *Current Directions in Psychological Science*, 14(3), pp. 135–138.

Boyatzis, R.E., Goleman, D. and Rhee, K. (2000). Clustering Competence in Emotional Intelligence: Insights from the Emotional Competence Inventory. In R. Bar-On and J.D.A. Parker (eds.), *The Handbook of Emotional Intelligence: Theory Development, Assessment, and Application at Home, School and in the Workplace.* San Francisco, CA: Jossey-Bass, pp. 343–361.

Caruso, D.R., Mayer, J.D. and Salovey, P. (2002). Emotional Intelligence and Emotional Leadership. In R.E. Riggio, S.E. Murphy and F.J. Pirozzolo (eds.), *Multiple Intelligences and Leadership.* Mahwah, NJ: Lawrence Erlbaum Associates, pp. 55–74.

Coates, J.M. and Herbert, J. (2008). Endogenous Steroids and Financial Risk Taking on a London Trading Floor. *Proceedings of the National Academy of Sciences of the United States of America*, 105(16), pp. 6167–6172.

Conger, J.A. and Kanungo, R.N. (eds) (1998). *Charismatic Leadership in Organisations.* Thousand Oaks, CA: Sage.

Day, A.L. and Carroll, S.A. (2008). Faking Emotional Intelligence (EI): Comparing Response Distortion on Ability and Trait-Based EI Measures. *Journal of Organizational Behavior*, 29(6), pp. 761–784.

Den Hartog, D.N., Van Muijen, J.J. and Koopman, P.L. (1997). Transactional versus Transformational Leadership: An Analysis of the MLQ. *Journal of Occupational and Organizational Psychology*, 70(1), pp. 19–29.

Dubinsky, A.J., Yammarino, F.J. and Jolson, M.A. (1995). An Examination of Linkages between Personal Characteristics and Dimensions of Transformational Leadership. *Journal of Business & Psychology*, 9(3), pp. 315–344.

Duckett, H. and Macfarlane, E. (2003). Emotional Intelligence and Transformational Leadership in Retailing. *Leadership and Organization Development Journal*, 24(6), pp. 309–317.

Erez, A., Misangyi, V.F., Johnson, D.E., LePine, M.A. and Halverson, K.C. (2008). Stirring the Hearts of Followers: Charismatic Leadership as the Transferral of Affect. *Journal of Applied Psychology*, 93(3), pp. 602–616.

Gardner, H. (1983). *Frames of Mind: The Theory of Multiple Intelligences.* New York: Basic Books.

Gardner, L. and Stough, C. (2002). Examining the Relationship between Leadership and Emotional Intelligence in Senior Level Managers. *Leadership & Organization Development Journal*, 23(2), pp. 68–78.

Gardner, W.L., Avolio, B.J., Luthans, F., May, D.R. and Walumbwa, F. (2005). "Can You See the Real Me?" A Self-Based Model of Authentic Leader and Follower Development. *Leadership Quarterly*, 16(3), pp. 343–372.

Goleman, D. (1995). *Emotional Intelligence.* New York: Bantam.

Goleman, D. (1998). *Working with Emotional Intelligence.* New York: Bantam.

Harms, P.D. and Credé, M. (2010). Emotional Intelligence and Transformational and Transactional Leadership: A Meta-Analysis. *Journal of Leadership & Organizational Studies*, 17(1), pp. 5–17.

Judge, T., Colbert, A.E. and Ilies, R. (2004). Intelligence and Leadership: A Quantitative Review and Test of Theoretical Propositions. *Journal of Applied Psychology*, 89(3), pp. 542–552.

Klenke, K. (2007). Authentic Leadership: A Self, Leader, and Spiritual Identity Perspective. *International Journal of Leadership Studies*, 3(1), pp. 68–97.

Knabb, J.J., Welsh, R.K., Ziebell, J.G. and Reimer, K.S. (2009). Neuroscience, Moral Reasoning, and the Law. *Behavioral Sciences and the Law*, 27(2), pp. 219–236.

Lindenbaum, D. (2009). Rhetoric or Remedy? A Critique on Developing Emotional Intelligence. *Academy of Management Learning & Education*, 8(3), pp. 225–237.

Locke, E.A. (2005). Why Emotional Intelligence Is an Invalid Concept. *Journal of Organizational Behavior*, 26(4), pp. 425–431.

Lowe, K.B., Kroeck, K.G. and Sivasubramanian, N. (1996). Effectiveness Correlates of Transformational and Transactional Leadership: A Meta-Analytic Review of the MLQ Literature. *Leadership Quarterly*, 7(3), pp. 385–426.

Lusch, R.F. and Serpkeuci, R.R. (1990). Personal Differences, Job Tension, Job Outcomes, and Store Performance: A Study of Retail Managers. *Journal of Marketing*, 54(1), pp. 85–101.

McCauley, C. (1987). Stress and the Eye of the Beholder. *Issues and Observations*, 7, pp. 1–16.

Mandell, B. and Pherwani, S. (2003). Relationship between Emotional Intelligence and Transformational Leadership Style: A Gender Comparison. *Journal of Business and Psychology*, 17(3), pp. 387–404.

Mann, R.D. (1959). A Review of the Relationship between Personality and Performance in Small Groups. *Psychological Bulletin*, 56(4), pp. 241–270.

Mayer, J. and Salovey, P. (1997). What is Emotional Intelligence? In P. Salovey and D. Sluyter (eds.), *Emotional Development and Emotional Intelligence: Implications for Educators*. New York: Basic Books, pp. 3–31.

Mayer, J.D., Salovey, P., Caruso, D.R. and Sitarenios, G. (2001). Emotional Intelligence as a Standard Intelligence. *Emotion*, 1(3), pp. 232–242.

Mayer, J.D., Salovey, P. and Caruso, D.R. (2002). *Mayer–Salovey–Caruso Emotional Intelligence Test (MSCEIT): User's Manual*. Toronto: Multi-Health Systems.

Mayer, J.D., Salovey, P. and Caruso, D.R. (2008). Emotional Intelligence: New Ability or Eclectic Traits? *American Psychologist*, 63(6), pp. 503–517.

Neisser, U., Boodoo, G., Bouchard, T.J., Boykin, A.W., Brody, N., Ceci, S.J., Halpern, D.E., Loehlin, J.C., Perloff, R., Sternberg, R.J. and Urbina, S. (1996). Intelligence: Knowns and Unknowns. *American Psychologist*, 51(2), pp. 77–101.

Newsome, S., Day, A.L. and Catano, V.M. (2000). Assessing the Predictive Validity of Emotional Intelligence. *Personality and Individual Differences*, 29(6), pp. 1005–1016.

Norman, S., Luthans, B. and Luthans, K. (2005). The Proposed Contagion Effect of Hopeful Leaders on Resiliency of Employees and Organisations. *Journal of Leadership & Organisational Studies*, 12(2), pp. 55–64.

Palmer, B.R., Walls, M., Burgess, Z. and Stough, C. (2001). Emotional Intelligence and Effective Leadership. *Leadership and Organisational Development Journal*, 22, pp. 5–10.

Paulus, M.P., Hozack, N., Zauscher, B., McDowell, J.E., Frank, L., Brown, G.G. and Braff, D.L. (2001). Prefrontal, Parietal, and Temporal Cortex Networks Underlie Decision-Making in the Presence of Uncertainty. *NeuroImage*, 13(1), pp. 91–100.

Reichard, R.J. and Riggio, R.E. (2008). An Interactive Process Model of Emotions and Leadership. In C.L. Cooper and N. Ashkanasy (eds.), *Research Companion to Emotions in Organisations*. Cheltenham, UK: Edward Elgar, pp. 512–527.

Salloway, S., Malloy, P. and Duffy, J. (eds.) (2001). *The Frontal Lobes and Neuropsychiatric Illness*. Arlington, VA: American Psychiatric Publishing.

Salovey, P. and Mayer, J.D. (1990). Emotional Intelligence. *Imagination, Cognition, and Personality*, 9(3), pp. 185–211.

Shamir, B., House, R.J. and Arthur, M.B. (1993). The Motivational Effects of Charismatic Leadership: A Self-Concept Based Theory. *Organisational Science*, 4(4), pp. 577–594.

Sosik, J.J. and Megerian, L.E. (1999). Understanding Leader Emotional Intelligence and Performance: The Role of Self–Other Agreement on Transformational Leadership Perceptions. *Group and Organizational Management*, 24(3), pp. 367–390.

Stogdill, R.M. (1948). Personal Factors Associated with Leadership: A Survey of the Literature. *Journal of Psychology*, 25, pp. 35–71.

Trice, H.M. and Beyer, J.M. (1986). Charisma and its Routinization in Two Social Movement Organizations. In B.M. Staw and L.L. Cummings (eds.), *Research in Organizational Behavior* (Vol. 8). Greenwich, CT: JAI Press, pp. 113–164.

Van Rooy, D. and Viswesvaran, C. (2004). Emotional Intelligence: A Meta-Analytic Investigation of Predictive Validity and Nomological Net. *Journal of Vocational Behaviour*, 65(1), pp. 71–95.

Wong, C.C. and Law, K.S. (2002). The Effect of Leader and Follower Emotional Intelligence on Performance and Attitude: An Exploratory Study. *Leadership Quarterly*, 13(3), pp. 243–274.

9

AUTHENTIC LEADERSHIP

"Success is a milestone and only a temporary moment. Similar to success in training and competition, it applies to a set benchmark that often moves or shifts as soon as it is reached."

– *Tammo Walter, CEO of ATAQ Fuel*[1]

On Saturday 27 October 2012, the UK *Financial Times* newspaper ran a cover story that UBS[2] was planning to cut 10,000 employees from its 16,000-strong global investment banking arm. Two days later, on Monday 29 October 2012, hundreds of employees of UBS London arrived at work. A lucky few swiped their ID card at reception and continued to their desks in the usual way. Most others discovered that their ID card simply did not work. And that is how they discovered that they no longer had a job.

In the world of business, stories of poor leadership and the unfair treatment of employees abound. Rarer are the tales of corporate leaders whose actions are shaped fundamentally by their values and guiding principles. One such example is Taddy Blecher, who has established six free-access higher education institutions in South Africa and has helped to raise 100 million Rand in cash and assets that have enabled almost 18,000 unemployed South Africans to move from poverty to the middle class – an incredible achievement. Blecher remains a pioneer in education, sitting at the helm of multiple innovative educational organizations such as the Maharishi Invincibility Institute, the Imvula Empowerment Trust and the Community and Individual Development Association. He is also the Chairperson of the South African National Government Council on Entrepreneurship, Education and Job Creation, co-founded the Branson Centre of Entrepreneurship alongside Sir Richard Branson, holds two honorary doctorates and was named South Africa's Man of the Year for Education in 2018. Such stories are inspirational – yet they remain in the minority.

The destruction of the global economy that originated from the wide-scale trading of toxic subprime debt in 2008, the ruinous consequences of the Deepwater Horizon oil spill in 2010 and the vicious alt-right propaganda – conspiracy theories targeting Jews, Muslims and political opponents (sometimes written or retweeted by the 45th President of the US himself) – are but a few examples of systemic moral failure that has led to renewed calls, by both practitioners and academics, for a new values-based approach to leadership. This chapter addresses the subsequent emergence of *authentic leadership*, a field that has developed as a means of answering this call.

Structure of the chapter

This chapter begins by defining *authentic leadership* (separating the field into *self-based* and *developmental* definitions), and by clarifying the current state of progress in the field. Four theories of authentic leadership are then presented. The first focuses on a theorized link between the positive relationship between authentic transformational leadership and heightened morality in followers (Zhu *et al.*, 2011). The second presents a self-based model of leader and follower development (Gardner *et al.*, 2005), and the third, a model based on the life stories approach to authentic leadership. Finally, the role of eudaemonia[3] in authentic leadership (Ilies *et al.*, 2005) is considered.

Issues associated with the measurement of authentic leadership are discussed, alongside a consideration of critiques of the approach. The expert insight for this chapter profiles ATAQ Fuel CEO Tammo Walter ("On the ATAQ") who explains how he turned his passion into his career. A case study, "Tour of duty" offers an insightful overview of the authenticity of the leadership of Robert Swan Mueller III. A quiz completes the chapter.

Introduction

In the greatest tradition of leadership studies, there is (as is the case with the term 'leadership' itself), no universally accepted definition for what exactly constitutes *authentic leadership* and, as a result, some conceptual confusions do exist (Cooper *et al.*, 2005). However, there has been no shortage of additive definitions that have, so far, prevailed within the literature (Avolio and Gardner, 2005; Shamir and Eilam, 2005), with authentic leadership appearing to have been defined as a trait, attribute and skill, and also at the dyadic level (i.e. as a relational process).

The concept of authenticity in leadership has gained significant momentum in the leadership literature in recent years (Luthans and Avolio, 2003), owing notably to a desire for greater moral accountability in leadership in the wake of corporate scandals. Recent gargantuan corporate fines – $76 billion (Bank of America), $5 billion (Facebook) – remind us that authenticity and moral accountability is often lacking in the leadership that we see. In fact, Wall Street institutions have paid around $243 billion in fines in total since the 2008 financial crisis. Politics does not appear to be faring any better in recent years; Donald Trump's campaign chair, deputy campaign chair, Foreign Policy Advisor, personal lawyer and National Security Advisor and long political advisor (as it stands in 2020) are all convicted felons.

Defining authentic leadership

The first definition of both authentic and inauthentic leadership was proposed by Henderson and Hoy (1983), who stated that a leader's authenticity is in part defined by the extent to which subordinates perceived them to take personal responsibility for their actions, outcomes and mistakes, and to be non-manipulative. Lance Armstrong was widely perceived as inauthentic during his seminal *Oprah Winfrey* appearance, as his admission of guilt was not perceived to be accompanied by an appropriate level of contrition. Furthermore, his extensive subterfuge in the use of performance enhancing practices made him appear manipulative. Conversely, Sir James Crosby, former CEO of HBOS, voluntarily gave up his knighthood and 30 per cent of his annual pension as a result of the collapse of HBOS, which ultimately required a multi-million-pound taxpayer-funded bailout by Lloyds. While Crosby had appeared to be accountable for extensive failures at the helm of HBOS, he nevertheless appeared authentic in his contrition, and in his wish to address the consequences of the failures in leadership that had occurred during his tenure at HBOS.

Differentiations have also been made between individual and organizational authenticity (Halpin and Croft, 1966; Novicevic *et al.*, 2006; Rome and Rome, 1967). Later definitions and approaches are multitudinous. It is not the purpose or aim of this chapter to list them all, but to highlight those that draw attention to the different schools of thought that exist within this field (namely, *self-based* constructs, *relational* constructs and *developmental* constructs).

Self-based definitions of authentic leadership centre upon the internal state of the leader and focus principally on the self-development of the leader. For example, George (2003) identifies the attribute of self-discipline, alongside purpose, values, heart and relationships, as key to the practice of authentic leadership. Red Auerbach, quoted earlier in the book in the context of transformational leadership (Auerbach and Webber, 1987, p. 85) provides an effective example of the value of such qualities, stating: "I don't believe in statistics ... You can't measure a ballplayer's heart, his ability to perform in the clutch, his willingness to sacrifice his offence or to play strong defence." Luthans and Avolio (2003) similarly point to the mediating effect of confidence, optimism, hope and resilience on the ability of the leader to be self-aware and to practise self-regulation effectively, viewing authentic leadership as dependent on both the existence of positive psychological capacities and a supportive organizational context. Nelson Mandela provides an excellent example of a leader whose confidence, optimism, hope and resilience carried him through extreme periods of difficulty and injustice, and who demonstrated true authenticity in action, regardless of the hardship that he was forced to endure as a result.

Kernis (2003, p. 13) identifies the role of self-identity, defining authenticity as the "unobstructed operation of one's true, or core, self in one's daily enterprise", a process that he views as being mediated by the possession of self-esteem and the subsequent ability to self-assess. The role of positive psychology in authentic leadership influences many other authors, who also identify the role of morals (Avolio *et al.*, 2004; Walumbwa *et al.*, 2008) as central to authenticity. The concept is eloquently summarized by Bennis (2003, p. 334), who views authentic leaders as people who "create their own legends and become the authors of their lives in the sense of creating new and improved versions of themselves". Certainly, one is able to refer once more to the example of Nelson Mandela who clearly and elegantly embodied the earlier words of Bennis (2003).

IDEA IN BRIEF

Act as I say, not as I do – the Yahoo! *Rebooting Work* mandate

A study conducted by Brigham Young University in 2010 found that employees working from home worked an average of 57 hours per week before feeling that they had neglected their home life – an impressive figure when compared to the 38 hours a week reported by their office-based counterparts. Some argue, however, that being physically available for last-minute meetings, engaging in informal water-cooler conversations and interacting with the boss – in person – are all factors that are more likely to lead to further career progression than working remotely would ultimately allow.

Certainly, the argument has become crystallized in the case of Yahoo! CEO Marissa Mayer, who issued a mandate in early 2013 that working from home was no longer allowed, and that employees must henceforth report to the office to carry out their work. The message carried a particularly painful sting in the tail for working mothers; while the new mandate undeniably made childcare arrangements more problematic for many Yahoo! employees, Mayer, who pledged to work throughout her pregnancy (with twins) and reportedly only planned to take two weeks off work, had installed a nursery next door to her office so that she could bring her own children to work with her. Mayer did, however, increase maternity benefits a few months afterwards. She resigned in 2017 after five years at the helm of Yahoo!, amid reports of low employee morale and slow growth, leaving after the sale of Yahoo! to Verizon sale to start her own tech company with a severance package reported to be worth, at that time, around $55 million.

The reader will recall Deci and Ryan's (1995) Self-Determination Theory (SDT), discussed earlier (Chapter 4, "Behavioural theories"). SDT stipulates that the leader must incorporate externally regulated behaviour into their own internal values and intrinsically regulated self in order to be authentic and to display congruence with both personal and organizational goals. Similarities between authentic leadership and emotional intelligence specifically relating to self regulation (for example, Gardner *et al.*, 2005) argue that authentic leaders possess the ability to self-regulate their emotions and to share their emotional feelings with followers as a means of demonstrating authenticity.

Authentic leadership can also be viewed as an essentially dyadic, *relational process*, where followers' perceptions of leadership play a critical role (Klenke, 2005), and where leadership is essentially an emotional process (George, 2000). In this sense, both leader and follower are able to exert a positive effect on each other.

Developmental definitions concentrate more closely on the way in which authenticity is developed in both leaders and followers. For example, Shamir and Eilam (2005) discuss the centrality of life stories in the development of the authentic leader, and Gardner *et al.* (2005) focus upon the role of life histories and trigger events as antecedents to the development of authentic leadership. For example, Eigel and Kuhnert (2005) measured the characteristics of 21 top executives, finding that the developmental maturity of the leader affected the mental and moral capacities, and, thus, the authenticity, of the executives surveyed. The *life stories* approach detailed later in the chapter extends the discussion of this concept (Ilies *et al.*, 2005).

DISCUSSION STARTER

Burns' (1978) conceptualization of transformational leadership identifies leadership as a social and mutual process between leader and follower. Trait research (Chapter 2, "Trait theories") reports upon how voters really are inclined to select political candidates on the basis of physiognomic and other physical markers.

Start the discussion: If both leader (political candidate) and follower (voter) are agentic forces in the practice of leadership, what does this tell us about the potential for leadership to be effective or ineffective?

Morality and the authentic leader

While some dissention exists regarding the role of ethics and morals in authentic leadership (Shamir and Eilam, 2005), many researchers nevertheless argue that morality remains a key part of the construct (Avolio and Gardner, 2005; Luthans and Avolio, 2003; May *et al.*, 2003; Walumbwa *et al.*, 2008). Conceptualizations of the dyadic effect on the development of morality in leadership reside clearly in the early work of Burns (1978). Describing transformational leadership as a social process, he explained the necessity for both leader and follower to be engaged in a mutual process of "raising one another to higher levels of morality and motivation"

(Burns, 1978, p. 20). Bass further extends conceptualizations of morality in transformational leadership in his explanation that:

> Authentic transformational leaders motivate followers to work for transcendental goals that go beyond immediate self-interests. What is right and good to do becomes important. Transformational leaders move followers to transcend their own self-interests for the good of the group, organization, or country.
>
> *(Bass, 1977, p. 133)*

Thus, a manager who inspires their team to be creative and take risks, who values their ideas and who acts as a positive role model, creates a culture so positive that they are able to transform the working environment into a positive place. By recognizing and raising employees' aspirations, they are able to lead their team to self-actualize and, by acting as a role model, create a supportive, ethical working environment.

The central role and importance of morals in authentic leadership has been highlighted extensively (Gardner *et al.*, 2004; Bass and Riggio, 2006; Bass and Steidlmeier, 1999), following Bass's (1985) and Burns' (1978) original conceptualizations of the ability of leaders to act as moral agents and as positive agents of change. However, it is possible that morals and ethics are not necessarily perceived in a uniform, universal way and that culture may be a mediator (Carlo and Edwards, 2005).

The reader will recall Bass and Steidlmeier's (1999) argument noted earlier in the book (Chapter 7, "Transformational leadership") that leadership must possess a moral foundation in order for it to be authentically transformational. The subsequent interest in extending this theoretical work led to the first publication in the area in 2003 (Luthans and Avolio, 2003), and has most recently culminated in a model developed by Zhu *et al.* (2011, p. 806), which identifies the role of: (1) moral values (for example, kindness and altruism); (2) modal values (such as honesty, integrity, trustworthiness, reliability and accountability); and (3) end values (which includes security, justice, equality and community) in authentic transformational leadership. The model theorizes the positive effect that authentic transformational leadership will exert on the moral identity and moral emotions of followers. The model (see Figure 9.1) draws on a range of theoretical areas, including social cognitive theory and authentic leadership development, to explain the way in which authentic transformational leadership might lead to the heightened moral decision making and action of both individuals and groups.

The reader is encouraged to engage with the case study of Donald Woods presented in Chapter 7 ("Transformational leadership"), for a real-world example of exactly what the model proposes. Woods was an authentic transformational leader, whose actions were defined by his moral values and principles. The ethical climate at the newspaper that he edited, the *Daily Dispatch*, was raised to an exemplary moral standard under his leadership, with the newspaper becoming a vociferous opponent of apartheid.

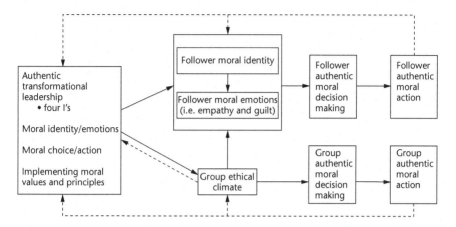

FIGURE 9.1 The effect of authentic transformational leadership on follower and group ethics.

Source: Zhu *et al.* (2011, p. 802).

Linking authentic leadership to followers' attitudes and behaviours

Answering calls by May (2004) for a closer examination of a possible relationship between authentic leadership and experienced meaning at work, and by other researchers for a recognition of the role of emotions in the leadership process (Ashkanasy and Tse, 2000; Brief and Weiss, 2002). Gardner *et al.* (2004), developed a theoretical model linking authentic leadership to positive changes in the attitudes and behaviours of followers, and on performance outcomes (see Figure 9.2).

The model indicates how, in an authentic leadership process, the follower experiences both *personal* and *social* engagement with the leader. Personal engagement relates to the process by which a follower (e.g. Apple salesperson) engages with the leader (in this case the late Apple CEO Steve Jobs) in a way that becomes self-defining or self-referential (Gardner *et al.*, 2004). This means, essentially, that a follower's self-identity might become strongly bound to that of the leader. While this can be considered a dangerous concept if it occurs in the presence of a psychopathic or narcissistic leader (such as David Koresh), it can nevertheless lead to greatly positive outcomes if the leader could be considered authentically transformational (e.g. Mahatma Gandhi). The effects of this type of engagement can be significant and highly positive; for example, followers of Gandhi become influenced by his moral strength and thus begin to embody these qualities within themselves. This also works effectively on a group or cultural level, as a group member is typically rewarded by others for exhibiting a high level of prototypical group behaviour (e.g. via promotion).

This reward often materializes in the form of the group member being regarded as a more competent leader by others (Hogg, 2001). Within a work environment, and in accordance with the '*in-group*' phenomenon discussed in Chapter 5 ("Situational

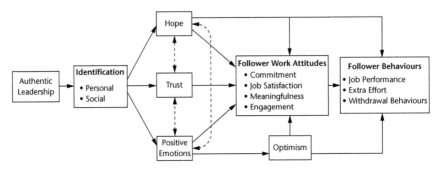

FIGURE 9.2 The process by which authentic leadership impacts follower attitudes and behaviours.

Source: Avolio *et al.* (2004, p. 803).

theories") in the context of Vertical Dyad Theory (Dansereau *et al.*, 1975), a moral employee working in an organization with a strong ethical and moral culture would be more likely to benefit from attributions of leadership by others due to their highly prototypical behaviour – and will be more likely to emerge as leaders in the eyes of their peers (Gardner *et al.*, 2004). The effects of this nature of *social* identification, at a cultural level (e.g. of prototypically moral employees being rewarded and promoted), is heartening, as it effectively promotes a culture of morality within an organization or society.

The model in Figure 9.2 explains how positive *personal* and *social* identification of an employee with an authentic transformational leader produces feelings of *hope, trust, positive emotions* and *optimism*. As stated by Luthans and Avolio (2003, p. 253), "the force multiplier throughout history has often been attributed to the leader's ability to generate hope." Mahatma Gandhi, Martin Luther King, Nelson Mandela, John F. Kennedy and Winston Churchill all possessed this ability and serve as useful examples of leaders with the ability to elicit such a powerful emotion. *Trust* is engendered via the establishment of open, transparent and authentic communication in the dyadic leadership process (e.g. by a leader communicating regularly with employees, keeping them informed of all aspects of a project, minimizing uncertainty, informing them of updates and asking for their input). Followers are empowered by authentic leaders who also act as moral and ethical role models, which in turn impacts the followers' inclination to experience feelings of trust in the leader. A high level of trust is associated with positive organizational outcomes (Dirks and Ferrin, 2001, 2002, cited in Gardner *et al.*, 2004). *Positive emotions* relates to all positive emotions, such as empathy. The model theorizes that authentic leaders are more likely to develop positive emotions within their followers, and that this will impact positively on the attitudes, behaviours (and, subsequently, performance outcomes) of employees. Specifically, the elicitation of positive emotions is theorized to lead to greater optimism among followers, which in turn is theorized to empower followers, lead to greater employee engagement and satisfaction and heighten their commitment to the organization (Gardner *et al.*, 2004, p. 814).

DISCUSSION STARTER

Andrew Carnegie, man of steel

I have known millionaires starve for lack of the nutriment which alone can sustain all that is human in man, and I know workmen, and many so-called poor men, who revel in luxuries beyond the power of those millionaires to reach. It is the mind that makes the body rich.[4]

Andrew Carnegie was one of the most successful business people of his era. By 1889, aged 53, Carnegie dominated the American steel market, eventually selling the company to JPMorgan for $480 million in 1901. Following the sale, Carnegie devoted his life to philanthropy, donating over $400 million to charitable causes. He believed that for a man to die rich meant to die disgraced and he gave away around 90 per cent of his personal wealth before his death.

Start the discussion: Was Carnegie correct in his beliefs that for a man to die rich is to die disgraced? Apply this logic to the philanthropic work (or lack thereof) of modern-day billionaires. What would Carnegie think of their work?

Authentic leader and follower development

The previous model (Figure 9.2) theorized the ways in which authentic transformational leaders are able to influence the attitudes and behaviours of their followers. But via which mechanisms are these behavioural and attitudinal changes facilitated? Building on the work of Luthans and Avolio (2003), Gardner *et al.* (2005) sought to further extend understanding of the authentic construct by creating a model that theorizes how authentic leaders and followers acquire the traits and behaviours of an authentic leader (see Figure 9.3). The model incorporates the four components of authentic leadership identified by Kernis (2003) – namely, awareness, unbiased processing, action and relational orientation – and adopts Luthans and Avolio's (2003, p. 243) definition of authentic leadership in organizations as one that "results in both greater self-awareness and self-regulated positive behaviours on the part of leaders and associates, fostering positive self-development".

The model theorizes authentic leadership and followership as reciprocal, where the authentic leader acts as a role model for followers, facilitating their authentic development, and where the development of the follower mirrors that of the leader. It also emphasizes the key role of an inclusive, ethical and caring organizational climate in allowing such developmental gains to be achieved. Theorized outcomes of authentic followership are greater feelings of trust, engagement and workplace well-being on the part of the follower, which in turn enhances their performance. The model draws heavily on *self-awareness* and *self-regulation*, and in this sense shares

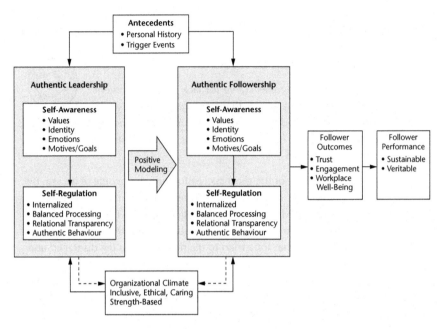

FIGURE 9.3   A conceptual framework for authentic leader and follower development.

Source: Gardner *et al.* (2005, p. 346).

notable similarities with Goleman's (1998) Five Components of Emotional Intelligence at Work model identified in the previous chapter (Chapter 8, "Emotional intelligence"). In the case of this model, *emotions* play a distinct role in self-awareness.[5]

The model adopts a self-based approach, proposing the centrality of the role of personal histories and trigger events as antecedents of both authentic leadership and authentic followership. In doing so, the theory draws on literature on the self and identity (Hoyle *et al.*, 1999; Leary and Tangney, 2003) in addition to work of Luthans and Avolio (2003) who propose that a leader's personal history and certain trigger events in an individual's history act as potential antecedents to the emergence of authentic leadership.

Two specific antecedents to the development of authentic leadership are identified, namely, *personal history* (education, familial influence, social status), and the existence of *trigger events* in the life history of the individual. Trigger events could be considered to be any kind of event to which an individual has been exposed, and which has exerted a developmental or transformative effect on the individual as a result. This could be as dramatic as a near-death experience, or as subtle as reading a book that inspires oneself in some way. This observation bears similarity to the recognition of the role of life stories in the development of authentic leaders (Shamir and Eilam, 2005).

Resistance to authentic leadership

It is possible that an authentic leader entering a new organization might face considerable resistance, particularly if the organization is a toxic one. Followers with low self-clarity, for example, might be especially defensive and might feel threatened by a leader who demonstrates both a high level of authenticity and transparency (Gardner *et al.*, 2005). Nevertheless, social contagion processes (Ilies *et al.*, 2005) allow for the spread of authenticity from leader to follower over a period of time, indicating that it is possible for a leader to reverse the effects of toxic leadership and to act as a positive agent for organizational change. This might require a level of transformational leadership ability on the part of the new leader, as the ability to *challenge the status quo* is required to transform the toxic workplace into one that is more positive. It would also require emotional intelligence, as the new leader would need to be willing to face the inevitable resistance that accompanies requirements for change (e.g. via demonstrating courage and self-belief in the face of hostile colleagues, and maintaining tenacity in applying new initiatives).

Pittinsky and Tyson (2004) comment that followers will look for authenticity markers in the life story of the leader in order to find validation for the authenticity of the leader and of their ability to lead them – something that Barack Obama or Steve Biko, for example, are able to demonstrate via their demonstrated commitment to engaging in transformative social programmes (their socially transformative 'track record') that can be observed over the course of their life histories. This suggests that a leader seeking to transform a toxic organization might benefit significantly not only from the articulation of messages of hope, or role modelling, but also via their demonstrated track record of authentic leadership that indicates both their moral and ethical strength and the true authenticity of their leadership.

Eudaemonia and authenticity

Eudaemonia, otherwise known as well-being, or personal expressiveness, occurs when one feels intensely alive and involved with a particular task. This has been likened to the achievement of a *flow state* (Csikszentmihalyi, 2003), and relates to the realization of one's true potential (Keyes *et al.*, 2002). As eudaemonia entails a state of living in accordance with one's true self, authentic behaviour will therefore lead to eudaemonia (Ilies *et al.*, 2005).

Ilies *et al.* (2005, p. 374) define authentic leaders as people who "are deeply aware of their values and beliefs, they are self-confident, genuine, reliable and trustworthy, and they focus on building followers' strengths, broadening their thinking and creating a positive and engaging organisational context'. Ilies *et al.* (2005) propose a model that theorizes authentic leadership influences on the eudaemonic well-being of leaders and followers, and which draws on the earlier quoted conceptualization of authentic leadership as the "unobstructed operation of one's true, or core, self in one's daily enterprise" (Kernis, 2003, p. 13), and theorizes that the integrity and self-awareness of the authentic leader engenders trust and an enhanced self-concept of their followers. According to the model (see Figure 9.4), authentic leaders act as positive role models, create a positive emotional atmosphere and encourage self-determination by creating opportunities for followers to be autonomous and to develop their skills.

The model identifies four components of eudaemonic well-being that are identical for both leader and follower: *personal expressiveness, self-realization/development, flow experience* and *self-efficacy/self-esteem*.

The model theorizes components of authentic leadership, and also identifies eudaemonic constructs that are influenced by authentic leadership. The model also illustrates a theorized relationship between a leader's authenticity and eudaemonic well-being, and proposes the ways in which authentic leadership can influence the eudaemonic well-being of followers.

Components of authentic leadership

The model (Figure 9.4) identified four components of authentic leadership: *self-awareness, unbiased processing, authentic behaviour/actions* and *authentic relational orientation* (Ilies *et al.*, 2005, p. 374). It is useful to again note the similarities between emotional intelligence and authentic leadership in the recognition of self-awareness as a key component of the theory, although it is also useful to note that in the context of this model, self-awareness is theorized to be predicted by a positive self-concept. *Unbiased processing* requires an individual to seek to engage in an objective assessment of one's strengths and weaknesses, and *authentic behaviour/actions* involves the ability of an individual to act in accordance with their core values and principles. The fourth component, *authentic relational orientation*, relates to the way in which an individual approaches their relationships. An individual who possesses authentic relational orientation is one who strives to achieve trust and honesty and to be truly genuine in their relationships.

Influence processes

The processes influencing followers' eudaemonic well-being are identified as *personal and organizational identification, positive emotional contagion, positive behavioural modelling, supporting self-determination* and *positive social exchanges*.

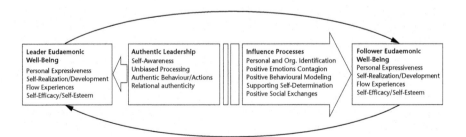

FIGURE 9.4 Authentic leader influence on eudaemonic well-being.

Source: Ilies *et al.* (2005, p. 377).

Personal and organizational identification (similar to the concept of *personal and social engagement* conceptualized in Gardner *et al.*'s [2004] model, described earlier), refers to the way in which a leader or employee's self-concept is affected by their identity as an employee of a particular organization, and the level to which the employee identifies personally with their leader. An authentic leader who communicates a message of trust, hope and optimism in their followers is likely to incubate a positive organizational culture via the process of *emotional contagion*, meaning that the work-place is likely to become more positive and satisfying for employees. The ability of the authentic leader to act as an effective *role model* further extends their ability to transform their employees and to empower them to act in a similarly authentic, moral and ethical manner. The concept of *self-determination* is a fascinating one, and is considered here within its role in facilitating eudaemonia. As it has been con-sidered at length earlier in the book (Chapter 4, "Behavioural theories"), it will not be subject to further discussion here. Finally, the authentic leader is able to promote eudaemonic well-being via developing high-quality relationships between themself and members of their team at a group and individual level.

Criticisms of authentic leadership

It can be observed that most of the work in this field has, thus far, relied on theoret-ical observation. Furthermore, empirical and theoretical work undertaken in the field remains relatively culturally homogenous, in that most studies have been undertaken by North American researchers.

Another criticism lies in the fact that, while perceptions of authenticity (by fol-lowers) can occur virtually instantaneously, the development and execution of such behaviours within the leader may have taken many years, particularly in regard to issues that involve a high level of transparency and moral and ethical conduct (Chan *et al.*, 2005). If the development of authenticity is, indeed, long term and complex, then this raises potential concerns in terms of how corporations might pragmatically seek to develop authentic leadership in their CEOs, managers and employees.

Life-story research remains very limited (Shamir and Eilam, 2005). Ilies *et al.* (2005) further caution that, while the proposition that underlies their model repres-ents testable hypotheses, it is still vital that a measure of authentic leadership is developed that can adequately evaluate the construct (something that the field cur-rently lacks). Studies of authentic leadership have, so far, been leader-centric and more studies of authentic followership are arguably required in order to further understand the phenomenon of authenticity in leadership.

Finally, Shamir and Eilam (2005) comment that all current definitions of authen-tic leadership are arbitrary, in the sense that there is currently no one universally accepted definition of the construct, nor is there any reliably valid means of testing propositions. In order for the field to advance effectively, it appears vital that further empirical work is undertaken. Only then can the claims and observations of authen-tic leadership theorists be tested, and the field advanced in a meaningful and efficient way.

Measuring authentic leadership

Henderson and Hoy (1983) were the first to develop a scale to measure authentic leadership. The 32-item Leader Authenticity Inventory has, however, been criticized for a lack of construct validity and generalizability. The most commonly used instruments currently used to measure authentic leadership are the ALQ (Authentic Leadership Questionnaire) (Walumbwa *et al.*, 2008) and the AI:3 (Authenticity Inventory) (Kernis and Goldman, 2005, 2006). Such critiques should be viewed within the context that authentic leadership (and its associated instruments of measurement) remains in its infancy, as it is a relatively new concept to emerge from the literature.

Summary

Avolio and Gardner (2005) conceptualize authentic leadership as a *root* construct that provides a foundation for all positive forms of leadership. This means, for example, that a transformational leader, or a socialized charismatic leader, can both be considered *authentic* if they demonstrate the moral and ethical nature of the authentic leader, or if they possess the traits or abilities (such as self-regulation) of the authentic leader. That is, the traits and abilities – and the centrality of moral and ethical consideration – that define authentic leadership provide a solid foundation upon which all forms of positive leadership can be based. This separates the *pseudo-transformational* from the *transformational* leader and stresses the need to locate a synergy between the values and actions of the leader in order to ensure that they are acting in an authentic way, and not simply creating an image of authenticity that will allow them to manipulate their followers to achieve their own self-serving and destructive aims.

The central focus of moral and ethical integrity of authentic leadership carries particular resonance when one is confronted by the ramifications of leadership devoid of authenticity – a concept that occupies the focus of the next chapter: toxic and destructive leadership (Chapter 10, "Destructive leadership").

 **Expert insight**

On the ATAQ

Tammo Walter is the CEO of ATAQ Fuel. A believer in pushing limits, his vision for innovating within the sport performance industry and the development of an extremely motivated, talented team has made ATAQ a powerful force to be reckoned with. Prior to founding ATAQ, Tammo worked as Creative Director with a wide variety of brands such as Nike, Motorola, UCLA (University of California, Los Angeles), American Eagle Outfitters, Miller Lite and Jeep.

The inspiration for ATAQ came from Tammo's own drive to improve his performance as a road cyclist. In this expert insight, Tammo shares his experiences of leading ATAQ, what leadership and success mean to him, and how he achieved the ultimate entrepreneurial dream – transforming his passion into his career.

Work hard, push limits

"A common question I get asked in job interviews is what it is like to work at ATAQ. It's very much like being part of a professional sports team. As in sports we are under constant pressure of our competition and if we don't give our best – all the time – we won't be successful. We are still a small fish in a big pond and as a start-up with limited resources we need to work smarter and harder.

The team with every single player in it is ultimately the key factor to our success. We have fun working hard and pushing the limits, we are respectful but straightforward and we have high expectations of each other.

Everyone understands the importance of the team, their role within it and the different skills everyone else brings to the table to get to a common goal. It's not a requirement, but all of our employees are athletes. I found that people that either are, or have been, athletes, to be great employees. The concept of getting out what you put in and having to work hard to succeed is something ingrained in them.

A lot of my approach to running a team has, in one form or another, been influenced by fitness and sports. In my view the parallels to success in business and sports are quite stunning, certainly in the way things are in our industry, which happens to be a highly competitive one. Team culture is a complex and dynamic organism influenced by many factors but without a doubt it is substantially influenced by the example the team leader sets. In our case sport has always played a crucial role in my life and the way I approach many aspects of it – including running a team.

Cycling and working out also helps to keep me sane. It helps me decompress, focus and be more energized throughout the day. I can feel the difference on days I've been working out versus not (for example, during business travel). As physically exhausting as some workouts are, they usually give me a great sense of mental cleansing and recalibration which keeps me a lot more balanced on hectic and stressful days.

Building leadership skills

I was born and raised in Germany. Coming out of high school I joined the German Special Forces (KSK) for a few years, then went to college studying graphic design and marketing. I founded a branding agency and B-2-C [business-to-consumer] e-commerce platform pooling consumer demand for electricity and gas after those markets opened up in Germany in 1999. In 2003,

I applied for the sixth time for a US permanent resident visa by entering the US Green Card Lottery. Persistence gave me the luck of the draw – I arrived in New York City in 2004 with only a suitcase and a backpack.

To hone my English skills, I started working as a greeter at a Club Monaco retail store in Manhattan. That also taught me a lot about the culture and people here before I had the opportunity to work as an Art Director for the advertising agency BBDO.

A few years later I switched to the corporate side and joined Motorola Mobile Phones as Creative Director for Global Advertising. A couple of years and many phone launches later I switched back to the agency side, joining branding agency 160/90, opening and running an office for them in California, helping Nike for many years to put the sport of tennis back into the minds of the teen market. Overall, I spent about 20 years in branding and advertising before my business partner and I started ATAQ in 2016.

With my move to California in 2012 I picked up road cycling and started working with a coach and nutritionist promoting a plant-based diet. Encouraged to get off any synthetic food and supplements I looked for clean, plant-based sports nutrition products but couldn't find what I was looking for. The general trend of people caring more and more about their food, bodies and health, coupled with becoming increasingly more active and competitive, provided a great opportunity to develop a brand and products. Our first line of cold-pressed drink products was launched in mid-2016, and we added a line of energy bars in mid-2017. That was followed by a line of electrolyte drink mixes and plant-based protein powders in early 2018. Initially we launched online before venturing into local specialty retail in early 2018, regional grocery retail in early 2019 and then national chains by the end of 2019. If things go as planned, we will be in over 3,000 stores by Q1 [the first quarter] of 2020.

Turning your passion into your business

My first advice in turning your passion into your job is to trust your gut. If you are really passionate about something and you have an idea that you are excited about and lets you turn your passion into your profession, then do it. It's not often that you come across such an opportunity and when it happens, grab it by its horns.

My second key piece of advice is – don't do it alone. Find a trusted companion and sparring partner with a complementary skill-set that can propel the business forward. I was in the fortunate position to have exactly that. My business partner has a supply chain management and operations background and it's the perfect addition to my set of skills. Building a business is always challenging, with plenty of amazing ups and steep downs. Being able to share the excitement and the burden along the way is incredibly helpful.

The importance of research

From the very beginning, we always put a lot of effort into our product development. Having clinical research to support the functionality and purpose of our products was and still is crucial. Because our products are plant-based, we naturally face more scrutiny by the general public and still fight against the stereotype that plant-based products aren't as effective or are inferior to synthetic products.

With a massive shift in nutritional consumer behaviour, particularly over the last couple of years, that perception is slowly changing – but when we started, we had to make sure we could scientifically back up our claims. However, the subject matter of sports nutrition, let alone clinical research data, is very complex. This, in turn, makes it hard to convey those key benefits in simple advertising messages. We find educating our audience on research and efficacy at and during events more effective than traditional advertising.

The power of sponsorship

We partner with high-performing athletes that fit to our brand, strategic approach and genuinely use and believe in our products. The right athlete partner simply functions as an opinion leader and can authentically represent us and stand behind our products. That is valuable as, generally speaking, the trust with a third party individual is always higher than with a business. In addition, we love to work with athletes to put our products to the test, get frontline and professional feedback, inform product advancements and new product lines.

Changing the game

Watch the just recently launched documentary "The Game Changers".[6] The producers did a great job breaking the advantages of plant-based sports nutrition down for a mass audience and using athletes to demonstrate its effects from a variety of sports.

Our bodies recognize natural ingredients as food which plays a crucial role in what we absorb whereas many synthetic supplements are left alone to be pushed through our digestive system. We aren't what we eat. Instead, we are what we absorb. If the fuel doesn't get to the engine it doesn't matter what we put into the tank. The research of the last two decades has shown and clinically proven what efficacy natural and plant-based ingredients and supplements can have. Our ability to develop high-end sports nutrition products is now so advanced that, especially with long-term use, it's better for the athletes' performance, their long-term health and the environment.

A view from the top

Within your business universe and its limits, you can do what you think is the absolute best thing to do and no one can tell you to do something different. You can dream up an objective and goal and go for it. You are in charge of defining the journey of your business. But with that freedom and flexibility comes the burden of having to carry any bad consequences if something goes wrong.

I truly care and that applies to all aspects of our business, whether it is about the people, brand, products, customers, business partners, vendors, you name it. I care a lot and I lead by example. In my experience that creates an environment of trust and respect which is a fantastic base to build a team from.

The road to success is paved with setbacks and speed bumps. It's just the nature of the beast but the less sparkly side of building a business. Most owners and entrepreneurs have a very high level of drive and determination. But externally they of course have to deal with everyone else that 'runs' on a normal pace. Accepting that and finding a way to not let that throw you off is key.

No one cares about your business as much as you, the owner. In consequence it means others, especially on the outside of your organization, don't care that much about your business. That's not always easy to accept and deal with, especially when your money and future is on the line.

Learning from others

I haven't been inspired by one particular person. For me, it comes down to an assembly of experiences I collected from a variety of different leaders over the years. When you observe, pay attention and analyse a little bit what others do well (or badly), there is a lot that can be learned from and applied to your own way of running a business or living life.

If you are open minded and receptive then leadership inspiration can come from many different people – a great high school teacher or college professor, a colleague or boss, CEOs of renowned or global companies, politicians … the list goes on and on.

Leadership in my view is a combination of a few personality traits – but ultimately it all funnels into the ability to motivate people to follow and achieve a common goal. In order to motivate people, you need vision, focus, determination, confidence, empathy, authenticity and above all you need to lead by example. Success is a milestone and only a temporary moment. Similar to success in training and competition, it applies to a set benchmark that often moves or shifts as soon as it is reached.

The best advice?

Trust your gut. **"**

Find out more

- ATAQ Fuel official website: https://ataqfuel.com/

Questions

1 How does this expert insight provide a compelling example of *eudaemonia* (a form of happiness that is inextricably linked to a person's achievement of their true calling) (Kernis and Goldman, 2006)?

2 Shamir and Eilam (2005) discuss the centrality of life stories in the development of the authentic leader. Apply this theoretical observation to the CEO profiled in this expert insight.

3 The model of eudaemonic well-being (Ilies *et al.* 2005, p. 374) identifies the need for self-awareness, unbiased processing, authentic behaviour/action and authentic relational orientation. Identify an example of each of these practices in this expert insight.

Case study: tour of duty

Robert Swan Mueller III is a quintessential all-American hero. Now in his seventies, he has demonstrated a consistency of commitment to public service, an upholding of moral and ethical responsibility and a track record of exemplary leadership that leaves him virtually unrivalled in the annals of FBI history.

Hailing from an affluent family, the son of a World War II former Navy submarine commander, Mueller attended a distinguished prep school. A high academic achiever and talented athlete, Mueller followed in the footsteps of his father by attending Princeton, before studying a master's degree in international relations at NYU (a degree, incidentally, that he engaged with while waiting to be cleared for active service in Vietnam).

He was 24 when he began his first tour of duty in Vietnam as a Second Lieutenant in the US Marine Corps, receiving a Bronze Star for bravery. He quickly won the deep respect of his platoon.

A leader built in battle

Mueller credits his time in Vietnam for shaping him as a leader, in allowing him to forge a character under fire, to feel confident in his decisions, to lead a team and to place all future challenges into perspective – nothing he would face after Vietnam, however tough, could ever rival the realities of war. As a lieutenant, he was considered a reserved soldier, meticulous planner, courageous, extremely well-prepared and a talented leader. He took the responsibility of leadership on the field of battle – and throughout every other role in his life – extremely seriously.

Mueller's time in Vietnam remains a defining experience in his life. He is a man who retains a pride to this day that the US Marine Corps entrusted him with the responsibility of leading other Marines into battle – and for whom no courtroom battle or government position will ever match the intensity and hardships thrown at him and his men in Vietnam. This, perhaps, offers us one explanation as to why Mueller remained consistently stoic, calm and immovable while investigating charges of Russian interference in the 2016 US Presidential election, despite a rising chorus of uproarious attacks on his character, competence and integrity by Fox News, Donald Trump, members of the Trump Administration and other Conservative comment-ators and alt-right figures.

Teflon Don: staging a breakout

After his successful military career, Robert Mueller enjoyed an equally distinguished prosecutorial career. For example, he sat at the helm of the US Criminal Division of the Justice Department at the time of the high-profile, politically sensitive Lockerbie bombing case. He also led the historic prosecution of the Gambino crime family boss John Gotti and became Director of the FBI only one week before 11 September 2001, successfully navigating the Bureau through one of its most challenging periods in modern history.

Mueller's investigation into, and prosecution of, the Enron board, meanwhile, remains a defining case in corporate law and led to wide-ranging changes in the way in which accounting regulations are enforced. Mueller's leadership style while at the FBI and as a lawyer at a private firm continued to mirror that of his time in active service in Vietnam – disciplined, dignified, private – a man who prioritized integrity, honesty, diligence and efficiency over all else.

The story of Mueller's prosecution of John Gotti, head of the infamous Gotti crime family in New York, is remarkably compelling. John Gotti was a ruthless figure who was acquitted three times in high-profile trials relating to federal racketeering, assault and conspiracy charges (prosecutors alleged that racketeering activities included organized murder, smuggling cigarettes, loan shark activity and truck hijacks), earning him the name Teflon Don (as no charges ever seemed to stick). He was also known as 'Dapper Don' due to his love of ostentatious suits and extravagant appear-ance. This extravagant lifestyle would end forever, however, in December 1990, when Gotti was arrested at the Ravenite Social Club (his headquarters) in the Little Italy neighbourhood of New York City.

From 1990–1991, Gotti was held in prison awaiting trial along with one of his top lieutenants, Frank Locascio and trusted hit man Salvatore 'Sammy the Bull' Gravano. In October 1991, Mueller signed off as US Assistant Attorney General on an operation that would require Gravano to be smuggled out of his cell to allow him to testify against Locascio and Gotti. At the time, Bruce Mouw, who headed up the FBI's C-16 team in charge of a years-long investigation into Gotti, and Mueller constructed a plan to remove Gravano from the cell under the auspices of requiring a voice analysis test. This enabled Gravano to meet with and confess to the FBI and federal prosecu-tors without Gotti and Locascio suspecting that he was turning against them. The plan worked; Sammy the Bull turned on his former boss and struck a plea deal.

Gravano, former underboss of the Gravano crime family, was now, in mob parlance, a rat. Gravano had killed 19 men (10 of whom were directly ordered by Gotti) but struck a plea deal that saw him sentenced to only 5 years in jail. Gotti, one of the most feared crime lords in modern history, was subsequently sentenced to life without parole on murder and racketeering charges.

Enron: the smartest guys in the room?

The collapse of the energy giant Enron represents what was, at the time, the largest corporate bankruptcy in the US. In December 2001, Enron filed for bankruptcy. Soon after, FBI Director Robert Mueller launched the Enron Task Force alongside Deputy Attorney General Larry Thompson and Assistant Attorney General for the Criminal Division Michael Chertoff. The Department of Justice aided the Task Force – a critical fact, as some Enron executives were, at the time, particularly close to the Bush family and to several other prominent Republicans, which raised the possibility that the Task Force might be held back by sensitive political associations or limited at the request of senior political figures. A close association with the Department of Justice went some way to mitigating that risk.

Despite pushback from higher level government figures, the Task Force charged the wife of Andrew Fastow, the Chief Financial Officer of Enron, with tax evasion relatively early in their investigation. The arrest placed pressure on Fastow who cooperated quickly. It was a move also designed to signal to high society that the investigation meant business and would not be swayed by political pressures. The strategy worked. Flipping lower level executives and persuading them to eventually testify against their bosses subsequently formed a major part of the Enron Task Force prosecutorial strategy. It is a strategy, under Mueller, that would be repeated effectively many years later as part of the indictments that swiftly emerged from the Russian interference investigation.

The role of the Task Force was to spearhead an investigation into crimes allegedly executed by Enron executives, which was an extremely complex task. The fraudulent acts committed by Enron executives were complex to identify, track and uncover, and when Mueller collected salient evidence proving evidence of fraud, Enron CEO Jeffrey Skilling and Chairman and Chief Executive Kenneth Lay attempted to shift the blame to other lower-level staff – for example, their employees, their attorneys and auditors.

One of the early successes of the Enron Task Force was to win a jury conviction of Enron's auditors Arthur Anderson on obstruction of justice charges. Mueller's strategy was to be rigorous, to work slowly and thoroughly. Five years into the work of the Task Force, former Enron CEO Jeffrey Skilling and Chairman and Chief Executive Kenneth Lay were eventually found guilty (although it is worth noting that the Supreme Court later overturned part of the Skilling verdict). The Task Force faced great scrutiny and political pressures throughout (a common feature of Mueller's investigations). As is the case with Mueller's more recent spearheading of the FBI investigation into Russian interference in the 2016 US Presidential election, Mueller stayed largely silent, seemingly unruffled by political and media pressures, instead committing to a long game and retaining an airtight control on leaks. Another feature of Mueller's work seems to be the ability to silently weather scrutiny and to accept that he and his team would need to exercise a high degree of patience in the investigative process – his investigations tended to take considerable time but always produced impressive outcomes.

US Russian interference

After completing his remarkably long and successful tenure at the FBI, Mueller became a partner at the law firm WilmerHale, but was in fact only away for four years – it was not long before US Deputy Attorney General Rod Rosenstein requested that he return to serve as Special Counsel in the Russia investigation, following James Comey's sudden firing by President Donald Trump. Mueller's name was thrust into the media spotlight during the years that followed and, for a time, the "Mueller Report" became the biggest topic of conversation in households across America.

To date, Mueller's 22-month investigation led to indictments against 34 people and 3 organisations on nearly 200 separate criminal charges. Six associates of Trump have been convicted. At the time of writing, one of those associates – Roger Stone – is awaiting sentencing. Prosecutions include Paul Manafort, who pleaded guilty to eight counts of tax and bank fraud for which he receive a custodial sentence of four years. He received a further 3.5-year jail sentence for charges related to secret foreign lobbying and witness tampering.

Rick Gates, an associate of Manafort, pleaded guilty in February 2018 on charges of lying to investigators and financial fraud. Lieutenant General Michael Flynn, a campaign adviser and briefly National Security Advisor to Trump was also convicted as was campaign advisor George Papadopoulos. Dutch attorney Alex Van Der Zwaan served a short prison sentence before being deported to the Netherlands.

In August 2018, long-time Trump lawyer and adviser, Cohen, pleaded guilty in federal court to multiple criminal charges, while Roger Stone, a long-time associate of Manafort and Gates, faces up to 50 years in jail for 7 felonies that include lying to Congress under oath, witness tampering and obstruction of justice. In July 2018, the Special Counsel also indicted 12 Russian intelligence officers on charges of hacking DNC (Democratic National Committee) and DCCC (Democratic Congressional Campaign Committee) servers and leaking data.

Find out more

- Special Counsel Robert S. Mueller, III (March 2019). Report on the Investigation into Russian Interference in the 2016 Presidential Election [Redacted]. US Department of Justice. Available at: https://cdn.cnn.com/cnn/2019/images/04/18/mueller-report-searchable.pdf.
- Shubber, K. (5 March 2019). The Big Read: Mueller Road Map: The Next Steps for the Trump Investigation. *Financial Times*. Available at: www.ft.com/content/a17b2ca8-3e67-11e9-9bee-efab61506f44.

- Thomas, C. W. (1 April 2002). The Rise and Fall of Enron. *Journal of Accountancy.* Available at: www.journalofaccountancy.com/issues/2002/apr/theriseand fallofenron.html.
- Blum, H. (1 December 2017). How Scared Should Trump Be of Mueller? Ask John Gotti or Sammy "The Bull". *Vanity Fair.* Available at: www.vanityfair.com/news/2017/12/how-scared-should-trump-be-of-mueller-ask-john-gotti-or-sammy-the-bull.

Questions

1 Robert Swan Mueller III demonstrated remarkable consistency in his approach to leadership throughout his life. What does this tell us about Mueller's authenticity as a leader?

2 Mueller seems to be motivated greatly by the idea of public service. Relate this motivation to authentic leadership theory.

3 Mueller's status as a decorated military veteran shows us that – even under fire – his values and behaviours did not waver. With reference to authentic leadership and emotional intelligence theory, explain why this might have been the case.

4 In today's media, tech-driven age, political leaks seem to have become an almost constant feature of campaigns and sensitive political projects. How do you think that Mueller managed to keep an airtight grip on data and information during the Russia investigation, despite its extremely high-profile nature?

5 Mueller seems unmoved by a need for public adulation or approval. With reference to McClelland's Theory of Motivation, explain why this might have made him more successful as a leader.

6 Mueller seems to have been clear as to what his values, beliefs and identity were from an early age. Comment on how this has not only made him a more authentic leader, but also more successful within his professional career.

CHAPTER 9 QUIZ

1 Avolio and Gardner (2005) conceptualize authentic leadership as a root construct. What exactly does this mean?

2 Self-based definitions of authentic leadership centre upon the internal state of the leader and focus principally on the self-development of the leader. Provide three examples of self-based definitions, taken from this chapter.

3 Developmental definitions concentrate more closely on the way in which authenticity is developed in both leaders and followers. Provide three examples of developmental definitions, taken from this chapter.

4 Summarize the role of morals and ethics in authentic leadership.

5 What is eudaemonia, and how can it be considered similar to the achievement of a flow state?

6 Luthans and Avolio (2003) propose that a leader's personal history and certain trigger events in an individual's history act as potential antecedents to the emergence of authentic leadership. Can you identify a leader whose life story contains a trigger event of this nature?

7 Name one self-based model of authentic leadership.

8 Identify the key components of the model identified in question 7.

9 Name one developmental model of authentic leadership.

10 Identify the key components of the model identified in question 9.

11 Identify two criticisms of authentic leadership.

12 Name the instrument most effective in measuring authentic leadership and identify its weaknesses.

Notes

1 Quote taken from an interview conducted for this book with CEO Tammo Walter, in the expert insight "On the ATAQ" that appears later in this chapter.

2 UBS is an investment bank with a presence in 50 countries.

3 A form of happiness that is inextricably linked to a person's achievement of their true calling (Kernis and Goldman, 2006).

4 Andrew Carnegie (1895). *The Bulletin of the American Iron and Steel Association*, 29–30, p. 253. American Iron and Steel Association.

5 Readers are encouraged to refer back to Chapter 8 for further elucidation concerning the role of emotions in the self-awareness of the leader and follower (as identified within the model) as it has already been discussed at greater length within this context.

6 "The Game Changers" is a documentary presented by James Cameron, Arnold Schwarzenegger, Jackie Chan, Lewis Hamilton, Novak Djokovic and Chris Paul. See the official website: https://gamechangersmovie.com/.

References

Ashkanasy, N.M. and Tse, B. (2000). Transformational Leadership as Management of Emotion: A Conceptual Review. In N.M. Ashkanasy, C.E.J. Hartel and W.J. Zerbe (eds.), *Emotions in the Workplace*. Westport, CT: Quorum Books, pp. 221–235.

Auerbach, A. and Webber, A.M. (1987). Red Auerbach on Management. *Harvard Business Review*, 65 (March–April), pp. 84–91.

Avolio, B.J. and Gardner, W.L. (2005). Authentic Leadership Development: Getting to the Root of Positive Leadership. *Leadership Quarterly*, 16, pp. 315–338.

Avolio, B.J., Luthans, F. and Walumbwa, F.O. (2004). *Authentic Leadership: Theory Building for Veritable Sustained Performance*. Working paper, Gallup Leadership Institute, University of Nebraska–Lincoln.

Bass, B.M. (1977). Does the Transactional–Transformational Leadership Paradigm Transcend Organizational and National Boundaries? *American Psychologist*, 52(2), pp. 130–139.

Bass, B.M. (1985). *Leadership and Performance Beyond Expectations*. New York: Free Press.

Bass, B.M. and Riggio, R.E. (2006). *Transformational Leadership*. 2nd ed. Mahwah, NJ: Lawrence Erlbaum Associates.

Bass, B.M. and Steidlmeier, P. (1999). Ethics, Character, and Authentic Transformational Leadership Behaviour. *Leadership Quarterly*, 10(2), pp. 181–217.

Bennis, W.G. (2003). The Crucibles of Authentic Leadership. In J. Antonakis, A.T. Gianciolo and R.J. Sternberg (eds.), *The Nature of Leadership*. Thousand Oaks, Sage, pp. 331–342.

Brief, A.P. and Weiss, H.M. (2002). Organizational Behavior: Affect in the Workplace. *Annual Review of Psychology*, 53(1), pp. 279–307.

Burns, J.M. (1978). *Leadership*. New York: Harper & Row.

Carlo, G. and Edwards, C.P. (2005). *Nebraska Symposium on Motivation. Moral Motivation through the Life Span* (Vol. 51). Lincoln, NE: University of Nebraska Press.

Chan, A., Hannah, S.T. and Gardner, W.L. (2005). Veritable Authentic Leadership: Emergence, Functioning, and Impacts. In W.L. Gardner, B.J. Avolio and F.O. Walumbwa (eds.), *Authentic Leadership Theory and Practice: Origins, Effects and Development*. Oxford: Elsevier Science, pp. 3–41.

Cooper, C., Scandura, T.A. and Schriesheim, C.A. (2005). Looking Forward but Learning from Our Past: Potential Challenges to Developing Authentic Leadership Theory and Authentic Leaders. *Leadership Quarterly*, 16, pp. 475–493.

Csikszentmihalyi, M. (2003). *Good Business: Leadership, Flow, and the Making of Meaning*. New York: Penguin Books.

Dansereau, F., Graen, G. and Haga, W.J. (1975). A Vertical Dyad Approach to Leadership within Formal Organizations. *Organizational Behavior and Human Performance*, 13(1), pp. 46–78.

Deci, E.L. and Ryan, L.M. (1995). Human Autonomy: The Basis for True Self-Esteem. In M.H. Kernis (ed.), *Efficacy, Agency and Self-Esteem*. New York: Plenum Press, pp. 31–49.

Dirks, K. and Ferrin, D. (2001). The Role of Trust in Organizational Settings. *Organization Science*, 12(4), pp. 450–467.

Dirks, K.T. and Ferrin, D.L. (2002). Trust in Leadership: Meta-Analytic Findings and Implications for Research and Practice. *Journal of Applied Psychology*, 87, p. 611.

Eigel, K.M. and Kuhnert, K.W. (2005). Authentic Development: Leadership Development Level and Executive Effectiveness. In W.L. Gardner, B.J. Avolio and F.O. Walumbwa (eds.), *Authentic Leadership Theory and Practice: Origins, Effects and Development*. Oxford: Elsevier Science, pp. 357–386.

Gardner, W.L., Avolio, B.J., Luthans, F., May, D.R. and Walumbwa, F.O. (2004). Unlocking the Mask: A Look at the Process by Which Authentic Leaders Impact Follower Attitudes and Behaviours. *Leadership Quarterly*, 15(6), pp. 801–823.

Gardner, W.L., Avolio, B.J., Luthans, F., May, D.R. and Walumbwa, F.O. (2005). Can You See the Real Me? A Self-Based Model of Authentic Leader and Follower Development. *Leadership Quarterly*, 16(3), pp. 343–372.

George, J.M. (2000). Emotions and Leadership: The Role of Emotional Intelligence. *Human Relations*, 53, pp. 1027–1055.

George, W. (2003). *Authentic Leadership: Rediscovering the Secrets to Creating Lasting Value*. San Francisco, CA: Jossey-Bass.

Goleman, D. (1998). *Working with Emotional Intelligence*. New York: Bantam.

Halpin, A.W. and Croft, O.B. (1966). The Organisational Climate of Schools. In A.W. Halpin (ed.), *Theory and Research in Administration*. New York: Macmillan, pp. 131–249.

Henderson, J.E. and Hoy, W.K. (1983). Leader Authenticity: The Development and Test of an Operational Measure. *Educational and Psychological Research*, 3(2), pp. 63–75.

Hogg, M.A. (2001). A Social Identity Theory of Leadership. *Personality and Social Psychology Review*, 5(3), pp. 184–200.

Hoyle, R.H., Kernis, M.H., Leary, M.R. and Baldwin, M.W. (1999). *Selfhood: Identity, Esteem, Regulation*. Boulder, CO: Westview Press.

Ilies, R., Morgeson, F.P. and Nahrgang, J.D. (2005). Authentic Leadership and Eudaemonic Well-Being: Understanding Leader–Follower Outcomes. *Leadership Quarterly*, 16(3), pp. 373–394.

Kernis, M.H. (2003). Toward a Conceptualization of Optimal Self-Esteem. *Psychological Inquiry*, 14(1), pp. 1–26.

Kernis, M.H. and Goldman, B.M. (2005). Authenticity: A Multicomponent Perspective. In A. Tesser, J. Wood and D. Stapel (eds.), *On Building, Defending, and Regulating the Self: A Psychological Perspective*. New York: Psychology Press, pp. 31–52.

Kernis, M.H. and Goldman, B.M. (2006). A Multicomponent Conceptualization of Authenticity: Research and Theory. In M.P. Zanna (ed.), *Advances in Experimental Social Psychology* (Vol. 38). San Diego, CA: Academic Press, pp. 284–357.

Keyes, C.L.M., Shmotkin, D. and Ryff, C.D. (2002). Optimizing Well-Being: The Empirical Encounter of Two Traditions. *Journal of Personality and Social Psychology*, 82(6), pp. 1007–1022.

Klenke, K. (2005). The Internal Theatre of the Authentic Leader. In W.L. Gardner, B.J. Avolio and F.O. Walumbwa (eds.), *Authentic Leadership Theory and Practice: Origins, Effects and Development*. Oxford: Elsevier Science, pp. 155–182.

Leary, M.R. and Tangney, J.P. (2003). *Handbook of Self and Identity*. New York: Guilford Press.

Luthans, F. and Avolio, B.J. (2003). Authentic Leadership: A Positive Developmental Approach. In K.S. Cameron, J.E. Dutton and R.E. Quinn (eds.), *Positive Organizational Scholarship*. San Francisco, CA: Barrett-Koehler, pp. 241–261.

May, D.R. (2004). The Flourishing of the Human Spirit at Work: Toward an Understanding of the Determinants and Outcomes of Experienced Meaningfulness at Work. Paper presented at the European Conference on Positive Psychology, Verbania Pallanza, Italy, 5–8 July.

May, D.R., Chan, A.Y.L., Hodges, T.D. and Avolio, B.J. (2003). Developing the Moral Component of Authentic Leadership. *Organizational Dynamics*, 32(3), pp. 247–260.

Novicevic, M.M, Harvey, M.G., Buckley, M.R., Brown, J.A. and Evans, R. (2006). Authentic Leadership: A Historical Perspective. *Journal of Leadership and Organisational Studies*, 13(1), pp. 64–76.

Pittinsky, T.L. and Tyson, C.J. (2004). Leader Authenticity Markers: Findings from a Study of African-American Political Leaders. Paper presented at the Gallup–University of Nebraska Leadership Institute Summit, Omaha, NE, 10–12 June.

Rome, B.K. and Rome, S.C. (1967). Humanistic Research on Large Social Organisations. In J.F.T. Bugental (ed.), *Challenges of Humanistic Psychology*. New York: McGraw-Hill, pp. 181–193.

Shamir, B. and Eilam, G. (2005). What's Your Story?: A Life-Stories Approach to Authentic Leadership Development. *Leadership Quarterly*, 16(2), pp. 395–417.

Walumbwa, F.O., Avolio, B.J., Gardner, W.L., Vernsing, T.S. and Peterson, S.J. (2008). Authentic Leadership: Development and Validation of a Theory Based Measure. *Journal of Management*, 34(1), pp. 89–126.

Zhu, W., Avolio, B.J., Riggio, R.E. and Sosik, J.J. (2011). The Effects of Authentic Transformational Leadership on Follower and Group Ethics. *Leadership Quarterly*, 22(5), pp. 801–817.

Other resources

See PowerPoint slides on the companion website at www.routledge.com/9780367374822.

10

DESTRUCTIVE LEADERSHIP

"I've been rolled out as a token more times than I care to count, and it is depressing."
— Anonymous senior executive[1]

Great leaders possess the ability to transform lives, to rescue nations, to fight great injustices and to lead the world to find a better way to live. But it is not enough to simply consider what makes a leader great. Once must also consider what makes a leader destructive; what causes a company such as Enron to become so toxic that it implodes in the most catastrophic way, ruining lives, stealing life savings and even leading to suicides. What leads a nation to become subsumed under the fascist leadership of Hitler, or for the evils of apartheid to have become so systematically and legally powerful in twentieth-century South Africa? To understand such a phenomenon is to recognize the need to deconstruct the way in which the leader, follower and environment interact to allow such destructive leadership to take place, and to comprehend how the subjugation of the many by the few can occur so frequently and with so much force – how, in the historic words of Steve Biko (1986, p. 92), "the most potent weapon in the hands of the oppressor is the mind of the oppressed".

While the 'Great Man' theory of leadership provided the reader with the first great question of contemporary leadership studies – Is a great leader born or made? – subsequent theories of leadership have sought to further understand this concept, asking whether the study of effective leadership should be leader-centric, dyadic or follower-centric in nature. Questions have been raised concerning how the impact of effective leadership can be defined, conceptualized and measured, and how it might be taught, and theories have been discussed in relation to the external situational variables that might affect the success of the leadership process.

While the study of charismatic leadership has furthered our understanding of the *dark side* of leadership, it is nevertheless surprising that the focus of leadership scholars has, thus far, neglected to fully consider the idea of *destructive* leadership – limiting itself to the study of what might make a leader great. The focus of this chapter is, therefore, to draw together emerging research in the relatively new field of *destructive leadership* studies, a field that has emerged since the late 1980s (Conger, 1990; Kellerman, 2004; Luthans *et al.*, 1998; Schaubroeck *et al.*, 2007), and to consider its impact on employees and organizations. The concept remains pertinent given the financial and economic costs of workplace stress (Xie and Schaubroeck, 2001), the frequency with which employees have cited their manager as a source of stress (Schabracq and Cooper, 1998) and the effects that bullying and other negative leadership behaviours exert on the success of the organization (Rayner, 1997).

Structure of the chapter

The chapter begins with an invitation to the reader to engage with a brief illustrative example of destructive leadership ("Enron and destructive leadership"), before considering competing definitions of *toxic* and *destructive* leadership. Readers are introduced to the mechanisms by which followers are drawn towards destructive leaders, how some followers are more susceptible than others, and how cultures are made toxic as a result. Three key models are then presented: a model of *constructive and destructive leadership* (Einarsen *et al.*, 2007), the *toxic triangle* (Padilla *et al.*, 2007) and the *susceptible circle* (Thoroughgood *et al.*, 2012). All three models enable the reader to advance their understanding of the way in which toxic and destructive leaders are able to attain and retain power over subordinates, and to consider ways in which such power might be challenged. A critique of destructive leadership theories is then provided, followed by an overview of ways in which destructive leadership can be measured.

The expert insight for this chapter is provided by a senior leader who shares with us an anonymized account of workplace racism. "Just show me the data" offers a case study of the compelling rise and fall of Theranos Inc. and its CEO Elizabeth Holmes. An end-of-chapter quiz completes the chapter.

Enron and destructive leadership

Enron was, at one time, the largest provider of natural gas in North America, and a powerful mediator between gas producers and utility companies. By year end 2000, Enron's market capitalization exceeded $60 billion. Previously rated the most innovative large company by *Fortune* magazine, the company boasted an image of an elite meritocratic, high performance culture (as evidenced by its internal *Vision and Values* training video (readers are advised to locate this video online using an appropriate media-based website such as YouTube).

Enron quickly extended its scope to trading in other energy markets such as electric power and coal and expanded overseas, hoping to capitalize on the success that it had experienced following North America's deregulation of energy markets. With the need to retain their first-mover advantage against aggressive competitors,

Enron quickly began to rely on the use of off-balance sheet financing vehicles and a range of questionable accounting practices in order to finance its activities, which were both costly and, ultimately, unsuccessful. In 2000, for example, Enron signed a 20-year entertainment on demand deal with Blockbuster. Despite the fact that the project failed at pilot stage, Enron recorded a $110 million estimated profit for the deal. Accounting standards were violated, and company value was misrepresented to investors.[2] This led to a situation where Enron grossly understated its liabilities and overstated its equity and earnings. Despite such questionable practices, the company was, for a long time, lauded as an example of ethics, innovation and corporate responsibility.

However, by 2001, questionable financial practices had been identified within the company and Enron was forced to announce a number of asset write-downs, to issue restated financial earnings reflecting a 23 per cent reduction in profits and an increased liability of $628 million, and reduced company equity by £1.2 billion over the financial period 1997–2000 (Healy and Palepu, 2003). While some analysts and institutions continued to recommend Enron stock to their clients for a number of months, the company was ultimately downgraded by major credit rating agencies to junk status by the end of 2001, and filed for bankruptcy shortly afterwards.

The toxic culture of Enron

Enron provides a powerful example of the potential for leadership to be both toxic and destructive. How was this destructiveness evidenced? First, the culture of Enron was largely leveraged on the awarding of heavy compensation for good performance in the form of stock options. This led to the profligate pursuit of personal financial gain on the part of management and individual traders – at the expense of the company, investors and the economy as a whole.

Second, accounting malpractice was undertaken complicit with the company's auditor Arthur Andersen, who failed to exercise due diligence with regard to Enron's financial affairs despite (or perhaps due to) their earning a $25 million audit fee from Enron in 2000 (Healy and Palepu, 2003).

Third, 'Car Day' saw the public awarding of sports cars and large bonuses to high-performing traders. The company was elitist, demonstrating a strong preference for the hiring of Ivy Leaguers, where the public naming and shaming of the bottom 5 per cent of employees (as measured by trading income) at each annual review was a common theme. Employees were required to aggressively outperform each other in order to belong. This combination of elitism, status symbols, individualism and self-aggrandizing behaviour suggests a strong permeation of personalized charismatic leadership behaviour within the company culture.

Fourth, the CEO and senior management actively engaged in unethical business practices. For example, Andrew Fastow, former Chief Financial Officer of Enron, occupied ownership positions of LJM Cayman LP and LJM2 Co-Investment LP, two of Enron's most important partners. This contravened Financial Accounting

Standards Board (FASB) rulings as it effectively rendered these companies subsidiaries, not partners (Sims and Brinkmann, 2003). In late 2001, and shortly before Enron had been forced to issue its restated finances, ex-CEO Jeffrey Skilling resigned, taking with him the $66 million that he had earned from the sale of his company shares. Employees who had previously been encouraged to invest in the company were not so lucky (Sims and Brinkmann, 2003). As role models, the CEO and Chief Financial Officer and other managers had undoubtedly allowed a negative culture of rule-breaking and individualistic, self-serving behaviour to proliferate and subsume the company. The destructive nature of this style and culture of leadership led to extreme consequences. Not only did former CEO Jeff Skilling face subsequently imprisonment, but a verdict of suicide was tragically recorded in the shooting of ex-Vice President J. Clifford Baxter only a month after Enron's bankruptcy had been filed.

Defining destructive leadership

Currently there is no universal agreement as to what constitutes destructive leadership, and the concept has been discussed at length under the auspices of different terms, such as abusive supervision (Tepper, 2000) and petty tyranny (Ashforth, 1994). Discussions also centre upon whether destructive leadership is an *outcome* or a *process*.

Einarsen *et al.* (2007) argue that any definition of destructive leadership should account for behaviour that is aimed at both the subordinate and the organization. The authors contend that destructive leadership can be both active and manifest, and also passive and indirect, and that intent to harm does not need to be a qualifying element within this definition; thoughtlessness might be as manifest an element of destructive leadership as ignorance or incompetence.

While recognizing the limitations of leader-centric approaches, the following definition of destructive leadership is adopted (Einarsen *et al.*, 2007) and used for the purposes of discussion throughout the remainder of this chapter: "The systematic and repeated behaviour by a leader, supervisor or manager that violates the legitimate interest of the organisation by undermining and/or sabotaging the organisation's goals, tasks, resources, and effectiveness and/or the motivation, well-being or job satisfaction of subordinates" (Einarsen, 2007, p. 208).

Although it is not completely clear exactly which behaviours and concepts should be subsumed under the mantle of destructive leadership, it is a contention of this chapter that bullying is without doubt considered destructive.[3] There has been a much larger body of work conducted to date in the field of studies of bullying in the workplace; as such, it deserves inclusion within this chapter, both in terms of a consideration of the characteristics of the targets of bullies (Matthiesem and Einarsen, 2001), personality traits of bullies (Adams, 1992), the situational variables that can foster bullying (Adams, 1992), the power distance that tends to exist between bullies and their victims (Ferris *et al.*, 2007; Hogh and Dofradottir, 2001) and the outcomes of bullying (Einarsen and Raknes, 1997; Rayner, 1997). In order to further define the concept of bullying as a destructive behaviour, the following definition has been adopted:

> Leader bullying represents strategically selected tactics of influence by leaders designed to convey a particular image and place targets in a submissive, powerless position whereby they are more easily influenced and controlled, in order to achieve personal and/or organisational objectives.
>
> *(Ferris et al., 2007, p. 197)*

Ferris *et al.* (2007) argue that bullying can be viewed as a political behaviour, and theorize that a workplace bully is often unable to recognize the power that is held by his employees in terms of their task-related expertise, which subsequently releases him from usual self-imposed constraints (i.e. respect and deference, where appropriate, to the knowledge and ability of others) to pursue power and reputation within the organization. Einarsen *et al.* (2007) propose a succinct model of destructive and constructive leadership behaviour that can be viewed in Figure 10.1.

Tyrannical leadership

Referring to the Enron example, the practice of publicly shaming (in addition to redeploying or firing) employees whose performance featured in the lowest 5 per cent that year bears the hallmark of tyrannical leadership, as does the organization's practice of requiring peer reviews that added to these performance ratings. Interestingly, this type of leadership did actually lead to pro-organization outcomes (but anti-subordinate behaviour) in the short term. Clearly, however, this was not maintainable. This culture of intimidation and bullying behaviour has been linked to

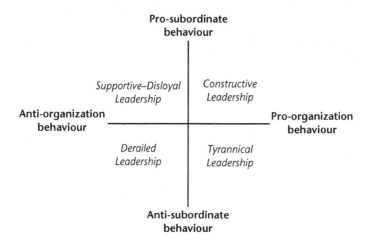

FIGURE 10.1 A model of destructive and constructive leadership behaviour.

Source: Einarsen *et al.* (2007, p. 211).

short-lived positive organizational outcomes that occur as a result of employee compliance (Zapf and Gross, 2001). This type of culture appears to bear many hallmarks of the effects of the personalized leader whose power through charisma is evident yet somewhat transient *in statu nascendi* (Chapter 6, "Charismatic leadership").

Derailed leadership

This behaviour involves behaviour that is both damaging to the employee and to the organization, a behaviour clearly demonstrated by ex-CEO Jeffrey Skilling in his simultaneous resignation from the company during its most difficult period and his profiteering through the sale of his $66 million shares in the company. A culture of fear is often evident in an organization led by derailed leaders.

Supportive-disloyal leaders

The supportive-disloyal leader is someone who, according to Einarsen *et al.* (2007), may lack strategic competence but is able to nurture friendly relationships with subordinates, sometimes through allowing them to commit or be complicit in theft, may be allowed to turn up late, fail to conduct their job efficiently or receive bonuses and perks to which they should not reasonably be entitled. This behaviour appears to carry theoretical similarities to McClelland's theory of needs motivation, specifically with respect to his conceptualization of a manager with a high need for affiliation (McClelland, 1975).

Constructive leadership

The constructive leader is one who is interested in the welfare of their subordinates, but who is also guided dominantly by achieving the goals and objectives of the organization (for example, Patrick Gelsinger, CEO of VMware, voted best CEO to work for by the 2019 Glassdoor survey).

DISCUSSION STARTER

The Wolf of Wall Street

Jordan Belfort's autobiopic *Wolf of Wall Street* recounts a debauched tale of corporate corruption at the helm of the New York boiler room brokerage outfit Stratton Oakmont Inc. – a company immortalized in the fictional movie *Boiler Room* and a role which ultimately earned Belfort 22 months in jail. By his own estimate, Belfort cheated investors out of as much as $200 million. In 2003, a US District Judge in Brooklyn ordered Belfort to pay $110.4 million in restitution to investors as part of his punishment. Belfort (the Chairman) and Daniel Porush, the former President of Stratton Oakmont, also forfeited around $16 million in properties. Both pleaded guilty to 10 counts of securities fraud and money laundering via a vast 7-year scheme to manipulate the stocks of at least 34 companies, costing investors hundreds of millions of dollars. Furthermore, the NASD (National Association of Securities Dealers) charged a total of 33 Stratton Oakmont Inc. employees with defrauding at least 70 customers through aggressive telemarketing and other rules violations.

Start the discussion: How can Einarsen *et al.*'s (2007) model of destructive and constructive leadership be used to explain the mechanics by which Stratton Oakmont Inc. became so embroiled in fraudulent activity?

Defining toxic leadership

Padilla *et al.* (2007, p. 176) identify the "toxic triangle" of leader, follower and environmental factors that make it possible for destructive leadership to occur. Their definition includes the need for susceptible followers and an environment conducive to destructive leadership, selfish orientation of, and the use of coercion and control by, the destructive leader, and a compromised quality of life for followers as a result of the leader's destructiveness. This definition led to the development of the toxic triangle shown in Figure 10.2.

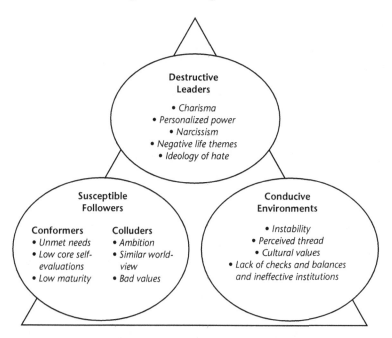

FIGURE 10.2 The toxic triangle: elements in the three domains related to destructive leadership.

Source: Padilla *et al.* (2007, p. 180).

Destructive leaders

The uppermost component of the triangle, "Destructive leaders", draws heavily from theories of *personalized power* (McClelland and Burnham, 2003), *charisma* (for example, the characterization of the threatening 'other' in Weber's conceptualization of charisma; Weber, 1947) and *authentic leadership development* (in terms of the impact of life histories in the formation of leadership authenticity). Drawing on a wealth of charismatic leadership research to underpin the model, Padilla *et al.* (2007, p. 180) comment that "not all charismatic leaders are destructive, but most destructive leaders are charismatic".

Some scholars argue that certain individuals are more likely to suffer at the hands of a destructive leader than others, either as a result of their own personality traits (Matthiesem and Einarsen, 2001) or as a result of situational variables such as during periods of change (McCarthy *et al.*, 1995).

Susceptible followers

The second component of the triangle, "Susceptible followers", raises a wider issue of a general lack of focus on the importance of followers in the leadership process. The model contends that there are two types of followers of a destructive leader: a *conformer* and a *colluder*.

Conformers are followers who try to minimize the detrimental effects of not conforming to the leader's destructive vision or behaviour; they share the world-views of the destructive leader and collude with the leader in order to satisfy their own ambitious, selfish motivations. Conformers tend to have unmet needs (Burns, 1978; Maslow, 1954) and demonstrate low psychological maturity rendering them more susceptible to manipulation. They are also likely to possess low self-esteem, a poor locus of control and low self-efficacy (Luthans *et al.*, 1998), all interesting concepts when one refers back to Deci and Ryan's Self-Determination Theory (Deci and Ryan, 2000) discussed in Chapter 4 ("Behavioural theories").

Colluders tend to be highly ambitious – a trait that can lead them to be more easily coerced and manipulated, as it can make them more willing to compromise personal boundaries in order to collect symbols of power, prestige and success. Personalized leaders (McClelland, 1975) are more likely to subjugate ethically motivated behaviours in order to achieve self-serving goals. Colluders also tend to possess unsocialized values and beliefs that are congruent with the destructive leader. Eatwell (2006) identified the role of *centripal* and *coterie* charisma in Hitler's inner circle that ultimately facilitated many atrocities and advanced his destructive and psychopathic causes.

The concept of *conformer* and *colluder* bear some resemblances to Kellerman's (2004) identification of a follower of a destructive leader as either a *bystander* (one who stands by and does not intervene or hold the leader to account) or an *acolyte* (someone who participates in the destructive acts of the leader).

Conducive environments

Padilla *et al.* (2007) recognize the key role of the situation in the destructive leadership process, identifying "Conducive environments" as the third component of the toxic triangle. The environment that is conducive to the emergence of a destructive leader is one which is characterized by *instability*, and by the existence of a *perceived threat* (Weber, 1947). Collectivist, uncertainty-avoidant cultures are more susceptible to destructive leadership, as are environments where there is an absence of *checks and balances*. Interestingly, it does appear that followers' susceptibility to destructive leadership might be countered if they experience job enrichment, finding their job to be intrinsically satisfying (Podsakoff *et al.*, 1993). Uhl-Bien and Carsten (2007) identify the impact of the hierarchical nature of the organization as a strong socializing influence on employees, causing them to become more obedient and passive.

IDEA IN BRIEF

Comrades and capos

In recounting his experiences of surviving a Nazi concentration camp, Dr. Viktor Frankl, creator of *logotherapy* (often referred to as the *Third Viennese School of Psychotherapy*) opened his account with a reference to the capos (inmates given special privileges and power over others by their captors), judging them on a similar psychological basis to the SS guards. He described them as being different to an ordinary prisoner, remarking that only the most brutal of prisoners were generally chosen for the role of capo. This conceptualization throws valuable light on one way in which prisoners (capos) were used to perpetuate the extreme toxicity and destructive nature of Nazi concentration camps (Frankl, 1984).

Personality traits of destructive leaders

Hostility and trait-negative affectivity have been identified as characteristic of destructive leadership, with trait-anxious individuals identified as people who tend to "live in a constant state of psychological vigilance and physiological arousal and tend to project their fears on to the environment" (Schaubroeck *et al.*, 2007, p. 238), and who are less likely to lead effectively. Referring to the charismatic leadership literature, it is viable to theorize that individuals who score highly in personalized power motivation and who possess narcissistic tendencies are most likely to display destructive leadership tendencies.

Susceptibility of followers of destructive leaders

> No matter how clever or devious, leaders alone cannot achieve toxic results.
>
> *Thoroughgood* et al., *2012, p. 901*

Earlier in the book, research was presented concerning the tendency for US, Finnish and Canadian voters to select political candidates on the basis of gender, physiognomic and other physical traits (Poutvaara *et al.*, 2009; Lawson *et al.*, 2010; Rule and Ambady, 2010). Studies of charismatic leadership identify the impact of the seductive nature of charisma, particularly for those individuals who display a dominant motivation for personalized power, and for the associated need to collect symbols of prestige and power.

The 'toxic triangle' model presented earlier (Padilla *et al.*, 2007) identified the key role of both *conformers* and *colluders* in the destructive leadership process. This work is extended by Thoroughgood *et al.* (2012), who developed a *taxonomy of followers* associated with destructive leadership (Figure 10.3). The taxonomy retains

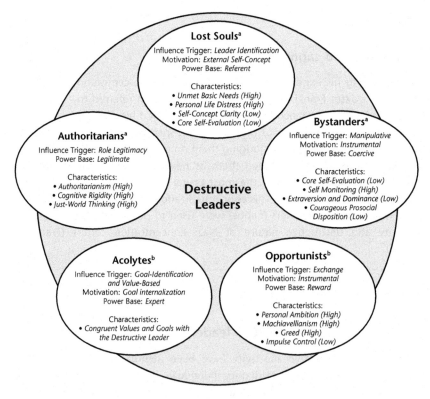

FIGURE 10.3 The susceptible circle: a taxonomy of followers associated with destructive leadership.

Source: Thoroughgood *et al.* (2012, p. 902).

Note
'a' denotes conformers and 'b' denotes colluders.

Padilla *et al.*'s 2007 *conformer* and *colluder* categories, extending both to include additional sub-types. Sub-types of conformers include *lost souls, bystanders* and *authoritarians*. Sub-types of colluders constitute *acolytes* and *opportunists*.

Sub-types of conformers

It is the lost soul who appears most vulnerable to the seductive power of the personalized charismatic leader. Their feelings of loyalty towards the leader, combined with a weak sense of self and a need for acceptance lead to a situation where their own self-identity and values become subsumed within those of the leader and their organization (for example, David Koresh). This makes them far more susceptible to the likelihood that they will comply with the unethical acts and orders of the destructive leadership. The lost soul is vulnerable to manipulation and control, as they are so motivated by an *external self-concept motivation* (Barbuto and Scholl, 1998). They are lost souls in part because they also have *unmet basic needs*, have encountered some kind of *life distress* that may make them temporarily vulnerable and experience both the *low self-concept clarity* and the *negative core self-evaluations* identified in the earlier referenced work of Padilla *et al.* (2007).

Authoritarians, by contrast, are motivated into conformity by a tendency to blindly accept legitimate power, to engage in "just-world thinking" (JWT; Lerner, 1980) and to obey orders within this context regardless of their ethical integrity. Just-world thinkers tend to deflect anxiety and fear by devaluing the victims that suffer at their hands as a consequence of the unjust acts that result from the authoritarians' compliance (Thoroughgood *et al.*, 2012). Bystanders, conversely, feel motivated by fear, as discussed earlier in Padilla *et al.*'s (2007) conceptual definition.

Colluders

Colluders include two sub-types: opportunists and acolytes. Opportunists are individuals who possess personal ambition and unsocialized characteristics, such as Machiavellianism and greed (Thoroughgood *et al.*, 2012). They tend to be ambitious, lack self-control and view their relationship with the destructive leadership as one motivated by *exchange triggers* – or, in other words, the likelihood that their compliance with the acts of a destructive leadership will lead to their own personal gain (Barbuto, 2000). Referring to Enron, many individuals colluded in the widespread fraud that occurred within the company, including the analysts that continued to recommend Enron stock, the failure of auditors Arthur Andersen to exercise due diligence in its compliance activities, Enron traders who broke rules in order to increase their own bonuses and Enron management who demonstrated significant conflicts of interest through ownership of Enron's most significant partnership companies. Acolytes are those who actually share the world-view of the destructive leadership – for example, Himmler and Goebbels, who were loyal servants of Hitler's Third Reich.

IDEA IN BRIEF

Walking in two worlds

Christine M. O'Bonsawin, PhD (Abenaki, Odanak Nation), Associate Professor of History and Director of the Indigenous Studies Program at the University of Victoria, explains how racist, colonial attitudes continue to hold back the Indigenous peoples of Canada.

"For Indigenous peoples in Canada, leadership concepts take on a multiplicity of meanings, which are grounded in both traditional understandings of governance as well as present-day lived-realities. In the pre-contact era, effective and revered leadership was central to the cultural, spiritual, political, social and economic prosperity of all Indigenous societies. Since first contact, Indigenous peoples have experienced centuries of colonial oppression, which can be categorized as nothing less than cultural genocide. Through the ongoing imposition of colonial policies and racist attitudes, Indigenous peoples remain the most marginalized group in Canada and continue to experience high levels of poverty, unemployment and inadequate housing. Furthermore, Indigenous peoples continue to heal from the physical, sexual and emotional abuses they experienced when forced to attend government-administered and church-run Indian residential schools, which operated throughout Canada between the 1820s to the late 1990s.

The capacity for Indigenous peoples to carry on with traditional leadership approaches (which are deeply embedded in cultural practices) as well as their ability to engage in any meaningful leadership role in the political and corporate apparatuses of mainstream Canada has been seriously hindered by ongoing colonial structures and racist attitudes. For example, within the Canadian federal structure there exists a government department that is responsible for overseeing the management of Aboriginal affairs (treaties, reserves, Indian registry, etc.). The management of 'Indian affairs' has been the responsibility of various federal departments since the 1830s as settlers sought to 'get rid of the Indian problem', which was administered through an aggressive process of assimilation. In recent years, the department responsible for Indian affairs has purportedly shifted its vision as it currently claims to support Aboriginal independence and decision making. Yet, an Indigenous person has never served in the primary leadership position of this department, nor do structures exist to ensure that Indigenous persons occupy senior and managerial positions. In fact, this department currently seeks to achieve a 50 per cent Aboriginal recruitment target within its civil service.

Sadly, such realities persist within political and corporate entities throughout Canada as structural barriers to leadership positions remain firmly in place for Indigenous peoples. It can be argued that Indigenous communities are losing potentially strong and effective leaders to mainstream organizations, which seek to meet employment equity quotas through the hiring of Aboriginal recruits. In all likelihood, such persons will never be provided with meaningful opportunities to reach influential positions of leadership. As long as such colonialist and racist attitudes prevail in Canada, the onus remains on Indigenous peoples to strive for a better life. This will undoubtedly depend on strong Indigenous leadership and those who have the foresight, ability and strength to successfully walk in two worlds."

Measuring destructive leadership

Shaw *et al.* (2011) recently developed a Destructive Leadership Questionnaire (DLQ) in order to empirically examine differences between conceptual definitions of destructive leadership. Given its infancy, further testing of the instrument is required in order to ascertain its validity and reliability.

Given the potential role of narcissism, charisma and Machiavellianism in destructive leadership, these scales could also be used to measure potential contributory traits of destructive leadership. Nevertheless, Padilla *et al.* (2007, p. 189) refer to the problem of destructive leadership as being as "much a practical problem as it is a theoretical one", referring to both the need for practitioners to focus more effectively on the identification of destructive leadership at the recruitment stage, and on the need for further theoretical development of destructive leadership itself.

Critiques of destructive leadership

To date, the field lacks any empirical substantiation of the difference between varying approaches to, and conceptualizations of, destructive leadership (for example, it has been referred to as bullying, destructive and toxic). This problem is exacerbated by the associated lack of instruments available to measure destructive leadership.

Thoroughgood *et al.* (2012) also call for further research into the psychometric properties of their taxonomy of toxic followers, and also call for the development of measures of sub-types of toxic followership. They also theorize that certain types of organization might mediate the level to which sub-types of follower demonstrate susceptibility to coercion and manipulation, indicating that further research is needed in this area.

Criticisms can be attributed, in large part, to the infancy of the field, and it is likely that, as the field matures, so too will the quality of the conceptual frameworks and instruments of measurements used to investigate and measure this phenomenon.

Summary

The emergence of destructive and toxic leadership as an academic field of study carries the potential to illuminate the conditions within which toxic and destructive leaders thrive; to shine a spotlight on the critical role of colluders and conformers; and to understand how and why certain individuals might be susceptible to its effects. Such an understanding allows individuals to gain a more detailed understanding of how to identify and counteract the effects of tyrannical leaders, toxic cultures and organizational bullies, and to develop strategies with which one can fight them.

 **Expert insight**

Ticking the box

This expert insight profiles the experiences of a leader who has experienced a high level of professional and academic achievement, yet still experiences racism on a day-to-day basis. It has been written anonymously so that the leader was able to speak without fear of retribution.

"People here often regard equality & diversity training as a 'tick box' exercise. I specialise in helping organisations and departments to improve their equality & diversity programme, and the problem is that leaders often see no problem in making employees sit through a generic diversity training package online. They think that's fine.

Sadly, no-one learns much from that kind of training because it is not applied or tailored to the organisation. It is often not even relevant. A lot of employees will also feel resentful at having been made to sit in front of a computer and complete the training. Employees end up as passive recipients of this generic, uninspiring 'training' which they then also do not have to repeat or update meaningfully in future years, meaning that it ultimately carries no impact in terms of influencing their professional practice. It is also too superficial to make any inroads into dealing with the complex nature of discrimination and people walk away thinking that they understand how to practice equality and diversity. But they don't. In reality, this reductionist approach leaves people unequipped to tackle diversity issues or even recognise what discrimination looks like.

Tokenism

What we often see is that a management or decision-making group will include one member of an ethnic group and other members then believe that the individual represents, and speaks for, everyone with that ethnicity. That is a form of tokenism. It is ineffective, and it reduces people to the colour of their skin or their ethnic status. Of course, we are all individuals and we all think and feel differently about a range of issues – a white leader doesn't represent the views of all white people, for example, so why should the Asian member of staff on your board represent all Asians? I've been rolled out as a token more times than I care to count, and it is depressing.

Understanding intersectionality

I find when I go into organisations that sometimes, the people leading diversity and cultural competency training think they are doing a good job yet can't even pronounce some of the key terminology. Or I ask them how they've included intersectionality into their training and they don't know what I am talking about. A lot of places have good intentions, but there are a lot of misunderstandings.

Walk in the shoes of others

Another huge problem is that there's a lot of people out there who just don't get the fact that racism is a big problem because they don't receive it them-selves. That's the biggest problem for me – how to make others see what is happening on a day-to-day basis. Unconscious bias, stereotypes, a culture where everything has been happening one way for a long, long time and no one sees a reason to change – it's hard to break through those things. To walk in the shoes of another person would be a powerful thing.

Often someone who is from a minority group won't want to speak up or complain exactly because they are in a minority and they don't want to cause problems for themselves or lose their job. And when organisations do have decent funding for diversity programmes, they don't know how to reach the people that they need to attract or speak to, they don't know what kind of diversity training is really needed and worse still, the consultants that are hired are usually white.

When you are talking about racial equality you simply cannot know the complexities of the issues that are faced if you have not faced them yourself. I remember talking to senior management of a major public service organisation recently and one board member was clearly resentful of our advice, asking why they should do anything to change their organisation as he didn't see any problems himself so thought that no problems existed. So yes, investments in diversity training are made but it is so often a waste because it is not conducted effectively.

Day-to-day racism

I think that one way of fighting this is to share stories and to tell people what day-to-day racism looks and feels like. One experience that I face regularly is when I go to high-level meetings. I have a very senior role and I am highly qualified but usually I am the racial minority in the room, and I always have to change into extremely smart clothing before I get there. The reason for this is that I usually get asked to fetch biscuits, or make the tea or direct a delegate to the toilet because they think that I am support staff for the function room or a junior assistant of some kind for one of the other attendees.

I remember a research meeting where another member of staff and his assistant – far more junior that I am – were quite rude when we were discussing a diversity-related issue. I was the only non-white person in the room and what was said was quite offensive, but it wasn't challenged.

I've learned from experience, sadly, that speaking out is more likely to lead to me facing problems, being ostracised or pushed out of my role, so often it is just easier to keep quiet. That's still the reality. In that situation I didn't challenge those particular individuals nearly as much as the situation deserved – but I would probably have come off worse if I had.

That kind of treatment has definitely gotten worse for me and others since Brexit and Trump. You sometimes see this play out in meetings when one or two individuals are present as members of under-represented groups, yet they say nothing for the entire meeting. I remember this happening recently – these individuals did not say one word. I often wonder whether they are simply being complicit to maintain their position. That's one way in which racism can be powerfully insidious. It doesn't just have to be a skinhead shouting at you to be racism. It takes different forms, many of which exert pressure on you to keep quiet and put up with it. Some of those are subtle so unless you are directly living it, you won't realise that it is there.

The role of activism

There is a lot more racist language out there in wider society now, on social media and so forth, with a lot of people emboldened because of Trump and Brexit. There is also a lot more student activism right now. All I can say about student activists is – WOW. So bright. So brilliant. Their courage astounds me. A lot of adults who have jobs, families, mortgages etc. are fearful of the ramifications if they speak out. I remember being in a meeting myself where my boss at the time referred to 'you lot' as being lazy. Given my ethnicity that comment is steeped in really ugly cultural connotations, so I challenged her on it and asked, 'What do you mean, you lot? Our team?'. She sneered at me, and said, 'No, you know exactly what I mean'. And I did.

I remember a situation where I witnessed racial abuse of another member of staff and I literally had to leave my role and move vertically into a similar role in order to formally lodge a complaint. I knew that if I had done that whilst in my original role, I would have faced so much blowback that my work life would have been too miserable to continue with. Even with the move it was bad. It was difficult and weird – two members of HR [human resources] were in the room when I was filing the complaint on behalf of the other person, trying to say that I was lying. It was like being cross-examined in court.

It's often the case that the minority group – whatever that minority is – tends to get ostracised when complaints are made. When I had to make a complaint one time in my own defence, I had clear evidence but the individuals in question then lodged complaints against me just to retaliate. Their complaints didn't hold water but in terms of my mental health and professional reputation it still became extremely stressful.

Creating meaningful change

The best advice I can give to young students heading out into the workforce is to try to become positive forces in their work culture. We can all be a part of positive change regardless of who we are or where we come from. One direct piece of advice is to form a group of some kind for people experiencing the same issues. That safe space to talk and support each other is crucial. Creating a diversity action group that anyone can join if they want to be a part of fighting inequalities of any kind is also a great idea. That kind of group is positive, inclusive, and inspiring. Also, network a lot.

Ultimately, finding narratives and sharing experiences can help you survive. Finding advocates via those channels can also be powerful.

Another piece of advice that you won't read in standard HR training – record everything. It is easy in our society to be gas lit – to self-doubt and to think 'Did he really say that?' after a meeting, or to think, 'Am I mis-reading that?'. Playing audio back to yourself and even asking a friend to listen to it can bring that level of objectivity and cancel out self-doubt that can be really debilitating. You can't use recordings in any kind of legal case as you can't record someone without their permission, so it wouldn't be admissible – but if you write up transcriptions of the conversation straight after the meeting, then present that to HR in a tribunal situation it's hard for them to backtrack and say that certain things weren't said.

I remember a case where I heard the words 'black stupid b**ch' in a meeting with senior figures. That's not uncommon to hear bad language like that. That's why I recommend leaving a recorder switched on in your bag. I wish there was no need for doing so but you have to protect yourself. In the grievance case that was made against me, one reason it got dismissed is because I was able to demonstrate such a great recall of events, which I was of course able to demonstrate because I had the transcript of a recording of actual events.

What you can do, right now

What is the most positive thing that students, black, white, any ethnicity, any nationality, from any under-represented group or majority can do tomorrow to make things better? Small concrete steps. Be nice to someone that is struggling and ask them if they are okay. Go out tomorrow and interact with someone from a culture you'd never usually spend time with. Often that's all it takes – to reach out to a different community and recognise that we aren't so different or that there isn't anything to be scared about or alarmed by.

Questions

1   The leader in this expert insight notes that racist behaviours have got worse "since Trump and Brexit" (research confirms that this is the case).[4] With reference to the *susceptible circle*, and the need for scapegoats in charismatic rhetoric (see Chapter 6), explain why minorities are so often the target in populist political campaigns.
2   This expert insight explains why simply changing the law often does not stop racist and discriminatory behaviour. With reference to theory, explain why.
3   With reference to the theory in this chapter, explain why 'walking in the shoes of others' and spending time with other cultures is the only way in which to understand what other people are going through.
4   If the suggestions of this leader interest you and you would like to take them further, form an action group within your classmates and decide how to take it further. Speak with your institution to find out how best they can support you.

Case study: just show me the data

On 14 December 2015, *The New Yorker* ran a story called *Blood, Simpler.*[5] It opened with a brief explanation of the expansive revenue earned by blood testing corporations before explaining how disruptive medical tech company Theranos was revolutionizing and disrupting the blood testing industry. Led by the enigmatic Elizabeth Holmes, who was fast gaining a reputation as medicine's answer to Steve Jobs, Theranos had, at that time, recently entered into a lucrative agreement with Walgreens which would have allowed Walgreen customers to obtain a pin-prick blood test quickly and cheaply (for as much as 90 per cent below standard Medicare rates).

Holmes spoke of how getting your bloods taken should be a wonderful experience, claiming the ability to offer quick and easy pin prick tests that carried the technical capabilities to diagnose everything from cancer to diabetes. While Holmes placed a great deal of effort into curating her own image as a charismatic, visionary force (something that Silicon Valley was primed, ready and – some might say – desperate for at the time), it remains amazing that Holmes cast such a powerful spell over investors, powerful, established figures and the media in the way that she did. For years, she was never really pushed to present the data needed to prove her claims by the investors ploughing hundreds of millions into her vision.

Beware the Gulfstream

Readers of the WeWork case study that also appears in this book (see p. 169) might enjoy drawing some similarities between the charismatic appeal of Adam Neumann and Elizabeth Theranos, and in the fact that both acquired a Gulfstream jet – presumably a must-have status symbol of the successful tech entrepreneur. (While Neumann's core business was real estate, investors SoftBank helped them to curate an image of a tech innovator-style company. Similarly, while medical innovation lay at the core of the Theranos model, Holmes styled herself as a Steve Jobs-style tech visionary.)

At the age of 30, Holmes was travelling by that ubiquitous symbol of entrepreneurial success – a Gulfstream jet. Famed for her curious Zen-like vegan diet and love of black polo necks (designed to invoke comparisons to Steve Jobs), her low voice and piercing, seemingly unblinking, eyes further fed into an enigmatic, utterly charismatic image. Many commentators, former associates and colleagues recalled the power of her charisma and what seemed to be an almost unshakeable self-belief, even when they presented her with data, time after time, that pointed to systemic failures of their prototypes. Later, onlookers would speculate as to whether the low voice (an orthodox signalling of dominance, often associated with leadership) was perhaps not her real voice at all.

The art of persuasion

Elizabeth Holmes was extremely persuasive. She had, for instance, persuaded Henry Kissinger and former Secretary of State George Shultz to sit on the board of Theranos alongside other luminaries such as Larry Ellison (founder of Oracle), who Holmes had persuaded to become an early investor. These legendary names added great kudos, respectability and networking potential to Holmes' venture. It was a savvy move by Holmes to create a powerful inner circle at such an early stage.

Another interesting fact is that nobody who sat on the board of Theranos possessed the medical acumen required to knowledgeably question Holmes on any aspect of her data, or on the reliability, validity or efficacy of her medical discoveries or innovations. To compound that board-level peculiarity, Theranos did not make its data accessible for peer review. This represented an extremely strange decision in the medical testing field. After all, medical breakthroughs of the kind claimed by Holmes represent those once-in-a-lifetime dream scenarios for any scientific researcher who hopes to stake their claim in history and win the respect and envy of their peers. No other scientist would have remained so silent.

While hindsight is a glorious thing, one can also now notice curious behaviours by Holmes. She recalled reading Moby Dick as a 10-year-old child, for example, talked of taking a Mandarin class at Stanford and owning a copy of *Meditations* by Marcus Aurelius. These insights were presumably meant to serve as early indicators of her genius, determination and inspiration, but do not represent much more than the inquiring mind of a healthy young person. Where were the prodigious medical interests and achievements, or tales of an unfailing excitement and passion for science? Even more interestingly, when pushed to explain the science that lay behind her revolutionary one-prick blood testing technology, one leading publication noted that "Holmes's description of the procedure was comically vague".[6] The words alarming, or clumsy could have been used equally effectively – Holmes once said that "A chemistry was performed" to describe the complexity of her medical testing innovation. This was not only bizarrely vague – something that a medical scientist would never say – but grammatically nonsensical.

From $9 billion hero to $zero

Nevertheless, Elizabeth Holmes did enjoy a meteoric rise – at least, for a time. Boasting a Forbes cover story, a Fortune profile, the desirable status as the world's youngest female billionaire and the enjoyment of basking in the glow of Silicon Valley, Holmes managed to transition (as is often the way with charismatic leaders whose stars shine brightest) from most celebrated CEO (with Theranos valued, at its peak, at $9 billion) to being discredited, in an extremely short space of time. Holmes resigned as CEO of Theranos Inc. on the same day that the Department of Justice charged Holmes with wire fraud. The company was closed down soon afterwards. Having once held a net worth of approximately $5 billion, Forbes re-adjusted Holmes' personal wealth to $0.

At the time when the FBI closed in, Holmes had spent 15 years chasing her dream. Her one pin-prick blood test technology had, in truth, never existed. Holmes currently faces a significant jail term if convicted of fraud in her upcoming trial, brought by the US Department of Justice against Theranos Inc.

In November 2019, Holmes' lawyers, Cooley, were given judicial approval to end their representation of Elizabeth Holmes as a defendant in a class action civil law suit against her company Theranos Inc. and Walgreens, after she failed to pay their legal fees. Holmes, alongside co-founder Sunny Balwani, former Theranos President and Chief Operating Officer, is a co-defendant. Allegations of fraud focus on whether Balwani and Holmes conspired to defraud investors, doctors and patients. Both face up to 20-years in prison and a $250,000 fine in restitution if found guilty.

Enforcing a dream

According to multiple former Theranos employees, Sunny Balwani acted as an enforcer figure within the company and, as a result, many feared him. Leaked video footage of company events aired as part of HBO's Theranos documentary "The Inventor: Out for Blood in Silicon Valley"[7] included chants of "F**k you" led by Balwani against people and organizations that he viewed as enemies. Court records also identified the fact that Balwani and Holmes had been in a romantic relationship for a long period of time – a fact never disclosed to investors. This, in turn, caused considerable consternation among investors when they did find out.

One of the first people to legitimately doubt Elizabeth Holmes and the one-prick concept was Dr. Phyllis Gardner – a Stanford medical school professor who had also, at one time, been a professor to Elizabeth. Before dropping out of her course at Stanford University, Holmes had sought Gardner's support for the innovation of an antibiotic patch that could scan the wearer for illnesses, automatically releasing medication when physiologically required. The idea was more the stuff of sci-fi than medical science – a great idea but with no grounding whatsoever in the capabilities and constraints of medical science. Gardner quickly explained to Holmes why the idea was, medically, an impossibility.

Soon after, Elizabeth, then 19 years old, switched tack, abandoning the patch concept, instead pouring her time and energy into touting her one-prick blood test concept. Amazingly, Holmes was soon able to drop out of Stanford, with $700 million in seed investment secured. Gardner suspected from the outset that Holmes' claims could not possibly be true – but Silicon Valley and a raft of high-profile names seemed impatient to get behind her, and her entrepreneurial star began to ascend. In truth, Gardner was not the only dissenter; but for many years, concerns about the company remained largely ignored.

It would ultimately take a high-profile front-page series of *Wall Street Journal* articles, published in 2015, and authored by Pulitzer Prize-winning investigative journalist John Carreyrou, to really shake things up and blast open major allegations and concerns about Theranos. Carreyrou would later go on to write a bestselling book, *Bad Blood*, that detailed his experiences of researching and writing those articles.

Find out more

- Carreyrou, J. (16 October 2015). Hot Start-up Theranos Has Struggled with Its Blood-Test Technology. *Wall Street Journal online*. Available at: www.wsj.com/articles/theranos-has-struggled-with-blood-tests-1444881901.
- The Inventor: Out for Blood in Silicon Valley (2019). HBO documentary trailer, "You Wanted It to Be True So Badly" (interview clip with whistle-blower Tyler Schultz). Available at: www.hbo.com/documentaries/the-inventor-out-for-blood-in-silicon-valley.

Questions

1 This case study is called "Just show me the data" because if everyone had done so, Theranos Inc. would never have got off the ground. With reference to destructive leadership theories and models, explain why this was the case.

2 How did Holmes use her charisma, and the power of her emotional bond with followers, to hold off doubters and criticisms? Relate your observations to theories of toxic and destructive behaviours.

3 Draw a *susceptible circle* and identify where you feel the names of key players in the Theranos Inc. story would fit (e.g. Elizabeth Holmes, Sunny Balwani).

4 Draw a toxic triangle and apply it to the Theranos organization.

5 What does Tyler Schultz's experiences of being pulled between the "tiled" and "carpeted" world (cited in the documentary trailer, "You Wanted It to Be True So Badly"; see "Find out more" above) tell us about the power of charisma and coercion in destructive leadership?

6 Form small groups. Find early videos (e.g. via YouTube) of Elizabeth Holmes sales

pitches, company adverts and news reports. Genuinely ask yourselves whether you would have been taken in by the grand claims of Theranos or if you would have said "just show me the data".

CHAPTER 10 QUIZ

1 Identify three different terms that have been used to describe destructive leadership.
2 Name three leaders that conform to Einarsen *et al.*'s (2007) definition of destructive leadership.
3 Why could it be argued that bullying can be considered a political behaviour?
4 Identify the three key components of the *toxic triangle* (Padilla *et al.*, 2007).
5 Name the two types of susceptible followers in the *toxic triangle.*
6 Name the additional types of followers included in the *susceptible circle* (Thoroughgood *et al.*, 2012) and explain the justification for their inclusion.
7 How is tyrannical leadership linked to charismatic leadership within this chapter?
8 How is the concept of *conducive environments* also linked to the emergence of charisma?
9 How are *exchange triggers* used to facilitate the process of destructive leadership between leader and follower?
10 Define *just world thinking* (Lerner, 1980) and explain why it is so debilitating to the formation of a healthy workplace culture.

Further questions relating specifically to the section "Enron and destructive leadership" (p. 197):

1 Locate and watch Enron's *Vision and Values* (1998) company training video (located at www.youtube.com/watch?v=tc-l9J6WiMY). How is it possible that the corporate ethos presented in the training video was so different from the reality?
2 "Despite such questionable practices, the company was, for a long time, lauded as an example of ethics, innovation and corporate responsibility." Why did the destructive nature of the Enron culture go unchecked – and even rewarded – for so long?
3 Apply the *toxic triangle* to the case of Enron, and clearly identify the presence of susceptible followers, destructive leaders and a conducive environment in your analysis.

Notes

1 Quote taken from an interview conducted for this book (anonymized due to the sensitive nature of the discussion), which features in the expert insight "Ticking the box" later in this chapter.

2 By this stage, large institutional investors owned around 60 per cent of Enron stock.
3 It should be noted that destructive leadership can also lead to toxic outcomes for leaders themselves (for example, former Enron CEO Jeffrey Skilling, Bernard Madoff) (Leslie and Van Velsor, 1996).
4 For example, British actor Stephen Fry voiced an insightful two-part podcast outlining the hate crime statistics reported post-Brexit. There is a great deal of academic and professional data that confirms this. See: www.independent.co.uk/news/uk/politics/brexit-hate-crime-rise-stephen-fry-youtube-video-facts-vs-fear-a8727411.html.
5 Auletta, K. (8 December 2014). Blood, Simpler. *The New Yorker*. Available at: www.newyorker.com/magazine/2014/12/15/blood-simpler.
6 Ibid.
7 The Inventor: Out for Blood in Silicon Valley. HBO documentary, directed by Alex Gibney. Available at: www.hbo.com/documentaries/the-inventor-out-for-blood-in-silicon-valley.

References

Adams, A. (1992). *Bullying at Work: How to Confront and Overcome It*. London: Virago Press.
Ashforth, B. (1994). Petty Tyranny in Organizations. *Human Relations*, 47, pp. 755–778.
Barbuto, J.E. (2000). Influence Triggers: A Framework for Understanding Follower Compliance. *Leadership Quarterly*, 11(3) (Autumn), pp. 365–387.
Barbuto, J.E., and Scholl, R.W. (1998). Motivation Sources Inventory: Development and Validation of New Scales to Measure an Integrative Taxonomy of Motivation. *Psychological Reports*, 82, pp. 1011–1022.
Biko, S. (1986). *I Write What I Like* (ed. A. Stubbs). New York: Harper & Row.
Burns, J. (1978). *Leadership*. New York: Harper & Row.
Conger, J. (1990). The Dark Side of Leadership. *Organisational Dynamics*, 19(2), pp. 44–55.
Deci, E.L. and Ryan, R.M. (2000). The "What" and "Why" of Goal Pursuits: Human Needs and the Self-Determination of Behaviour. *Psychological Inquiry*, 11, pp. 227–268.
Eatwell, R. (2006). Explaining Fascism and Ethnic Cleansing: The Three Dimensions of Charisma and the Four Darks Sides of Nationalism. *Political Studies Review*, 4(4), pp. 263–278.
Einarsen, S. and Raknes, B.I. (1997). Harassment in the Workplace and the Victimisation of Men. *Violence and Victims*, 12(2), pp. 247–263.
Einarsen, S., Aasland, M.S. and Skogstad, A. (2007). Destructive Leadership Behaviour: A Definition and Conceptual Model. *Leadership Quarterly*, 18(3), pp. 207–216.
Enron. 1998. *Vision and Values* [training video]. Available at: www.youtube.com/watch?v=tc-l9J6WiMY.
Ferris, G.R., Zinko, R., Brouer, R.L., Buckley, M.R. and Harvey, M.G. (2007). Strategic Bullying as a Supplementary, Balanced Perspective on Destructive Leadership. *Leadership Quarterly*, 18(3), pp. 195–206.
Frankl, E.E. (1984). *Man's Search for Meaning*. New York: Simon and Schuster.
Healy, P.M. and Palepu, K. (2003). The Fall of Enron. *Journal of Economic Perspectives*, 17(2) (Spring), pp. 3–26.
Hogh, A.R. and Dofradottir, A. (2001). Coping with Bullying in the Workplace. *European Journal of Work and Organisational Psychology*, 10, pp. 165–184.
Kellerman, B. (2004). *Bad Leadership. What It Is, How It Happens, Why It Matters*. Boston, MA: Harvard Business School Press.
Lawson, C., Lenz, G.S., Baker, A. and Myers, M. (2010). Looking Like a Winner: Candidate Appearance and Electoral Success in New Democracies. *World Politics*, 62, pp. 561–593.

Lerner, M.J. (1980). *The Belief in a Just World: A Fundamental Delusion*. New York: Plenum Press.

Leslie, J. and Van Velsor, E. (1996). *A Look at Derailment Today*. Greensboro, NC: Center for Creative Leadership.

Luthans, F., Peterson, S.J. and Ibrayeva, E. (1998). The Potential for the "Dark Side" of Leadership in Post-Communist Countries. *Journal of World Business*, 33, pp. 185–201.

McCarthy, P., Sheehan, M. and Kearns, D. (1995). *Managerial Effects and Their Effects on Employees' Health and Well-Being in Organisations Undergoing Restructuring*. Report of Worksafe Australia, Griffith University, Brisbane.

McClelland, D.C. (1975). *Power: The Inner Experience*. New York: Irvington.

McClelland, D. and Burnham, D.H. (2003). *Power is the Great Motivator*. Harvard Business Review (January). Boston, MA: Harvard Business School Publishing.

Maslow, A. (1954). *Motivation and Personality*. New York: Harper.

Matthiesem, S.B. and Einarsen, S. (2001). MMPI-2 Configurations among Victims of Bullying at Work. *European Journal of Work and Organisational Psychology*, 10, pp. 467–484.

Padilla, A., Hogan, R. and Kaiser, R.B. (2007). The Toxic Triangle: Destructive Leaders, Susceptible Followers, and Conducive Environments. *Leadership Quarterly*, 18, pp. 176–194.

Podsakoff, P.M., Niehoff, B.B., MacKenzie, S.B. and Williams, M.L. (1993). Do Substitutes for Leadership Really Substitute for Leadership? An Empirical Examination of Kerr and Jermier's Situational Leadership Model. *Organisational Behaviour an Human Decision Processes*, 54, pp. 1–44.

Poutvaara, P., Jordahl, H. and Berggren, N. (2009). Faces of Politicians: Babyfacedness Predicts Inferred Competence but Not Electoral Success. *Journal of Experimental Social Psychology*, 45, pp. 1132–1135.

Rayner, C. (1997). The Incidence of Workplace Bullying. *Journal of Community and Applied Social Psychology*, 7(3), pp. 199–208.

Rule, N.O. and Ambady, N. (2010). Democrats and Republicans Can Be Differentiated from Their Faces. *PLoS ONE*, 5, e8733.

Schabracq, M.J. and Cooper, C.L. (1998). Towards a Phenomenological Framework for the Study of Work and Organisational Stress. *Human Relations*, 51(5), pp. 625–648.

Schaubroeck, J., Walumbwa, F.O., Ganster, C. and Kepes, S. (2007). Destructive Leader Traits and the Neutralizing Influence of an "Enriched" Job. *Leadership Quarterly*, 18(3), pp. 236–251.

Shaw, J.B., Erickson, A. and Harvey, M. (2011). A Method for Measuring Destructive Leadership and Identifying Types of Destructive Leaders in Organizations. *Leadership Quarterly*, 22(4), pp. 575–590.

Sims, R.R. and Brinkmann, J. (2003). Enron Ethics (or: Culture Matters More than Codes). *Journal of Business Ethics*, 45(3), pp. 243–256.

Tepper, B.J. (2000). Consequences of Abusive Supervision. *Academy of Management Journal*, 43(2), pp. 178–190.

Thoroughgood, C.N., Pailla, A., Hunter, S.T. and Tate, B.W. (2012). The Susceptible Circle: A Taxonomy of Followers Associated with Destructive Leadership. *Leadership Quarterly*, 23, pp. 897–917.

Uhl-Bien, M. and Carsten, M. (2007). Being Ethical When the Boss Is Not. *Organisational Dynamics*, 36(2), pp. 187–201.

Weber, M. (1947) *The Theory of Social and Economic Organization* (trans. A.M. Henderson and T. Parsons). New York: Free Press.

Xie, L. and Schaubroeck, J. (2001). Bridging Approaches and Findings across Diverse Disciplines to Improve Job Stress Research. In P.L. Perrewé and D.C. Ganster (eds.), *Research in Occupational Stress and Well Being* (Vol. 1). Oxford: Elsevier Science, pp. 1–53.

Zapf, D. and Gross, C. (2001). Conflict Escalation and Coping with Workplace Bullying: A Replication and Extension. *European Journal of Work and Organisational Psychology*, 10(4), pp. 497–522.

11

SELF-LEADERSHIP

"Courage is not always done on the battlefield. Courage is done when someone has the courage to right a wrong, even if it is not popular."

— Gunnery Sergeant and former Marine of the Year,
David A. Oswell[1]

Recalling the emotive words of Thomas Henley, Churchill once commented that, "We are still masters of our fate. We are still captains of our souls."[2] From the literary eloquence of *Invictus*, from whose tomes Churchill's words originate, via the indomitable rhetoric of Churchill himself and through the resilient words of Gunnery Sergeant Oswell that open this chapter,[3] we are able to present this penultimate chapter of the book as one which ultimately poses the greatest relevance to the reader – that of *self-leadership*, and how one can actively and diligently seek to use the theory contained in this book to develop the ability to self-lead, to achieve performance beyond expectations and to excel as a leader of both oneself and others.

It is useful to note that Bennis (2003, p. 334) views authentic leaders as people who "create their own legends and become the authors of their lives in the sense of creating new and improved versions of themselves", and it is ultimately the objective of this chapter to help the reader achieve such a goal.

Structure of the chapter

The chapter begins by presenting an overview of the emerging academic field of self-leadership. Competing definitions and models of self-leadership are presented, alongside a consideration of strategies (for example, *anticipatory coping* (Aspinwall and Taylor, 1997) that facilitate the ability of an individual to self-lead.

The chapter then adopts a *transtheoretical* approach to the study of leadership. The purpose of this approach is to *identify* key leadership trends that have emerged across the previous ten chapters of this book, and to communicate their *pragmatic* value in the context of enhancing one's own ability to self-lead. This approach reflects the contention of this book that the scholastic endeavour should ultimately – in the context of leadership studies – empower a scholar to not only retain information, but to become a better leader as a result of the knowledge and wisdom that they have acquired. After all, how is one able to confidently lead others if one cannot first lead oneself?

The chapter then presents critiques of self-leadership theory, before identifying ways in which self-leadership can be measured. The expert insight for this chapter is provided by Gunnery Sergeant David A. Oswell of the US Marines ("Military lessons in self-leadership"). A case study entitled "Frank talk" follows, providing a compelling and inspiring insight into the leadership style of Steve Biko, father of the South African Black Consciousness Movement, and arguably one of the greatest leaders of the twentieth century.

Defining self-leadership

Self-leadership essentially speaks to our ability to self-manage the finite resources (psychological, physical, social, financial, temporal) that we each possess, in order to maximize success within every facet of our lives. Self-leadership strategies have been found to lead to higher levels of performance across clinical, sports, educational and employment contexts (Neck and Manz, 1992, 1996; Stewart *et al.*, 1996).

Self-leadership is a concept that involves the process of influencing oneself to establish the self-direction and self-motivation needed to perform (Manz, 1983; Manz and Neck, 1999). It has been applied within the context of self-managing teams and with regard to the empowerment of followers, to the concept of *Super-Leadership* (Manz and Sims, 1989) and to the concept of *thought self-leadership* (Neck and Manz, 2007).

Self-management

Manz and Sims (1980) conceptualized *self-management* as the practice of an employee who autonomously manages his performance in a way that exceeds the basic requirements of his role. This might, for example, involve an employee not only being punctual, but arriving at work consistently early in order to practise a major presentation, or to deal with minor administrative matters (such as answering emails received the previous evening, or completing timesheets) so that their schedule is clear for the onset of a new working day. *Self-management* acted as a precursor to the development of *self-leadership*, extending its focus to include the cognitive abilities of self-regulation and self-control (Neck and Manz, 1992), the role of strategies such as imagery and positive self-talk in its development and the recognition of the need for intrinsic motivation in order for such a process to occur (Manz, 1986).[4]

SuperLeadership

Manz and Sims (1989) suggest that a manager can develop 'SuperLeadership' within their employees via the use of six specific practices. The first, *modelling self-leadership*, requires the leader to effectively act as a role model, by demonstrating the ability to self-lead effectively.[5] The manager should also facilitate self-goals and productive thought patterns, reinforce self-leadership, constructively reprimand employees (where required), facilitate a culture that fosters self-leadership and design socio-technical systems and teams. Parallels between SuperLeadership and Hersey and Blanchard's Situational Leadership Theory (SLT) have been acknowledged in the literature (Markham and Markham, 1995).

Self-leadership strategies

According to Neck and Houghton (2006), self-leadership strategies can be grouped into three strategies:

1 *Behavioural strategies.* This involves the setting of goals for oneself, and the management of one's behaviour in order that the goal is achieved, via practices such as self-monitoring, self-control and self-regulatory behaviours (self-observation, self-reward). For example, an executive might plan a weekend hiking trip with friends if specific sales targets are met, which subsequently makes a few days of prioritizing work over all else far more palatable.
2 *Natural reward strategies.* These strategies involve the increase of self-motivation to complete a task, by either (a) making the task more naturally rewarding to oneself by adapting it in some way, or (b) refocusing one's perceptions on the inherently rewarding and positive aspects of a task, and away from its less attractive features.
3 *Constructive thought pattern strategies.* These strategies require the development of constructive thought patterns via the use of positive self-talk, visualization and other mental strategies that together positively impact performance, a concept developed at length within the sport psychology literature and to which the reader is directed for further elucidation (e.g. Hanrahan and Andersen, 2012).

Learning to self-lead

Interestingly, it has been theorized that self-leadership can be learned (Manz and Sims, 1987). Positive increases in self-efficacy[6] were reported one month after self-leadership training (Prussia *et al.*, 1998) and, under the aegis of '*thought self-leadership*' (Manz and Neck, 1991) and *SuperLeadership* (Manz and Sims, 1989), self-leadership has been theorized to empower individuals and to help them to develop the skill to lead themselves.

Aspinwall and Taylor (1997) similarly argue that self-leadership can be taught, and that its use is primarily valuable as a means of developing anticipatory coping abilities, and as a means of enhancing performance. *Anticipatory coping* allows an individual to anticipate potential stressors, and to then minimize them via the implementation of necessary cognitive, behavioural and emotional strategies. For example, a senior executive is asked, the evening before her company's annual symposium, to deliver the following morning's keynote address. Previously developed anticipatory coping skills allow her to use positive *self-talk* strategies to motivate herself to perform, and to manage stress. She uses *self-control* and *self-regulation* to ensure that she finalizes work on her presentation with adequate time to sleep (conscious, as she is, of the detrimental effect that a lack of sleep exercises on one's performance), and takes advantage of the conference hotel gym in the morning for a brief workout (to dispel heightened levels of cortisol and adrenaline). She is subsequently able to approach the keynote address feeling as calm as possible, having also used *visualization* techniques that morning as a means of undertaking a brief mental rehearsal. The combined used of anticipatory coping techniques thus enabled her to perform to her highest potential, given the limits of the situation.

When used together, self-leadership strategies have been shown to lead to positive performance outcomes and enhanced career success. They have also been shown to diminish levels of stress (Unsworth and Mason, 2012), as individuals who are able to self-lead experience less stress and anxiety when anticipating difficult tasks. The resulting outcome is an individual who is far more capable of facing complex tasks and of performing under pressure without becoming overwhelmed.

Self-leadership: a transtheoretical approach

While self-leadership continues to emerge as an academic field in its own right, it nevertheless remains youthful in its conceptualization (at least within the context of organizational studies). This prompts the need for leadership scholars, managers and executives to adopt a multidisciplinary approach to the study of self-leadership (e.g. by addressing the sport psychology literature, such as Hanrahan and Andersen, 2012) in order to gain further elucidation of the intricacies of such an exciting and potentially valuable topic. It also requires the leadership scholar to revisit key theories of leadership discussed over the course of the previous ten chapters, and to recognize their value in developing one's own self-leadership.

Consequently, the remainder of the chapter focuses on key trends that have arisen from the leadership literature – trends which, when viewed together, form a foundational base for the effective practice of self-leadership.

The ten trends, discussed in greater detail below, constitute:

1 the need to *establish a vision*
2 the need to *chase power, not popularity*
3 the ability to *define your principles and align your actions to them*
4 the ability to *seek to maximize your genetic potential*
5 the requirement to *acquire skills conducive to leadership*
6 the need to *develop anticipatory coping strategies*
7 the vital importance of *practising effective followership*

8   the benefits of *developing your emotional intelligence*
9   the need to *challenge the status quo*
10 the need to *seek to transform yourself and others.*

1 Establish a vision

Leadership requires the establishment of, and commitment to, a vision (Giampetro-Meyer *et al.*, 1998). *Values-based leadership* posits the importance of a passionate articulation of a vision in order to command great commitment and performance beyond expectations from followers (House, 1996; House and Shamir, 1993). The presence of a vision (Bennis and Nanus, 1985; Conger and Kanungo, 1987) emerges as the most commonly emphasized behaviour possessed by a charismatic leader, and as an important element of transformational leadership.

Vision creation, articulation and communication have been theorized to be the most important factors in predicting leadership effectiveness (Bass, 1990; Bycio *et al.*, 1995; Simons, 1999), and carries similarities to the need for goal-setting identified in the self-leadership literature (Neck and Houghton, 2006).

Effective self-leadership thus requires the articulation of a vision, and the ability to guide oneself towards its realization via the use of relevant self-management strategies (such as self-control and self-assessment). Without a vision, one lacks direction and focus and risks squandering potential.

2 Chase power, not popularity

To return to the earlier words of Sergeant Oswell, "Courage is not always done on the battlefield. Courage is done when someone has the courage to right a wrong, even if it is not popular."

House and Howell (1992) identify a low need for affiliation[7] as characteristic of the need for personal power, with the latter gaining empirical support as a predictor of leader effectiveness (House *et al.*, 1991; McClelland and Boyatzis, 1982; McClelland and Burnham, 1976). The need to be respected – as opposed to liked – emerges with clarity as a practice exercised by the successful leader. The leader who is held back by the need for employees to like them risks compromising their values and principles, and is more likely to circumvent organizational rules and goals in order to satiate this egoistically driven need. This can be contrasted strongly with a leader such as Donald Woods who regularly threatened resignation if he felt that the newspaper for which he worked, the *Daily Dispatch*, had reneged in a substantial way on its stance as a vocal opponent of apartheid. Expressed succinctly by the divisive yet successful former British Prime Minister Margaret Thatcher, "If you just set out to be liked, you would be prepared to compromise on anything, wouldn't you, at any time. And you would achieve nothing!".[8]

Thus, the development of self-leadership requires the ability to reject the egoistic need to be liked, and to instead prioritize the need to realize one's vision in the most effective way possible.

3 Define your principles and align your actions to them

Kernis (2003, p. 13) defines authenticity as the "unobstructed operation of one's true, or core, self in one's daily enterprise". It is theorized to be a *root* construct of leadership that provides a foundation for all positive forms of leadership (Avolio and Gardner, 2005). True self-knowledge and the ability to be led by one's defining principles (all components of authentic leadership) empower an individual to become the best version of themselves that they can be, by ensuring that they chase their goals without compromising their own personal moral and ethical code.

It is interesting that individuals with unmet or unaddressed needs (Burns, 1978; Maslow, 1954), low psychological maturity, low self-esteem and a poor locus of control (Luthans *et al.*, 1998) are more susceptible to manipulation by destructive, narcissistic leaders (Padilla *et al.*, 2007; Thoroughgood *et al.*, 2012). This suscepti-bility can be minimized via an honest self-assessment of one's own unmet needs, and the ability to define both one's own principles and boundaries in the achieve-ment of a personal goal, vision or ambition.

Most importantly, however, is the idea that practising true authenticity in one's life leads to a state of *eudaemonic well-being* (Ilies *et al.*, 2005) – in other words, happiness. Consider the case of a law graduate who is offered a top-flight internship in a global law firm, an appointment likely to lead to a permanent contract and an enviable salary. She is aware, however, that a future career prac-tising law might never truly fulfil her, as her true calling lies in opening an elite surfing academy in her native Australia (an ambition built on her previous com-petitive status as a surfer, and love of the ocean). This raises a philosophical ques-tion as to *why* a person chases success; if one's goal is true happiness, then one must be prepared to resist societal pressures and expectations to remain true to the (earlier quoted) idea of achieving the "unobstructed operation of one's true, or core, self" (Kernis, 2003, p. 13).

4 Achieve your natural potential

To return to the earlier quoted Turkheimer (2000, p. 160), "Everything is herit-able". The role of neurological traits discussed in the context of trait theory (Chapter 2, "Trait theories") clearly underlines the role of brain chemistry, serotonin and endogenous steroids (e.g. testosterone and cortisol) in decision making, risk taking, management of stress, the articulation of a vision (Morse, 2006), and the regulation of risk and responses to fear and other emotions. It is also interesting that McClel-land (1985) reported an association of a high motivation for power with raised levels of adrenalin, dopamine and endorphins (Paulus *et al.*, 2003), that right frontal brain dysfunction predisposes an individual to poor social skills, poor emotional regulation and poor self-awareness (Salloway *et al.*, 2001) and that frontal cortex activity affects moral judgement (Knabb *et al.*, 2009). Practising a healthy diet, regular exposure to nature, adequate sleep and exercise all positively impact IQ and EQ while drug use harm both. Excitation transfer (the biological transfer or emotion) also identifies the need to spend time with positive, life-affirming individuals as emotional states can be contagious!

5 Acquire skills conducive to leadership

Many view Churchill as the archetypal great orator, but the reality is that his natural ability fell far below that which is most commonly ascribed to him. In actuality, it is said that he spent one hour preparing for every one minute of his speeches – a fact that somewhat clouded his ability to participate in the cut and thrust of parliamentary debate as a young MP, but which played a highly effective and historic role in his prime ministerial role during World War II.

It is the contention of this book that leaders such as Winston Churchill may have been born with certain innumerable traits, but that it also – critically – lies within the individual's ability and commitment to the nurturing and maximizing of their abilities to be able to unlock leadership brilliance. In the previously quoted words of Katz (1955, p. 40),

> We talk of "born leaders", "born executives", "born salesmen". It is undoubtedly true that certain people, naturally or innately, possess greater aptitude or ability in certain skills. But research in psychology and physiology would also indicate, first, that those having strong aptitudes and abilities can improve their skill through practice and training, and, secondly, that even those lacking the natural ability can improve their performance and effectiveness.

There is no doubt that Churchill's power of oratory and commanding rhetoric greatly increased the attributions of charisma that were afforded him by his followers. While limited evidence currently exists to suggest that charisma can be taught, it is nevertheless possible to develop skills of oratory (as Churchill did, so successfully), which might, as a result, enhance a leader's ability to communicate charismatic rhetoric (Shamir et al., 1993; Shamir et al., 1994). Such an achievement would hold great value in terms of one's ability to lead, as attributions of charisma have been seen to be related positively to leader effectiveness (Lowe et al., 1996) and perceived and actual organizational performance (Wilderom et al., 2012), a predictor of leadership effectiveness (Howell and Avolio, 1993) and a positive agentic force of organizational change (Bass and Avolio, 1993).

6 Develop anticipatory coping strategies

There will come a time when things do not go to plan, and a vital part of self-leadership is the ability to cope positively with a perceived loss or failure. The development of *anticipatory coping* (Aspinwall and Taylor, 1997) strategies allows an individual to achieve such a goal. It also empowers a leader by heightening their ability to cope with stress (Wong and Law, 2002). Anticipatory coping strategies require the use of *constructive thought pattern strategies* (positive self-talk, visualization) and can effectively accompany the use of *behavioural* (self-reward) and *natural reward strategies* (finding ways to increase the inherent appeal of a task) in an individual's holistic approach to self-leadership.

7 Practise effective followership

Voters play a powerful role in the leadership process, but evidence indicates that we often vote emotionally, not rationally. For example, candidates rated as "more attractive" in a Canadian election achieved the highest levels of election success (Efran and Patterson, 1974, p. 352), and US military cadets with a "dominant appearance" were more likely to achieve promotion (Mazur *et al.*, 1984). The 2016 US Presidential election and UK 2016 Brexit referendum were undoubtedly geared towards engaging voters emotionally, including fear and anger inducing propaganda, charisma and microtargeted 'us and them' tribalism.

The emotional bond established between leader and follower is seductive and powerful, and is particularly potent in times of crisis and uncertainty (Shamir *et al.*, 1993; Trice and Beyer, 1986), especially when negative feelings such as fear of persecution are present (Burns, 1978; House, 1977, 1996; House *et al.*, 1991; Weber, 1947). This is one reason why the Trump and Brexit campaigns relied so heavily on emotional appeals stoking fear, persecution, scapegoating and anger. Research tells us that we are most susceptible to the appeal of a charismatic leader in periods of personal uncertainty or stress, where powerful charismatic rhetoric is designed to appeal directly to our unmet needs (Maslow, 1954; see the expert insight "Life after hate", Chapter 7, for an applied view on this) – one reason why President Trump, for example, consistently relies on battle rhetoric. Our susceptibility to this type of manipulation can lead to ruinous consequences (for example, losing one's life savings after investing in Allen Stanford or Bernard Madoff's Ponzi schemes). Research in the area of destructive leadership (Padilla *et al.*, 2007; Thoroughgood *et al.*, 2012) further identifies the fact that some individuals are far more susceptible to the allure of a destructive leader than others. Practising effective self-leadership will allow an individual to be adequately *self-aware* and to effectively *self-assess* whether they are being swayed by destructive rhetoric. Most people might want to be a leader, but followership is, undoubtedly, also an important skill.

8 Develop your emotional intelligence

Emotional intelligence (EI) has been positively linked to skills identified as valuable in a manager, leader or employee (Barling *et al.*, 2000; Bass, 1990; Caruso *et al.*, 2002; Dubinsky *et al.*, 1995; Goleman, 1998; Lusch and Serpkeuci, 1990; Mandell and Pherwani, 2003), and it can be noted that much of the self-leadership literature bears similarity to models of EI. For example, Goleman's (1995, 1998) popular model of EI identifies *self-awareness* and *self-regulation* as two of the five components of emotional intelligence at work, which bears striking similarity to the *self-monitoring, self-control* and *self-regulatory* behaviours proposed by Neck and Houghton's (2006) approach to self-leadership.

Developing EI heightens one's ability to self-lead, as it fosters the ability to manage emotions (for example, fear or frustration) within the workplace. It also allows an individual to engage in honest self-evaluation of one's strengths and weaknesses in the pursuit of self-improvement. Consider the case of rogue traders Nick Leeson of Barings Bank, Kweke Adoboli of UBS and Jérôme Kerviel of Société Générale, who cost their banks billions in unauthorized trades. Trading decisions, which became increasingly risky, were executed on the basis of uncontrolled emotion (i.e. fear at their financial losses being discovered), rather than rational action, a situation that snowballed uncontrollably and led to unmitigated disaster for both themselves (prison sentences) and their employers (for example, UBS received a £30 million fine from the Financial Services Authority).

9 Challenge the status quo

The most admired leaders in business (Steve Jobs, Richard Branson, Jeff Bezos) and politics (Mahatma Gandhi, John F. Kennedy, Nelson Mandela) have been those that have challenged the status quo or, as it is known in the context of *transformational leadership* (Bass, 1985), demonstrated a high level of *intellectual stimulation*. Intellectual stimulation constitutes a leader's ability to stimulate followers to be more curious and creative in thinking and problem solving (Doherty and Danylchuk, 1996; Weese, 1994). One such example is Steve Jobs' technological brilliance in innovating new products and in driving the Apple brand forward. Similarly, Jeff Bezos's intelligent and creative vision for Amazon Inc. made him a defining force in the emergence of e-commerce.

However, it is not only the emergence of *intellectual stimulation* in Jobs or Bezos that facilitated their respective ascensions to the uppermost echelons of corporate royalty. What was also critical was that they possessed the *self-leadership* necessary to overcome the inevitable barriers and competition that they would face on the journey towards the realization of their respective visions. Such a concept was voiced eloquently by Steve Biko (the subject of the case study "Frank talk" later in this chapter) in his call to:

> take off our coats, be prepared to lose our comfort and security, our jobs and positions of prestige, and our families, for just as it is true that "leadership and security are basically incompatible", a struggle without casualties is no struggle.
>
> *(Biko, 1986, p. 97)*

Those that dare to raise their head above the parapet will undoubtedly become a target for detractors. Self-leadership therefore requires an acknowledgement that one might encounter hostility in the pursuit of a vison or goal, and that this hostility or hardship should be strategically countered and planned for as much as is practicably possible.

10 Transform yourself and others

While there are many leadership development strategies and approaches available to today's discerning leadership scholar, it is imperative that one identifies an approach that not only demonstrates effective outcomes, but which can also exhibit a high level of validity, reliability and generalizability.

Transformational leadership remains dominant in its presence within the leadership literature, and features as a hallmark of many of the inspirational leaders discussed in this book. The theory has been subjected to extensive testing across a diverse range of cultures and settings, within which it is frequently and consistently reported to exhibit a positive relationship to the elicitation of successful leadership.[9] While the roles of *charisma* and *intellectual stimulation* in self-leadership have already received specific consideration, it is nonetheless only in the presence of the two remaining transformational behaviours (*inspirational motivation* and *individual consideration*) and specific transactional behaviours (*contingent reward*) that their contribution to performance beyond expectations can be realized. Seeking to develop one's transformational leadership ultimately represents an efficacious investment in the maximization of one's human capital, as it provides a sound, empirically grounded framework for leadership development.

In the context of self-leadership, the use of *behavioural strategies* (Neck and Houghton, 2006) allows an individual to develop a structure whereby their designation of a *self-reward* is contingent on their achievement of a specific goal (i.e. self-leadership strategies can be used in the elicitation of successful *contingent reward* behaviour). The securing of 360-degree feedback from friends, peers, colleagues, subordinates and superiors using the MLQ Form 5x (alongside self-ratings) enables the individual to engage in the self-leadership behaviour of *self-assessment*. Finally, a commitment to improving one's leadership ability via development of transformational behaviours allows the individual to benefit from the use of an approach that possesses a high level of empirical robustness, validity, reliability and generalizability – a sound and effective use of one's human capital.

Measuring self-leadership

The first instrument to be devised was the Self-Leadership Questionnaire (SLQ), a 50-item self-leadership scale developed by Anderson and Prussia (1997), based on the work of Manz and Sims (1991) and Manz (1992). This preceded the development of Houghton and Neck's (2002) Refined Self-Leadership Questionnaire (RSLQ) that addressed the critiques of its forebear and subsequently possessed greater reliability and construct validity than the SLQ. The more recent Modified Self-Leadership Questionnaire (MSLQ) (Ho and Nesbit, 2009) partially addresses the issue of cultural differentiation in its measurement of self-leadership across both Western and Eastern cultures, with early empirical work indicating internal reliability and partial scalar invariance of the MSLQ.

Criticisms of self-leadership

Self-leadership theory has been criticized for a lack of empirically robust measures with which the construct can be measured. Additionally, it is unclear as to whether self-leadership carries specific benefits at both an *individual* and a *dyadic* level, and whether the level of seniority of a leader (e.g. Junior Team Leader or Managing Director) mediates both the need for, and beneficial effect of, self-leadership. The field is also relatively underdeveloped within the context of organizational studies, and scholars are subsequently guided towards other disciplines (such as sport psychology) within which the concept has received a far greater level of academic consideration.

Summary

This book began its consideration of leadership with the 'Great Man' theory, asking whether great leaders are *born* or *made*. It is actually possible to answer, with complete certainty, that great leaders are, in fact, *born*, for if they are not born, then, metaphysically, they do not exist! Metaphysical arguments aside, however, it is also possible to comment that leaders are both facilitated and constrained in their ability to lead by the existence of both external factors (such as gender discrimination or racism) and internal factors (anticipatory coping and other self-leadership strategies, or a motivation for socialized power) – and by the pre-existence of social structures (for example, an apartheid government). So, to an extent, it is valid to argue that every leader is to some extent *shaped*. Whether that is commensurate with the idea of being *made* is another story, but it is hoped that the case studies, expert insights and academic theory within this book have, to some extent, at least enlivened the debate in the mind of the reader.

Nelson Mandela once said that "education is the most powerful weapon which you can use to change the world".[10] It is hoped that the reader has gained a valuable insight into key theories of leadership throughout their journey traversing the eleven chapters of this book, and that this knowledge and education will empower them to both seek and realize their own potential as a leader.

The final chapter now invites the reader to move into a new phase of knowledge acquisition – to move beyond the desk research of other scholars to actively research leadership themselves. Before we do so, however, the reader is invited to engage with the expert insight, case study and quiz that conclude this chapter.

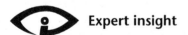 **Expert insight**

Lessons in self-leadership

Twenty-one years of active service in the US Marine Corps has given Gunnery Sergeant David A. Oswell great exposure to leadership. Now retired from active service, Gunnery Sergeant Oswell is a former United Services Organization (USO) Marine of the Year (2001) and honor graduate of the Marine Corps Military Police. He holds a range of accolades, including achievement and good conduct medals, a Meritorious Mast and Navy commendation medals.

"I learned that to be a good leader you must lead by example and practise self-sacrifice, and practise what you preach. My toughest challenge was to place mission first over family. I also found that courage is not always done on the battlefield. Courage is done when someone has the courage to right a wrong, even if it is not popular.

I was not always happy with the Marines around me. I have sometimes worked in a hostile workplace. To overcome this, I set my own standards, encouraged others to follow and set the example. I would also encourage others to be better than myself – to move beyond what I have accomplished. A true leader will create better leaders for the future.

I learned in my 21 years of service in the Marine Corps that you will not make everyone happy with your decisions. Your role is not to be there to make everyone happy, but to accomplish the mission and task at hand by following the Marine leadership principles and by leading by example. I learned when making decisions to never ask someone to do something that you would not do yourself. I always tell myself that I am being lazy so that I will continue to move forward with my goals and daily tasks to reach those goals.

Marines follow a strict code of conduct, using the eleven Marine 'Leadership Principles': to know yourself and seek improvement; to be technically and tactically proficient; to know your marines and look out for their welfare; to keep your Marines informed; set the example; to ensure the task is understood, supervised, and accomplished; to train your Marines as a team; to make sound and timely decisions; to develop a sense of responsibility among your subordinates; to employ your command in accordance with its capabilities; and to seek responsibility and take responsibility for your actions. Additionally, Marines are expected to demonstrate specific traits: bearing, courage, decisiveness, dependability, endurance, enthusiasm, initiative, integrity, judgement, justice, loyalty, knowledge and tact.

The first Marine 'Leadership Principle' – to know yourself and seek improvement – requires the use of these traits. Knowing yourself will allow you to practise self-leadership; to honestly evaluate your strengths and weaknesses, to determine the best way to lead in any given situation and to seek 360-degree feedback to evaluate your performance as a leader. This knowledge will empower you to seek improvement in your ability to lead.

Marines walk around with what others view as a sense of arrogance, but this is actually a high self-esteem and confidence, fuelled by the belief that they are able to accomplish anything through the use of hard work and dedication. In my opinion, the Marine 'Leadership Principles' and traits can be used and applied to everyday life. This needs to be used as early as elementary or high school. It builds self-confidence and establishes self-esteem among young adults. Everyone – whether at school or in the workplace – can benefit from using them to develop their self-leadership and to become a better leader."

Questions

1 With reference to self-leadership theory, identify ways in which Gunnery Sergeant Oswell demonstrates self-leadership.
2 Identify how Gunnery Sergeant Oswell's approach reflects the values communicated in two of the transtheoretical statements presented in this chapter.
3 Identify ways in which Gunnery Sergeant Oswell employs *behavioural* and *constructive thought pattern strategies* in the elicitation of self-leadership.
4 Do you agree that the US Marines' 'Leadership Principles' could be used effectively to develop the leadership skills of students and executives?

Case study: frank talk

Throughout the preceding eleven chapters of this book, the reader will have identified the most successful leader as one who is transformational, who demonstrates authenticity in his/her actions, who possesses a strong vision and charisma and whose actions are motivated by a socialized need for power. This case study subsequently presents an eloquent example of such a leader: Steve Biko (also mentioned in the Chapter 7 case study, "Sikhahlela Indoda Yamadoda").

Biko: a brief history

Stephen Biko was born in Kingwilliamstown, in the Cape Province of South African in 1946. In 1966, he matriculated at the medical school of the University of Natal, Durban, where he quickly became involved with the National Union of South African Students (NUSAS). He was to leave NUSAS in 1968 in order to form a blacks-only student organization – the South African Students' Organisation (SASO) – in 1969. SASO was committed to the philosophy of Black Consciousness and quickly gained strength within South Africa's black university campuses.

Biko left NUSAS as a result of frustrations with the white liberalism that shaped and led the actions of the organization. One such example of the negative effects of a white liberalist ideology can be found with reference to the 1967 NUSAS Conference hosted at Rhodes University. The Group Areas Act prohibited racially mixed accommodation. The response of NUSAS was to condemn the university but, at the same time, to instruct black members to act in accordance with the law. Biko argued that what was required to transform South Africa was for black South Africans to become agents of change, and not have their futures shaped by white liberal voices. The Black People's Convention (BPC), formed in 1972, provided a route for graduating SASO members to continue political action.

Black consciousness

Biko was thrown out of the University of Natal in 1972. It was at this time that he devoted himself fully to the development of Black Consciousness and related activities, becoming involved with the BCP (Black Community Programmes) in Durban and in other institutions, such as the BPC and The Zimele Trust Fund to assist political prisoners, and the Ginsberg Educational Trust to aid black students. While Biko was no longer able to pursue a medical education, he pursued a Law degree by correspondence with UNISA (the University of South Africa).

Biko's vision was of a South Africa that was "an open society, one man, one vote, no reference to colour" (Biko, 2002, p. 123).[11] Steve Biko is widely regarded as the father of Black Consciousness, defined as being, in essence,

> the realisation of the black man of the need to rally together with his brothers around the cause of oppression – the blackness of their skin – and to operate as a group in order to rid themselves of the shackles that bind them to perpetual servitude.
>
> *(2002, pp. 91–92)*

In February 1973, Biko was banned without trial, which meant that he was not allowed to enter an educational institution, to write for any publication, to attend any gathering of any kind other than a bona fide church service, to be quoted in any publication, to receive any visitors in his home (aside from a doctor), speak in public or be in the company of more than one person at any time. The banning order also required him to leave Durban and return to Kingwilliamstown, the town of his birth. It is clear that the security forces had enforced these bans as a means of breaking up the BPC so that it would cease operations, and also to cease communications between leaders and followers of the BPC. Herein lay the true virtue of Black Consciousness, a philosophy that transcended the need for the physical presence of a leader (as would have been the case in charismatic leadership that exists only *in statu nascendi*; Weber, 1947) – a necessary condition, given the constant threat of violence and banning that existed in apartheid-era South Africa. It also transcended the need for a bricks-and-mortar organization (again, a necessary condition, since security forces came down with such brutal force on such organizations). Instead, it embodied fully the spirit of what Bass (1985) and Burns (1978) refer to as transformational leadership – the empowerment of the follower, by the leader, to such an extent that the leader's presence would not be necessary in order for the transformational effect to be maintained. Black Consciousness ultimately empowered its followers to become true agents of change.

Biko was a charismatic figure, with a 'burning inner spirit' with great physical presence, vitality and power – one who commanded great loyalty from his followers. His vision for South Africa was greatly socialized and intellectually powerful, where the transformative message of Black Consciousness aimed to empower individual followers as well as the nation as a whole.

One of the many projects that Biko spearheaded was the development of the Zanempilo Community Health Centre, an ambitious project developed by the BCP in Zinkoya, five miles outside of Kingwilliamstown, which aimed to provide essential health services that were independent of Government control – a centre that was "utterly different in spirit from any other clinic or hospital in the country ... the incarnate symbol of Black Consciousness" (Biko, 2002, p. 169). This was funded in part by the Anglo–American mining corporation, with Dr. Mamphela A. Ramphele appointed as Chief Medical Officer.[12] Despite his ban, Steve Biko was to create a transformative effect on his home town, where he became Branch Executive of the Kingwilliamstown BCP office in addition to assisting the foundation of the Zanempilo Community Health Centre. Dr. Ramphele stated that the founding of the clinic was essentially a statement intended to demonstrate how little (with the use of proper planning and organization) it would take to deliver the most basic of services to South Africans living within townships.

Biko discussed the idea that South African blacks were denied the chance to even accidentally prove their equality with white men via the legitimized concept of 'job reservation': a lack of training in skilled work and a tight ring-fencing around the professional possibilities that were open to blacks, meaning that the professions – such as lawyers, engineers, economists, politicians – were exclusively open to whites. This perpetual state of servitude led to Biko's observation, which opened Chapter 10 ("Destructive leadership"), that "the most potent weapon in the hands of the oppressor is the mind of the oppressed" (Biko, 2002, p. 92). He goes on:

> If one is free at heart, no man-made chains can bind one to servitude, but if one's mind is so manipulated and controlled by the oppressor as to make the oppressed believe that he is a liability to the white man, then there will be nothing the oppressed can do to scare his powerful masters. (Ibid.)

A martyr of apartheid

Biko spoke eloquently of the dangers involved in being part of a true bid for change. He spoke of the need to

> take off our coats, be prepared to lose our comfort and security, our jobs and positions of prestige, and our families, for just as it is true that "leadership and security are basically incompatible", a struggle without casualties is no struggle. We must realize that prophetic cry of black students: "Black man, you are on your own!".
>
> *(Biko, 1986, p. 97)*

During cross-examination in May 1976, in a trial that later became known as the Trial of Ideas,[13] Biko explained to the prosecuting attorney Mr L. Atwell and to the presiding Judge Boshoff that the goals of SASO were to liberate the black man, first from their own psychological oppression meted out to themselves through the adoption of an inferiority complex (as a result of apartheid), and second from the physical oppression that resulted from living in a white racist society. It was partly as a result of this trial that Black Consciousness spread to South African schools via the formation of SASM (the South African Students Movement), which in turn played an important role in the student uprisings of 1976.

Charged numerous times under security legislation, Biko was detained, but never convicted, of a crime. In August 1977 he was detained under Section 6 of the Terrorism Act and taken to Port Elizabeth. He was to die under interrogation, with the cause of death attributed to brain damage. An article printed in the *New Republic* in 1978 after his death carried some of Biko's final thoughts: "You are either alive and proud or you are dead, and when you are dead, you don't care anyway. And your method of death can itself be a politicizing thing" (Biko, 2002, p. 153).

Certainly the political ramifications of Biko's death caused reverberations around the world. His words and actions, and the enduring legacy of Black Consciousness played a significant role in ultimately causing the fall of the apartheid regime; they provide an inspiring example of how one man can truly make a difference to the world in which he lives.

Questions

1   Biko was often consulted by the BPC (Black Peoples' Convention) despite being banned from holding a formal position in the organization. Comment on the types of power held by/attributed to Biko by colleagues and followers, in the context of French and Raven's (1959) theories of power.

2   Biko once stated that, "Township life alone makes it a miracle for anyone to live up to adulthood" (Biko, 2002, p. 109), a quote revisited under Biko's cross-examination in May 1976. What did Biko mean by this statement, and what does it suggest about the role of environment in the development of one's skills and competencies?

3   Path–Goal Theory identifies the role of the leader in removing barriers from the path of his/her followers, in order to allow them to achieve their goals. Identify an example from the case study above that illustrates the effective demonstration of path–goal behaviour.

4   Leadership could be argued to be a process that occurs between leader, situation and follower. With reference to Weber's (1947) conceptualization of charisma *in statu nascendi*, argue a case for why Biko was not only charismatic, but transformational.

5   How are Biko's actions authentic? Refer to an example from the case study in your answer.

6   Comment on the way in which Biko demonstrated effective self-leadership throughout his life – for example, through the demonstration of courage and intellectual strength.

7   Steve Biko was only 30 years old when he died. Despite his age, he demonstrated great wisdom in his political and social life. Discuss the level to which his leadership *traits* (e.g. intelligence) and his pursuance of leadership *skills* (e.g. acquiring knowledge via undergraduate study) intersected in order to facilitate great leadership.

8   How did Biko demonstrate *intellectual stimulation?*

9 Identify why self-leadership was crucial to Biko in the pursuance and realization of his vision.

10 What can you, personally, learn from this case study, in terms of your own self-leadership development?

CHAPTER 11 QUIZ

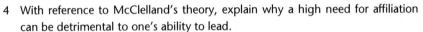

1 Provide two competing definitions of self-leadership.
2 What is *SuperLeadership*?
3 Can self-leadership be learned, or is it a trait? Refer to theory in your answer.
4 With reference to McClelland's theory, explain why a high need for affiliation can be detrimental to one's ability to lead.
5 Self-regulation is considered to be a behaviour associated with self-leadership. Which other theories include self-regulation?
6 Provide an example of an anticipatory coping strategy that an executive might use in order to improve their performance.
7 List three critiques of self-leadership theory.
8 Identify a reliable means of measuring leadership.
9 How do Manz and Sims (1987) define *self-management*?
10 Why is the alignment of one's principles with one's actions a valuable pursuit in the practice of leadership?

Notes

1 Quoted in an interview conducted for this book for the expert insight "Lessons in self-leadership" that appears later in this chapter.
2 House of Commons speech, 9 September 1941.
3 This also forms the basis of an expert insight later in the chapter.
4 The value of intrinsic motivation in the performance of an employee is conceptualized at far greater length as part of Deci and Ryan's (2000) Self-Determination Theory. As this has been discussed at some length earlier in the book (Chapter 4, "Behavioural theories"), it will not be subject to further consideration here. However, the reader is encouraged to revisit the chapter and to compare Deci and Ryan's Self-Determination Theory, and other theories of motivation, to self-leadership theory, and to consider the ways in which both fields might inform one another.
5 The need to act as a role model is also prevalent within theories of socialized charismatic leadership, and transformational and authentic leadership.
6 An individual's "perception of their ability to perform across a variety of different situations" (Judge et al., 1998, p. 170).
7 Affiliation = the need to be liked.
8 Interview for the Press Association, 5 March 1989.
9 Avolio and Howell (1992), Avolio and Yammarino (2002), Barling et al. (1996), Bass (1998), Bryman (1992), Bycio et al. (1995), Gardner and Cleavenger (1998), Hater and Bass (1988), Kelloway et al. (2000), Lowe et al. (1996), Pillai et al. (1999), Podsakoff et al. (1996), Ross and Offermann (1997), Shamir et al. (1998), Sosik and Godshalk (2000).

10 Quoted by Nelson Mandela in a speech delivered at the launch of the Mindset Network at the Planetarium, University of the Witwatersrand, Johannesburg, South Africa, 16 July 2003.
11 Readers are guided to Biko (1986) for a fuller appreciation of his life and leadership. For further reading, it is recommended that readers visit the Steve Biko Foundation: www. sbf.org.za/Main_Site/index.php.
12 Dr. Ramphela Mamphele served as a member of the Anglo–American board from 2006 to 2012.
13 Leading SASO and BPC members were charged with inciting unrest and used the ensuing 17-month trial as a platform to promote Black Consciousness.

References

Anderson, J.S. and Prussia, G.E. (1997). The Self-Leadership Questionnaire: Preliminary Assessment in Construct Validity. *Journal of Leadership Studies*, 4(2), pp. 119–143.

Aspinwall, L.G. and Taylor, S.E. (1997). A Stitch in Time: Self-Regulation and Proactive Coping. *Psychological Bulletin*, 121(3), pp. 417–436.

Avolio, B.J. and Gardner, W.L. (2005). Authentic Leadership Development: Getting to the Root of Positive Leadership. *Leadership Quarterly*, 16(3), pp. 315–338.

Avolio, B.J. and Howell, J.M. (1992). The Impact of Leader Behaviour and Leader Follower Personality Match on Satisfaction and Unit Performance. In K.E. Clarke, M.B. Clarke and D.R. Campbell (eds.), *Impact of Leadership*. Greensboro, NC: Center for Creative Leadership.

Avolio, B.J. and Yammarino, F.J. (2002). *Transformational and Charismatic Leadership: The Road Ahead*. London: Elsevier Science.

Barling, J., Weber, T., and Kelloway, E.K. (1996). Effects of Transformational Leadership Training on Attitudinal and Financial Outcomes: A Field Experiment. *Journal of Applied Psychology*, 81(3), pp. 827–832.

Barling, J., Slater, F. and Kelloway, E.K. (2000). Transformational Leadership and Emotional Intelligence: An Exploratory Study. *Leadership & Organisational Development Journal*, 21(6), pp. 157–161.

Bass, B.M. (ed.) (1985). *Leadership and Performance Beyond Expectations*. New York: Free Press.

Bass, B.M. (ed.) (1990). *Bass & Stogdill's Handbook of Leadership*. New York: Free Press.

Bass, B.M. (1998). The Ethics of Transformational Leadership. In J. Cuilla (ed.), *Ethics, The Heart of Leadership*. Westport, CN: Praeger, pp. 169–192.

Bass, B.M. and Avolio, B.J. (1993). Transformational Leadership: A Response to Critiques. In M.M. Chemers and R. Ayman (eds.), *Leadership Theory and Research: Perspectives and Directions*. San Diego, CA: Academic Press, pp. 49–80.

Bennis, W.G. (2003). The Crucibles of Authentic Leadership. In J. Antonakis, A.T. Gianciolo and R.J. Sternberg (eds.), *The Nature of Leadership*. Thousand Oaks, CA: Sage, pp. 75–85.

Bennis, W. and Nanus, B. (1985). *Leaders: The Strategies for Taking Charge*. New York: Harper & Row.

Biko, S. (1986). Black Consciousness and the Quest for a True Humanity. In C. Basil Moore (ed.), *Black Theology: The South African Voice*. London: Hurst & Co.

Biko, S. (2002). *I Write What I Like* (ed. Aelred Stubb). 1st ed. Chicago, IL: Chicago University Press.

Bryman, A. (1992). *Charisma and Leadership in Organisations*. London: Sage.

Burns, J. (1978). *Leadership*. New York: Harper & Row.

Bycio, P., Hackett, R.D and Allen, J.S. (1995). Further Assessment of Bass's Conceptualisation of Transactional and Transformational Leadership. *Journal of Applied Psychology*, 80(4), pp. 468–478.

Caruso, D.R., Mayer, J.D. and Salovey, P. (2002). Emotional Intelligence and Emotional Leadership. In R.E. Riggio, S.E. Murphy and F.J. Pirozzolo (eds.), *Multiple Intelligences and Leadership*. Mahwah, NJ: Lawrence Erlbaum Associates, pp. 55–74.

Conger, J. and Kanungo, R.S. (1987). Towards a Behavioural Theory of Charismatic Leadership in Organisations. *Academy of Management Review*, 12(4), pp. 637–647.

Deci, E.L. and Ryan, R.M. (2000). The "What" and "Why" of Goal Pursuits: Human Needs and the Self-Determination of Behavior. *Psychological Inquiry*, 11(4), pp. 227–268.

Doherty, A.J. and Danylchuk, K.E. (1996). Transformational and Transactional Leadership in Interuniversity Athletics Management. *Journal of Sport Management*, 10(3), pp. 292–309.

Dubinsky, A.J., Yammarino, F.J. and Jolson, M.A. (1995). An Examination of Linkages between Personal Characteristics and Dimensions of Transformational Leadership. *Journal of Business & Psychology*, 9(3), pp. 315–335.

Efran, M.G. and Patterson, E.W. (1974). Voters Vote Beautiful: The Effect of Physical Appearance on a National Election. *Canadian Journal of Behavioural Science*, 6, pp. 352–356.

French, John R.P. and Raven, B. (1959). The Bases of Social Power. In D. Cartwright (ed.), *Studies in Social Power*. Ann Arbor, MI: University of Michigan, pp. 150–167.

Gardner, W.L. and Cleavenger, D. (1998). The Impression Management Strategies Associated with Transformational Leadership at the World-Class Level. *Management Communication Quarterly*, 12(1), pp. 3–41.

Giampetro-Meyer, A., Brown, T., Browne, M.N. and Kubasek, N. (1998). Do We Really Need More Leaders in Business? *Journal of Business Ethics*, 17(15), pp. 1727–1736.

Goleman, D. (1995). *Emotional Intelligence*. New York: Bantam.

Goleman, D. (1998). *Working with Emotional Intelligence*. New York: Bantam.

Hanrahan, S. and Andersen, M.B. (2012). *Routledge Handbook of Applied Sport Psychology: A Comprehensive Guide for Students and Practitioners*. London: Routledge.

Hater, J.J. and Bass, B.M. (1988). Superiors' Evaluations and Subordinates' Perceptions of Transformational and Transactional Leadership. *Journal of Applied Psychology*, 73(4), pp. 695–702.

Ho, J. and Nesbit, P.L. (2009). A Refinement and Extension of the Self-Leadership Scale for the Chinese Context. *Journal of Managerial Psychology*, 24(5), pp. 450–476.

Houghton, J.D. and Neck, C.P. (2002). The Revised Self-Leadership Questionnaire: Testing a Hierarchical Factor Structure for Self-Leadership. *Journal of Managerial Psychology*, 17, pp. 672–691.

House, R.J. (1977). A 1976 Theory of Charismatic Leadership. In J.G. Hunt and L.L. Larson (eds.), *Leadership: The Cutting Edge*. Carbondale, IL: Southern Illinois University Press. pp. 189–207.

House, R.J. (1996). Path–Goal Theory of Leadership: Lessons, Legacy, and a Reformulated Theory. *Leadership Quarterly*, 7(3), pp. 323–352.

House, R.J. and Howell, J.M. (1992), Personality and Charismatic Leadership. *Leadership Quarterly*, 3(3), pp. 81–109.

House, R.J. and Shamir, B. (1993). Toward the Integration of Charismatic, Transformational, Inspirational and Visionary Theories of Leadership. In M. Chemmers and R. Ayman (eds.), *Leadership Theory and Research Perspectives and Directions*. New York: Academic Press, pp. 81–107.

House, R.J., Spangler, W. and Woycke, J. (1991). Personality and Charisma in the US Presidency: A Psychological Theory of Leader Effectiveness. *Administrative Science Quarterly*, 36(3), pp. 364–396.

Howell, J.M. and Avolio, B.J. (1993). Transformational Leadership, Transactional Leadership, Locus of Control, and Support for Innovation: Key Predictors of Consolidated-Business-Unit Performance. *Journal of Applied Psychology*, 78(6), pp. 891–902.

Ilies, R., Morgeson, F.P. and Nahrgang, J.D. (2005). Authentic Leadership and Eudaemonic Well-Being: Understanding Leader–Follower Outcomes. *Leadership Quarterly*, 16(3), pp. 373–394.

Judge, T.A., Erez, A. and Bono, E.J. (1998). The Power of Being Positive: The Relation between Positive Self-Concept and Job. *Performance Human Performance*, 11(2–3), pp. 167–187.

Katz, R.L. (1955). Skills of an Effective Administrator. *Harvard Business Review*, 33(1) (January–February), pp. 33–42.

Kelloway, E.K., Barling, J. and Helleur, J. (2000). Enhancing Transformational Leadership: The Roles of Training and Feedback. *Leadership and Organizational Development Journal*, 21(3), pp. 145–148.

Kernis, M.H. (2003). Toward a Conceptualization of Optimal Self-Esteem. *Psychological Inquiry*, 14(1), pp. 1–26.

Knabb, J.J., Welsh, R.K., Ziebell, J.G. and Reimer, K.S. (2009). Neuroscience, Moral Reasoning, and the Law. *Behavioral Sciences and the Law*, 27(2), pp. 219–236.

Lowe, K.B., Kroeck, K.G. and Sivasubramanian, N. (1996). Effectiveness Correlates of Transformational and Transactional Leadership: A Meta-Analytic Review of the MLQ Literature. *Leadership Quarterly*, 7(3), pp. 385–426.

Lusch, R.F. and Serpkeuci, R.R. (1990). Personal Differences, Job Tension, Job Outcomes, and Store Performance: A study of Retail Managers. *Journal of Marketing*, 54(1), pp. 85–101.

Luthans, F., Peterson, S.J. and Ibrayeva, E. (1998). The Potential for the "Dark Side" of Leadership in Post-Communist Countries. *Journal of World Business*, 33(2), pp. 185–201.

McClelland, D.C. (1985). *Human Motivation*. Glenview, IL: Scott, Foresman.

McClelland, D.C. and Boyatzis, R.E. (1982). Leadership Motive Patterns and Long-Term Success in Management. *Journal of Applied Psychology*, 67(6), pp. 737–743.

McClelland, D.C. and Burnham, D. (1976). Power Is the Great Motivator. *Harvard Business Review*, 54(2) (March–April), pp. 100–110.

Mandell, B. and Pherwani, S. (2003). Relationship between Emotional Intelligence and Transformational Leadership Style: A Gender Comparison. *Journal of Business and Psychology*, 17(3), pp. 387–404.

Manz, C.C. (1983). *The Art of Self-Leadership: Strategies for Personal Effectiveness in Your Life and Work*. Englewood Cliffs, NJ: Prentice-Hall.

Manz, C.C. (1986). Self-Leadership: Toward an Expanded Theory of Self-Influence Processes in Organizations. *Academy of Management Review*, 11(3), pp. 585–600.

Manz, C.C. (1992) Self-Leadership. The Heart of Empowerment. *Journal for Quality and Participation*, 15(4), pp. 80–89.

Manz, C.C. and Neck, C.P. (1991). Inner Leadership: Creating Productive Thought Patterns. *Executive*, 5(3), pp. 87–95.

Manz, C.C. and Neck, C.P. (1999). *Mastering Self-Leadership: Empowering Yourself for Personal Excellence*. 2nd ed. Upper Saddle River, NJ: Prentice Hall.

Manz, C.C. and Sims, H.P., Jr (1980). Self-Management as a Substitute for Leadership: A Social Learning Theory Perspective. *Academy of Management Review*, 5(3), pp. 361–367.

Manz, C.C. and Sims, H.P., Jr (1987). Leading Workers to Lead Themselves: The External Leadership of Self-Managing Work Teams. *Administrative Science Quarterly*, 32, pp. 106–128.

Manz, C.C. and Sims, H.P., Jr (1989). *SuperLeadership: Leading Others to Lead Themselves*. San Francisco, CA: Berrett-Koehler.

Manz, C.C., & Sims, H.P., Jr (1991). SuperLeadership: Beyond the Myth of Heroic Leadership. *Organizational Dynamics*, 19(4), pp. 18–35.

Markham, S.E. and Markham, I.S. (1995). Self-Management and Self-Leadership Reexamined: A Levels-of-Analysis Perspective. *Leadership Quarterly*, 6(3), pp. 343–359.

Maslow, A. (1954). *Motivation and Personality*. New York: Harper.

Mazur, A., Mazur, J. and Keating, C. (1984). Military Rank Attainment of a West Point Class: Effects of Cadets' Physical Features. *American Journal of Sociology*, 90, pp. 125–150.

Morse, G. (2006). Decisions and Desire. *Harvard Business Review*, 84, pp. 42–51.

Neck, C.P. and Houghton, J.D. (2006). Two Decades of Self-Leadership Theory and Research: Past Developments, Present Trends, and Future Possibilities. *Journal of Managerial Psychology*, 21(4), pp. 270–295.

Neck, C.P. and Manz, C.C. (1992). Thought Self-Leadership: The Impact of Self-Talk and Mental Imagery on Performance. *Journal of Organizational Behavior*, 12, pp. 681–699.

Neck, C. and Manz, C.C. (1996). Thought Self-Leadership: The Impact of Mental Strategies Training on Employee Cognition, Behavior, and Affect. *Journal of Organizational Behavior*, 17, pp. 445–467.

Neck, C.P. and Manz, C.C. (2007). *Mastering Self-Leadership: Empowering Yourself for Personal Excellence*. 4th ed. Upper Saddle River, NJ: Prentice-Hall.

Padilla, A., Hogan, R. and Kaiser, R.B. (2007). The Toxic Triangle: Destructive Leaders, Susceptible Followers, and Conducive Environments. *Leadership Quarterly*, 18(3), pp. 176–194.

Paulus, M.P., Rogalsky, C. and Simmons, A. (2003). Increased Activation in the Right Insula during Risk-Taking Decision Making Is Related to Harm Avoidance and Neuroticism. *Neuroimage*, 19(4), pp. 1439–1448.

Pillai, R., Schreisheim, C.A. and Williams, E.S. (1999). Fairness Perceptions and Trust as Mediators for Transformational and Transactional Leadership – A Two Sample Study. *Journal of Management*, 25(6), pp. 897–933.

Podsakoff, P.M., MacKenzie, S.B. and Bommer, W.H. (1996). Transformational Leader Behaviours and Substitutes for Leadership as Determinants of Employee Satisfaction, Continent, Trust and Organizational Citizenship Behaviours. *Journal of Management*, 22(2), pp. 259–298.

Prussia, G.E., Anderson, J.S. and Manz, C.C. (1998). Self-Leadership and Performance Outcomes: The Mediating Influence of Self-Efficacy. *Journal of Organizational Behavior*, 19(5), pp. 523–538.

Ross, S.M. and Offerman, L.R. (1997). Transformational Leaders: Measurement of Personality Attributes and Work Group Performance. *Personality and Social Science Bulletin*, 23(10), pp. 1078–1086.

Salloway, S., Malloy, P. and Duffy, J. (eds.) (2001). *The Frontal Lobes and Neuropsychiatric Illness*. Arlington, VA: American Psychiatric Press.

Shamir, B., House, R.J. and Arthur, M.B. (1993). The Motivational Effects of Charismatic Leadership: A Self-Concept Based Theory. *Organisational Science*, 4(4), pp. 577–594.

Shamir, B., Arthur, M.B. and House, R.J. (1994). The Rhetoric of Charismatic Leadership: A Theoretical Extension, a Case Study, and Implications for Research. *Leadership Quarterly*, 5(1), pp. 25–42.

Shamir, B., Zakay, E., Breinin, E. and Popper, M. (1998). Correlates of Charismatic Leader Behaviour in Military Units: Subordinates' Attitudes, Unit Characteristics, and Superiors' Appraisals of Leader Performance. *Academy of Management Journal*, 41(4), pp. 387–409.

Simons, T.L. (1999). Behavioral Integrity as a Critical Ingredient for Transformational Leadership. *Journal of Organizational Change Management*, 12(2), pp. 89–104.

Sosik, J.J. and Godshalk, V.M. (2000). Leadership Styles, Mentoring Functions and Job-Related Stress: A Conceptual Model and Preliminary Study. *Journal of Organizational Behaviour*, 21(4), pp. 365–390.

Stewart, G.L., Carson, K.P. and Cardy, R.L. (1996). The Joint Effects of Conscientiousness and Self-Leadership Training on Self-Directed Behavior in a Service Setting. *Personnel Psychology*, 49(1), pp. 143–164.

Thoroughgood, C.N., Pailla, A., Hunter, S.T. and Tate, B.W. (2012). The Susceptible Circle: A Taxonomy of Followers Associated with Destructive Leadership. *Leadership Quarterly*, 23(5), pp. 897–917.

Trice, H.M. and Beyer, M. (1986). Charisma and Its Routinisation in Two Social Movement Organisations. In B.M. Staw and L.L. Cummings (eds.), *Research in Organisational Behaviour* (Vol. 8). Greenwich, CT: JAI Press, pp. 113–164.

Turkheimer, E. (2000). Three Laws of Behavior Genetics and What They Mean. *Current Directions in Psychological Science*, 9(5), pp. 160–164.

Unsworth, K.L. and Mason, C.M. (2012). Help Yourself: The Mechanisms through Which a Self-Leadership Intervention Influences Strain. *Journal of Occupational Health Psychology*, 17(2), pp. 235–245.

Weber, M. (1947). *The Theory of Social and Economic Organization* (trans. A.M. Henderson and T. Parsons). New York: Free Press.

Weese, W.J. (1994). A Leadership Discussion with Dr Bernard Bass. *Journal of Sport Management*, 8(3), pp. 179–189.

Wilderom, C.P.M., van den Berg, P.T. and Wiersma, U.J. (2012). A Longitudinal Study of the Effects of Charismatic Leadership and Organisational Culture on Objective and Perceived Corporate Performance. *Leadership Quarterly*, 23(12), pp. 835–848.

Wong, C.C. and Law, K.S. (2002). The Effect of Leader and Follower Emotional Intelligence on Performance and Attitude: An Exploratory Study. *Leadership Quarterly*, 13(3), pp. 243–274.

Other resources

See PowerPoint slides on the companion website at www.routledge.com/9780367374822.

12

RESEARCHING LEADERSHIP

"In order to be an effective CEO, I have had to employ elements of research to every single aspect of my job."

— Dr. Laslo-Baker, CEO, DeeBee's Organics[1]

Great research should begin with great passion. Whether you are tackling your first project for a research methods module or embarking on the momentous, life-changing journey of a PhD, passion is what will keep your research journey focused, even in the toughest of times. If it doesn't go wrong at least once then you should be surprised! As Barack Obama stated in his 2013 Ohio State Commencement speech, "You can't give up on your passion if things don't work right away."

The key is to throw yourself into the immersive experience of a research project with the goal of learning literally everything you can about research along the way, making a positive contribution to knowledge (and perhaps, even, to your local community) as you do so, and embracing any mistakes, learning curves or adaptations that you need to confront along the way. You might start out feeling that research methods are a little abstract or confusing but by the end of this chapter you should feel far more confident in taking the first step on your personal research journey.

This chapter walks you through the steps of researching leadership in as entertaining and clear a way as possible. As always, you will then have the opportunity to apply theory to practice, first, via engagement with a compelling case study entitled "Financial markets meltdown: the case of Value at Risk" and then via the fascinating expert insight "Passion, meet science" – a profile of Dr. Laslo-Baker, a PhD researcher-turned-CEO who recently raised $6 million in seed funding for the innovative Canadian health company DeeBee's.

A research blueprint

A little later in the chapter you will have the opportunity to brainstorm concepts and work out what makes a great research question or objective. But first you need to map out the structure of your research. To help you achieve this, a blueprint (Figure 12.1) is provided below.

The blueprint begins with a research question or statement that is generally based on initial observations of a phenomena. Here's an example. You have observed a swift increase in usage of a relatively new social media platform among classmates, but complaints about online bullying seem (anecdotally, at least) to have increased concomitantly. You take a brief look at research data and find current reports confirming the prevalence of bullying on social media. However, the platform is too new for research to have been included in these studies, so you conclude that replicating an existing online bullying study is justified. This might take the form of a statement such as "An investigation of perceptions and experiences of online bullying among 18-year-old collegiate freshmen on the social media platform Instagram".

You have your working title! The next step is to perform a literature review (desk/secondary research) that confirms the efficacy of your study. Using the previous example, you might come across some studies that highlight a gap in the research suggesting that the neurological immaturity of the teenage prefrontal cortex makes teens more vulnerable than adults to tech addiction and the effects of bullying. This offers an interesting new angle – you can replicate a previous study

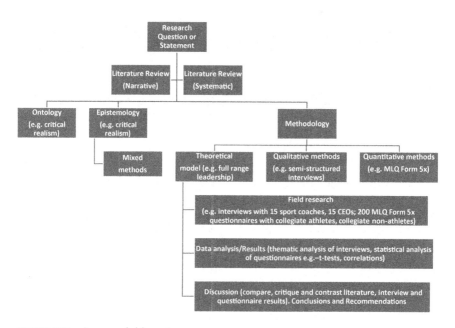

FIGURE 12.1 A research blueprint.

and add to it by including interviews with neurologists to gain their insights into existing theory. Or you might have found an existing study but not one that has been conducted in your country. So, you construct a study talking to the right people – a great start would be selecting a sample of 18-year-old freshmen. Talking to them will require qualitative methods (e.g. interviews) while a simple quantitative study (e.g. survey) would expand your target group and offer you the opportunity to present some basic descriptive statistics (e.g. bar charts). Adopting the correct methods of analysis ultimately leads to a well-thought out results and discussions chapter and viable recommendations and conclusions.

Find your inspiration

But first you need to undertake what most people think of as the fun, easy part (which can be surprisingly difficult when you try to achieve it!) – and that is identifying your research statement or question.

Leadership scholars are extremely fortunate, in that there are multiple examples of incredible – and terrible – leadership on a virtually day-to-day basis, so there are plenty of opportunities to get inspired. The trick is to think of something that you feel real passion for. Here's an example. If you are a student athlete, you might wonder whether collegiate sports participation develops leadership competencies. Alternatively, if you are a political science major, you might be interested in the way in which different social groups – your classmates, parents, teachers, etc. – receive differentiated microtargeted political data, and why. If you hold dreams of becoming a speechwriter, you might want to analyse charismatic political speeches; alternately you might choose to research issues of gender or ethnic diversity (or lack thereof) in the executive boards and faculties of your institution. You might even choose an auto-ethnographic study (where *you* are the case study) if you are embarking on a challenging leadership-focused project (e.g. representing your country at a sports event).

Regardless of your choice it must be theoretically viable and researched through the lens of a relevant theoretical framework (e.g. equity theory).

First – brainstorming!

Before you read any further, take a few minutes to discuss ideas with your peers and see if you can inspire each other, then decide which theoretical framework you are likely to utilize (NB browsing through previous chapters will provide a lot of inspiration!). A theoretical framework is the 'lens' that you use to analyse your research through. You might use the susceptible circle discussed in Chapter 10 ("Destructive leadership"), for example, to discuss the experiences of executives who have experienced workplace bullying.

Share your thoughts with your peers and ask for feedback. It is always useful to submit a rough outline of your overall strategy to your supervisor as early as possible so they can alert you to any issues straight away. And remember – there is no shame in going back to the drawing board if an initial idea does not seem viable. This is all part of the process.

Enjoy the journey

Research rarely runs smoothly. From the outset, it is useful to recognize research as an immersive, iterative process, with exciting parts (identifying your research topic, for example), frustrating parts (how do you narrow down your subject to a specific research objective?) and slightly boring parts (typing out transcriptions of interviews). The skill is in practicing effective self-leadership, strategizing and prioritizing your time to ensure a high-quality completed piece of work. Do not give up until you reach the finish line and do not leave anything to the last minute.

Defining your research philosophy

Most young researchers have little to no knowledge of what a research philosophy is, or why it is important. It is, in fact, critical. There are notable reasons for this. First, it justifies your entire research design. Second, it intellectually challenges you and requires that you challenge your own conceptions of what constitutes reality. Third, it may even alter the way in which you view the world. Finally, it showcases your skills as a researcher effectively, which can only lead to positive academic outcomes – most notably, the potential for a higher grade.

So ... what is research philosophy?

Often when philosophy is discussed it is viewed as pretentious, abstract or impossible to understand. This is a shame; research philosophy offers simple tools that ultimately allow you to construct something quite beautiful. The trick is in finding a place that communicates it to you in relatively simple terms (no mean feat). Think of it like this; a QB (quarterback) could not be without a football. A researcher cannot, and should not, be without his/her research philosophy.

The word *philosophy'* is derived from the French *filosofie*, the Latin *philosophia* and from the Greek *philosophos*, which means "lover of wisdom". Metaphysics, a branch of philosophy, requires that we consider the nature of what reality is (also known as ontology). Once we have defined what reality consists of, we can devise a research strategy that provides us with the most effective means of investigating it (our epistemology).

Whereas natural scientists (biologists, medics, physicists, chemists, etc.) tend to focus exclusively on empirical investigation of the *physical* world, (e.g. observing the effects of small doses of tryptophan in the treatment of depression in adults), leadership scholars tend to focus on human and social variables (e.g. why did the Robert Mueller-led FBI investigation of Russian interference in the 2016 US Presidential election lead to so many arrests – and what does this tell us about the role of opportunism in destructive leadership?). Natural scientists and social scientists (of which leadership scholars are a sub-group) are subsequently bound by different philosophical assumption and rules, with the latter depending mostly on qualitative methods (that allow us to explore human thoughts, perceptions and beliefs) and the former reliant on quantitative methods.

Natural sciences

For example, natural scientists follow a *positivist* research philosophy – a belief that reality consists only of that which is directly observable and empirically testable (e.g. human lung volume can be measured using a VO2 Max test [a physiological test usually performed on a treadmill that measures lung capacity]). In contrast, leadership scholars would, metaphysically speaking, be considered *post-positivists* as they believe that reality consists not only of the empirically observable, but also of causal powers and mechanisms that we cannot see (e.g. emotions, perceptions, beliefs, cultural assumptions, unconscious racial bias).

In practice many of us fall somewhere in the middle of that metaphysical spectrum and the choice of philosophy is often, in reality, situationally dependent. It is certainly useful to understand a little more, so that you can present this wider landscape in your own methodological chapter, and so you can also understand where the leadership scholar 'fits'.

Positivism

Positivism (see Figure 12.2) was founded in the nineteenth century by a philosopher named Auguste Comte, and is known as a doctrine of realism: "A philosophical system that holds that every rationally justifiable assertion can be scientifically verified or is capable of logical or mathematical proof, and that therefore rejects metaphysics and theism."[2] Natural scientists are bound by the rules of the scientific method – a set of rules ensuring adherence to specific scientific procedures and standards that ensure generalizability, validity and reliability and an extremely high standard of scientific rigor – and which includes the generation and testing of a hypothesis. Conforming to the scientific method allows hypotheses to be tested and findings to be generalized to a wider population. This allows research scientists at other institutions to repeat, compare, critique and/or analyse the data to further the goals of science. The epistemology used is known as empiricism and we can see below that a deductive approach is always used.

As one can note from Figure 12.2, research starts with an observation of a phenomena. A hypothesis is formulated about the phenomena, which is then tested. Data taken from the study is analysed and the stated hypothesis is accepted or rejected. We refer to this approach as a *hypothetico-deductive* or *falsificationist* approach.

Whilst positivist–empiricist approaches assume objectivity, in practice this can be tough to maintain – usually because humans are involved at the observation and inference stages and humans can make mistakes or disrupt what is being observed!

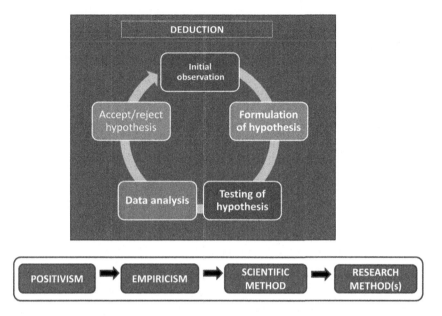

FIGURE 12.2   Positivism and deduction.

Famed scientist and philosopher Thomas Kuhn, for example, noted that followers of revolutionary research philosopher Karl Popper would be inclined to read his own work through a "*special pair of spectacles*" (Kuhn, 1965, p. 3). It remains a fascinating quirk of nature itself that atoms act differently when they are being watched. Leadership scholars might well want to include a quantitative study in their overall research design and it might be that you therefore need to conform to the scientific method for this specific part of your study – as you will see later in the chapter, mixed methods approaches are actively encouraged.

Leadership research is subjective!

Now on to the fun part (leadership research can be a lot of fun!).

Put down your books and ask everyone in your class to write down the name of the best political leader alive today. You might experience anything from a fully-fledged argument, a minor entertaining disagreement, or a hugely life-affirming motivating call to arms when you find out the results! But most importantly you will find major subjective differences, motivations, beliefs and justifications among your class for the choices that have been made.

Differences in beliefs are simply reflections of the diverse nature of our species and they reflect a life lived through a truly unique lens – our own. Each one of us is a complete individual, shaped by different experiences, influences and even brain chemistry. Acknowledging the existence of these differences – and the reasons why different beliefs exist – places us firmly in metaphysical terms as post-positivists because we are stating our belief that reality consists of more than what can be empirically observed and tested. Sure, we can test political allegiances by taking a tally of who classmates would vote for but finding the *why* behind the numbers is also critical to us.

These kinds of studies can create fascinating outcomes. What, for example, are the stop-and-frisk rates of black American males as compared to white American males, and why? What makes some people – such as Swedish diplomat Raoul Wallenberg whose rescue efforts saved tens of thousands of Hungarian Jews from the Holocaust – stand up against great evil while others actively court opportunities to benefit from it? Understanding these powerful social anomalies can carry major ramifications for the ways that we shape and live our lives, enact laws and perform social practices.

The Innocence Project

Here's a great example of a mixed methods model of research that has vastly altered the direction of many people's lives for the better, righting historic wrongs in the process: the case of The Innocence Project.

The DNA molecule or genome carries the entire genetic code of an individual, subsequently offering a powerful means of identifying a criminal if that individual has left behind DNA evidence (e.g. sweat, hair, blood) at the scene of a crime. DNA analysis is relatively new, meaning that in former times many individuals were wrongly convicted of crimes, often on the basis of flawed witness statements, from which the accused could not be exonerated due to a lack of opposing testimony. DNA technology offered exactly that opportunity, with a number of wrongful incarceration cases sadly emerging in recent years. An organization called The Innocence Project, founded in 1992 by Barry C. Scheck and Peter J. Neufeld at the Benjamin N. Cardozo School of Law at Yeshiva University in New York City dedicates itself to exactly this process – the exoneration of innocent men and women, via the retrospective application of DNA technology to decades-old evidence.

The Innocence Project has, at the time of writing, reported 273 post-conviction DNA exonerations in the US alone. Of these 273 convictions, 17 prisoners served time on death row, with an overall average length of wrongful incarceration of 13 years. The average age at time of incarceration was 27. In 123 of these cases, the real perpetrator was also identified.

Seventy-five per cent of wrongful convictions exonerated by DNA testing were based on incorrect eyewitness statements. Unvalidated or improper forensic scientific studies also played a role in approximately 50 per cent of wrongful convictions. False confessions were found to have secured a wrongful conviction in 25 per cent of cases. Furthermore, 35 per cent of those exonerated were under 18 and developmentally disabled. The majority, 166, were African-American. A further 81 were Caucasian, 20 of Latino origin, 2 Asian-American and 4 identified as race unknown.

Those last statistics are critical. Use of the scientific method in DNA testing opened a watershed of reversals in wrongful convictions. Use of qualitative analyses can seek to understand the extremely skewed racial profile in those wrongful conviction data sets.

Investigating irrationality

Have you ever heard of the Darwin Awards? They exist to "salute the improvement of the human genome by honoring those who accidentally remove themselves from it in a spectacular manner!".[3] Put another way, they ironically highlight the crazy, irrational and ridiculous things that human do, that are, by nature, *so* irrational that they led to the tragic and premature death of that individual.

These cases are, of course, extremely tragic and should be no cause for the entertainment or vilification of others. There is no one in your classroom or lecture theatre – right now – who hasn't done something silly at some point in their lives. It is (curiously) the nature of the human condition.

What the Darwin Awards do achieve is in the communication of the fact that humans are hard-wired to act emotionally and irrationally, often favouring short-term gratification to our detriment. As leadership scholars, we cannot assume the study of humans and society to be rational, partly because humans are so frequently irrational; so we require a method of observation and study that theorizes the existence of the rational and observable (conducting DNA testing, for example) as well as acknowledging the existence of the less rational and unobservable (the unseen causal powers and social structures that drive our world – e.g. greed, sensation-seeking, racism). Only then can we begin to fully understand much of the phenomena that surrounds us.

Investigating emotions

When we investigate emotions, beliefs and perceptions, we are intuitively expressing a *metaphysical belief* that reality is not only what the positivist–empiricist sees (i.e. an objective, observable, testable reality). You cannot, for example, directly observe a belief. You would need to ask a research subject what they perceive to be true and that allows you to record an unobservable entity (the belief) which has been expressed entirely subjectively (through the lens of personal experience of the subject you are interviewing).

You can ask someone to explain how they feel about anything – and that data can be extremely useful to you – but what if all you receive in terms of data is a curated version of what they *want* you to hear? They might not tell you how they really feel – perhaps the truth would embarrass them, or they are ashamed of how they feel. Perhaps they are about to run for college president. Or they have a crush on you and want to impress you. Either way, as a leadership scholar you cannot just stop at *doing* the research. You need to explain that you are aware of each of these limitations as a successful *post-positivist* researcher, or else the research will hold limited value.

Post-positivism

To understand post-positivism further, note the simple diagram below (Figure 12.3) that illustrates in clear, very basic terms the relationship between natural sciences and positivism, and between social sciences and post-positivism (worded in this diagram as the "study of humans and society"). As you now know, leadership scholars come from a field that originated in management science. As a result, many of us may already feel comfortable with the idea of empirical, quantitative analysis, which occupies a valid place in leadership research – but we obviously need to add layers of investigation to those results to find out the *why* and *how* behind the quantitative data that we might initially observe.

Put another way, reality, to the leadership scholar, is multi-dimensional. One dimension is represented ably in the world of the positivist–empiricist.

This might be starting to feel quite abstract. You are the QB with your football – so let's dial this back and make it as clear as we can. When you have spent some time absorbed in research, you might adopt your own philosophical approaches, but the perfect springboard when you are starting out is an excellent research philosophy known as critical realism, which champions mixed methods and clearly sets out the many layers of reality that the leadership scholar needs to acknowledge in their work.

Critical realism

Several post-positivist approaches exist, all of which share the same critiques of positivism (i.e. that reality is subjective, and that reality consists of unobservable as well as observable dimensions). One approach, interpretivism, offers a popular inductive approach that embraces idealism, and often involves the researcher immersing himself/herself in what is being researched. It stresses the use of qualitative methods, arguing that access to reality is only possible via social constructions (such as language). Interpretivism offers an umbrella for diverse approaches such as phenomenology, social constructivism and hermeneutics that focus on meaning, and reject the idea of meaning existing independently of human consciousness. It is a wide, rich field but not the springboard that we will begin with.

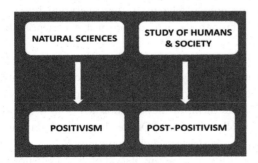

FIGURE 12.3 Positivism and post-positivism.

Critical realism: a springboard to further research

Critical realism is not based on idealism; conversely, it assumes that reality exists independently of our conscious experience of it. It is often regarded as 'sitting between' interpretivism and positivism, offering a flexible vehicle for mixed-methods research which suits the leadership scholar extremely well.

For most leadership scholars familiar with empiricist management science focused studies (and who also wish to investigate more intangible concepts such as perceptions, beliefs, bias, irrationality, etc.), critical realism subsequently offers a very natural fit and a logical choice. So how, exactly, does it work?

Reality: a multi-layered phenomenon

While much debate exists in the field of critical realism, a philosopher named Roy Bhaskar offered a really useful stratification of reality that we will adopt here using a handy iceberg diagram (Figure 12.4).

Bhaskar stratified reality into three distinct dimensions that are labelled in Figure 12.4. The first level is the *empirical* level (observable tangible objects and phenomena that we can see, test or touch – DNA, photosynthesis, blood platelets). The second is the *actual* level (where we witness events caused by 'real' level phenomena). The third is the *real* level (phenomena that remain largely unseen, but which drive and shape the human and social world). Applying this to the work of The Innocent Project offers an excellent example. Measurement of DNA and racial and ethnic status of wrongly convicted inmates (empirical level), observation of these incarcerated individuals in their prison cells (actual level) and investigation of

Empirical level: phenomena that are directly observable and testable. Phenomena at this level exist as a result of the causal powers that exist at the 'real' level

Actual level: events that occur as a result of the causal powers that exist at the 'real' level

Real level: a 'deep' understanding of phenomena, using retroduction to theorize about the existence of causal powers, structures and mechanisms that make possible what we observe at the actual and empirical levels. Both society ('structure') and persons ('agency') are sources of power.

FIGURE 12.4 The philosophical iceberg.

causal powers that caused significant over-representation of non-white inmates within the empirically observed group, leads to the argument that racism is a leading root cause of this observed phenomena (the real level).

Induction

Whereas positivist–empiricists use deductive logic, critical realists use something known as inductive logic. This involves the leadership scholar moving from an initial observation to (usually mixed-methods) research, to theory building (and for this you need to re-visit the iceberg!).

This theory building is referred to as "retroductive inference", where empirical and actual level observations (the DNA results of The Innocent Project, for example) are used to form the basis of theorizations about causal powers and structures that enabled that data to be collected in the first place (e.g. retroductively inferring the existence of racism as a root cause of wrongly convicted inmates). According to Sayer (1992, p. 107), retroduction is a "... mode of inference in which events are explained by postulating (and identifying) mechanisms which are capable of producing them ...". It is recognized as the key epistemology related to critical realism (Easton, 2010).

Objectivity vs subjectivity

While we mentioned earlier that positivist–empiricists (positivists) claim objectivity of data, social science researchers (and, subsequently, leadership scholars) cannot reasonably make the same claim. Why?

The reader might have cottoned on by now to the idea that this difference is generally attributable to the fundamentally different properties of phenomena researched in the natural and social worlds. A medic examines the lungs of a smoker using a chest x-ray, analyses the patient's arterial blood gases and concludes that the patient has emphysema. As an objective statement of fact, based on empirically viable quantitative data, the doctor has done an effective job. There are no hidden social realities of interest here.

But consider the next part of the picture. The patient leaves the clinic and continues to smoke even though the doctor has told him that if he does so, he will probably die very quickly. The clinic despairs – it has noticed that a vast percentage of emphysema patients simply fail to stop smoking, leading to very high mortality rates within months of diagnoses. A health researcher is drafted in to investigate the habits, beliefs, practices and everything else that might cause these emphysema patients to continue risking their life by smoking. This requires the health researcher to embrace the investigation of unobservable phenomena (e.g. peer pressure, boredom, anxiety, distrust of medical science) to find out how best to help emphysema patients stop smoking and subsequently prolong their lives. That would require different qualitative approaches such as focus groups and interviews. As we can see natural and social research would, in this case, be extremely complementary.

Structuration theory

An interesting theoretical lens to adopt when using a critical realist ontology is structuration theory, which argues that agents (a research term for human beings) produce and reproduce social structures, consciously and unconsciously. You do this all the time in your own life. Do you own a passport? You are consciously reproducing national identity and unconsciously endorsing and facilitating the Western concept of a nation state. We often do not stop and think about these structures and how they facilitate and constrain us.

Structuration theory posits that structures are in fact 'structured practices' which are made manifest by social conduct (a set of moral and procedural rules and resources that are adhered to and which, as a result, continually reproduce patterns of actions). Some can facilitate evil; others can allow mechanisms for charitable and altruistic acts. Others facilitate general law and order. What remains interesting is how unconsciously we accept so many of them. Should we be doing so?

Bourdieu's Theory of Practice

Another really interesting theory is Bourdieu's Theory of Practice, which revolves around the concepts of '*habitus*', '*fields*' and '*capital*'. Habitus refers to the mental structures and internalized schemes that agents use to perceive, understand and act in the social world (greatly affected by structures such as social class and education). Field relates to the social arena within which agents exist (a system of social positions based on power relationships where some agents occupy positions that are more powerful than others, and where agents in all walks of life compete for scarce resources in order to multiply their capital). Finally, capital refers to the economic, social, symbolic or cultural (in other words, anything that is desirable or significant and thereby can be traded for power – financial capital in the form of banknotes, for example, or thousands of Instagram likes that can be traded for influencer power).

In Bourdieu's theory, agents bring their capital with them to the field to compete for resources, a practice mediated by their specific habitus (e.g. the Instagram influencer). In this context, fields are often conceptualized as a marketplace, offering us an equation to explain specific motivations for human behaviour: *[(Habitus) (Capital)] + Field = Practice* (Bourdieu, 1984, p. 101). Some historians speculate that the incredible altruism and courage of the Swedish diplomat Raoul Wallenberg, mentioned earlier in this chapter, was mediated partly by the confidence afforded to him by his public school upbringing, relative wealth and aristocratic status.

Choosing your research methods

Let us apply these theories, just for fun, to your own practice. By reading and understanding everything in this chapter thus far, you have already improved your ability to compete for resources (academic grades) by increasing your capital (knowledge) as a researcher. Bourdieu would be proud.

Leadership scholars reading this book are, in fact, already in an advantageous position with regard to their practice, because each chapter of this book has already included a critical presentation of the most efficacious and robust instrument(s) that one should use in the investigation of each distinct leadership (or management) theory. The reader is therefore already in a very beneficial position having been provided with a research-focused roadmap from the outset. One simply needs to find the theory or leadership concept that interests them the most (the theoretical framework), browse the examples in this book (or find one's own inspiration in terms of *what* to research) and apply that knowledge to one's own practice, explaining how post-positivism offers the only logical route to do so.

Entering the home strait

So now you have a very clear approach; you can argue a case as to why you are a post-positivist critical realist researcher. You have identified critical realism as your philosophical (ontological and epistemological) approach, justifying a mixed-methods design. You will have located your theoretical framework and associated instrument(s) of analysis in earlier chapters. The instrument (quantitative or qualitative) will dictate the specific method of analysis utilized, which makes your life a lot easier, too.

Reading journal articles that have used that particular instrument and/or theory offers a viable next step in seeing how other fellow researchers have approached similar studies (but bear in mind that you might have to pay a licence fee to use some instruments, such as the MLQ Form 5x).

Structure of a thesis

Pulling it all together, you need to write your dissertation, research project or thesis. There are many generic research methods texts out there that do a great job in explaining the minutiae of a focus group, for example, or a survey. Consequently, we will not reinvent the wheel here. But what is always useful is a basic check list in terms of the steps that need to be taken to complete your work, just to make sure that you haven't left anything out.

You are likely to require the following chapters (although some courses and professors might deviate slightly so do check!):

1   An *Abstract*. This chapter requires you to briefly summarize your work from start to finish. As a result, seasoned researchers tend to write this last.
2   You will need an *Introduction*. This requires you to clearly state your research aims and objectives. It is common practice to separate the Introduction and Statement of Aims and Objectives into distinct, relatively brief chapters, but you can exercise personal judgement here.
3   The *Literature Review*. While there is more than one kind of review, a Narrative Review is generally well-suited to a leadership-focused study.

4   A *Methodology* chapter offers you a brilliant opportunity to showcase your new philosophical knowledge and justify every step of your study.

5   The *Results*, where you clearly set out the – wait for it – results of your study. Just as different quantitative and qualitative approaches require strict rules in terms of how you conduct them, they also require stringent conformation as to how you analyse and present them – make sure that you do not undermine results by neglecting quality of presentation.

6   The *Discussion*. This offers an excellent opportunity to provide an in-depth consideration of your results, inter- and intra-study comparisons and analyses and desk research. You will need to make inferences – a hard task, as an incorrect inference (which often occurs when the researcher does not know their subject) can undermine everything that you have, so far, achieved. This reflects the need for a genuinely in-depth literature review using top notch sources and research parameters (e.g. the time that journal articles were written, quality of journal, geographic location of publisher, relevant search terms).

7   Your *Conclusions and Recommendations* must include limitations of the research and recommendations for how your research can be taken forward by others. It is often relatively short, but this section can nevertheless carry significant weight.

Summary

In summary, bring your passion to the table, engage with philosophy and research design, and there will be no stopping you. Brush off set-backs (all great researchers experience these), learn a lot and who knows – you might make a meaningful change to yourself, your community and your school with the work that you produce. Just remember that you need to leave far more time than you think you need to complete a great study, so do not leave it until the last moment to complete.

Good luck!

Case study: financial markets meltdown: the case of Value at Risk

How can positivist assumptions (e.g. those that underpin financial research) be complemented by post-positivist approaches (e.g. critical realism)? This case study offers a fascinating take on the way in which the limitations of a reliance on Value at Risk – a core method of analysis in orthodox economics and finance theory – could have been hugely mitigated by blending post-positivist critical  realist approaches into research, development and organizational decision making.

The financial crisis: Why did nobody see it coming?

The financial crisis of 2008 seemingly came out of nowhere, blindsiding the Federal Reserve and many leading Wall Street banks. It led to catastrophic failures within the global financial markets, triggering widespread recession, the liquidation of powerful financial institutions (e.g. Lehman Brothers) and unprecedented levels of government intervention.

The origins of the crisis were undoubtedly complex, but what remains of great interest is the way in which orthodox economics failed to predict this, or any other major crisis, of the last century. The status of economics as a science is conflicting, and new fields of research such as behavioural finance are drawing back the curtains on assumptions of rationality and objectivity (classic positivist–empiricist assumptions).

For a critical realist, finance offers an amazingly interesting field; at the empirical level, mathematical models, equations and algorithms tell one hugely valuable story. But it seems that we should not stop there. A sociological study of human agency, for example, also seems imperative if we wish to play a part in predicting and interpreting key contributors to future financial crises and their effects. What might application of the susceptible circle tell us, for example, about the temptation to take opportunistic risks when large bonuses are in play? What might Bourdieu's theory tell us about the predominance of Goldman Sachs ex-employees in the Federal Reserve and the subsequent orthodoxy of thought that this might have caused? When hedge funders like Michael Burry of Scion Capital warned the Federal Reserve of the impending crisis, they did not take him seriously, yet he was able to track the crisis so closely that he predicted the specific month in which it would hit (his experiences are now immortalized in the movie *The Big Short*). Such theoretical questions are really fascinating for a leadership scholar and allow effective utilization of quantitative and qualitative methods.

Managing risk: Value at Risk

One of the empirical mathematical tools used by financial risk analysts to model and predict financial risks is Value at Risk (VaR). VaR allows financial analysts to assess the potential risk of a loss of value of a given portfolio of assets that are held by their financial institution.

Assessment of risk using VaR uses historical simulation, an approach where data taken from a recent historical period (e.g. the previous five years) is analysed and used as a basis to predict future financial trends. VaR is accompanied by stress testing, a form of historical simulation where various events over a recent period (e.g. the terrorist attack on the US on 11 September 2001, Russian debt default in 1998 and the Asian crisis in 1994) are analysed and used to illustrate worst-case scenarios. This is designed to ensure that the bank is appropriately capitalized to manage such risks, and also to ensure that it complies with its regulatory capital requirements.

VaR captures risks including interest rates, equity prices, currency rates and commodity prices. So, for example, if we looked at any date at random – the Goldman Sachs half year 2011 report, for example, their average daily VaR amounted to $110 million, assuming a one-day time interval and a 95 per cent confidence level. The 95 per cent confidence level means that there is a 1 in 20 (5 per cent) chance that daily trading net revenue losses on a particular day will exceed the reported VaR. As such, VaR theoretically allows the bank's risk managers to make effective risk allocation decisions to increase or decrease the bank's risk-taking appetite.

Financial analysts also utilize credit risk models which assess the risks associated with lending products, such as loans. These models use two parameters to assess credit risk; first, the probability of default (i.e. how likely is it that the borrower will not repay the loan?) and, second, the so-called 'loss given default' (i.e. how much money will the bank lose on its loan if the borrower defaults?), sometimes referred to as *loss assumptions*.

The 2008 financial crisis came as a shock to Wall Street, leaving governments and financial institutions (banks, hedge funds, etc.) completely unprepared. Why did VaR and other orthodox approaches fail to predict the onset of the 2008 global crisis?

Origins of the 2008 financial crisis

To understand why they did not work, we first need to walk through a very basic overview of the origins of the financial crisis, which began with excess financial liquidity held by China, resulting from robust economic growth over a number of years and from the subsequent acquisition, by China, of considerable amounts of US dollar denominated foreign exchange reserves. Over the same period of years, Middle Eastern oil exporting countries had enjoyed the benefits of high oil prices, which in turn precipitated acquisition of considerable US foreign denominated foreign exchange reserves. While all of that was happening, the US was experiencing signi-ficant government deregulation in the home purchasing sector, which led to a huge boom in mortgage lending to the subprime (i.e. substandard) mortgage sector, most specifically, to a group of borrowers known as 'NINJAs' (borrowers with *No Income, No Job or Assets*). Securitization of that subprime debt offered massive paydays to financial institutions who could not package up subprime debt fast enough to trade on the global markets in huge volumes as financial vehicles known as CDOs (Collat-eralized Debt Obligations). The huge boom in subprime lending also led to a massive expansion in real estate and associated fraud (classic opportunism as identified in the susceptible circle).

In what later became known as 'exploding ARMs' (adjustable rate mortgages), many of these subprime NINJA mortgages had a two-year grace period built in. This meant that no mortgage repayments were made – at all – for the first two years. If the borrower could not make the mortgage payments after that time, they simply handed back the keys to the property (one reason why Michael Burry was able to forecast the crisis to a specific month – he had analysed ARM data to identify that a huge percent-age would mature in the same month and that borrowers would have an extremely high likelihood of default immediately after). Defaults occurred in huge volumes at the end of that two-year period, exactly as Burry had predicted.

The two scenarios – Chinese excess liquidity and subprime debt – intersected when the Chinese Government and Middle Eastern investors chose to invest heavily in the US real estate market (one of the largest US denominated markets aside from

US Government bonds) due to its apparent growth and profitability. These investors did not, however, initially appreciate the complexity of issues arising from the significant emergence of subprime lending to the NINJAs' demographic. One leadership studies researcher recalled, at the time just before the financial crisis hit, that he had been visiting a friend in Las Vegas and got talking to a couple who had purchased the property next door. The neighbours turned out to be a stripper and her unemployed boyfriend. Perplexed as to how they could afford such an incredible home, the couple mentioned that they were in the process of designing and commissioning a swimming pool for their large back garden. The researcher subsequently wondered if the plans for that swimming pool ever saw the light of day.

CDOs and securitization

So how does securitization work, exactly? In simple terms, financial institutions 'bundled' the risky subprime debts into CDOs, so that they could trade them and de-risk, or hedge, their own balance sheets. CDOs allowed traders to combine toxic subprime assets with 'good' assets, or to combine supposedly uncorrelated subprime assets from different regions of the US, enabling the (effectively toxic) CDO to obtain a positive overall credit rating. A major problem occurred here: a strong credit rating from a respectable rating agency (such as Standard & Poor's, Moody's or Fitch) was essential for any CDO/liquid asset to be traded on the international financial markets, as it would denote quality and value. Nobody wanted 100 per cent toxic subprime on their balance sheets and everybody needed to hedge their risk to some extent, which is why the toxic subprime debt always had to be bundled up with a range of higher-rated assets in a CDO. What happened, in reality, is that ratings agencies often gave completely toxic CDOs an AAA (top) rating, suggesting that subprime debt was higher quality than it really was. After the crisis, many ratings agency staff spoke to the press complaining about unacceptable pressure from management to give top ratings to toxic assets. It would be very interesting for leadership scholars to see how ratings agency staff feel these days.

Toxic assets

The use of CDOs led to a flooding of the markets with subprime toxic assets, and the multiplication of asset exposure (a risk multiplier) for financial institutions. This also resulted in non-transparency in accounting (due to debt tranching[4]) as the CDO structures, due to their higher credit rating, allowed institutions to hold toxic assets on their balance sheets without having to recognize them as toxic. Institutions thus became critically overexposed to risk.

Ultimately, the influx of subprime NINJA credit within the US housing market led to an inevitable and detrimental slide in performance of the US housing market, as widespread defaulting on loans (mortgages) by the NINJAs started to occur. As investors in subprime assets realized that the assets that they were holding were – in reality – much riskier than they thought, they started selling assets, which led to a crippling effect on the markets and widespread panic, which, in turn, resulted in a significant drop in the market price for CDOs in the secondary market. We now know from studies of behavioural finance that traders tend to act as 'herds' with trading becoming vastly emotional and irrational when a market is experiencing a major boom or bust. And at this point, the panic was extremely high. Many institutions were, by this point, hugely and critically exposed to toxic debt that they could not sell. AIG, a huge insurance company that had insured hundreds of thousands of CDOs, simply could not pay out. The US Government was forced to arrange a major bail-out of AIG using public funds – a source of anger among regular taxpayers that still exists today.

This drop in the value of CDOs, in turn, increased the pressure on financial institutions to reduce any and all risk as quickly as possible. However, it became intensely problematic for financial institutions to sell them, due to their status as toxic assets. There was very little liquidity in the markets at this point as no financial institutions were willing to lend money to anyone else. By this point, individual savers were panicking, queuing outside retail banks to withdraw their funds. As a result of the ensuing mass demand for financial withdrawals, banks literally ran out of money.

The fall of Lehman Brothers

At the time of the widespread NINJA defaults, Lehman Brothers was recognized as one of the most powerful financial institutions in the world, with a balance sheet of $650 billion. However, the bank was extremely thinly capitalized (and highly leveraged) to commercial (subprime) real estate, and had overexposed themselves by taking on considerable subprime risk on their balance sheet. To make matters far worse, Lehman Brothers had previously acquired five mortgage lenders, including the subprime lenders BNC Mortgage and Aurora Loan Services, which specialized in 'Alt-A' loans (loans made to borrowers without full documentation required). As a consequence, Lehman's high leverage made it increasingly vulnerable to volatile market conditions. The bank was subsequently unable to continue operating and funding itself when the crisis hit, entering bankruptcy liquidation on 15 September 2008.

In many ways, the game was up. Other leading financial institutions recognized their extremely vulnerable position, similar to that of Lehman Brothers (Merrill Lynch was acquired by Bank of America soon after). The failure of AIG and Lehman Brothers – two powerful institutions – further spooked the market and led to fears of market meltdown.

Widespread panic

An unexpected ban on hedging (shorting[5] bank stocks) was imposed by governments in a bid to stem further market drops – which at the same time led to further losses for those investors who were rightly sceptical of (and who had 'bid against' the subprime investments of) financial institutions. This included investors such as Michael Burry who had attempted to warn the Federal Reserve of the nature and timing of the crisis – but was roundly ignored, partly because orthodox economics analyses showed no signs of an impending crisis. In reality, what Burry had done – extremely efficiently – was to take the empirical data pertaining to exploding ARM expirations and apply it to current market conditions, and then provide a perfect case study (for leaderships scholars, anyway!) of efficient human agency in his attempts to directly warn the Federal Reserve. Social science scholars could find value in applying Bourdieu's theory of social capital to explain orthodoxy and dogma in the Federal Reserve, while the monumental diffusion of fraud that extended throughout the mortgage lending industry as a result of government deregulation would offer another great case study. The human stories that sit behind these headlines no doubt carry far reaching outcomes, of great value to leadership scholars.

Strong correlations across asset classes meant that all assets, except the US dollar and gold, were fundamentally and detrimentally affected and lost a great deal of their value. The panic was now truly widespread. Uncertainty spread, and capacity utilization and earnings of many companies deteriorated, which further detrimentally affected shareholder confidence and drove down share prices. Ultimately, many countries went on to experience recessions that carried very real political, social and economic consequences.

Closed vs open systems

The application of VaR and credit models assumes that the world is a *closed* system (i.e. where the analysis of finite variables under test conditions can lead to generalizable predictions of future events), whereas a critical realist approach would allow a researcher to take that valuable VaR data and combine it with additional qualitative studies that together interpret the world as a complex *open* system – one that is far more fluid and dynamic than economic orthodoxy would generally allow.

VaR models typically only forecast a 95 per cent probability – which means that the likelihood of 5 per cent of events occurring in the future is completely unknown. If these 5 per cent were extreme events (such as the emergence of the subprime mortgage market bubble, combined with excess liquidity and poor asset quality that led to the crisis), the impact of such extreme events could render the calculated 95 per cent VaR result almost entirely meaningless. It is true that VaR is most effective in estimating risk exposure in markets where there are no sudden fundamental changes or shifts in market conditions; but such shifts can, and do, happen – and many of these shifts can relate to complex human and social events, such as the sudden onset of a catastrophic health emergency such as the COVID-19 pandemic. Such a concept ultimately underscores the importance of investigating human and social factors alongside mathematical predictive data.

Questions

1   This case study makes a great case for the adoption of a post-positivist approach in finance. Why?

2   Do you feel that human error or methodological shortcomings were princi-
     pally at fault in the failure of orthodox economics approaches in predicting the
     2008 financial crisis?
3   In groups, devise a basic research study that investigates the lived experiences
     of one sub-group involved in the 2008 financial crisis (e.g. exploding ARM
     borrowers, traders who worked at Lehman Brothers in September 2008, sub-
     prime mortgage lenders, ratings agency staff, Federal Reserve staff) and explain
     why your study would propose to constitute an original contribution to
     knowledge.

 ## Expert insight

Passion, meet science

Dr. Dionne Laslo-Baker, CEO and founder of
DeeBee's, obtained her PhD in the field of
medical sciences with a focus on maternal-
fetal toxicology. After winning multiple awards
and enjoying a successful career as a
researcher, Dr. Laslo-Baker founded DeeBee's
Organics, an innovative Canadian organic

natural snack company. Successfully raising over $6,000,000 in capital, DeeBee's is
expanding fast across North America and recently partnered with Disney to create Dee-
Bee's Organic Ice Wands in conjunction with the release of the movie Frozen II.

What started as a tiny idea in Dr. Laslo-Baker's kitchen has grown into a distribution
network of approximately 15,000 US and Canadian retail locations including Whole
Foods, Sobeys, Walmart, Kroger's and Loblaws, and a growth rate of close to 200 per cent
over the last 12 months. In Dr. Laslo-Baker's words, "The most brilliant thing is also the
most terrifying thing – that I am in control of this company." She shares her exciting,
inspirational story with us, detailing what she has learnt about leadership and how she
has dealt with hurdles along the way.

A view from the top

*//*The most brilliant thing is also the most terrifying thing – that I am in control
of this company. I have the ability to make DeeBee's soar, and that is something truly incredible. It's also very scary! – because if anything goes wrong, it's
ultimately my responsibility.

Passion, meet science

At my core, I will always be a researcher and research scientist, thus I feel that
research has been and will continue to be integral to the inception and success
of DeeBee's Organics. I firmly believe in the power of using one's education

creatively, which is what I have done by leveraging my background as a researcher and medical scientist.

The focus of my doctoral research was on the effects of exposure to chemicals during pregnancy on fetal development and child neurocognitive health. Through my education, I studied the association between exposure to chemicals and negative consequences to fetal development evidenced as neurocognitive challenges, deficits or lack of ability to attain optimal intellectual development as a result of exposure. My own work, alongside the breadth of research in this area, has led me to firmly believe that there is no place for synthetic pesticides and herbicides in our food system.

As a result of the years of study, 'always organic' became a core DeeBee's promise that I refuse to compromise on. This principle, and the research behind it, helped guide our initial products and impacts every step of our current product innovation process. Today, I am lucky to work alongside a talented research and development team that ensure we are creating the best possible products with the cleanest, shortest labels for our families, our team, and DeeBee's customers.

I believe that my research experience has really informed how I choose to run my company. While academic research has a different set of requirements to that of a CEO, I approached learning how to run DeeBee's through the lens of a research scientist. For example, in order to be an effective CEO, I have had to employ elements of research to every single aspect of my job. This ranges from understanding the financial requirements of running a business, to ensuring the highest level of quality assurance and understanding the production requirements for each of our products, to assembling and managing a core group of people, to studying how to accomplish any task. Learning how to learn, being humbled by the vast amount of information that I don't know and figuring out how to learn the tools to conquer any challenge has never left me, and those abilities have subsequently helped shape the person I am today.

A core tenet of research is being curious and, while running DeeBee's, it is essential that I am consistently curious. This curiosity might be about how to optimally transport a product from one end of the globe to the other, how to make something a bright colour using only organic fruits or vegetables, how to empathically empower a team, how to stimulate young minds who join the team to reach for the stars and succeed or how to innovate disruptive products that the world needs. I believe that the more we learn, the more we discover how much we truly don't know – and the more we learn how exciting it is to go and learn it!

Overcoming hardships

Especially early on, I experienced moments of real doubt and real periods where I felt quite down, but being financially committed to the business, and remaining true to a personal promise that I had made to myself to never give up, means that I made it through. Having passion for DeeBee's was something I held on to during those times. I have a very supportive husband who encouraged me to follow my passions and to this day, I believe that I should not settle for anything less than a life full of passion. That is certainly something that I have found via creating and running DeeBee's.

There was initially so much learning when I founded this company. I often joke that I went to school to become a PhD researcher, but I went to the school of hard knocks to become an entrepreneur! The first few years were a massive undertaking and huge sacrifices were made in every part of my life. When we got started, I was doing everything with our own funds and I did every job at the company from raising capital to mopping office floors. It felt overwhelming when our team began to grow quickly, and I had to learn to find a balance between being very hands-on and giving my team the space that they needed to grow.

Leading with passion

My leadership style is naturally quite passionate. I always strive to transfer my energy to the rest of my team, which I use to rally everyone around our common goals to ensure they are feeling positive and inspired. I am also a very equilateral leader in that I work hard to ensure that no one feels like I am more important than them. I am always willing to spend time with any member of our team, no matter who they are or what they are focused on, to build a strong personal connection with them and to provide them with guidance when it is needed. Members of our team tell me that I am a very positive problem solver – that instead of pointing blame I am solution focused and I work with our team to help find the best possible outcome to challenges. At DeeBee's, we work through challenges together.

Big dreams need clear strategies

I would advise those who dream of starting their own company to get a strong grasp of the financial necessities of their dreams. Capitalizing a company that manufactures on a large-scale can be very challenging. I would recommend getting a sober sense of what the true scope of your growth vision entails and understanding what it will actually take to get from point A to point B. Once you build this picture, it is wise to also ensure that your product is ripe for success. Is the margin excellent? Is there a strong demand? Is there a void that your product, idea or service is filling? Is it suited for e-commerce?

There are many factors to consider, and I have navigated all these challenges as they have arisen with DeeBee's. Looking back, now that I have a good understanding of the industry we are in, I know I could have achieved my goals more efficiently if I had done this up-front analysis which really underscores the importance of developing sound research skills. I am also a firm believer in mentorship – to seek advice and guidance from those already experienced in your field.

Breaking through barriers

Data suggest that all-male business teams are four times more likely to receive funding[6] than all-women teams, and that when it comes to raising capital, women face many barriers, including misogynistic unconscious biases, unequal access to influential social networks and gendered assessment criteria biased towards traditionally male qualities. This leads to far fewer women involved in early stage entrepreneurial activities and established business ownership, and disadvantages those who attempt to scale their businesses.

I personally experienced this type of challenge, especially in the earlier years of the business. Once, for example, a male banker told me that my desire to be a successful entrepreneur was 'disrupting the peace' of my husband's career and family life. Presumably, he could never and would never have thought to make that kind of comment to a man. I left that meeting feeling disempowered and disengaged. I am certainly not alone – whenever I share these kinds of experiences, other female entrepreneurs all have similar experiences to match mine.

Raising capital

As a female leader who has successfully raised capital both through equity and debt with large banks, I ultimately feel a responsibility to help educate women [about] what they should be prepared for. Women need to have the tools that will increase the likelihood that their efforts to raise capital are successful, so understanding the financial aspects of their business is critical. These financial tools include, but are not limited to:

1   Profit and loss statement – understand each line item in detail and be able to accurately describe each line item to back up the numbers.
2   Forecast – it is essential to thoroughly understand and be able to explain in detail:
    a   gross and net sales
    b   COGS (cost of goods sold)
    c   gross and net margin – critical to be honest about this and ensure that all costs including items like transport and trade marketing are factored into this number
    d   Each line item broken down into categories that correspond accurately to the accounting system used
    e   EBITDA (earnings before interest, taxes, depreciation and amortization)
    f   Cash flow analysis – be able to accurately describe the cash flow

forecast, why need for capital arises, specifically what period of time the need will arise, method of paying the loan/debt back

g   Balance sheet.

When well-educated and armed with this type of information, the likelihood of successfully raising capital increases. Lenders and investors are savvy and intelligent and if they see a weak point, holes in the data presented to them or a poor understanding of the information at hand or how the business will be managed, it is unlikely that you will secure funding. Admit when you do not know something and seek advice from an expert when you need to.

A blockbuster from the get-go

One of our biggest challenges to date has been creating a product that sustains a healthy margin – something that is very difficult to accomplish across the food and beverage industry, and especially in the natural foods industry. Our initial product didn't have the margin we needed so we innovated to create the SuperFruit Freezie – an organic, shelf-stable, freezer pop made with no added sugars, artificial flavours or preservatives – which has been extremely successful. Being shelf-stable, the product is convenient to store and very easy to retail, requiring no refrigeration or special handling. It was a blockbuster hit from the get-go; the SuperFruit Freezie has been embraced by retailers and consumers alike. In fact, when we launched this product with a major Canadian retailer in 2017, it became the highest velocity product ever launched in its category! So we turned what could have been seen as a failure into a major success.

What I would have done differently

If I were to start a new company knowing what I know today, I would focus far more on the financial aspects of the company and build a strong multi-year capital raising plan. It makes you face the financial reality of running your company; it provides an (often uncomfortable) reality check. If I'd done this earlier, we would have become financially sustainable far quicker.

I also would have focused on taste far more from the beginning; if a food product doesn't taste good, it will never become profitable, no matter how healthy it might be, and scaling up production can change that product in a major way. A major learning moment for me was discovering that a product taste changes when you scale to larger production – a batch of one hundred pops tastes very different than a batch of a million, for example, even when you use the same recipe. Now, we have strong taste parameters established, and we are continually working to improve the taste of new iterations of our current products, as well as products that are in development, allowing us to scale effectively but retain taste, quality and flavour.*"*

Find out more

- DeeBee's Organics: www.deebeesorganics.com.
- Dr. Dionne Laslo-Baker. *Women of Influence*. Available at: www.womenof influence.ca.
- Laslo-Baker, D., Barrera, M., Knittel-Keren, D., Kozer, E., Wolpin, J., Khattak, S., Hackman, R., Rovet, J. and Koren, G. (2004). Child Neurodevelopmental Outcome and Maternal Occupational Exposure to Solvents. *Archives of Pediatrics & Adolescent Medicine*, 158(10), pp. 956–961.

Questions

1 How has a passion for research enabled the CEO profiled to drive her business forward, from acquiring $6 million in seed funding to developing a truly innovative product?
2 Find out more about DeeBee's and explain how a research-formed approach allowed the CEO profiled in this expert insight to innovate and identify a niche within her industry.
3 In small teams, devise a product or service that you feel passionate and excited about. Identify a top-level research plan that you would need to execute to bring this product to market.

CHAPTER 12 QUIZ

1 Provide a definition for the following terms: research philosophy, ontology, epistemology and metaphysics.
2 What are the top-level differences between positivism and post-positivism?
3 Define your research philosophy.
4 In small groups, plan a mini-study, identifying the research question, philosophical approach and research methods that you will use. Share with the class.

Notes

1 Quoted in an interview with Dr. Laslo-Baker conducted for this book, as featured in the expert insight "Passion, meet science" that appears later in this chapter.
2 Merriam-Webster Dictionary [online]: www.merriam-webster.com/dictionary/reality#:~:text=Definition%20of%20reality,nor%20dependent%20but%20exists%20necessarily.
3 Darwin Awards website: https://darwinawards.com/darwin/.
4 Tranches are usually portions of mortgage-backed securities separated by risk and maturity.
5 'Shorting' is a colloquialism that refers to the practice of short selling – speculating on a decline in the price of a stock or security.

6 Brush, C., Greene, P., Balachandra, L. and Davis, A. (2018). The Gender Gap in Venture Capital – Progress, Problems, and Perspectives. *Venture Capital*, 20(2), pp. 115–136.

References

Bhaskar, R. (1975). *A Realist Social Theory of Science*. London: Leeds Books.

Bourdieu, P. (1984). *Distinction: A Social Critique of the Judgement of Taste*. London: Routledge.

Bourdieu, P. (1990). *The Logic of Practice*. Cambridge: Polity Press.

Burr, V. (1995). *An Introduction to Social Constructionism*. London: Routledge.

Easterby-Smith, M., Thorpe, R. and Lowe, A. (2002). *Management Research: An Introduction*. 2nd ed. London: Sage Publications.

Easton, G. (2010). Critical Realism in Case Study Research. *Industrial Marketing Management*, 39(1), pp. 118–128.

Giddens, A. (1984). *The Constitution of Society: Outline of the Theory of Structuration*. Cambridge: Polity Press.

Kuhn, T.S. (1965). Logic of Discovery or Psychology of Research? In Imre Lakatos and Alan Musgrave (eds.), Criticism and the Growth of Knowledge. *Proceedings of the International Colloquium in the Philosophy of Science*, London, Vol. 4. Cambridge: Cambridge University Press.

Sayer, A. (1992). *Method in Social Science: A Realist Approach*. 2nd ed. London: Routledge.

INDEX

Page numbers in **bold** denote tables, those in *italics* denote figures, those followed by 'n' refer to notes.

Printed in the United States
By Bookmasters